The Latin Beat

Also by Ed Morales

*Living in Spanglish: The Search for
Latino Identity in America*

The Latin Beat

• • • • •

The Rhythms and Roots of
Latin Music from Bossa Nova
to Salsa and Beyond

ED MORALES

Da Capo Press
A Member of the Perseus Books Group

Copyright © 2003 by Ed Morales

Interior design by Lisa Kreinbrink
Set in 10.5-point Janson Text by The Perseus Books Group

Library of Congress Cataloging-in-Publication Data

Morales, Ed, 1956-
   The Latin beat : the rhythms and roots of Latin music from bossa nova to salsa
and beyond / Ed Morales.—1st Da Capo Press ed.
      p.   cm.
   Includes bibliographical references (p.   ) and index.
   ISBN 0-306-81018-2 (pbk.)
   1. Popular music—Latin America—History and criticism.   I. Title.
ML3475.M67 2003
781.64'098—dc22

                                                                                    2003016423

First Da Capo Press edition 2003

Published by Da Capo Press
A Member of the Perseus Books Group
http://www.dacapopress.com

Da Capo Press books are available at special discounts for bulk purchases in the
U.S. by corporations, institutions, and other organizations. For more information,
please contact the Special Markets Department at the Perseus Books Group,
11 Cambridge Center, Cambridge, MA 02142, or call (800) 255-1514 or
(617) 252-5298, or e-mail j.mccrary@perseusbooks.com.

   2 3 4 5 6 7 8 9—07 06 05 04

La música es amor.

Héctor Buitrago and Andrea Echeverri

Contents

Acknowledgments

Thanks to my editors: Andrea Schulz, for her initial belief and dedication; Joan Benham for tireless review; and Ben Schafer for bringing it all back home. To my agent Daniel Mandel. To Bryan Vargas for careful critiques and challenging discussion and to Bobby Sanabria and Conrad Herwig for passionate insights. To Adriana for putting up with endless piles of CDs and smoky clubs. To the legions of industry types who are out there every night—you know who you are. To all the musicians who have sat patiently with me and put into words what is often impossible to describe: *la música.*

Introduction

Trying to define Latin music is like trying to define Latinos in the United States. We are far from a monolithic consensus— there may be more styles and variations of being Latino than there are different Latin American countries. Including Spain, there are twenty-two predominantly Spanish-speaking countries, and there are many more styles of Latin music. The only things that hold together the concept of Latin music are the same things that unify Latinos—a language, Spanish; Spain's cultural traditions; and large helpings of African and indigenous traditions that vary by region. The discussion of Brazil as Latin music in this book is based on Portugal's and Portuguese culture's proximity and affinity with Spain's, as well as the similarly hybrid construction of Brazilian culture.

Latin music, like Latin American culture, comes across as exotic to North American and European listeners, with its vaguely "hot" rhythms and emotional vocalists. While for Latinos our music constitutes an essential part of our identity, it appeals to non-Latinos because of its wild complexity and expressive possibilities. The purpose of *The Latin Beat* is to unravel some of Latin music's mystery, to demystify its tangible aroma. In general we can say that Latin music is influenced by Spanish song forms, African

and indigenous rhythms and harmonic structures, European classical and popular music, and, increasingly in the twentieth and
twenty-first centuries, North American ballad, rhythm and blues,
jazz, rock, reggae, electronica, Afro-pop, and hip-hop.

To the uninitiated or non-Spanish speaking listener, the varieties of Latin music can seem indistinguishable. But just as Latinos
in the United States vary in character by virtue of their country of
origin—whether it is Mexico, Puerto Rico, Cuba, the Dominican
Republic, and now, increasingly countries in Central and South
Americas—different regions of Latin America produce different
strands of music, and those strands can be identified even further
by a particular country, and then a particular region within that
country. The music of the Caribbean generally differs from the
music of Mexico and Central America, which in turn is different
from the northern and southern regions of South America, and
Brazil is, of course, a very different story.

While by no means definitive or all-inclusive, the Latin
Grammy awards, unlike its somewhat stodgy forefather, the mainstream Grammys, have sought to present the various musics in all
their diverse glory. The awards, administered by the Latin Academy of Recording Arts and Scientists, a group of musicians, producers, and engineers modeled after the National Academy of
Recording Arts and Scientists, were created in 2000 in response to
the growing popularity of Latin music. The Latin Grammys are
awarded in several categories that point to regional differences.
Mexican regional music is distinguished from Brazilian music.
Separate categories are assigned to genres like tango, associated
with Argentina, and flamenco, associated with Spain. The "tropical" categories refer to music that generally originates in the
Caribbean islands or in countries that border on the Caribbean
and are divided between contemporary and traditional versions.

The Latin Grammy awards are perhaps the first formal attempt
by the music industry of Anglo and Latin America to codify the wide
varieties of the music and present them alongside of each other. But

different regional tastes sometimes hinder marketing all of these forms in all areas. Even MTV Latin America, which confines its programming to rock, hip-hop, and pop, divides its signal when broadcasting to the northern and southern regions of Latin America.

Beyond these geographical differences, which are most clearly expressed in different traditional music (Colombia is the home to cumbia and vallenato, for instance; the Dominican Republic gave birth to merengue, Puerto Rico to the bomba and plena), are genres that have been consolidated in the modernization process of the twentieth century. Slickly recorded versions of traditional music like cumbia and merengue are lumped into the "tropical" category with salsa, which fuses Afro-Cuban son, a popular song form, with elements of Afro-Cuban jazz, North American R&B, and other Caribbean beats. Latin pop has roots in traditional boleros and other song forms, and Latin alternative fuses almost the entire repertoire of Latin music with modern rock and hip-hop.

Given the dizzying array of traditional and modern styles, it can seem difficult to prioritize among the varieties of Latin music made in the countries of Latin America, as well as Spain, for the purpose of crystallizing the notion of what "Latin music" is. But it's helpful to consider two factors. One is the impact that traditional genres like merengue or cumbia or modern or hybrid genres like salsa or Latin pop can have on the music consumers of Latin America and Spain as a whole—that is, which genres become popular across national boundaries. The other is what kind of Latin music breaks through to both English- and Spanish-dominant listeners in the United States. These factors address the idea of what Latin music means to the larger listening public and distinguish it from regional variations.

This book is intended to be a useful and compact survey of Latin music, focusing on the main branches of its manifestation as a popular music—salsa/Afro-Cuban music or tropical, Latin pop, rock, and hip-hop, and Brazilian music—while also shedding light on regional genres from Mexico and South America such as ranchera, cumbia, Andean music, and tango. The attention given to each branch or genre corresponds to its ability to transcend regional and national boundaries, as well as its absorption into modern forms of popular music. In other words, it seems important to focus on the kind of music that listeners worldwide identify most strongly as Latin (that is, on the ubiquitous use of Afro-Cuban and Brazilian forms in advertising or dancing settings or on Latin pop stars such as Enrique Iglesias, Ricky Martin, and Shakira). But it is also important to understand something of the traditional and indigenous genres from the periphery of Latin music that continue to be re-discovered and re-incorporated into more popular forms. Latin music is best understood as an *American* music, that is, a music of the New World, which is manifested in continually evolving permutations involving the interplay between European, African, and indigenous cultures.

The conception of Latin music begins with Spain's and Portugal's colonization of the New World, but was presaged by the 500-year Moorish occupation of the Iberian Peninsula that began at the start of the last millennium. The various North African dynasties that held sway in the Spanish province of Andalucía, as well as southern Portugal, allowed for a number of different ethnic cultures, such as Spanish Christian, Jewish, Moorish, and gypsy, to intermingle. The influence of traditional Arabic music, through instruments like the laud, (lute, a predecessor to the guitar), fiddles, flutes, and kettle drums, as well as a signature high-pitched and nasal vocal style and a penchant for improvisation, informed the oral tradition of Spain and Portugal (and to a lesser extent, more northern Germanic and Celtic cultures).

At the beginning of the second millennium, Spain, like much of Europe, was overrun by various wandering tribes. The gypsy tradition, which originated in northern India, brought a sense of nomadic loss to Iberia, and the characteristic vocal trill from North African Arabic culture (a western extension of the same

Islamic cultural influence) seemed to belong to a similar emotional register. The troubadour influence from France, in the
twelfth and thirteenth centuries, became central in Spanish literature and greatly affected its song forms. By the sixteenth century, the troubadours of Castile were also declaiming in the
octosyllabic *décima* style, featuring ten lines of eight syllables
each, that was pioneered by a mixed culture of Spaniards and
Arabs who often spoke a hybrid language known as Mozárabic
during the Moorish occupation. The *décima* form survives today
in the modern Latin ballad, known as bolero, the Mexican corrido, the Colombian vallenato, the Puerto Rican décima or seis,
the Cuban trova, and even the folk songs of Argentine nueva
canción.

According to Felipe Pasamarick, writing in *The Latin America
Music Review*, the décima was well-suited to evolve in connection
with African drum patterns that were important in Cuba because
of a "curious and ambiguous inherently rhythmic pattern of
stressed syllables and pairs of rhymes repeated unequally yet regularly." The favored rhythmic pattern of Spanish décimas became
the espinela, named after sixteenth-century poet Vicente Espinel.
The espinela pattern can be understood as a "mirror" in the way
two successive five-line stanzas reverse the pattern ABBAA, which
was used in seminal works like *La Vida es Sueño* by the playwright
Pedro Calderón de la Barca. The espinela form of décima was
enormously popular in Andalucía and was transmitted to early
colonial outposts like the Canary Islands. The Islands were a primordial site for the creation of the mixed-race, Creole ethnic
strand that would eventually become a major component of the
mestizo and mulatto culture of the Spanish New World. A sizable
number of the Creoles of the Canary Islands emigrated to Cuba
in the eighteenth and nineteenth centuries and became part of
the core of Cuba's guajiros, a group of yeoman country farmers
and workers whose sustained interaction and intermarriage with

African slaves and freemen were at the center of the development of Afro-Cuban music.

Example of décima, metrical scan: the first five lines are ABBAA, the second five are CCDDC:

Yo sueño que estoy aquí	I dream that I am here
de estas cadenas cargado,	Weighed down by these chains
y soñé que en otro estado	And dreamt that in another state
más lisonjero me vi	more pleasing, I saw myself
¿Qué es la vida? Un frenesí.	What is life? A frenzy
¿Qué es la vida? Una ilusión.	What is life? An illusion
Una sombra, una ficción	A shadow, a fiction
y el mayor bien es pequeño,	And the greatest good is small
Que toda la vida es sueño,	And that all of life is a dream
y los sueños, sueños son.	And dreams are also dreams

Calderón de la Barca,
La Vida es Sueño

When the Iberians colonized the Americas, they were not the unified Christian culture that the mythos of the Inquisition and the Castillian conquering monarchs Ferdinand and Isabela implies. Iberian culture was a complex mix of the influences engendered by the Moorish occupation, and when it came into contact with new influences in the Americas, a new set of hybrid impulses would come into play. Through their ventures in the Cape Verde Islands, a way station for the trafficking of slaves off the coast of Africa, the Portuguese, like the Spanish, were spreading an early Creole, or mixed culture of West Africans and Iberians, to the New World. In addition, many of the first Africans brought to Cuba were not shipped directly from Africa but from Seville, Spain, where they had been in contact with Andalusian culture and the tradition of the *décima* long enough to absorb them.

Latin music in the New World resulted from a mixing of cultures that gradually took place between the European conquerors, African slaves, and indigenous people. While European song forms and instrumentation were essential to its creation, and indigenous instrumentation and rhythms had a fair amount of influence, African music is central to the evolution of the major, internationalized forms of Latin music. In Cuba, African music was expressed through rumba, in Puerto Rican music through bomba, in Colombian music through cumbia, and in Brazil through samba. Even the Argentine tango derives from the Cuban habanera, which uses a five-beat cinquillo rhythm that again has roots in Africa, as well as from the musical traditions of Afro-Argentines like the candombe. Although Mexican regional and norteño music has more influence from the German polka, many of its traditional rhythms, like the son jarrocho, the huapango, and other Mexican son variations, are most likely borrowed from Afro-Cuban music.

Another central characteristic of Latin music is the widespread use of syncopation. The standard definition for syncopation is the shifting of musical accents from the strong to the weak beats in a measure. In the five-beat Afro-Cuban clave, an essential rhythm in Latin music, the accents are shifted between two bars. Although syncopation has been traced to fourteenth century French-originated *Ars Nova* and was used by classical composers like Beethoven and Bach, it came into prominence in North American music through the jazz of the early twentieth century, which we shall see later was strongly influenced by African rhythms that arrived in New Orleans from Havana, among other sources. Syncopation isn't technically used in the Arabic music tradition, although the stressing of the downbeat that can happen might be taken to be reminiscent of jazz syncopation.

Syncopated clapping is also pronounced in flamenco music from Spain, which continued to influence the development of Latin music in the Latin American capitals, as it also absorbed Latin American influences. It is the syncopation of the five-beat clave rhythm that most strongly distinguishes Latin music from the military march-style 4/4 rhythm and the 3/4 waltzes that have been central to U.S. popular music.

New Orleans had been under alternating periods of Spanish and French rule in the years preceding the Louisiana Purchase of 1803, giving the Latin influence an entrée into modern American popular music long before jazz was born there. The considerable commercial and cultural interchange between New Orleans and Latin American port cities like Havana, Veracruz, Mexico, Cartagena, Colombia, Caracas, Venezuela, Santo Domingo, Dominican Republic, and San Juan, Puerto Rico, was enormously influential on the U.S. city's development, and there was a reciprocal influence on music in Latin capitals as well. British and French Caribbean islands like Jamaica, Haiti, Trinidad, the Bahamas, and the Lesser Antilles, whose cultures are African-dominant, also contributed to the Caribbean mix.

During the Haitian revolt at the beginning of the nineteenth century, as many as 6,000 refugees of both French and African descent came to New Orleans by way of Havana. The city became a Franco-Spanish-African-Caribbean melting pot, and its culture allowed for tolerance for African-based traditions like circle dances and carnival parades, which were performed openly in a way unheard of in most of the United States. This kind of openness—the ability of African culture to stand on its own—was parallel to the relative cultural autonomy of urban freed slaves and rural escaped slave communities in Latin America and allowed elements of African music to begin to mix with North American music.

The introduction of what pianist Jelly Roll Morton called "the Latin Tinge" into the New Orleans style of piano-playing was crucial to the development of jazz in America. The division of labor between left and right hand, to carry out rhythmic figures known in Cuban music as tumbaos (originally played on the drums and upright bass) with the left hand and percussive improvisation with the right, was an element of Latin music that Morton adapted for his own piano technique. This strategy ultimately became one of the bases for his inimitable stride piano-playing. The interplay between rhythm and melody in Scott Joplin's ragtime piano also has echoes of Afro-Cuban playing—in ragtime, the melody itself is syncopated.

There were other ports of entry of Latin music to the United States, most notably New York, which began experiencing immigration from Latin American countries at the turn of the twentieth century. Most of these immigrants were from Caribbean islands like Cuba and Puerto Rico. Many came to work in factories and as cigar workers, and there was a sizable influx of intellectuals and political activists who had been involved in the effort to throw off Spanish colonialism until the United States stepped in and acquired the islands as booty from its war with Spain. Along the border between the American Southwest and Mexico, there was a continuing influence of Mexican music styles on the hybrid culture that had been forming since the mid–nineteenth century, and in the late 1940s and 1950s, Los Angeles, with its many Mexican immigrants, became captivated by the mambo sound of Cuban bandleaders like Pérez Prado, who had taken Mexico City by storm.

The evolution of jazz in the twentieth century was intertwined with the growing popularity of the Argentine tango and of Afro-Cuban-derived dance forms like mambo, providing Latin music with an entry point into the popular tastes of North America. Led by big band leader Xavier Cugat and the international popularity of Argentine singer Carlos Gardel, Latin music began to have commercial success in North America. From the rustic rumbas played on boxes by descendants of slaves, Afro-Cuban music had evolved to an elegant orchestra format for showcasing dances like the stately *danzón* and the ecstatic *guaguancó*, a sensual dance rhythm that had a major impact through the 1950s and 1960s mambo era.

Supporting the aims of the Good Neighbor Policy, a government public relations ploy designed to form an alliance between the Americas to head off the influence of countries like Germany, a number of Hollywood films from the mid-1930s to the 1950s began to depict several different forms of Latin music, from the hybrid Brazilian-Hispanic music popularized by Carmen Miranda to the Afro-Cuban bands led by Cugat. More recording studios opened their doors to a growing number of immigrant musicians, who saw greater opportunity for superior facilities and opportunities in cities like New York, where clubs like the Stork Club and El Morocco, featuring watered-down versions of the music, became de rigueur for the elite.

After World War II, the Good Neighbor Policy waned, but the mambo era of the 1950s kept Latin music alive on radio, in recordings, and in the clubs. But in the late '50s, Cuba experienced a socialist revolution, and Latin music's influence lessened in North America, which was turning away from the ballroom dancing that paved the way for the acceptance of styles like tango and mambo. However, many ethnomusicologists point to the link between the bass patterns in Afro-Cuban music from the *danzón* to mambo and the way the instrument was eventually played in 1950s rock and roll—the strong African tendencies in the improvisatory sections in mambo were important antecedents to African-American popular music from jazz to rhythm and blues to funk.

In the early '60s, following the reign of Mambo kings Pérez Prado, Tito Puente, and Tito Rodríguez, funky Latin rhythms thoroughly permeated American pop—Afro-Cuban piano figures form the basis of the Isley Brothers' *Twist and Shout*, and the five-beat rhythm that pervades Buddy Holly's *Not Fade Away*, although parallel to one found in the American south, is essentially Afro-Cuban clave. The Latin sound influenced the shaking and rattling behind rock and roll through New Orleans pianist/vocalist Fats

Domino and the traces of *habanera* found in the early stages of rockabilly. There were also musical influences from Mexico. The *corrido* tradition, based on Spanish ballads and important along the Texas-Mexico border, probably had an influence on Texas native Woody Guthrie, Bob Dylan's forebear. The curious sound of the Farfisa organ, used as a novelty in late-1950s conjunto (Mexican-American popular dance group) music, would become a signature of American psychedelic music half a decade later.

Latin styles had slipped out of the U.S. mainstream post-mambo, but in New York, Latin musicians continued to reproduce the latest fad from Cuba. They had been just been reinventing the fast-paced charanga and pachanga when suddenly Castro's socialist revolution cut them off from the island and they were left to their own devices. Out of New York Latinos' growing interaction with the African-American community, a fusion between R&B and Latin called bugaloo appeared as charanga declined. But led by in-novations by pianist Eddie Palmieri, trombonist/arranger Willie Colón, and bandleader Johnny Pacheco, New York Latinos in-vented their own music, salsa, which incorporated newer, faster arrangements, jazz and R&B influences, and dance styles from places like Puerto Rico, Colombia, and Panama. The Cuban- and Argentine-based *nueva canción* (new song) movement also had an influence on songwriters like Rubén Blades, who wrote some of the New York salsa school's most socially conscious lyrics. The Golden Age of Salsa was a revelation for New York Latinos in the mid-1970s, but it happened completely outside the mainstream, thriving in the same inner-city neighborhoods (the South Bronx, East Harlem) that later nourished hip-hop, house, and freestyle dance music. The salsa years allowed for the solidification of a new, bicultural mindset for U.S.-born Latinos, one nurtured in the pan-Latin urban metropolis rather than the provincial Latin American town and countryside.

In the glitzy '80s, salsa's promoters saw handsome leading men singing songs of love as being more commercially viable than

musicianship and socially conscious lyrics. Predictable and formulaic, salsa lost its edge of social protest; its *soneros*, or lead singers,
became reflections of the telenovela idols or pop stars that dominated the Miami-created version of Latin Hollywood, called *La
Farándula*. The Spanish national Julio Iglesias laid the groundwork
for the middlebrow Latin pop genre by selling millions of records
of remade and original ballads across Latin America. Iglesias's success helped establish the Latin pop radio niche in the United
States, allowing for the creation of national playlists and eroding
tropical music's popularity. With its roots in the bolero tradition
that was widespread in Latin America from the 1920s to the 1970s,
the Latin pop market produced stars in the '80s and '90s like Luís
Miguel, Juan Gabriel, José José, and Ricardo Montaner.

Latin music's reemergence as a commercial force in the 1990s
was signaled when Mexican-Americans, whose love for Tejano and
norteño regional genres based in northern Mexico and Texas,
made Selena Quintanilla, a charismatic icon of pop-cumbia, a
megastar. Regional and Tex-Mex norteño music had been evolving
from the folkloric music played since the absorption of Texas into
the United States. A popular genre first in the mid-'50s, Tejano
had a second golden age in the early '90s when a surge in immigration increased demand for the music, which continued its dynamic evolution in the border regions of El Paso/Juárez and
Tijuana/San Diego. Mexican regional/Tex Mex also got a major
boost from the introduction of Soundscan, an electronic information system that tracks music sales, in the mid-1990s, but the market boom was largely created by Selena's massive sales, which
accelerated even faster after she was tragically killed in 1994 at age
twenty-three. Her posthumous fame, exemplified by a million-
selling issue of a special edition of *People* magazine, showed that
Latin music could be a major force even when produced in a
highly regional ethnic style, a point not lost on the major labels.

Latin music grew in the twentieth century as a result of the interplay between it and North American forms, and Latin musicians

who lived in the United States accelerated the pace of its evolution. But the music also evolved through its spreading between different Latin American countries. Mexico absorbed Cuban styles like the bolero and the mambo first through the connection with coastal cities like Mérida and Veracruz, and then in the 1940s and 1950s when Cuban musicians relocated to Mexico City to take advantage of that metropolis's rapidly growing film industry. Dominican merengue (which evolved in part from meringue music from neighboring Haiti) found its way into Puerto Rico, affecting music and dance styles there, and the Cuban danzón traveled all over the Caribbean. Music from the Caribbean was also adapted by Colombian musicians like Lucho Bermúdez, who invented a genre called merecumbé, a fusion between merengue and cumbia. The Colombian cumbia became enormously popular in northern Mexico, which plays it so idiosyncratically now that many have forgotten its Colombian origins. The tango was an international phenomenon in Latin America and greatly affected the evolution of the bolero, particularly in Mexico.

By the end of the 1990s, the pop music worlds of Anglo and Latin America overlapped, generating a phenomenon that became known as the Latin Pop Explosion. When Ricky Martin suddenly appeared on millions of television sets shaking his *bon-bon* and singing his riotously infectious *Livin' La Vida Loca*, he brought the idea of Latin pop music to the forefront of the North American scene in a way no one else had done since the 1950s. Martin was the leading edge of a new crop of singers, including Marc Anthony, Enrique Iglesias, Jennifer Lopez, and Christina Aguilera, who, if not steeped in the traditions of Latin music, traded on Latinness.

When Martin released *Livin' La Vida Loca*, he expanded his audience, but he didn't put his core base of fans at risk. Most young Latinos are bilingual and would follow him, or any other major Latino pop star who dabbled in English, something that wouldn't have happened ten years before. About half of the U.S. Latino population is under twenty-five, and growing numbers prefer their information in English over Spanish. In 1999, New York's salsa-oriented La Mega became the first Spanish-language radio station to take number one in the area's Arbitron ratings, and much of its success was attributed to its occasional use of bilingual and English content. But preference for English doesn't mean that young Latinos want to ditch their roots entirely. In a phenomenon that academics and advertising wonks call "reverse assimilation," bilingual Latinos, who grew up on a diet of R&B, hip-hop, and rock, are going back to their roots. Martin, a young, bilingual Latino trying to make contemporary music without burying his native rhythms, is emblematic of a new generation in America. These are the fans at the core of Latin music's resurgence, filling salsa dance clubs from the Copacabana in New York to the Congo Room in Hollywood, and fueling the sales of Tejano, norteño, and its newest variant banda (a fast-paced dance music characterized by rapid-fire tuba grunts).

The Latin Pop Explosion was only the crest of a wave of Latin musical incursions on the North American market. The surge in interest in Cuban music, crystallized by nostalgia groups like the Buena Vista Social Club, and the popularity of highly stylized dance music called salsa had been setting the stage for Martin for several years. Latin pop's return to prominence was also influenced by the growing Latin alternative music movement (sometimes called *rock en Español*), in which rock angst was framed in a Romance language, influenced by both the North American blues and rock tradition and the Latin American bolero tradition.

The success of Latin pop also had to do with a synergistic interaction between North and Latin America in part brought about by the free trade climate of the turn of the twenty-first century. In a confluence between music and marketing, Latin America is becoming more American and the United States is getting more Latin. Having strengthened its bases in Miami and New York, the Latin music industry has helped create a demand that is growing at twice the rate of the mainstream American music market. In the United States, massive immigration over the last ten years has made Latinos the largest minority group. Through sheer numbers, Latinos have created possible markets for all types of Latin music, and the major record labels have organized themselves to take advantage of this growing Latino consumer spending.

Several trends among young Americans have created a new non-Latino listenership as well. The cocktail lounge fad prepared young listeners to embrace the sexy-smooth Brazilian bossa nova, and swing-dance revivalism paved the way for a late–1990s salsa-dancing craze. Meanwhile, the thawing of relations with socialist Cuba has allowed an avalanche of innovative Afro-Cuban dance and jazz-fusion bands to tour the United States. The stunning expertise of these musicians, many trained in government-sponsored conservatories, seemed to lift Latin music from its "ethnic" status, attracting a more mainstream audience. In New York, a new generation of Nuyorican and Dominican youth followed club-music-oriented idols like Marc Anthony and La India back to their roots and helped create a second golden age of salsa. The energy in the Latin clubs from English-speaking Latino youth spilled into the general population, making salsa-dancing classes de rigueur for a broad swath of college-aged kids.

In California, which 150 years ago was a sprawling northern outpost of Mexico, a new ska fad grew in the late 1990s. Mexican and Mexican-American youth fused *rock en Español* bands like Maldita Vecindad and Los Fabulosos Cadillacs, who were inspired by 1980s English bands like the Specials and Madness, with Southern California skateboard punk culture. Through Jamaica's proximity to Spanish-speaking Caribbean neighbors, ska penetrated countries like Mexico and Argentina easily—ska's rhythmic similarities to Latin music like *cumbia* and some of the more rustic African beats translated well for young people looking for a synergy between tropical beats and modern rock.

Perhaps Latin music's resurgence in the late 1990s was inevitable, given the decade's embrace of hybridization across all music and culture. It was a period that mixed hardcore punk with salsa, dancehall with merengue, and British progressive rock with Mexican folk music. It was a time when Marc Anthony sang salsa with a new jack twist, when Puff Daddy dropped Spanglish rhymes, and Beck shared a producer with Mexican rockers Plastilina Mosh. American music went Latin because it was trying to acknowledge its long-ignored roots and to fuse back together its musical history into one swinging, soulful *loca*-motion.

In the pages that follow, I will try to illuminate those roots, while at the same time recounting the significant developments that made Latin music what it is today. Much of what is written or testified to about the African origins of Latin music and its subsequent mixing in Latin American cities is constantly debated. A famous tension exists between the work of Cuban writers Alejo Carpentier and Fernando Ortiz on exactly what genres originated in Latin America, Africa, and Spain. Owing to the lack of scholarly work and the vagaries of oral traditions that pass on the history of the music there is a general lack of accuracy. This book will try to pass on as many interpretations as possible, while recognizing that at times specificity can be lost in different, sometimes conflicting sources.

From the beginnings of the intermixing between the modern Cuban son (a early merging of the street-flavored, drum-oriented rumba and the country-folk, guitar-driven son) and American swing and bebop, through the mambo craze of the 1950s, the bugaloo beat of the 1960s, and the emergence of Nuyorican salsa in the '70s, *The Latin Beat* explains how the already hybrid forms of Latin music changed once they were part of the American pop milieu. The first few chapters, "The Beat Is in the Blood," "The

Evolution of Cuban Music into Salsa," "The Story of Nuyorican Salsa," and "Contemporary Cuban Music," tell the story of how the central strand of Latin music begins and ends with the hybrid developments between the European contradanza (a dance originally known in England as country dance, picked up by France as contradanse), the above-mentioned son, and the African rumba (ritual Western African religious music that became secular in places like Havana). These chapters focus on the central story of what we know superficially as "Latin music," particularly the way the North American pop cultural mythology frames it as a succession of dances starting in the 1930s and culminating with the mambo movement of the 1940s and 1950s.

Chapters 5 and 6 capture the ancillary stories of music that became popular in Latin America in a kind of symbiotic relationship to Afro-Cuban music. "The Latin Ballad from the Bolero to the New Latin Pop" describes the development of the bolero in the early part of the century and that pop music's evolution into the current form, which constitutes a major radio format on both sides of the border. "Latin Jazz" follows the progress of a revolution started by Afro-Cuban musicians like Mario Bauzá and Israel Cachao López after they came to New York and began playing side-by-side with African-American jazz musicians. "Re-imagining Brazil" is an attempt to boil down into one chapter the vast history of Brazilian music, which is based on an entirely different strand of Iberian and African culture. While the samba was also developed by ex-slaves, it has an entirely different feel, and is less anchored to a clave beat. But there are some parallel developments with Afro-Cuban-derived music, as its interaction with and influence on North American jazz and popular music is crucial.

"Other Latin Beats" focuses on the major Latin music genres, again somewhat different from Afro-Cuban music, which became national symbols for their respective countries: the Dominican Republic, Colombia, Puerto Rico, and Mexico. The last two chapters, "The Hidden History of Latinos in Rock and Hip-hop" and

"Latin Alternative" follow the course of Latin music as it becomes increasingly intertwined with North American pop music. The hidden-history chapter details the ways that Latin music and/or Latino musicians played major roles in the development of North American genres like rock and roll, garage rock, punk rock, hip-hop, and electronica.

In demonstrating the wide breadth of what can be considered Latin music today, *The Latin Beat* draws distinctions often more for the sake of clarity than to illuminate strong qualitative differences. The reason for the emphasis on Afro-Cuban and African-derived music is not an aesthetic one. It simply reflects the wide range of popularity these forms of music have. While today's Latin music market is dominated by the sales of Mexican regional and Tejano music, that is more of a reflection of Mexican-American buying power than of the acceptance of the music across the Americas. If you are in a bar or club or taxi in Buenos Aires, Bogotá, Mexico City, San Juan, or Miami, you are much more likely to hear a syrupy bolero or a frenetic salsa tune than Mexican regional or Andean folkloric music. Latin music as we know it today colloquially, casually, is an international music, the one with the swing and the soul that transcends borders and languages.

The Beat Is in the Blood

Latin music is the product of a culture that has combined influences from Europe, Africa, and the indigenous people of Latin America, as well as its North American neighbors, and its variety reflects all these inputs. Historically Latin music, like Latin culture, has had a pronounced influence from African and indigenous cultures, and it displays a great fluidity in cultural mixing. The important genres of Latin music, such as Cuban son, danzón, mambo, and bolero, Brazilian samba, Argentine tango, Colombian cumbia, Puerto Rican bomba and plena, and Dominican merengue, all have a distinctive tonal and rhythmic quality that derives from African and indigenous influences. These rhythmic and harmonic tendencies are what distinguish Latin music from European and North American music (despite its own African influence), for example, and ground our understanding of its uniqueness.

Although perhaps the most important, internationally recognized Latin music at the beginning of the twentieth century was the tango, by the 1920s and '30s, the music that dominated the rest of the Latin music field was Afro-Cuban music. The context of Afro-Cuban music is the Caribbean nucleus of diasporic African cultural forms, which also gave birth to genres like merengue, cumbia, and samba. Afro-Cuban music is the most highly developed music of a genre that the music industry now calls tropical. It is also the most recognizable form of Latin music because of the various well-known dance forms it spawned, its influence on North American jazz, its transformation into what is now called salsa, and most of all, its pronounced, five-beat clave rhythm, which is the closest to a generic understanding of Latin music as there is.

The central importance of Cuba in Latin music owes to its geographic location, which made it an important maritime way station for all kinds of human travel and trade from the sixteenth to the twentieth centuries. From its beginning as a stopping off point for adventurers on their way to Cortés's Mexico, to its relatively brief intermingling between the indigenous Arawak Indians and early Spanish settlers, to the influx of French and Haitian free blacks and slaves in the late eighteenth century, Cuba was a major cultural crossroads. Its major cities, Havana and Santiago, were centers of Hispanic culture in the Caribbean, and they were centers for absorbing and recontextualizing music from the Andalucía region of Spain and from European cities like Paris and Naples (under Spanish rule in the sixteenth and seventeenth centuries, Naples was the birthplace of opera buffa, an influence on nineteenth century Cuban music). At the same time these forms were recombined with influences from other African diasporic centers like New Orleans, the Caribbean coastal Colombian region, the Dominican Republic, and Puerto Rico.

While many European popular and classical influences were absorbed into Afro-Cuban music, the element that is most distinctive about it, and Latin music in general, is its rhythmic structure, or beat. The centrality of the drum in creating and maintaining the Latin beat, which is in actuality a wide range of rhythms, is the essence of Latin music. The panoply of African drums that can be found in neighboring countries such as Puerto Rico, the Dominican Republic, Venezuela, Colombia, and Mexico are more or less variations on similar-sized instruments. In Cuba, a specific set of instruments became associated with the creation of a native Cuban music.

Combining the influence of European instruments, such as the guitar, mandolin, and lute, and Yoruba drums like the batá, used for religious ceremonies, Cubans fashioned the tres, typically a small guitar with three sets of doubled strings; the timbal, bongo, and conga drums; and small clave sticks used to keep time. Since most of Cuba's Arawak and Taino tribes had died from disease brought by the conquering Spaniards, as well as from the hardships of slavery, by the end of the seventeenth century, their influence was limited to accompanying instruments such as the güiro, a hollowed-out gourd that is scraped as incidental percussion, and the maracas, but versions of both instruments also previously existed in Africa. As Cuban music evolved in the nineteenth century, stringed instruments, flutes, and pianos imported from Europe and the United States began to play important roles. The use of the piano in particular was emblematic of submission of the musicians to rhythmic imperatives—the ultimate composing tool of European music in Cuba was transformed into the ultimate rhythmic instrument.

The Afro-Cuban beat is actually a complex array of several kinds of rhythms, derived from a number of different African cultures, most notably Yoruban and Congolese. The African drumming at the root of Afro-Cuban music is partly a form of communication, the religious invocation of a pantheon of West African gods called *orishas*, used to call them down to earth during ceremonies. These religious traditions were established in the eleventh century in the city-states of Oyo and Ife, in what is now Nigeria. Oyo was an important center of slave trade in the eighteenth and nineteenth centuries, as it controlled the port of Lagos. Many of the slaves brought to Cuba were of Yoruba ethnic origin, followers of the *orishas* of Oyo and Ife. Another sizable importation of slaves was from the Congo-Angola area Bantu tribes, who were more dominant in other islands of the Caribbean.

The earth-based religions of West and Central Africa were brought to the New World through slavery, beginning in Cuba in the early sixteenth century. When Bartolomé de las Casas recommended the importation of African slaves after the hard work of mining for gold decimated the Arawak Indians of the Greater Antilles, he unwittingly set the stage for the creation of "Latin" music. (Although towards the end of his life de las Casas denounced all forms as slavery as against the teachings of Christ, by that time the transatlantic slave trade had already begun.) The arrival of tribes from the Yoruba and Efik nations of Nigeria and the Arará and Ewe-Fon from Dahomey and Bantu from the Congo put Cuba on a path toward a radically new kind of music.

The legacies of the various strands of African populations brought to Latin America were so intertwined when they got to the New World that a direct lineage to cultural traditions is difficult to establish. Yorubans brought to the New World a complex system of religious belief that incorporated dance and drum ritual. The religions of Ife and Oyo combined with the external trappings of Roman Catholicism to become what is now popularly known as Santería. Three major ethnic groups from West Africa laid the foundation for Afro-Cuban music: the Lucumí, from what is now Nigeria, the Arará speaking tribes of Benin or Dahomey, and the Abakuá, who descended from an interior river region called the Calabar and whose sects are extremely secretive and exclusively male. The various West African tribes brought with them several antecedents to what would become the Afro-Cuban clave, each based on specific rituals in Yoruban religion. The basic structure was consolidated in Cuba—the clave's two-bar, five-beat rhythm varies in terms of accenting and pauses. The Congolese Bantu traditions were crucial in helping to transform this religious music into secular music. Terms like conga, bongó, and mambo come from the Bantu language, and Bantu dances became the root of what would become known as the rumba. The adaptation of the Yoruban clave onto these Congo-derived rhythms is essential to Afro-Cuban music.

Since the Spaniards were motivated by Roman Catholicism, they were more interested than their Protestant counterparts in North America in converting their slave and indigenous populations in an attempt to "save" them. This made it relatively easier for Africans to retain their original cultures under the Spaniards than under the North Americans—the Spanish empire was also less efficient in preventing the creation of escaped slave communities. In seventeenth-century Cuba, the colonial government tolerated *cabildos* or "houses" created by freed slaves or indentured servants that allowed some semblance of regional cultures to remain intact and in the long run helped some slaves and servants to raise enough money to buy their freedom. These *cabildos*, situated on the outskirts of major cities like Havana, became powerful institutions in which the Santería religion was incubated, attracting not only Africans, but also lower-class whites and mulattos who lived in urban areas.

Santería was and is a way for Yorubans to worship their gods by cloaking them in the identities of Catholic saints. For instance, the fiery, lustful Changó merged with Santa Barbara; the tricky middleman Elegguá with St. Anthony. Each initiate into the religion undergoes a process by which is discovered the saint to which his or her soul should be devoted. More than just being objects of worship, the *orishas* corresponding to individual believers actually "own" their bodies. In the Santería rituals called *bembés*, any variety of corresponding *orishas* are called down to "possess" individual believers. Wielding the thundering *batá* drum (as well as other instruments that today are still not revealed to nonbelievers), the drummers at *bembés* create a trance-inducing frenzy that lasts for hours. These rituals, originating as early as the first slaves' arrival in the New World, are still held throughout Cuba today.

From the religious *toques* (musical performances conforming to rhythmic patterns designed to call down specific *orishas*), evolved a more secular tradition of rumbas, popular gatherings in which revelers perform dances derived from Santería rituals, not to be confused with rhumba, a Latin-style music popular in North America and Europe in the early twentieth century. Rumbas, which grew out of nineteenth century carnivals, took hold in the communities near the sugar mills of Havana and Matanzas in the twentieth century. They are similar to *toques* in musical content, but are less formal in their religious function. The *orishas* are praised, and the centrality of the drumming remains, but the celebration is not necessarily for initiates—it's more like a block party, and the erotic Bantu fertility dances are central. The dances performed at these gatherings are also called rumbas—specific styles known as guaguancó, yambú, and columbia. The 6/8 time signature that is found in classic mambo of the 1950s and 1960s is present in the "columbia" rumba. The guaguancó would eventually became the most popular form of rumba, but in its primal form it contains a call-and-response sequence between two vocalists as well as a chorus and a dance segment in which a male and female couple is surrounded by a circle of dancers. The male gyrates his body in imitation of a rooster trying to impregnate a hen, a kind of courting and mating ritual. Lyrics accompanying this dance often make reference to a "vacuna" or vaccination, a somewhat crude and humorous metaphor. The columbia features a single dancer, who performs rhythmic, aggressive thrusting moves similar to Brazilian capoeira or even contemporary breakdancing. The yambú tells a story with two dancers enacting the characters, often using the espinela form of décima inherited from Spain.

Clave, the Key to Latin Music

Appropriately enough for music built on the drum, the organizing principle of Latin music is a five-beat pattern called the clave: Two wooden clave sticks are used by musicians to tap out the underlying rhythm of a song, whether it's a slow bolero or an out-and-out guaguancó. The sticks are called "clave" sticks most likely because they embody the function of unlocking the "code" of Afro-Cuban music. The word *clave* is taken from the Spanish word meaning key and also the musical term clef. Fernando Ortiz, a Cuban musical historian, said that the claves doubled as "pegs of hard wood used in the making of ships," adding another meaning—*clavo* in Spanish means nail. Ortiz felt that the clave attained a kind of mystical quality through its evolution in Cuba: "Aside from its rhythmic importance in musical practice, the Cuban clave is itself, by virtue of its simplicity and striking timbre, a melodic exclamation filled with emotion . . . There is something about [the clave] which eludes the typically opaque sound of wood. Although made of vegetable, its vibrations create an almost crystalline or metallic resonance."

Most Afro-Cuban musicians refer to two main types of clave, the *son* clave and the rumba clave. The son clave, most often associated with orchestra dance styles, has a 3/2 pattern, and the rumba clave, associated with older carnaval rhythms, has a 2/3 pattern. In the son clave, the three-beat measure is the strong or tresillo measure, and is the site where syncopation occurs, on the second note. In the rumba clave, an additional note is syncopated, something that allows for a funkier sound when played by modern salsa orchestras. The two forms are also referred to as forward and reverse clave, which implies an interactive tension between them that pops up in the evolution of Afro-Cuban music, and their juxtaposition is an interesting parallel to the "mirror" phenomenon inherent in the Spanish espinela form of décima, which was transmitted through mixed-race peasants in the process of Cuban cultural evolution. The clave began evolving in Cuba as soon as interaction began between the major ethnic groups during the peak period of the slave trade from the late-seventeenth to mid-eighteenth centuries. The earlier forms of clave were usually rumba clave, with *son* clave slowly evolving as a result of increased contact between African ritual traditions and secular influences from Cuban Creole society.

The sociologist/novelist Alejo Carpentier, in *La música de Cuba*, recounted that although in Cuba various forms of percussive accompaniment were used, from the güiro to the Afro-Haitian catá and bran-bram sonettes, the clave sticks enforced a rhythm that "is the only one that can always adjust itself, without variation, to all types of Cuban melodies, thereby constituting a kind of constant rhythmic element."

According to Columbia University Professor and trombonist Chris Washburne, the two "diametrically opposed" measures of clave pattern are not at odds, but rather, are balanced opposites, like positive and negative, expansive and contractive, or the poles of a magnet. In this view the clave pattern is not only a metaphor for the interaction between races, it actually functions as a mathematical vehicle for the resolution of these contrasts.

The clave retained key African notions: The clave's pattern never changes throughout a song; and the melody of the song determines whether it's son or rumba clave, once it's established whether a song should be played in forward (3/2) or reverse (2/3) clave. Given its relatively flexible rhythmic necessity, clave sets the stage for improvisation in a wide harmonic range.

As long as Cuba was still a European colony, the continued influence from European styles encouraged the evolution of new syncretisms between African and European cultures. Cuba was coming into its own in the mid-to-late eighteenth century; a bourgeois class was developing, sometimes enjoying a standard of living that exceeded that of influential families back in Spain. The strength of Cuban agriculture and its plantation-based economy fed the vitality of the ports of Havana, Matanzas, and Santiago. A class of Creoles, descendants of Spaniards, sometimes mixed with indigenous and African blood, began to create a unique Cuban cultural identity.

Slavery did not end in Cuba until 1886, although liberal laws instituted by the Spanish colonial government had allowed for a free-black population almost as high as the slave population. As

Alejandro Carpentier wrote, blacks would be celebrated in the *décima*-based songs of the mid-eighteenth century as worthy opponents to the brief British occupation of Havana. (*La audacia y valentia/de los pardos y morenos/que obraron/nada menos/que blancos sin cobardía*–"The audacity and courage/of the browns and blacks/who fought with valor/no less than whites"–went a popular *décima* of the time.) Blacks made up about 40 per cent of the island's population, and about 40 per cent of these blacks were free. At the end of the eighteenth century, the Haitian revolution had sent thousands of French, their slaves, and escaped slaves to various locations in Cuba, bringing their own hybrid forms of African and European music with them. Carpentier stated that in the first half of the nineteenth century, blacks were "the clear majority of the professional musicians," and the island's premier maker of musical instruments, Juan José Rebollar, was black.

The development of music in Cuba up to the early twentieth century followed several lineages. In the nineteenth century, there was the salon music of the bourgeoisie, which was played first in cathedrals, then theaters. This salon music ranged from French opera like Molière to the Spanish traditions of *tonadilla* and *trípili-trápala*, which were predecessors to the nineteenth century *bufo* tradition. The *bufo* operas, derived from Neapolitan opera buffa, were akin to Spanish *zarzuelas*. Through innovators like Havana native Francisco Covarrubias, bufo began to focus on local Cuban characters, highlighting regional origins (Galicia, Catalonia), and class standing (country peasant guajiro, urban types). Another strand of Cuban music, the guaracha, originating in the eighteenth century as a kind of lower-class, humorous song, up-tempo and highly choreographed in the bufo tradition, reached the peak of its popularity in the mid-nineteenth century.

The nineteenth century also saw the evolution of the *contradanza*, which was derived from the French contredanse, a salon dance style brought by French fleeing the Haitian revolution. In towns like

Matanzas at the end of the nineteenth century, dancers and musicians began to reject the rigidity of the contradanza, and the increasing improvisation of their styles gave birth to the primary Cuban form, the danzón. Finally, the cabildo houses, established by free Africans beginning in the seventeenth century, had been participating in their own version of Christian religious processions, the Caribbean carnival. Groups of cabildo members sang and danced to the percussion of drumming groups, which performed an up-tempo dance (not dissimilar to Brazilian samba) in 4/4 time called cocoyé, based on the rhythmic unit called the cinquillo, a five-beat, one-bar pattern. (The cinquillo would become vastly important to Cuban, and, by extension, all Latin music.)

At the beginning of the twentieth century, all these traditions in Cuban music, which until then had existed more or less discretely in the dynamics of the island's major cities, began to mix together. The most galvanizing development was a new kind of street music that would ultimately become the basis of Afro-Cuban music in the same way that blues would become the basis for rock and roll. The rumba—the name can literally mean "form a path," or figuratively, "let's get going"—came from the surviving African culture that evolved from slaves on the plantation to workers in the sugar mill to the cabildos and finally the narrow alleyways of urban centers like Havana, Matanzas, and Santiago.

The oft-repeated legend of rumba is that slave descendants were not permitted by local authorities to play drums except on Sunday, so they used a range of different packing boxes (most famously those for codfish), each with a different pitch. In fact, a string of Cuban presidents from 1909 to 1933 (notably Alfredo Zayas) issued edicts to prohibit various manifestations of African culture such as carnival *comparsas*, secular rumbas, and the bongó drum. To this day in certain performances, rumbas are played on "cajas," literally, boxes.

Small percussive instruments augment the rumba clave, such as the cata, a cane-like stick, and the maranga, an iron rattle. Additional patterns, such as the cáscara, which sounds like the clopping sounds of horses; and the bombó, a strong accent played on a bombó drum with a resonant sound, flesh out the rumba. The guaguancó, perhaps the most modern of rumba patterns, incorporated the metric feel of 4/4, while retaining a polyrhythmic 6/8 character, ultimately becoming one of the more esoteric beats in classic salsa.

Although other African-Spanish or African-Spanish-indigenous musical hybrids were developing in countries like Puerto Rico, the Dominican Republic, Venezuela, Colombia, Panama, Mexico, and Peru, Cuban music became the standard for an "international" form of Latin music. Havana's centrality as a maritime port, combined with the extraordinary mixing and remixing of European and African traditions going on in Cuba, allowed for easy export of a continually evolving strand of Latin music that began affecting the rest of Latin America. Through Mexico's port of Veracruz, Cuban styles like contradanza began to penetrate that country's musical tradition by the mid–nineteenth century, leaving an indelible imprint that would continue when the mambo was popularized in the mid–twentieth century.

One of the strongest examples of the influence of Afro-Cuban music through export is the habanera, whose name, according to some researchers, was given to it only when it left Havana. According to some accounts, the first habanera was written in 1836, but the style hit its peak in 1884 when Sebastian Yradier's *La Paloma* became a hit in Mexico and in the United States. The Argentinian port city of Buenos Aires absorbed the habanera rhythm, which had evolved from Cuban ballroom styles like the danzón and contradanza, to create its quintessential national music, the tango. The habanera rhythm was also exported to New Orleans, where it had a major effect on the development of the nascent North American music known as jazz, which in turn returned to Havana and its elements of phrasing and orchestration had yet another influence on Latin music.

By the end of the nineteenth century, several different orchestra styles playing ballroom dance music were popular in Cuba. The styles had roots in several European influences that began to arrive in Cuba. First was the Haitian revolution of the late eighteenth century, which had displaced French aristocracy and their servants to the eastern half of Cuba. Their favorite popular dance music was the contradanza, originally an English country dance that caught on in France and in turn was infused by African influences during the French colonization of Hispañola, the island that is today divided into Haiti and the Dominican Republic.

Small orchestras played the Cuban contradanza, which was driven by strings and brass. The French contredanse, from which the Cuban contradanza had evolved, featured piano, violins, and flutes, as well as a strong tradition of couple-dancing. The contradanza took on more Cuban characteristics, mixing European and African instruments as the colonial Creole culture mixed influences from both antecedents, as local musicians combined European string instruments with reeds (clarinets, saxophones), brass (mostly cornet), and African percussion instruments that were used in the son.

These groups, known as *orquestas típicas*, literally, "typical orchestras," began to incorporate into the contradanza a rapid-fire five-beat, one-bar pattern known as cinquillo, a repeating bass figure of African derivation that had most likely been transmitted from Haiti, on the piano and in the rhythm section. Thus was born the contradanza habanera, a term eventually shortened to habanera. The habanera rhythm, in addition to becoming the basis for the Argentine tango, was such a widespread influence that it showed up in Bizet's *Carmen*. (The original tango orchestras of Argentina had basically the same instrumental lineup and shared the same name with the Cuban *típicas*.)

In 1877, Matanzas cornet player Miguel Failde was credited with originating the danzón, which was designed for more improvisation by dancers. According to Isabelle Leymaire's *Cuban*

Fire: The Story of Salsa and Latin Jazz, one of Failde's early danzones, *Las Alturas de Simpson*, referred to a Matanzas neighborhood known for its rumbas and cabildos. By the early twentieth century there was a proliferation of orquestas típicas in Havana that played the danzón, a dance music often invoked as the Cuban counterpoint to the increasing popularity among the bourgeoisie of North American dances like the fox trot. The danzón is now more of an archaic dance, still performed in Veracruz, Mexico, and the Philippines, and is related to the Puerto Rican danza.

The Cuban bolero, or romantic love song, also became popular fodder for típica orchestras. The bolero, which evolved from the trova, a song form from Santiago that was influenced by Italian operas, French romances, and ultimately the troubadour tradition, was distinguished by a syncopated strumming technique (alternately called *rasqueado*, or scratching, reflecting its roots in Africa or Andalusian flamenco) and its use of clave. The bolero tradition was developed by singers like José Pepe Sánchez, said to be the father of this style, and emphasized melody and poetry (a famous example is the bolero *Aquellos Ojos Verde*, with lyrics by the poet Adolfo Utreta). As is the case with much of Cuban music, the sophistication that bolero gained in conjunction with the dance orchestras of Havana ultimately projected it onto an international stage.

Another branching of the típica orchestras came in the early twentieth century when pianist Antonio María Romeu formed the first charanga orchestra. Charangas played lighter, faster versions of the danzón, eliminating the brass section and emphasizing French flutes, violins, and the piano. By the mid-1930s, the charanga movement climaxed with the work of flautist Antonio Arcaño, whose Las Maravillas orchestra came to rule Havana's dance clubs.

The creation of North American jazz came about in large part as the result of a free-flowing relationship between New Orleans and Havana that dates back to the mid-nineteenth century. As

John Storm Roberts wrote in *Latin Jazz: The First of the Fusions*, it is difficult and almost self-defeating to untangle the European and Afro-Caribbean influences on New Orleans piano-playing during that era, because various genres had been cross-fertilizing for a century. During that era, New Orleans pianist and composer Louis Moreau Gottschalk traversed various Caribbean cities, mining the predominantly Latin styles of each country. He was primarily responsible for the transmission of the *habanera* rhythm to New Orleans, which was known as the "tango bass." In a World's Fair exhibition of 1884–1885, in New Orleans, a Mexican military band had its music transcribed by a sheet music printer, and its repertoire, which included the danzón *Ausencia* (not to be confused with the bolero written by Jaime Prats in the 1920s) became part of the local lore.

John Storm Roberts has identified the use of the habanera in Scott Joplin's ragtime piano in 1908, and by the mid-1920s, New Orleans jazz pioneer Jelly Roll Morton had also incorporated habanera bass lines, creating the stride piano style in which a rhythmic pattern akin to the Cuban *tumbao* (a repeating bass figure) was played on the left hand, with the right used for extensive improvisation. Morton was recreating the dynamic in basic Cuban sextetos, transposing rhythmic percussive parts to the piano. Morton called this the "Spanish tinge," stating "if you can't manage to put tinges of Spanish in your tunes, you will never be able to add the right seasoning, I call it, for jazz."

As Isabel Leymarie observed, Latin musicians were playing all over New Orleans at the turn of the century. Latin syncopations could be found in Jesse Picket's *The Dream*, Neil Moret's *Cubanola*, and Robert Hampton's *Agitation Rag*, as well as in the work of Scott Joplin. W. C. Handy, an early blues giant, had traveled to Cuba in 1910 with the U.S. army and was exposed to the típica orchestra. His famous composition *St. Louis Blues* incorporated the habanera rhythm. During this time the trumpet was added to the Cuban orchestras, giving Cuban music at least a superficial similarity with jazz and ragtime. In 1912, three years after W. C. Handy did the same, Antonio Romeu added a saxophone to his danzón orchestra.

Around the turn of the twentieth century, various strands of Cuban music began to come together in popular dance music halls. American corporations, after the Spanish-American War, had free rein in Cuba, and record companies soon began recording Havana acts, which drew more musicians in from other parts of the island. The son, a polyrhythmic popular song form originally developed in Santiago, the bolero, a ballad-like, slower-paced romantic song form, and the danzón were all being recontextualized with new influences from Havana, North American popular music and jazz, and the rawer African rumba. Like the rumba, the son is more than just a particular song form, it is an ambience, an atmosphere that expresses something essential about Cuban culture.

Like rumba, the word *son* itself has multiple associations, though in this case not denotative but connotative. It resonates with *sonido*, literally *sound*, can also be read as "they are," as in the state of a particular popular culture (a famous son, *Son de la Loma*, plays with this meaning to refer to the singers' origin—"they are from the mountains" forms a pun with "son from the mountains"), and to the English speaker, it suggests simply "song." To think of *son* as primordial Cuban "song" is helpful, especially if one takes to heart Alejo Carpentier's assertion in *La música de Cuba* that the earliest version of the Cuban son appeared in the sixteenth century, penned by a free African woman named Tedoroa who moved to Santiago from the Dominican Republic. *Son de la Ma' Teodora* tells the story of a woman who performed with a violinist from Seville, among other collaborators, and featured the call-and-response vocals that exemplified both the African influence and the mandolins typical of Spanish instrumentation of the period.

Some historians say that a Colombian tune predated *Son de la Ma' Teodora* and that the *guajiros*, largely responsible for creating the contemporary son, were at least partly descended from indigenous people from the Colombian coastal region of la Guajira, which might explain the name given to them. Such mixed ancestry is typical in the development of Latin music, particularly in the Caribbean. The important point is that because of Cuba's pivotal, dynamic nineteenth century Latin culture, musical forms like son were crystallized on the island and brought to their highest form of sophistication before they were exported and popularized elsewhere. The modern son first appeared in the Eastern Oriente Province of the island in the late nineteenth century, an area that contained not only a high population of African descendants because of its importance to sugar cultivation but also Cuba's second-largest city, Santiago, which was largely Afro-Cuban.

The structure of the son is relatively simple—first, there is an introduction, the "song" part, which has a verse usually containing octosyllabic four-line stanzas, a slight variation on the décima and most likely of Andalusian origin. Secondly, in the *montuno* section, the elements established in the introduction are developed, and a chorus sings a refrain. The Spanish and African antecedents to the son came from the racial miscegenation between poor Spanish-ancestry peasants and African laborers and tenders of the land (with perhaps some traces of Taíno and South American indigenous groups present). The décima was central to the son's verse structure and the Iberian laud had evolved into the Cuban tres, which had three sets of double strings. (The laud's shape changed from a more triangular one to guitarlike, and the sound became more like a guitar's.) The clave, played with sticks, set the rhythm, and the call-and-response pattern comprised the rhythmic break often called the *montuno*, a reference to the mountainous areas like the Sierra Maestra. The percussive instruments *güiro* and *maracas* represented a shared musical tradition between Africans and indigenous people.

As Rebecca Mauleón described the son in her *Salsa Guidebook for Piano and Ensemble*, the form allows for the juxtaposition of three rhythmic patterns: the *tumbao*, a syncopated bassline; the rhythm section, played by the guitar, bongos, and maracas; and the clave. These elements are central to Cuban music, but as Mauleón stated, the signature of the son belonged to the melodic guitar lines. Still, the competitive nature of the call-and-response vocal patterns (sometimes called *controversias*) and the variations of these African traditions echo throughout the history of North American music from jazz to hip-hop.

In the early twentieth century, the son began to establish itself in Havana, which had become a magnet for migrants from the rural countryside. During this era, several regional forms of son existed, including the changüí (which some say is actually a predecessor), which had a harder, more rhythmic-oriented African sound from the southern Guantanamo area that contrasted with the slightly more genteel guajira son, which is also related to the son montuno, both generally played at a slower pace and known for telling stories of rural nationalism.

The son had the function of telling the news of the countryside, and as a song form adapted the ten-line décima style from medieval Spanish poetry, a form that was to later inspire the improvisational break in contemporary salsa called the *coro*. Neatly intertwined with the European influence in son, the improvisational montuno break that was added onto the traditional son song form was a call-and-response pattern steeped in African tradition. A related genre, the guaracha, a kind of satirical song form that had its origins in the eighteenth century, was updated to the son format with its own improvisational break.

The son became so popular in Havana that groups playing it were increasingly displacing the danzón orchestras. Sextetos, which included two vocalists—the first a tenor who played clave sticks, the second a baritone shaking maracas—a tres, bongó, güiro, and bass, became the quintessential son unit. They played their songs in son clave, which was easier for dancers to move to than rumba clave and ultimately changed the course of Latin music, since it allowed for smoother integration of European melody, as well as the simpler steps of European-style dancing.

The Sexteto Habanero, led by bassist Ignacio Piñeiro, became popular among urban dancegoers by the early 1920s, and when Piñeiro added a trumpet, his group became the enormously influential Septeto Nacional. With the increase of recording facilities in Havana, as well as the opportunity provided by American record companies for orchestras to travel to places like New York to record, Cuban music, as well as Havana itself, began to attract worldwide attention. Piñeiro's band, which recorded numerous hits such as *Échale Salsita*, was one of the first septetos to gain international acclaim.

In the late 1920s and early 1930s, the same time that the son was revolutionizing the Cuban music scene, classically trained musicians like the master pianist Ernesto Lecuona were beginning to synthesize forms like danzón, bolero, and jazz. Lecuona combined danzón with bolero on *Siboney*, one of the first Cuban songs heard widely in North America and Europe, and went on to write many songs that would become classics of early twentieth century Cuban music. Lecuona, who has influenced Latin pianists from Michel Camilo to Chucho Valdés (see chapter 6, "Latin Jazz"), had a melodic insight that could be compared to George Gershwin's. Lecuona used classical harmonic shadings that were more Debussy than Scott Joplin, and his themes were more Cole Porter than Jelly Roll Morton. He wrote danzas and recorded zarzuelas, and Gershwin called him "the Cuban Chopin." But his ability to incorporate Afro-Cuban influences (he is said to be one of the earlier musicians to use that term) including abakwá music, is what made him a worldwide sensation. He led some of the first major Cuban orquestas to perform in the United States and Europe in the 1920s and 1930s. He also studied with the composer Ravel, whom he met while on tour in Paris in 1928, and co-founded the Havana Symphony after he returned to Cuba in the 1930s.

Lecuona and his contemporaries—Ignacio Piñeiro, Beny Moré, and Antonio María Romeu, another danzón pianist—were the best-known creators of a new era for Cuban music. It was no longer simply influencing North American music through jazz, but actually was appearing on the mainstream music scene as "Latin music." When Don Azpiazu's Havana Casino Orchestra arrived in New York in 1930, it almost immediately scored a huge hit with *El Manicero* ("The Peanut Vendor"). The song was so immensely popular that jazz trumpeter Louis Armstrong (among many others) covered it. Azpiazu's band's multiracial lineup (including Humberto "Chino" Lara, a Chinese Cuban, and Antonio Machín, an Afro-Cuban singer who tossed peanuts into the crowd during live performances) broke racial and cultural barriers in New York.

Ernesto Lecuona's danzón *Siboney* and *The Peanut Vendor* set off a full-fledged trend on the Broadway circuit in the early years of the 1930s. A rhumba fad began in the United States in the early '30s with several Hollywood movies featuring stars like George Raft boogying around like they just didn't care. The rhumba fad was supported by extensive radio play as well as its popularity in New York's dance clubs. Lecuona's work, as well as many early Latin classics, was published by U.S.-based names like Oliver Ditson, E. B. Marks, and Leo Feist, the latter publishing *Siboney*. That rhumba music was a watered-down version of the authentic Afro-Cuban son purveyed by Ignacio Piñeiro's Septeto Habanero is attributed by some to the demands of North American publishers. Classic rhumbas include Xavier Cugat's *Begin the Beguine*, and other attempts such as composer George Gershwin's *Cuban Overture ("Rhumba") for Orchestra*. The rhumba fad was a precursor to the kind of Latin music that was performed by Brazilian singer Carmen Miranda in the 1940s.

The Cuban music boom piqued an interest from Hollywood, which began with 1931's *Cuban Love Song*, featuring Lecuona's orchestra, and, in 1935, George Raft's famous *Rumba*. Cugat, a bandleader from Spain who first came to the States playing hybrid tango habaneras, became one of the most popular Latin music acts. Members of Cugat's band included Desi Arnaz, Miguelito Valdés, and Tito Rodríguez. Flaccid Afro-Cuban music, rearranged to accommodate show-tune lyrics and with little room for improvisation, became the norm for "Latin music" in the 1930s and 1940s. In 1946 Desi Arnaz broke off from the Cugat band and scored a hit of his own, a cover of *Babalú*. In the 1950s, Arnaz became a fixture on prime-time U.S. television in the show *I Love Lucy*, and the song's constant exposure through reruns was the ultimate mainstreaming of Cuban music. Originally known as *Babalú Ayé* and performed by Cuban vocalist Miguelito Valdés (another veteran of the Cugat orchestra), *Babalú* was written about the orisha Babalú Ayé, the healer.

Cuban music had evolved from the semi-religious ritual rumbas and toques, from slave music, to Hollywood, and few North American observers had more than a vague notion of the underpinnings of Cuban music or understood what had happened. The Afro-Cuban tradition had come to New York, and it was going to stay there for a while.

While in the twentieth century Afro-Cuban music became the dominant force in what we know as Latin music, there was a wealth of regional music being produced around Latin America. These styles of music also involved a process in which African, indigenous, and European influences were fused to create a music that came to represent a regional identity. Chief among these styles were merengue, which was strongly influenced by the French-African culture of Haiti before it became the national music of the Dominican Republic; the Colombian cumbia, a rare fusion of Spanish, African and indigenous musical traditions on South America's northern coast and European popular music; the Brazilian samba, perhaps the most dynamic Afro-European music outside of the Cuban orbit; and the Argentine tango, a curious amalgam of African traditions and Cuban influence.

Merengue

A relative late bloomer in the pantheon of Latin American beats, merengue, traditionally played on accordion, saxophone, box bass with metal plucked keys, a guayano, a metal scraper, and, most importantly, a two-ended tambora drum, was the most influential style that developed in the Dominican Republic. As in most Spanish-colonized Caribbean islands, the Dominican Republic was also home to the Cuban-derived styles of son, bolero, and guaracha, as well as its own local Yoruban religious styles such as salve and música de palos. The Yoruban musics paralleled Afro-Cuban music in its utilitarian function to create a trance state, often with increasing tempo, but they were less integrated with Spanish influences. Merengue, a hip-shaking dance in which partners rotate in place driven by the thudding beat of the tambora drum, has a quick 2/4 dance rhythm that likely originated both in rural regions of Africa (where the tambora drum seems to be from) and in the Haitian part of the island of Hispañola, which was colonized by both the French and the Spanish. Since Haiti revolted against France at the end of the eighteenth century before the Dominican Republic broke away from Spain, Haiti became a magnet for runaway slaves throughout the Caribbean region. In the Dominican Republic, an anti-African reaction set in to the extent that by the twentieth century, its official culture (constructed by dictator Rafael Trujillo) denied the African root in merengue, even when it was obviously related to the very similar Haitian meringue. Most of the early nineteenth century merengue (often called "salon" merengue) was played with guitars, though eventually the accordion became a prominent feature. According to Paul Austerlitz in *Merengue: Dominican Music and Dominican Identity*, the accordion was adopted in the 1870s because Germany was an important trading partner with the Dominican Republic, and accordions were often bartered for tobacco. There was even a distinction between the danzón-like merengue orchestras of Cibao, home to the country's lighter-skinned or Creole elite, and the more popular forms of merengue.

Merengue was established in the Dominican Republic as a national music in an almost parallel fashion to the way samba was established in Brazil, with backing from governmental and educational figures trying to establish a New World identity for Latin America. Music and art in general has significance in Latin America beyond its cultural function—it acts as a powerful symbol for the successful integration of cultural influences in a region where national stability is fragile. In the twentieth century, countries like Brazil, Mexico, and the Dominican Republic searched for a national identity that was not tethered to Europe or North America. While Mexico looked more to art and architecture to valorize its indigenous communities, Brazil embraced black culture by making samba its national music. But the institutionalization of merengue in the Dominican had more sinister overtones because of the influence of Rafael Trujillo, one of the worst dictators in the Americas in the twentieth century. At one point he ordered the wholesale slaughter of Haitians and the repression of Haitian culture within the Dominican Republic, reflecting a need to assert his power by fending off the Cibaon elite. Orchestra leader Luis Alberti was promoted by the Trujillo regime because he included traditional instruments like the percussive güira and tambora in his band, which was already emphasizing more rustic versions of merengue, in direct contradiction of the Cibaon preference for guitar-driven merengue.

Cumbia

The cumbia is often ascribed an African origin, because of its name's similarity to the cumbe dance practiced in Guinea, Africa. But the cumbia's origin is as firmly rooted in the indigenous traditions of northern Colombia as it is in African influences. Many

Colombian musicologists have theorized that the cumbia evolved from the Taino-Caribe Indians' tradition of areito, a circle of dance, poetry, and music widely practiced by the indigenous people of the Caribbean region. Some of the songs from Juan Luís Guerra's 1992 album *Areíto*, in which he celebrates the pre-Hispanic indigenous culture of Hispañola, hint at this theory. The rhythms found on these songs are reasonably similar to cumbia. Another field of thought hypothesizes a fusion between indigenous and African culture that occurred during carnaval celebrations in Cartagena de las Indias, the Caribbean colonial port of Colombia. Rituals similar to areítos (the Taino and Caribe influence is rooted in northern Colombia through interaction and possible kinship relations between Caribbean tribes and the Magdalena River group, los Chibchas) were held there, and Africans joined in them, since African peoples had a similar circle-dance tradition. It is said that African artisanry was more advanced than that of the indigenous and that Africans helped construct more effective drums, driving the indigenous' gaita flutes in a heavier rhythmic direction. African polyrhythms also influenced dance styles.

The cumbia is a unique rhythm in Latin America—unlike in Caribbean countries such as Cuba, Puerto Rico, and the Dominican Republic, in Colombia the indigenous presence was not wiped out and is felt along with the African and European influences. Cumbia evolved in Colombia along the coastal areas, a product of interchange between European settlers, African slaves, and indigenous people, and was propelled by Spanish conquerors into the interior of the country.

Cumbia has a lightness, a headiness that is not achieved by the mere possibility of improvisation, as it is in Cuban music, but rhythmically, by its stressing of the upbeat rather than the downbeat, unlike both Cuban music and the blues. Cumbia can become hypnotic when its subtle rhythm is properly absorbed on the dance floor and the haunting gaita (long flute), which is the main indigenous influence, works its spell.

The early form of cumbia, often referred to as gaitero music (referring to those who play the gaita flutes), has been played for centuries in the Caribbean coast region. In its essential folkloric form, where it is played on three varyingly sized drums (one as large as the one used in merengue), maracas, and the gaita flute, cumbia dates back at least to the time of Simon Bolívar, in the early 1800s. The ethereal melodies of gaitero, still heard today among the Cuna and Kogi Indians, are played in counterpoint to each other and are combined with the steady, hypnotic beat of a small drum, the high-spirited and skillful improvisations of the other two drums, and the embellishing rhythms of the maraca. One of the gaita players holds the gaita in one hand and the maraca in the other, and with amazing agility and rhythm plays the two simultaneously, his lips only leaving the flute to sing.

In the nineteenth and twentieth centuries, cumbia evolved in a way similar to Cuban music. New, modern instruments were added and influences from recording techniques and trends in other Latin American countries made cumbia faster and more modern. Early 1930s cumbia orchestras, like La Sonora Cienaguera, under the influence of North American swing bands, added saxophones and trumpets. In the mid–twentieth century, Colombian orchestra leaders such as Lucho Bermúdez tried to combine cumbia with various forms of Afro-Cuban music with little success outside of Colombia (probably due to a lack of recording sophistication and the lack of familiarity the rest of the world had with Colombian rhythms), and the "orquesta" configurations familiar to salsa were adopted by cumbia outfits like La Sonora Dinamita.

Today cumbia is one of the more popular beats in Latin America, particularly in Mexico, which also shares the corrido, a sort of folk-protest song played with guitar, with Colombia. (Colombia has always been fond of Mexican musical styles and imported them freely—it's often easier to find mariachis in Colombia than anywhere outside of Mexico and Central America). Much of what is known as Tejano music, the contemporary music of Texas and northern Mexico made famous by Selena, is actually a pop version of cumbia. Perhaps most importantly, cumbia is one of the most important influences on contemporary tropical pop music manufactured in state of the art studios in Miami.

Samba

The samba appeared on the scene in the early twentieth century in Rio de Janeiro. It is descended from the lundú, a Bantu-Angolan style brought by Africans to Brazil during the peak of slavery in the eighteenth and nineteenth centuries, but eventually internalized influences from ragtime (from New Orleans), habanera (from Cuba), and even German polka (through Mexico and German immigration). Like the Cuban rumba, samba is mainly a percussive music played in a shuffling 2/4 rhythm, using several different kinds of drums, such as the surdo and the batería, and percussive accessories like the cuíca, the reco-reco, and the agogô, which have functions similar to those of the Cuban instruments like the cáscara and the chékere. The thunderous sounds of samba drums are a tad reminiscent of high school marching bands, and the whistles characteristically used in carnaval parades give it a unique flavor.

A particularly large migration of blacks to Rio, dominated by Portuguese descendants, in the late nineteenth century (brought about by the failure of northern Brazilian coffee plantations) led to the establishment of many Afro-Brazilian communities in Rio. Like the Cuban rumba, samba was originally promulgated in Brazil in the rundown neighborhoods called favelas, which were populated by the descendants of slaves, and it was often repressed by governmental authorities. The candomblé religion, one parallel to Santería, grew to have a more mainstream, secular following in Brazil, as the country grew more tolerant of African customs. The favelas' tradition of batucadas (drumming jams) and ritual performances in connection with the widespread candomblé religion led to the development of ecolas de samba, or schools. The ecolas were less schools than clubs, although they did foster an environment of learning and perfecting of the craft.

Samba schools were on display during the yearly carnavals of Rio, which were taken over by samba in the 1920s and 1930s, and became famous worldwide. The celebrations, which take place on the Tuesday before Ash Wednesday of the Christian calendar, are regarded as one last chance for excess before the austere season of Lent. But they are also a chance for Afro-Brazilians to demonstrate their loyalty to the Yoruban orishas through candomblé, in which the gods are camouflaged as Christian saints in the same way they are in Afro-Cuban Santería.

The numbers of drummers involved in a large Brazilian samba batería (group of drummers) are staggering. During a typical winter carnaval, hundreds of sambistas are playing a wide variety of drums, most of which have rough equivalents in various other Latin American traditions, but some of which are unique to Brazil. Brazil has more varieties of percussion instruments than any other country in the Western Hemisphere. Surdos are very much like Dominican or Venezuelan tamboras, the caixa is similar to snare drums, the agogô is like the salsa cowbell, the pandeira like the Puerto Rican pandareta (a tambourine-like instrument played during Christmas celebrations). The samba is a call to wild, mass movement, an orgy of percussion, not the structured rhythmic base for improvisation that came from the fusions of African rhythms and courtly European dances in Cuba. Perhaps because of its Bantu influence, samba is more like the "chaos in tempo" that Arsenio Rodríguez drew on to create his idea of mambo.

Like merengue in the Dominican Republic, samba became an expression of national identity. In Brazil's case, this followed a long period of soul-searching by intellectuals for constructive ways to prepare for the country's mixed-race future. Theorists, politicians, and other cultural figures encouraged the adoption of samba as the country's national dance. But unlike what happened in the Dominican Republic, the adoption did not come about as a show of force by a dictator but as an almost spontaneous eruption of urban experimentation, more akin to the emergence of jazz in New Orleans a few years earlier or salsa in New York many years later.

Tango

The tango is Argentina's most significant form of popular music, evolved from a number of different influences—Argentina's ties to Europe, its repressed African past, and the legacy of its capital city (Buenos Aires) as a port town with a colorful seedy side. Tango originated as a dance style, one of the more curious and sensual in the Latin American dance tradition. On the wall of the National Academy of Tango in Buenos Aires it is written that tango is "a sad thought you can dance." Said to have been created in brothels and dance halls, the tango was taken up by the popular classes just before World War I. In *The Latin Tinge*, John Storm Roberts wrote that the name tango "is found everywhere in the Latin world, from the dance from Spain (called the tango Andaluza) to the Cuban tango congó (also known as tango habanera)." Its name probably comes from a Congolese word, tanga, meaning "festival" or "party." Other theories cite the word *tambo*, possibly short for *tambor*, the Spanish word for drum, as referring to a place where freed blacks and slaves could dance—ultimately clubs in the black sections of Buenos Aires were called tambos. Finally, some Congolese languages define tango as a circle, probably for dancing or ritual.

Tango is generally believed to owe its European root to the peregrinations of the milonga, a song and dance form popular in the late nineteenth century. Originally the milonga was a solo song sung by gauchos, cattle ranchers similar to the cowboys of the American Southwest who lived in the vast rural area known as the pampa. In turn the milonga is said to derive from the payada de contrapunto, in which two singers (payadores), accompanying themselves on the guitar, improvised in a competition-like practice. The verses had a format similar to décima—that is, octosyllabic quartets structured in a musical period of eight measures in 2/4. The term milonga refers to the African-Brazilian word for the lyrics sung by the payadores.

Traditional polkas, waltzes, and mazurkas were mixed with the Cuban habanera to form a new dance and music, which merged with the vocal pyrotechnics of the milonga. In 1880, the Argentine government confiscated much of the gauchos' land in the pampas and redistributed it to bourgeois Argentines and European immigrants, displacing the gauchos to the poorest suburban areas of Buenos Aires. Like the guajiros of Cuba, they made alliances with the African population, which was by this time diminishing through deaths in a war with Paraguay, an outbreak of yellow fever, and race-mixing with lighter-skinned Argentines and new European immigrants.

The tango started as a kind of satire of an African dance, the candombe (unrelated to the Brazilian religion candomblé), created by the displaced gauchos. The mixture of the rural gaucho milonga (which had a 2/4 syncopated rhythm), with the habanera brought by new European immigrants and with African dances like the candombe, is what ultimately yielded tango. Other root styles of tango were dances like fandangos, from Spain, and Argentine vidalitas (folk songs and dances with lyrics relating to rustic life on the pampa) and cifras (folk songs written in décima meter). A major development in the tango occurred with the arrival of the bandoneón, an accordion-like instrument with German origins, which replaced the guitar as the harmonic and rhythmic center of the music. Besides its famously dramatic impact as a dance style, the tango genre produced one of the most influential Latin singers of all time, Carlos Gardel, who reigned in the 1920s and 1930s. In Gardel's wake, from the mid-'40s on, Astor Piazzolla pioneered "the New Tango," a conglomeration of jazz, Brazilian, and North

American blues influences that continues to influence international tastes to this day.

Even more national genres have had a significant impact on Latin music and continue to be discovered and internationalized to this day. As we shall see in subsequent chapters, the Puerto Rican genres bomba and plena, as well as the Christmas songs called aguinaldos, have made their way into mainstream Latin music through salsa, Latin jazz, and revival groups like Plena Libre and Los Pleneros del 21. Additionally, folkloric and creolized dance genres from Colombia, like the pasillo, porro, vallenato, and bambuco, as well as the Venezuelan joropo are growing in importance either through their adaptation to the Latin pop formula that holds sway in Miami or through jazz musicians like Danilo Pérez or folk singers like Irene Farrera.

Several music genres in Latin America that are not as well known as the above have also had a considerable influence on contemporary Latin music. In fact one of the characteristics of present-day Latin music is the increasing incorporation of lesser-known styles into modern music forms like jazz, rock, and Latin alternative music. The less-Hispanicized regions of the Caribbean have musical styles that are often influential on Latin music—obvious examples are reggae, soca (also known as soul calypso), zouk, and punta, a very important music of the Honduran coastline that reflects the Garifunda culture of escaped slaves going back to the early days of the slave trade. The Andean regions of Ecuador, Peru, and Bolivia share common cultural ground and a series of danceable genres called charango, pasillo, danzante (*El Chulita Quiteño*, a danzante, is a second national anthem of Ecuador), albazo, sanjuanero, huayno, yaravi, chicha, and the infamous lambada, which was ironically made famous by a Brazilian group in the late 1980s. Peru's Pacific Coast reflects a little-known African influence, as well as indigenous roots, with genres like marinera resbalosa, marinera norteño, and the vals criollo, all danceable genres with lyrics composed in a way reflecting the influence of the Spanish tradition. Recently the work of Afro-Peruvian vocalists like Susana Baca, Eva Allyón, and Cecilia Barraza has been distributed internationally, shedding light on that country's relatively unexplored musical treasures.

Another sphere of cultural influence in South America is the Andean region encompassing Bolivia, northern Chile, and northern Argentina. Popular genres from this region include the bailecito, vidala, the zamba (pronounced like Brazilian samba, but not related), chacarera, and cueca. Some of the least well known Latin music genres are from Paraguay, including the guarania, galopera, and chamamé. But the Rio Plata region (which overlaps both the Buenos Aires and Montivideo, Uruguay, areas) provides an overlooked repository of African-based music in the Southern cone, which is often not associated with such music.

Many musical genres that were considered important only in the regions where they originated are beginning to project an international presence through assimilation into contemporary Latin music. The most famous example of this was *Llorando se fue*, ("Crying he departed"), an old Bolivian saya or folk song that was adapted in the early 1980s by Peru's Cuarteto Continental and finally recorded as *Lambada* in 1989 by the Brazilian group Koama. Similarly, in an echo of the journey made by *La Bamba* in the 1950s from Mexican son jarrocho to international rock hit by the Californian Ritchie Valens, the folkloric charango style of the Andean region was adapted by a Bolivian group, Azul Azul, and made into a hugely popular single, *La Bomba*, in 2000.

The next phase of Latin music may very well lie in the transnational journeys of traditional songs, readapted for the needs of the international pop marketplace. Sometimes this process sets off controversy and court battles: The Gipsy Kings' *Bamboleo* was said to have been pirated from Venezuelan composer Simón Díaz's joropo *Caballo Viejo*; Azul Azul's *Bomba* was similarly "borrowed" by an Argentinian living in Spain called King Africa. But when a flamenco-pop novelty group called Las Ketchup incorporated an improvised rap from the Sugarhill Gang's *Rapper's Delight* on its international hit *Aserejé*, it seemed that Latin music would be at the root of many fusions to come.

•2•

The Evolution of
Cuban Music into Salsa

Salsa is the first Latin music genre founded in an Anglo metropolis, albeit one with a dizzying mix of transplanted Latinos. The migration of Afro-Cuban music to New York ultimately begat salsa, the music that dominates dance floors in Latin clubs from New York to Buenos Aires and is the essential pulse of Latin music. While many Afro-Cuban music purists continue to claim that salsa is a mere variation on Cuba's musical heritage, the hybridizing experience the music went through in New York from the 1920s on incorporated influences from many different branches of the Latin American tradition, and later from jazz, R&B, and even rock.

In the 1930s, '40s, and '50s, as Cuban son and various rumba-derived guaguancó and guaracha elements embedded in it were helping to drive both the "rhumba" era and the mambo era, Afro-Cuban music was already becoming something else in New York, independent of what was going on in Havana. Musicians from the Caribbean and South America had been playing together in New York since the 1920s, at times mixing with African-American musicians and audiences. They came from various countries in the

Caribbean and South America. They played boleros, Puerto Rican danzas, tangos, sones, and guarachas to often-segregated audiences (Uptown and Downtown), and African-American jazz musicians were influencing their orchestras. Bands like Cuarteto Caney and Cuarteto Victoria, made up of predominantly Puerto Rican and Cuban musicians (with occasional members from the rest of Latin America), held sway in the slowly emerging precincts of Latin New York.

But the growing popularity of Latin music in North America had a ripple effect on Havana, causing increased tourism to Cuba and increasing the competitive nature of its capital's hotel and casino circuit. Beny Moré, one of its biggest stars, would use that circuit as a platform for a career that took him to Mexico City and North America, where he made a central contribution in the recording history of both mambo and bolero music.

Perhaps the key moment in this "Americanization" of Latin music came when the master Cuban arranger Mario Bauzá, who arrived in New York in the 1930s, and his percussionist cohort, Chano Pozo, flourished together in a way that might not have been possible in their native Havana. Their collaboration with trumpeter Dizzy Gillespie, which cemented the jazz influence on Latin music, helped propel mambo, a major development in Afro-Cuban music, to the center of America's musical stage.

The Mambo Era

Mambo appears to be a word of Congolese origin, which some have translated as simply "conversation," and others as "to speak with the gods." It was first used in the context of dance music when Cuban dancers in the 1930s began to refer to an extended percussion break as a mambo. Mambo is generally son and danzón writ large—a singer tells an often urban story and the percussion and brass sections interact like a jazz orchestra, varying 4/4 and 6/8 time signatures, always in clave. An improvisational break at the song's climax allows the various sections of the orchestra to converse with each other, and the dancers, inspired by what's going on, push the dialog even further. Like so many species of Latin music, mambo is less a formal pattern than a constellation of tendencies—the Afro-Cuban son and conjunto of the '30s, new influences from jazz, and the "internationalized" New York version of Latin music created several different incarnations of mambo.

In its original version the mambo was dance music that evolved from the son and guaracha that was played in Cuba sometime in the late 1930s, when septetos began to include extra trumpets, a piano, and the conga drum, an instrument central to the African carnaval marches performed in the major cities. Although he was preceded by groups like La Sonora Matancera and Septeto Cuba, Arsenio Rodríguez, a blind tres player, broke new ground by adding the conga drum, cementing the importance of the classic Cuban conjunto.

Rodríguez, whose music dispensed with the son's introductory passage and went straight to the montuno section, and Israel "Cachao" López, who played bass for Antonio Arcaño, are both credited as early mambo innovators. That the creation of mambo is attributed to Rodríguez, a conjunto leader playing son, and Arcaño, a charanga leader, symbolizes the sharing of repertoires between son and charanga bands in the '30s and '40s and their mutual influences. In the 1940s, increased contact between Cuban and Cuban-influenced musicians and American big band jazz, epitomized by the relationship between the great Cuban bandleader Mario Bauzá and his close friend Dizzy Gillespie, took mambo in a second direction. The last branch, the most popular among North Americans, was a streamlined dance music created by Cuban bandleader Pérez Prado in his journey to Mexico City and points north (mainly Los Angeles and New York) and by his sometime vocalist Beny Moré.

Arsenio Rodríguez, the López Brothers, and the Arcaño Orchestra

Arsenio Rodríguez, sometimes known as *El Ciego Maravilloso* (The Marvelous Blind Man), grew up near Matanzas, about thirty miles outside of Havana, where he would eventually migrate. His grandfather was a former slave and taught him the secret rhythms of the abakwá sect of Santería. His band included, in various stages, the influential trumpeter Felix Chapottín and a future Buena Vista Social Club pianist, Rubén González. Rodríguez's twangy, rapid-plucking tres playing, although based on the tres-laud style that ultimately came from Andalucía, was grounded in his knowledge of ritual drumming from the Congo's abakwá tradition—it had a mournful tone but was played with rhythmic complexity. Rodríguez's innovative spirit allowed him to expand the rhythmic improvisations in the son's montuno section, and he also pioneered the use of multiple trumpets. Rodríguez inspired much contemporary homage (notably 1990s avant-garde jazz guitarist Marc Ribot's Cubanos Postizos recordings, *Marc Ribot y Los Cubanos Postizos* and *Muy Divertido*). He insisted on the mambo's origin being the Congo region of Africa and once characterized it as "anarchy in tempo." One of his most famous songs, covered by Ribot, is *La Vida es Sueño*, a song that evokes the Spanish décima and directly refers to Calderón de la Barca's classic seventeenth century play. Cuban music historian Isabelle Leymaire recounted that Rodríguez wrote the song in a moment of despair when, after being invited to New York in 1947 by Miguelito Valdés to seek treatment for his blindness, he was told that there was no cure.

Israel "Cachao" López was born in 1918 to a family of bass players—his parents were players and teachers of the instrument, and his nephew Orlando went on to star with the Buena Vista Social Club. As a teenager he played with his father and his brother Orestes, a cello player in the Havana Philharmonic, and in the late 1930s the brothers joined Arcaño y sus Maravillas. The band's repertoire consisted mainly of danzónes until it began experimenting with a faster-paced improvisational section anchored by the López brothers and became known as a mambo orchestra.

In 1938, Cachao López composed a danzón he called *Mambo*, so that the dancers would be freer to improvise with his mambo breaks, which featured faster tempos. As a signal to band members that they could start their solos, Arcaño would call out, *Mil veces mambo!* (A thousand times mambo!) The ostinato of Cachao's tumbao bass lines infused the mainstream danzón/charanga style of Arcaño's band with a strong percussive influence. López's original tunes were referred to as *danzón con Nuevo ritmo* (danzón with a new rhythm). Eventually a conga drum was added to the band, which completed the shift toward percussion-oriented mambo. Cachao López and his brother Orestes went on to write hundreds of mambos.

The reaction of Cuban dancers to the less-structured mambo innovations was mixed. Mambo wasn't even known as a separate genre yet, but something had clearly taken hold of the music. In the early 1940s, the frenetic interplay of pianos, basses, and congas that produced dance-floor climaxes was catalytic in the invention of what came to be known as Latin jazz. It also set off an era of mambo-oriented big bands in which great pianists like Peruchín (Pedro Justiz) played with bandleaders like Arsenio Rodríguez and Armando Romeu and percussionists Patato Valdés and Mongo Santamaría, as well as Cachao.

In the 1950s, the improvisational energy partially created by Cachao's nuevo ritmo and the heightened interest in North American jazz in Cuba opened up the *descarga* (jazz jam) scene in Havana. The descarga was based on son changes and punctuated by extended riffing. The informal jam sessions were held in small clubs and the living rooms of participating musicians, who mostly played the hotel circuit.

A classic series of albums called *Cuban Jam Sessions in Miniature*, in 1957 on Panart, celebrates the descarga era, which also saw the creation of a jazz-influenced bolero style called *filin* (see Chapter 4). With a lineup of bass, güiró, trumpet, bongós, timbales, and conga, the Cachao sessions emphasized the interaction between bass and percussion, duplicating the call and response between vocalists and the band in mambo, son, and guaracha. The word *descarga*, although now widely translated as "jam," literally means "to discharge, to get something off one's chest." The improvisational bias built into mambo encouraged dancers to kick into an eternal high gear. But at the same time it attracted players who wanted to play a more serious music, and when descarga reached New York, this would have a major impact on the direction of jazz music.

López became a disillusioned exile from Cuba in 1962, unlike Arcaño, a committed socialist, and was still revered forty years later when he played in concert. He released several albums in the 1990s, lived in Miami, Florida, and was the subject of a documentary film made by actor Andy Garcia in 1993. His 2000 release *Cuba Linda* is an excellent new treatment of his classics with a strong lineup of older and new generation players.

Mario Bauzá and Cubop

Perhaps the most important early ambassador of Afro-Cuban music, the inventor of Cubop jazz, Mario Bauzá was a restless, fiery man whose intensity was matched only by the warmth he conveyed by his generous smile. Bauzá was quoted as saying that New Orleans jazz and the music from his native Cuba were two strands of the same music that had come to the New World from West Africa. The Yoruban batá ensemble, which performed at ritual ceremonies to communicate with Santería orishas, had essentially the same function as a New Orleans jazz band: They were both playing a funeral dirge.

Bauzá was born in Havana in 1911 and was raised by a pair of wealthy godparents, neighbors who asked his original parents whether they could raise him, since they were childless. His god-father taught voice, and when he deduced Bauzá had talent, he quickly enrolled Bauzá at the Havana Conservatory. He was a clarinet prodigy who played in the Havana Philharmonic Orchestra at age sixteen, something that gave him the chance to travel the world. In 1926, he was playing with Antonio Romeu's orchestra, as many philharmonic members would do to supplement their income, and accompanied Romeu on a trip to New York. He visited Harlem and thrilled to the Fletcher Henderson band, and in Midtown, he caught Paul Whiteman. He was inspired to pick up the saxophone and vowed that when he turned eighteen he would return to New York.

In 1930, he got wind of Don Azpiazu's move to New York and immediately left for Manhattan. He played with the band of Nobel Sissle, a Eubie Blake collaborator (substituting for Puerto Rican saxophonist Moncho Usera), as well as with uptown Latin bands. When Antonio Machín left Don Azpiazu's band to form his own Cuarteto Machín, Bauzá heard that he needed a trumpeter. He convinced Machín to buy him a trumpet, learned to play it in two weeks, and became one of New York's hottest new jazz trumpeters.

In 1932, he auditioned for jazz drummer Chick Webb's Orchestra, who was so impressed he made Bauzá musical director, a startling achievement for a newcomer and one that placed him at the center of the scene. Webb agreed to teach him jazz phrasing in exchange for Bauzá's arranging ability. During his stay with Webb, Bauzá introduced him to vocalist Ella Fitzgerald and helped arrange Webb's signature *Stompin' at the Savoy*, on which Bauzá played lead trumpet and also took a clarinet solo. By 1939 he was playing trumpet with Cab Calloway, whose band was disciplined and so successful that they were able to avoid racism at hotels on the road by traveling in their own Pullman coach. Bauzá's time with Calloway was fruitful—he was invited to play with both Duke Ellington and Count Basie. But the most important thing that happened was sitting next to trumpeter Dizzy Gillespie, who would later join him in his dream project.

In 1940 Bauzá became the musical director of a band led by his brother-in-law, and fellow Cuban expatriate, Machito (a.k.a. Frank Grillo), who had come to New York in 1937 as a vocalist in a band called La Estrella Habanera. Machito called his orchestra the Afro-Cubans, a seminal moment in the racial identification of this strand of Cuban music in New York. Machito's Afro-Cubans changed New York's idea of Latin music. From then on, it would no longer be watered-down rhumba. Bauzá imported arrangements he helped develop in the Chick Webb band and drilled the Afro-Cubans with North American jazz arrangements. Bauzá was the first key Latin musician who helped translate the worlds of North American jazz and Afro-Cuban music to each other.

The rhythm section of the Afro-Cubans was the first to incorporate the three-drum structure of conga, bongó, and timbales into New York-style Latin orchestras, which allowed for the same kind of percussive improvisation that was being generated in the mambo's extended section. The early Machito orchestra produced two of the classics of the big band orchestral mambo: *Afro-Cuban Jazz Suite* and *Tangá*. The jazz suite was a de facto blueprint for Latin jazz, in the way that it rattled off several rhythmic styles— mambo, guaguancó, jazz swing, and the original Cuban rumba. Built around a swirl of clashing trumpet and percussion themes, *Tanga* evoked the kind of hypnotic energy that embodied the spirit of mambo.

Charlie Parker sat in on these sessions on saxophone, as did the charismatic Cuban percussionist Chano Pozo, who was brought into the mix by Bauzá. The merging of African-American and Afro-Cuban styles by Pozo, Bauzá, and Dizzy Gillespie can be seen as the missing link between the big band period and bebop. Bebop developed during the period of absorption of Cuban music into jazz bands, and it has been argued that there are Cuban elements embedded in bebop itself. The complex rhythms that Cuban music provided seemed a perfect match with Parker's groundbreaking improvisational genius. Even his own compositions written in the same era, like the classic *Donna Lee*, seem playable in clave. Cubop, strongly influenced by Bauzá's rhythmic arrangements in the Dizzy Gillespie Orchestra and essentially bebop with a stronger Afro-Cuban focus, was born at this time as well, largely during jam sessions at the midtown Manhattan club Birdland, right down the street from the mecca of mambo, the Palladium club.

According to music historian Robert Palmer, Bauzá explained how his sessions with the Gillespie crew might have indirectly helped give birth to bebop. While many jazz commentators think that the Charlie Parker–Gillespie partnering was the essence of bebop, and that it was Parker's unique playing ability that allowed the "feel" of bebop to come through, there may have been a space opened up by Afro-Cuban techniques. "I'd stay up with Dizzy and the band's drummer, Cozy Cole, teaching them how to feel some of the simpler Cuban rhythms," said Bauzá. "Dizzy would sing the drum patterns using nonsense syllables, like 'oop-bop-sh'bam.' Be-bop, the name they gave to the new kind of jazz Dizzy started in the '40s, was itself a drum pattern."

By 1942 Gillespie was sitting in with the Afro-Cubans and by 1947 he was ready to record *The Manteca Suite*, his first Latin jazz recording. The forceful swing themes and thundering Afro-Cuban rhythms of the recording make it, along with *A Night in Tunisia*, a milestone in jazz history. The interconnection between North American jazz and Afro-Cuban music was now taken for granted, and the stage was set for the emergence of mambo music in New York, where music fans were becoming accustomed to innovation.

Beny Moré

More than anyone else, Beny Moré captured the essence of the vocal style that would help catapult Cuban music to its U.S. success.

Moré could be oversimplified as a cross between Frank Sinatra and Nat King Cole, but such comparison can't convey Moré's charged, authoritative presence on vinyl and in the ballroom. His nickname, *El Bárbaro del Ritmo* (The Barbarian of Rhythm), is indicative of how different Moré was from Sinatra or Cole. It was the aggressive swing in the rhythms of Afro-Cuban music, which was coming into its own in the 1930s and 1940s, that determined Moré's impact.

Moré was born in 1919 in a small town called Santa Isabel de las Lajas in Las Villas province, in the south side of Cuba. A Santería devotee from a family of ex-slaves, Moré made the typical journey from Las Villas to Havana, where he sang in the streets near the port of Havana. In the mid-'40s, he joined a trio led by Miguel Matamoros, a highly influential bolero-son singing group that later expanded to a septet, conjunto, and an orchestra. Moré and the Matamoros trio moved to Mexico City in 1945, attracted by a burst of growth in Mexico's film industry, which had become the biggest in Latin America. With Matamoros he recorded the all-time Cuban son classic *Son de la Loma* (originally recorded by the trio in 1926) and played a crucial role in the spread of Cuban music to the North. The Afro-Cuban phenomenon traveled through Latin America through the Mexican movies and heightened the appetite for the music by North American Latino immigrants as well. Eventually Matamoros decided to return to Cuba, but Moré was about to have new doors opened up for him. In 1948, Mario Rivera Conde, the director of RCA/Victor Mexico, discovered him and teamed him up with bandleader Pérez Prado, a relationship that would cement Moré's fame.

What made Moré's style so compelling was his blend of the folkloric nostalgia of Cuban guajiro music (the kind you hear in the thousands of versions of *Guantanamera*) with the smooth texture of the bolero, flowing over the rhythm-dominated arrangements of the bands he sang with. The inflections of the storytelling guajiro in his sharply seductive voice created an intimacy that transcended borders. On *Bárbaro del Ritmo*, arguably his signature song, he sang "Look how beautifully Mexicans dance the mambo," while in *Dónde Estabas Tú*, (Where Were You?), written by bandleader Ernesto Duarte, he scolded a tres player for fouling up a bembé.

Moré's songs captured the intensity of mambo's peak years—he was a bandleader as well as a vocalist, even though he didn't read music. Songs like *Yiri Yiri Bon*, *San Fernando*, and *Dónde Estabas Tú* (performed with the Matamoros and Pérez Prado bands) play with the onomatopoetic sounds of Afro-Cuban scat; the vocalist reigned, often augmented by almost Benny Goodman-style reeds and brass. But he had a softer side as well. It was when he wasn't recording or playing with Pérez Prado that Moré made the transition from up-tempo singer to balladeer. While his characteristic tenor has been identified with Prado's brass indulgences, the bolero side of Moré is heard on tunes like *Como Fue*, which he recorded with the Ernesto Duarte orchestra after he returned to Havana in the 1950s. Moré's technique of sliding up the scale with his already formidable tenor would be widely copied in contemporary salsa. It gives the sensation of flight, with all the evocative power that implies, as if to express the desire to lift Cuba, and the dreams of a family of ex-slaves, into unprecedented heights. His ability to hold these flights of vocal dexterity for seemingly endless moments suggested the wild leaps of faith that prefigured the Cuban revolution itself. Moré returned to Cuba in 1953 and unlike Celia Cruz and some others, refused to leave after Castro's revolution.

Pérez Prado

The most recognizable leader of the 1950s mambo craze, pianist-bandleader Pérez Prado, is often credited with bringing mambo to North American audiences. A native of Matanzas, Cuba, he began his career in the '40s playing with legends like Arsenio Rodríguez and Miguelito Valdés, a Havana-born singer/percussionist bandleader, in Havana's renowned Orquesta Casino de la Playa. The somewhat conservative hotel casino atmosphere in Cuba did not welcome his jazz-inspired eccentricities and abrupt shifts in tempo, and in a move that may have facilitated his success in the United States, in 1944 he formed his own group and moved to Mexico City, where he immediately became known as the "Glenn Miller of Mexico."

In 1949, during his collaboration in Mexico with Beny Moré, Prado produced a multi-million selling album, *Que Rico el Mambo*. Prado's Mexico City base helped him catch on with the Mexican-American community in Southern California, which was beginning to develop a distinct identity, and by 1950, to cross over onto mainstream pop radio in Los Angeles. In 1951, Prado made his first U.S. appearance at Teatro Puerto Rico in the Bronx, New York, beginning a long series of tours of the United States in which he played up to twenty-five cities each. *Que Rico el Mambo* was followed in 1955 by *Mambo Mania*, which included the No. 1 single *Cherry Pink, Apple Blossom White*.

When in New York, he played in the same venues as the Machito Orchestra, as well as emerging mambo kings Tito Puente and Tito Rodríguez. New York crowds responded less enthusiastically to Prado than did mainstream America. To fans of the densely layered music of Afro-Cuban jazz mambo king Machito, Prado's music lacked richness and depth, since he eliminated instrumental solos and wrote extremely simple arrangements. But he was one of Latin music's great showmen, and his stage presence, which featured his signature grunting to mark a percussion break, was a major force in the popular breakthrough of mambo. Prado's genius lay in his way of presenting Latin music to a public that didn't really understand it. His "mass market" mambo, with histrionics, grunts, growls, and hysterical horns, put Afro-Cuban music on the map in the mainstream, and if it was less elegant than the brand offered by Machito and his successors, it was certainly not watered down. The Prado mambo, with its difficult tempo shifts and harmonic complexity, is considerably more cerebral than it seems on first listen.

Prado's next album, *Havana, 3 A.M.*, recorded in Hollywood in 1956, is one of the great masterpieces of mass-market tropical music. Buoyed by his stunning success on the U.S. charts and his work recording film soundtracks, Prado was calling the shots in Hollywood when he recorded this album, leading an orchestra that featured world-class trumpeter Maynard Ferguson. Many Cuban and Latin classics, such as Ernesto Lecuona's *La Comparsa*, Agustín Lara's *Granada*, and the classic bolero *Historia de un Amor* were covered on *Havana, 3 A.M.* Played in the fashionable commercial mambo style of the mid-1950s, lavished with Prado's eccentrically entertaining flourishes, these tunes are a time capsule of America as it was learning to shake its hips. The drummer bangs out the rhythm to introduce *La Faraona*, the trumpet section pronounces its melody with rude brassiness and saxophones bring a polite chamberlike rejoinder. Prado's yelping on the *Freeway Mambo* (one of three original tunes on the album) uncannily infuses mambo with the spirit of the nascent California car culture by creating a soundtrack for the steady march of freeway traffic.

New York as Incubator of the Mambo

While Pérez Prado made mambo palatable to the vast expanses of mid-America and the West Coast, in New York the music was evolving as a less commercial, more organic art form that spawned a cultural phenomenon. From the late 1940s to the mid-1960s, the place to hear and dance to Latin music in Manhattan was a club in Midtown called the Palladium. Converted from a dance academy in 1946, it had become a kind of multicultural haven for dancers from New York's Latin, African-American and European-American communities, and it drew the mixed crowd because of its location on Fifty-Second Street, just down the street from the celebrated jazz clubs of the swing, big band, and bebop era. The Palladium had three dominant bands: Machito's Afro-Cuban Orchestra, Tito Rodríguez's band, and the band of Tito Puente, perhaps the most famous talent to emerge from that era. Unlike Machito, who was born in Cuba, the Titos Rodríguez and Puente were both of Puerto Rican stock, a fact that would be significant in the move from mambo to salsa in the coming decade.

Cubans had been immigrating to New York since the turn of the century, but a massive influx of Puerto Ricans in the late 1940s made that group the dominant Latino ethnic group in the city. The timing was not coincidental: Puerto Rico, which had been an unincorporated territory of the United States since America's defeat of Spain in 1898, was subjected to an island-wide industrialization in the late '40s. Called Operation Bootstrap, devised in conjunction with the U.S. government, the project was intended to stabilize employment on the island by creating factory jobs. But for it to succeed, millions of Puerto Ricans (often whole families) were encouraged to move to New York through cheap plane fares so that they wouldn't overcrowd the island's industrial urban centers. Titos Rodríguez and Puente were not part of that migration, having arrived earlier in the century, but the public that would flock to their shows was all but created by Operation Bootstrap.

The main rhythmic forms of Puerto Rico, bomba, plena, and jíbaro music (of similar lineage and parallel to Cuba's rumba and guajiro music), had never coalesced in as dynamic a way as rumba and son did in Cuba. These dance forms were played by smaller band configurations and weren't added on to with an array of jazz or orchestra instruments as frequently as had happened in Cuba. Recording facilities in Puerto Rico were also substandard. Because of its immense popularity, the Cuban conjunto style, as well as the bolero style, discussed in Chapter 5, came to dominate Puerto Rican orchestras playing on the island. Looking for new opportunities and better recording facilities, Puerto Rican musicians began arriving in New York in the 1920s, joining an early migration

of tobacco and factory workers, and were exposed to the urban sophistication of jazz. By the time Tito Rodríguez and Tito Puente
emerged in the '50s, Latin music had absorbed the influence of experimenters like Machito, Mario Bauzá, and Dizzy Gillespie. New
arrivals, mostly from Cuba, continued to bring the latest styles.
Son and guaracha had come under the spell of Machito's newer,
hipper way of playing jazz music, and the crowds Rodríguez and
Puente were playing for were even more demanding than the ones
in Havana.

Tito Rodríguez

Singer/percussionist Pablo "Tito" Rodríguez has been one of the
most overlooked talents of his time. His bands, with their impeccable arrangements, crisp, tight playing, and displays of improvisational bravura while remaining focused on creating great dance
music, turned mambo into high art over and over again. Born in
1923 in San Juan, Rodríguez moved to New York in 1939, working when he arrived with Xavier Cugat and Noro Morales, a
Puerto Rican who had come to New York in the mid-1930s and
led swing-era big bands. After a brief stint with another Cugat
alumnus, José Curbelo, in 1946, during which he first played the
Palladium, Rodríguez formed his own band. It was first known as
the Mambo Devils, then the Mambo Wolves, then finally the Tito
Rodríguez Orchestra. In the 1950s, he recorded four albums on
the Tico label. After one record for RCA, at decade's end he
signed with United Artists, and he thrived as that label's only Latin
artist. Rodríguez's drive for musical perfection as leader of one of
the Palladium's top bands created a body of recorded work from
the 1950s to the 1960s that ranks with the best of the mambo era.

Rodríguez recorded several successful albums in the '50s, notably *Three Loves Have I*, *Señor Tito Rodríguez*, and *Mambo Madness*.
Like his predecessors Mario Bauzá and Machito, as well as Puente,

he gave special attention to maintaining the high standards of American jazz musicians, a devotion epitomized by famous tunes like *Mama Güela*, found on *Tito Rodríguez Live at the Palladium* (1960), and *Cuando, Cuando*, probably his best known, from *Back Home in Puerto Rico* (1962). Rodríguez's tight horn section announces *Mama Güela* with three plaintive, almost anthemic notes, and then explodes into the mambo beat, which shapes a series of sax, trumpet, and piano solos. The insistent rhythms are further propelled by the vocal chorus, and it all happens in 2:36. Swing classics like *Satin and Lace*, composed by Rodríguez, and George and Ira Gershwin's *Liza* feature chirpy Benny Goodman-like clarinet solos and razor-sharp arrangements by Ray Santos. Despite the carefree groove of cha-chas like *Te Comiste un Pan* and *El Monito y La Jirafa* and mambos like *El Sabio*, there is some serious jamming going on—playing that would influence both the hard salsa of the 1970s and the Latin jazz of the 1980s. Rodríguez's desire to take the orchestra toward jazz would be fulfilled in 1963 with the release of *Live at Birdland*, which featured Zoot Sims.

Tito Puente

Master percussionist/arranger/bandleader Tito Puente, born in 1923, was ahead of his time in many ways, but perhaps the most important was the fact that his parents came to New York and settled in East Harlem in 1921, about thirty years before the peak of Puerto Rican immigration. That Puente grew up in New York made him an early "Nuyorican," or Puerto Rican whose upbringing in the city gave him more access to a wider variety of cultural influences as well as a more cosmopolitan edge than his island counterparts. During Puente's childhood there was a relatively equal concentration of Puerto Ricans and Cubans in New York, which allowed young Tito to be influenced by a range of styles in places like the New York School of Music in Harlem and

Harlem's clubs, the Park Plaza Ballroom, the Golden Casino, and club Cubanacán. Bordered by Italian-Americans to the east and African-Americans to the west, the neighborhood he grew up in was just beginning to establish itself as Latino. In his teen years he was influenced by pre-R&B groups like the Ink Spots and went to the Paramount Ballroom to see the great big bands of Benny Goodman, Artie Shaw, Duke Ellington, and Count Basie. He especially admired the drummer Gene Krupa.

But Puente's main tutelage came under a Latin banner. He took private piano lessons with Victoria Hernández, the sister of the legendary Puerto Rican singer Rafael Hernández, and later with Luís Varona, a pianist from the Machito orchestra. Puente's first gig was at sixteen, a one-night stand as a drummer with bandleader pianist Noro Morales. In 1939 he met pianist José Curbelo, who would eventually become his mentor. Puente's association with Curbelo gave him entry to the upscale New York circuit, places like the Stork Club and El Morocco, and he also performed with Curbelo's band for several months in Miami. But a year later he went back to Morales's band as a permanent member, and in 1941, he traveled to Hollywood with Morales to perform in the Latin exploitation classics *The Gay Ranchero*, *The Mexican Jumping Bean*, and *Cuban Pete*. The following year, back in New York, he landed a regular gig with Machito and his Afro-Cubans, which solidified his grounding in ambitious, orchestral treatments of mambo and Latin big band jazz. Contemporary percussionist Bobby Sanabria credits Puente with being the first Latin drummers to "kick" big band figures with a combination of drums, timbales, and cymbals. His prominence in the orchestra was soon rewarded when Machito placed him at the front of the stage to feature his unique talents.

Puente spent World War II in the Navy, where he learned more about arranging by playing in a big band on his ship, the USS *Santee*. According to Steve Loza, writing in *Tito Puente and the Making of Latin Music*, he learned more arranging techniques from a saxophonist who had played with Charlie Spivak (coincidentally, a trumpeter who had once tutored Mario Bauzá). When the war was over Puente picked up where he had left off in the now-thriving New York club scene, which featured venues in Harlem, the Bronx, and Midtown. He used the G.I. Bill to attend the Juilliard School of Music, where he studied the Schillinger system (a mathematical system of permutating melodies used by Stan Kenton, a Puente influence) with Richard Bender. His formal study of arranging and composition would figure importantly in his lengthy career, during which he would also become an accomplished vibraphonist, pianist, and saxophone player. After spending two years as musical director with the Pupi Campo Orchestra, he formed his own group, the Picadilly Boys, and he would soon be ready to vie for the title of Mambo King.

Unlike Machito and Rodríguez, Puente was not his own lead singer, but he used singers like Cuban-born Vicentico Valdés (Puente's favorite singer, and a great improvisational talent), Macucho, Vitín Áviles, and Gilberto Monroig. Puente had many regulars in his band, but most of the memorable names were percussionists, like Mongo Santamaría, Patato Valdés, Willie Bobo, Johnny Pacheco, and Ray Barretto. The band was basically a mambo (and by the mid-1950s, a cha-cha) dance band, but Puente's arrangements synchronized the percussion and brass charts, something that made the music a kind of maddening, heart-racing blast of musical chaos.

Puente made the first of his more than 100 recordings in 1949, called *Abaniquito*, which featured his first hit, with the same title, sung by Vicentico Valdés. His early career featured obviously titled releases like *Mamborama*, *Mambo With Me*, and by the mid-'50s he followed the current dance-floor fashion with cha-cha albums like *Cha Cha Chas for Lovers* and *Dance the Cha Cha Cha*. (The cha-cha, a slower, more shuffling version of the mambo, appealed to dancers who had trouble with the more frenetic mambo pace.)

His more representative records of that decade include *Para los Rumberos, Ran Kan Kan,* and 1958's *Dance Mania,* which introduced Santos Colón, the lead singer most strongly associated with Puente for the next twenty years. Puente's music represented the final stage of the modernization of Afro-Cuban music—the Latin dance tunes being played in New York at the time were now clearly hybrids, strongly influenced by jazz, and its tempo was speeding up to suit the fast pace of the metropolis. The combination of the attitude, the sophistication of the arrangements, and the Puente orchestra's role as training ground for the musicians who would emerge in the 1960s and 1970s made it as strong an influence as any on what would later become salsa music.

Tito Rodríguez and Tito Puente both tried to claim the middle ground between the frenetic mambo of Pérez Prado and the Machito sound, which was devoted to serious big band jazz arrangements. Their struggle to push themselves to the forefront of mambo resulted in one of the great rivalries in Latin music. The competition and one-upsmanship that exploded on the stage of the Palladium night after night not only created loyalty from dancers and listeners, but had the effect of making the quality and precision of the music even better.

Puente and Rodríguez shared some teenage years in East Harlem—they lived on the same block of 110th Street and played baseball together. In 1949, at the same time Puente was recording *Abaniquito,* he was hired by Rodríguez to arrange charts for Rodríguez's first recording. The tenuous alliance between Puente and Rodríguez bubbled over into rivalry prompted by a struggle over top billing at the Palladium in the early 1960s. Although battling between bands were encouraged to create better performances from the bands, the standoff between Rodríguez and Puente went beyond the bounds of friendly competition. Both bandleaders had scored chart-topping hits in the prior decade, with Puente's usually claiming dominance. But when Rodríguez pulled ahead with hits like *Vuela La Paloma, Cuando Cuando,* and *Cara de Payaso,* he filed a grievance with a musicians' local asking that he receive top billing instead of Puente for a spring dance at the Palladium. (Rodríguez later claimed in a radio interview that they both had top-billing provisions written into their contracts.) In order to hold on to these magnets of drawing power, the Palladium's manager and booking agent made sure that both Titos would no longer be on the same bill. In a fit of anger, Puente resigned from the union.

As a percussionist Puente couldn't promote himself as easily as Rodríguez, since vocalists were naturally front men. But thanks to Machito, Puente had taken the unprecedented step of putting his timbales in the forefront of his orchestra. More than just a public relations stunt, Puente's move was a powerful statement that would always keep the rhythmic roots of Afro-Cuban music in full view. He was admired by fellow musicians for the complexity of his arrangements, but like all great artists, he brought them off without a hint of the difficulty involved. His audiences were completely enthralled with his showmanship as a player, as well as the way he danced around his timbales.

In his ability to play so many different and cosmopolitan styles of music, Puente was a quintessential Nuyorican musician. His work in the 1950s and 1960s, which helped mainstream mambo and cha-cha, also included collaborations with Woody Herman, a master of the Catskills circuit that was the summer home of New York's Jewish middle class. In his late 1950s–early 1960s RCA period alone (collected on *The Complete RCA Recordings, volumes 1 and 2*, released 2000 and 2002, respectively), he recorded songs like *Puente at Grossinger's*, *Miami Beach Cha Cha*, *That Old Devil Moon*, *Take the A Train*, and *Tuxedo Junction*. In 1962's *Bossa Nova*, he championed that Brazilian pop style, which combined elements of traditional samba with West Coast cool jazz, by recording mambo variations of three of Antonio Carlos Jobim's most famous tunes, *O Pato*, *Desafinado*, and *One-Note Samba*.

But in songs like *Elegguá Changó*, *Son de la Loma*, and *Yambeque*, Puente tapped into and further developed the deep African rumba roots in Cuban music. He first became interested in Afro-Cuban religion when he recorded *Top Percussion* (BMG), with percussionists like Bobo, Santamaría, and Francisco Aguabella, another Cuban legend, embellished by the spiritual choruses of Mercedita Valdés. Eventually, Puente became a Santería devotee.

The mambo era climaxed with Puente finally winning out over his rival Tito Rodríguez, and the Palladium Club, where their careers were nurtured, was closed forever when a New York police detective who suspected drug use had it raided in 1966. Rodríguez was a superior vocalist who sang boleros and fashioned a playboy image; Puente was such a distinguished percussionist that Rodríguez felt compelled to learn timbales and vibes to compete. But Rodríguez's rivalry with Puente took a great toll, forcing Rodríguez to abandon New York and start a second career as a bolero singer.

After disbanding his group in 1966 because of the waning popularity of mambo, he decided to pursue his lifelong ambition to record ballads and torch songs with a string orchestra much like those used by North American crooners. This second career produced a number of successful albums, such as *From Tito Rodríguez with Love*, which featured the syrupy hit single *Inolvidable*, and a whole new fame in the Latin music world. In 1971 he moved to Florida, where he worked in Spanish-language television and formed his own label, TR. His last appearance, with fellow mambo king Machito at Madison Square Garden, came about a month before he died of leukemia, at fifty years of age, in 1973.

Although he demonstrated his fascination with jazz as early as 1956's *Puente Goes Jazz*, Puente began to turn away from the dance-floor gigs and toward the Latin jazz format with a recording contract signed in 1981 with California's Concord Jazz label, on which he released eighteen albums from 1982–2002. But perhaps because many of the players in his 1950s and 1960s bands, most notably Johnny Pacheco and Ray Barretto, became central figures in the development of a new genre called salsa, Puente never lost touch with his dance-floor roots. During the '70s, '80s, and '90s, he backed the most popular singers of the era, including Celia Cruz, La Lupe, and even the much younger star Marc Anthony.

Tito Puente's death in 2000 was a national news story. It seemed to come at the peak of a period of public visibility in which he was recognized as the centerpiece of Latin music. He had bridged the gap from Latin music's stirrings in New York in the early 1920s, through the quintessential mambo era, to the salsa era. Puente's multicultural outlook and reformulation of Cuban music would inspire a new generation of musicians who created a new mixture, a "sauce" called salsa.

•3•

The Story of
Nuyorican Salsa

In some ways it's obvious what we mean by salsa. Salsa is a style of music that dominates dance floor tastes in Latin music clubs throughout the United States and Latin America, with extravagant, clave-driven, Afro-Cuban-derived songs anchored by piano, horns, and rhythm section and sung by a velvety voiced crooner in a sharkskin suit. On the other hand the definition of salsa is the subject of endless dispute in Latin music circles. If mambo was a constellation of rhythmic tendencies, then, as leading salsa sonero (lead singer) Rubén Blades once said, salsa is a concept, not a particular rhythm. But although salsa is nothing more than a new spin on the traditional rhythms of Cuban music—son, cha-cha, mambo, guaracha, guaguancó, and danzón—it is also at once a modern marketing concept and the cultural voice of a new generation. Though the quicker, almost synthetic-feeling tempo salsa is played at gives the music a new feeling, it is still based on the traditional Cuban son structure—a basic melody is introduced, followed by a coro section in which both the singer and the band are allowed to improvise.

Salsa is different from its forebears because it represents the crystallization of a Latino identity in New York in the early 1960s.

By the time people became conscious of it, the crystallization was complete. The man who first used the term salsa to publicize New York-based Latin music, a magazine editor and graphic designer named Izzy Sanabria, pointed out that many musicians who are now associated with the genre worked hard to innovate new styles without knowing that they were playing what would become known as salsa. Many musicians actively rejected the term. Mambo bandleader Machito said salsa was nothing but a new version of what he had been playing for forty years. When Tito Puente was asked about salsa, he commented sourly, "I'm a musician, not a cook." But salsa as sauce is an excellent metaphor for cultural mixing, and a reference to a special kind of spiciness. And as Sanabria said, if he had been completely honest and said that salsa was nothing but the same old music that bandleaders like Machito and Puente were playing, would the world have paid attention to New York Latin music?

Several urban legends surrounding the creation or coining of the term salsa are worth reflecting on, if only because they locate the energy that informs the genre. In the most simplistic sense, salsa refers to a mixture of ingredients that "spices up" the proceedings. Most food eaten in Latin American countries would be unthinkable without local sauces, or salsas. So when in 1932 Ignacio Piñeiro, the pioneering Cuban bassist and orchestra leader, shouted out "salsa" on *Échale salsita*, he was saying "Put some salsa on it," telling his band to shift the tempo and put the dancers into high gear. Later in that decade, renowned vocalist Beny Moré would merely shouted "salsa!" to acknowledge a musical moment's heat, as well as perhaps to express a kind of cultural nationalist sloganeering, celebrating the "hotness" or "spiciness" of Latin American cultures. (Celia Cruz continued this tradition in a similar vein with her own, perhaps more feminine slogan, *Azucar* [Sugar]!) Finally, "salsa" was legendarily invoked by Izzy Sanabria as a way to categorize the modern version of Afro-Cuban music being made in New York in the late 1960s and early 1970s. The ingredients brought from Cuba to New York were given a different flavor by a multinational group of Latino, African-American, and sometimes Anglo-American musicians who were essential to the creation of salsa.

The mambo era of the '40s and '50s was critical to Latin music in the United States because it popularized the basic Afro-Cuban sound, while introducing an array of international contributors operating within the context of the New York and Los Angeles jazz scenes. Mambo was a significant force in keeping the jazz big band alive, albeit in a different context, during a period when the smaller configurations of the bebop era took jazz in a different direction. But as the 1950s wound down, two important shifts occurred: The Latin big bands began to shrink in members, going the way of the old jazz big band; and the 1959 Cuban revolution greatly reduced contact between the island and New York musicians. The domination of the New York Latino community by Puerto Ricans, which had begun in the post World War II era, now entered a new dimension. Afro-Cuban music being played in New York began to evolve into something different.

The post-mambo-era Latin music that prevailed in New York in the 1960s, played by bands led by percussionist Ray Barretto and pianist Eddie Palmieri, for example, had two major influences. The first was music fads like charanga and pachanga from Cuba, which continued to provide the latest in styles and arrangements for New York-area players until the political economic and cultural blockade that set in after the Cuban Missile Crisis of 1962. The second was the growing interaction between New York Latinos and African-Americans in the working-class neighborhoods of Manhattan, Brooklyn, and the Bronx. The result of that interaction, the so-called Nuyorican or New York Latino identity, would be a hybrid culture, basically Puerto-Rican inspired, but incorporating influences from many of the existing U.S. Latino groups, mostly from Cuba and from Caribbean cities like Panama City, Cartagena and Barranquilla, Colombia, Caracas, Venezuela, and Santo Domingo, Dominican Republic.

The big fad from Havana in the late 1950s and early 1960s was the reborn charanga style, a throwback to the early part of the century that was a kind of reaction to the slick mambo ballroom style. Led by the extremely precise and swing-strong Orquesta Aragón, the charanga bands helped popularize cha-cha and several variations of mambo, guaracha, and guaguancó. Charanga's main features were the use of flute and violins in the role that the horn section would otherwise play. The charangas that were imported to New York by Cuban migrants like bandleader Gilberto Valdés were super-fast versions of the stately, traditional danzón. Their speed allowed for a flippant delivery by the vocalists, and the high-range flutes embellished the jams like up-the-neck electric guitar solos.

Charanga orchestras maintained a strong influence over the New York Latin music scene through the mid-1970s. But in their early years, they trained musicians who would play a major role in what became known as salsa. After Gilberto Valdés's first percussionist, Mongo Santamaría, left in 1957 to become involved in the Latin-fusion experiments on the West Coast spearheaded by vibist Cal Tjader, Valdés took on Johnny Pacheco, a young Dominican congero who would galvanize the core players of salsa in the years to come.

In 1959 Pacheco, who had arrived in the city ten years before, left the Valdés group with the New York-born Puerto Rican pianist Charlie Palmieri to form Charanga Duboney, a charanga orchestra dominated by flutes and violins. It only lasted eight months, but its album, called *Viva Palmieri*, set the stage for the new harmonic and arranging trends that would eventually become the standard for salsa orchestras. The band was smaller; the harmonies used by backup singers became tighter, sharpening the call and response. Pacheco would move on to form his own band, releasing *Johnny Pacheco y su Charanga Vol. 1* on Alegre Records in 1962. In an attempt to distinguish himself from Charlie Palmieri's Charanga Duboney, he began to call his music *pachanga*, despite the fact that it didn't vary from the charanga style. (Duboney released a charanga album in 1962 called *Salsa Na' Ma*, meaning, "it just needs a little salsa, or spice," which also anticipated the use of the word salsa.)

Pacheco was taking advantage of a dance fad called the pachanga, which lasted for a few years in the early to mid-1960s and involved a hopping and sliding turn that recalled the North American Charleston. Eschewing trips downtown to the trendy Palladium, the dancers who flocked to see Pacheco's and Palmieri's bands were remaining in their local Bronx and East Harlem neighborhoods and going to clubs like Teatro Puerto Rico and the Park Plaza. Smaller and more flexible than the Latin big bands of the mambo era, the charanga orchestra created a new style, but also set musicians off in a search for ever-more different fusions in what had been a static post-Tito Puente-Machito world. The Pacheco-Palmieri era, as well as the move away from Midtown to the barrios, ushered in a sensibility called típico, a rustic, simpler, funkier feel that coincided with nostalgia for the Caribbean lands left behind.

Conga-playing bandleader Ray Barretto was also a significant contributor to the charanga craze, especially on albums like *Charanga Moderna*. Barretto, a Brooklyn native of Puerto Rican descent, took up playing the conga while stationed with the U.S. Army in Germany. On *Charanga Moderna*, the flute-playing characteristic of the genre seems to fly wildly off the rhythm section and urgent bursts of Alfredo de la Fe's violin. The simple cha-cha rhythms of *El Watusi*, however, presaged the soul-psychedelic path that Barretto would follow in the mid to late-1960s. His version of psychedelia had more to do with extended recording time than with actual rock-influenced sonic tendencies, but it still expressed a preoccupation with spiritual inner growth.

La Perfecta, an eight-piece band led by pianist Eddie Palmieri, Charlie Palmieri's brother, continued the trend toward consolidation and a return to the típico. The band at its peak in the early 1960s featured the invigorating tenor of Puerto Rican-born Ismael

Quintana and an unusually emphasized trombone section of Barry Rogers and the Brazilian-born Joao Donato. The basic Cuban son piano riffs that ran through both charanga and bugaloo were the backbone of La Perfecta's dance sound. Another key member of La Perfecta was percussionist Manny Oquendo, who went on in the 1970s to form Libre, an orchestra that would carry the essence of the golden age salsa sound well into the 1990s.

Eddie Palmieri's hard-driving and classical- and jazz-influenced piano style personified the cutting edge of salsa and Latin jazz. He and Charlie, who died at sixty-two in 1988, were gifted and innovative pianists, giants in the genre. In his early teens Eddie was already developing a highly original soloing technique that opened the door to improvisation. Eddie's first major gig came in 1958, when he joined Tito Rodríguez's band. Two years later he left to go solo, and in 1961 formed La Perfecta. La Perfecta's frontlining of the trombone section was a precursor to the signature sound of the 1970s Golden Age of Salsa.

In his 1980 book *El Libro de la Salsa* (The Salsa Book) Venezuelan scholar César Miguel Rondón observed that Palmieri arranged the trombones "in a way that they always sounded sour, with a peculiarly aggressive harshness." The combination of this attitudinal shift from the Afro-Cuban style and the institution of the trombone as a constant counterpoint to the lead vocalist is one of the key staples of the New York salsa sound. Palmieri's own style of frantic, bluesy piano runs worked to a climax with the sassy-sounding brass section, giving a hard New York edge to the Cuban sound.

Palmieri also played with Johnny Pacheco's longest-lasting group, Johnny Pacheco y su Nuevo Tumbao. Pacheco's band returned to the Afro-Cuban style conjunto format, which goes back to the days of Arsenio Rodríguez, but featured two trumpets in the lead instead of Rodríguez's tres. About the same time that Pacheco formed the group, he befriended the man who would become salsa's main impresario, Jerry Masucci, an Italian-American lawyer.

The two formed a record label, Fania, which would become synonymous with the best salsa players. Johnny Pacheco y su Nuevo
Tumbao's debut album, *Cañonazo* (coincidentally the name of a
nightly ritual still held in Havana involving the setting off of several cannon blasts in the tradition of the Spanish regime), was the
first of fourteen to be released between 1964 and 1973.

Palmieri released eight albums with La Perfecta, including
two in collaboration with Cal Tjader, until Palmieri disbanded it
in 1968. In his subsequent solo career, he collaborated with legends like trumpeter Chocolate Armenteros, Cachao López, and
the vocalist Cheo Feliciano. In the early 1970s Palmieri flirted
with R&B fusion and also cut a classic record with the African-
American players Benard Purdie and Ronnie Cuber in 1971
called *Harlem River Drive*.

Although Eddie Palmieri was not as accomplished an arranger
and orchestral innovator as his brother, his unusually experimental
improvisatory style was a major force in the creation of salsa as a
New York-based movement. Palmieri was influenced by European
classical music, especially Debussy, and he was also mentored by
McCoy Tyner, a jazz-fusion experimentalist. He had a kind of
Thelonius Monk-esque style of stressing weak beats, as if he were
playing between notes and spaces in the rhythm, as well as a European impressionist shading that was bordering on, and perhaps an-
ticipatory of, the psychedelia that swept the Latin, jazz, and rock
worlds in the 1960s.

Salsa's Afro–New York Essence

In Piri Thomas's novel *Down These Mean Streets* and Richard
Brooks's film *Blackboard Jungle*, we can see evidence of New York
Puerto Ricans forming part of the core constituency of a black-
oriented urban culture, which would ultimately explode as hip-
hop culture in the late 1970s. The antecedents to black-Latin

fusion were in the doo-wop era (two of Frankie Lymon's Teenager backups were Latino) and R&B. In the mid-1960s, a new sensibility crystallized in Nuyorican barrios—house parties began playing James Brown funk as well as traditional Latin music. Nuyoricans had the ability to retain the traditional roots of their music while simultaneously incorporating and modernizing African-American influences, which in turn had the effect of influencing soul and R&B.

Bugaloo, its name derived from the same African-style scat onomatopoeia as cha-cha, was the first Latin music to regularly use English lyrics, epitomizing the changing sensibility of a Latino population that was beginning to use English as its dominant language. The creator of the first million-selling Latin music hit, Joe Cuba (Gilberto Miguel Calderón) was one of the primary practitioners of bugaloo. One of the first generation of New York Puerto Rican musicians, Cuba grew up in East Harlem and learned to play music with peers like Cuban percussionists Patato Valdez, Changuito (who would return to Cuba and become a central piece of the Cuban band Los Van Van), and future West Coast jazz figure Willie Bobo. Cuba began his career in the 1950s by taking over leadership in the Joe Panama Quintet, renaming it the Joe Cuba Sextet. Members of the old Panama crew, who had been playing stripped-down variations of mambo and conjunto music, had been experimenting with the use of English lyrics, and the Cuba edition continued this tendency, expanding its audience by playing at Jewish and Italian dances.

Despite the mix-it-up nature of Cuba's approach, the songs on classics like *Wanted Dead or Alive* are mostly in Spanish, with tunes like *Mujer Divina*, and *La Malanga Brava* capturing the raw feeling of the early Havana-style rumbas. With its lilting vocals and improvisational break, *Así Soy* is a prototypical salsa song. *Triste* is a pretty, unassuming ballad that functions like an R&B slow jam. The sextet's first big success, released in 1965, was a hit single, *El Pito* (I'll Never Go Back To Georgia), from their fourth release for the Tico label, *Estamos Haciendo Algo Bien/We Must Be Doing Something Right*. But the real breakthrough came from the group's main vocalist, Jimmy Sabater, who co-wrote *Bang! Bang!*, an easygoing, vibes-dominated party song that appeared on the 1966 hit album *Wanted: Dead or Alive*, and became one of the most significant top forty Latin hits since rock and roller Ritchie Valens's 1959 hit *La Bamba*. Sabater's *Oh Yeah* also placed on the U.S. charts; he later recorded three solo albums. Cuba went on to record four more albums, the last in 1979, but he was never able to recapture the success of bugaloo's crowning moment in the early 1960s.

Joe Cuba also used slowed-down cha-cha and son rhythms, as well as some catchy English-language choruses, and played up electric keyboards and particularly the vibraphone. His Spanglish classics like *Bang! Bang!* have the feeling of being recorded live at a party, with many background voices like much of the early work of 1970s R&B group Kool and the Gang. With its irresistible yet simple beats, *Bang! Bang!* might be the easiest Latin song to dance to ever recorded. *Oh Yeah* has the feel of a Ramsey Lewis Trio song, with its easy groove, call and response, and cool, vibes-driven melody. *Push, Push, Push* is pretty much more of the same, but its welcome, relentless invitation to groove captures the essence of bugaloo's short but happy life.

Joe Cuba's work is at the core of the Spanglish bugaloo sound, but others made their mark. Johnny Colón, a bandleader and Latin music educator based in East Harlem, released two albums in 1967, *Bugaloo Blues* and *Bugaloo '67*, that are nothing short of state of the art. Other bugaloo classics include *I Like It Like That*, by Cuban vocalist Jimmy Sabater, and *El Watusi*, by rapidly ascending congero-bandleader Ray Barretto. *I Like it Like That* opens a conversation between Afro-Cuban son and Ray Charles-style stride piano. It paved the way for much of the Latin-tinged American pop music by instrumental groups in the mid-1960s. Rock classics like *Tequila*, *Wipe-out*, and the garage classic *96 Tears* sprang from bugaloo's attitude.

The Golden Age of Salsa—The Fania Years

The closing of the Palladium in 1966 signaled the official end of the mambo era, and the energy and direction of Latin musicians in New York was clearly changing. Promoters like Jerry Masucci became central players, booking groups in a new, Manhattan-oriented club circuit that included places below Ninety-Sixth Street like the original Cheetah Club, Casino 14, the Corso, and the Village Gate. A new magazine, *Latin New York*, appeared, with Izzy Sanabria at the helm.

Musically, Eddie Palmieri's La Perfecta and other groups were moving closer to salsa, as elements of bugaloo and charanga battled with elements of rock and rhythm and blues, all in an environment suddenly bereft of Cuban influence. As a marketing term and social phenomenon, salsa is inextricably linked to Fania Records. Fania's debut album, *Cañonazo*, recorded in 1964 by Pacheco's Nuevo Tumbao group (featuring Pete "El Conde" Rodríguez, who became a Fania All Star, on vocals), is often referred to as the formal beginning of the salsa era, if for nothing else than its decided break from charanga. But with the exception of releases by Bobby Valentín (a Pacheco bassist and trumpeter) and Larry Harlow (a pianist known as *El Judio Maravilloso* (the Marvelous Jew), perhaps because of his fondness for the work of "El Ciego Maravilloso," Arsenio Rodríguez), Fania's output did not gather momentum with the listening public. In 1967, Fania embarked on an aggressive and phenomenally successful program of recording and promotion to push the new music and corner the market for itself, signing many new bands and booking them for appearances on the New York club circuit.

Fania also put together all-star shows containing members of its best groups. Live recordings of two of Fania All-Stars' early shows, at the Red Garter and the Cheetah Club, became enormously popular releases in 1968 and 1971, respectively. Fania All-Star concerts were not quite a promotional appearance for a hot group, nor an overwrought "concert" of earnest rock poetry—

they were tribal jams perhaps influenced by the 1960s counterculture and explosions of improvisational creativity. Overwhelming
percussion sections that included Ray Barretto and Johnny
Pacheco fed off trombone-dominated horn sections. A four-to-
five member choral section, often teaming up vocalists Hector
Lavoe, Ismael Miranda, Santos Colón, and Adalberto Santiago,
took turns improvising the coro section with the rest of the band.

The formula for the Fania sound was not different from the
Afro-Cuban mambo promulgated by Cachao and Orestes López
or Arsenio Rodríguez. What was new was the personality and style
of the vocalists, and what they were singing about. The text for
these songs was often ancestral memories and nostalgia for Puerto
Rico. On *Anacanoa*, from *Live at the Cheetah*, *Vol. 1* (1971) the All
Stars invoked Puerto Rico's oral tradition—they riffed barrio
memories and salutes to Taino goddess Anacanoa in the declama-
tory style of décima poets. The concerts became a dazzling display
of the energy and style of salsa in its golden age (usually dated
from 1971–1978). In various incarnations, the Fania All Stars also
recorded ten other studio albums. Some, like *Crossover* and *Delicate
and Jumpy*, were attempts to commercialize the band through collaborations with jazz fusion and rock musicians.

At the center of the Fania movement was trombonist and salsa
innovator Willie Colón. Born in 1950 and raised in the Bronx's
hardscrabble Latino barrios, Colón was influenced by American
pop music and the inner-city toughness of his youth, as well as the
pop and folkloric music of his parents' native Puerto Rico. He was
not content with simply reproducing the music that was coming
out of the Caribbean. Colón combined two previous innovations,
making them characteristic of his brand of salsa. First, like
Palmieri, he used the trombone as a lead instrument—like Puente,
he even moved his instrument to the front and center of the stage.
Second, he went outside the traditional clave to incorporate several South American beats, most notably Panama's murga, a
cumbia-like dance rhythm, into his music.

Colón's recording career began in the late 1960s when he was still a teenager. He formed his first band at age fourteen, as a trumpeter, but soon discarded his trumpet for a trombone, heavily influenced by the powerful sound of this instrument and the dynamic style of Barry Rogers and José Rodrigues, trombonists in Eddie Palmieri's La Perfecta. By comparison, Colón's style was grittier and less mannered. In 1968, he recorded *El Malo* (The Bad Guy) for Fania, the first in what became a series of albums that epitomized the Fania style at its best, capturing the restless energy and aggressive dynamism of early salsa. Colón's band always had the most impressive singer, or sonero, on the scene, beginning with their first, Hector Lavoe. Lavoe had emigrated to New York from the city of Ponce, Puerto Rico, in the early 1960s, at age seventeen. He brought with him the traditional styles of island singers like Bobby Capó and Ismael Rivera.

When they finally teamed up, an encounter immortalized on records like *El Malo*, *The Hustler* (1969), and *Cosa Nuestra* (1971), Colón and Lavoe were electric, especially on tunes like *El Malo*, *Que Lio*, and *Che Che Cole*. Lavoe brought a rural soul feel and Colón the cutting edge of the street intellectual, ambitious to make his music American and international. *Che Che Cole*, like *La Murga de Panama*, was one of Colón's "world-salsa" experiments, and a highly successful one. Combining jazz, samba, and elements of Puerto Rican bomba and plena, as well as a chorus that hinted at Central African language (*Che che cole/che che cofisa/cofisa langa*), it was an internationalizing song that broke salsa out of previous New York Afro-Cuban models.

Because of his lifelong battle with drug and alcohol addiction, Hector Lavoe was salsa's ultimate tragic figure, acquiring a martyr-like aura in his embodiment of the new dynamism of the Nuyorican identity. It was as if the sudden rush to modernity had burned out the self-styled country *jíbaro*. When Lavoe sang *Mi Gente* (My People) at Yankee Stadium as a member of the Fania All Stars in the Massucci-produced *Salsa* documentary in August 1973, it was a cathartic moment, one that marked the birth of this new identity—Nuyoricans had found a way to reconcile their island and New York points of view. When Lavoe, fighting through a drug-induced haze and a fantasy of returning to his native Puerto Rico, sang the line, *Yo soy un jíbaro de Puerto Rico* (I'm a country guy from Puerto Rico), the effect on Nuyoricans was not unlike the effect on Cuban exiles when they hear *Yo soy un hombre sincero* (I'm a sincere man), which begins the classic *Guantanamera*. The strong identification with Caribbean culture by newly established populations in North America began a new kind of identity, one in which nostalgia became a permanent state of mind for a transplanted individual.

By declaring himself a jíbaro, Lavoe allowed thousands of transplanted Puerto Ricans to connect to their island roots while at the same time feeling a new sense of homeland in the middle of the South Bronx, which at the time was being ravaged by the phenomenon known as white flight, which was hastened by the deterioration of New York's industrial economy. The psychological devaluation of Nuyoricans and African-Americans was accompanied by a rash of arson, used by landlords to collect money for buildings they didn't want to rent to blacks and Latinos. The music of the Fania era, and particularly the collaboration between Lavoe and Colón, helped restore pride to the community through an era of struggle that culminated in the riots following the 1976 New York blackout and the fiscal crisis.

In 1976, Hector Lavoe's problems with drugs and health came to a head, and he had to leave Colón's band. His spot was taken by Panamanian sonero/songwriter Rubén Blades, who soon became a central figure in his own right. Blades was a fascinating figure in that he passed for a Nuyorican even though he was from a relatively middle-class family in Panama and did graduate studies in law at Harvard. He had a passion for the great soneros of Puerto Rico (such as Cheo Feliciano and Ismael Miranda), and Panama has a similar colonial relationship with the United States. But

Blades got deep into the city's heartbeat, starting out as a stock boy with Fania Records and prowling New York clubs like the Corso, the Village Gate, and Casino 14.

As Lavoe's replacement, Blades had enormous shoes to fill, but his collaboration with Colón continued Colón's status as the strongest of the Fania Records lineup in the mid-1970s, during which he produced classics like *Siembra*, an album that became a staple for a generation of socially conscious Latin New Yorkers. Although Blades wrote most of the songs for their collaboration, the two shared a creative bond that made them the Lennon and McCartney of salsa, an unprecedented team that produced groundbreaking tunes. *Siembra* included *Pedro Navaja*, a barrio reworking of *Mack the Knife*, from the *Three-Penny Opera*, and *Plástico*, a song that warned against the evils of the materialist culture of the North. *Pedro Navaja* became the *Stairway to Heaven* of salsa, the most requested song of the genre.

Siembra is one of those albums that defines a crowning moment in a genre—it contained several classic songs that functioned like mini-documentaries of the New York Latino experience. While the basic subject matter of salsa (and most of Latin music), dancing, and romance, was represented here, through songs like *Ojos* (Eyes) and *Dime* (Tell Me), both laments of a lost love, the album also included a strong political statement in *Plástico*, and island nostalgia in *Buscando Guayaba*. Colón's maturing, swing-filled arrangements and steady trombone act both as a rhythmic accompaniment and a second melody.

Siembra's extraordinary ability to symbolize a time comes from tunes like *Plástico*, which begins with a funk-disco bassline and evolves into a politicized critique of consumer materialism. But its crowning moment is a roll call of Latin American nations at the end of a long jam. *Pedro Navaja*, perhaps the most famous salsa song ever, is a poetic narrative flashback about the downfall of a small-time gangster on a barrio street corner. The hooks and edgy chemistry between the horn section, the piano, and the rhythm sections are flawless Fania. Sentimental nationalism has never been such partying fun as on this record, and *Plástico's* chanting of Latin American country names is a fixture in salsa concerts to this day.

Salsa continued to enjoy a great popularity after *Siembra*, but it began to go on the wane in the next decade. Blades and Colón continued their reign, recording several albums like 1981's excellent *Canciones del Solar de los Aburridos* (Songs From the Neighborhood of the Bored), but they went their separate ways after making the Latino-exploitation movie *The Last Fight* in 1982. Blades became highly successful as a world-music artist, performing and acting in over fifteen films alongside the likes of Jack Nicholson and Harrison Ford. In the film *Crossover Dreams*, directed by a New York-based Cuban, León Ichaso, Blades played a less successful singer. *Crossover Dreams* is one of the most significant U.S. Latino films of the 1980s, because it portrays the pain of assimilation and the increasing marginalization of New York salsa culture.

In the 1980s, Blade was able to extricate himself from his contract with Fania records, and he signed with Sony. His superior voice, now liberated from earlier criticisms that it was a carbon copy of Cheo Feliciano, a former singer for Eddie Palmieri and the Fania All Stars, and his ability to market himself to an Anglo audience, intensified tension between Blades and Colón, who seemed to lose luster without his star vocalist. Blades's career continued into the 1990s, when he released strong efforts like 1991's *Caminando* and 1992's *Amor y Control*. After an unsuccessful bid for the presidency of Panama in 1994, he reemerged at the turn of the twenty-first century with two superior albums, 1999's *Tiempos* and 2002's *Mundo*. These two releases, recorded with Costa Rican jazz fusion group Editus, evidenced Blades's maturity as a poet and a master of a variety of world musics.

Colón was less successful than Blades at keeping himself in the limelight, but he put out some extremely important work in the 1980s, such as *Doble Energía* with Ismael Miranda and *Vigilante* (1983), his last album with Hector Lavoe. His best albums of the late 1980s to the early 1990s, *Altos Secretos* and *Color Americano*, continued the social commentary that began during his collaboration with Blades. A song from *Altos Secretos*, titled *El Gran Varón*, was a huge success because it confronted for the first time in a salsa tune the issue of homosexuality and AIDS in the Latin community. While it's hard to argue that Colón ever faded away, these early 1990s albums constituted something of a comeback. Colón also appeared in commercials and television and in 1993 ran, unsuccessfully, as a Democrat for state representative in Westchester County, New York. In 1995, Colón and Blades, realizing that their fans made it lucrative for them to renew their collaboration, recorded *Tras la Tormenta*—in separate studios. They finally staged a tumultuous reunion in a concert at the Hollywood Bowl in 1997. As the century drew to a close, Colón continued to perform sporadically, starred in *Demasiado Corazón*, a Mexico City-based soap opera in 1998, and ran for public advocate of New York in 2001, where he finished second in the Democratic primary with 17 percent of the vote. His next CD, *Contrabanda*, issued on the independent Sonographica label, demonstrated that he was still a stirring force in Latin music.

Típica '73

With the crystallization of the Fania sound in the late 1960s and early 1970s, there was a rush to a new conformity in Latin music. Salsa's upfront horns and percussion section had wiped out the violins and flutes of the charanga era. It was more soulful and funky and left more room for extended improvisation by percussion and chorus. But it also lost some of the discipline of the traditional Cuban dance orchestra. In the early 1970s a change got under way that would restore some of that discipline, break apart one of salsa's most successful bands, and reunite the New York tradition with Havana for the first time since the Cuban revolution.

A series of jam sessions held in Manhattan in 1972 by a young session percussionist named Johnny Rodríguez Jr., the pianist Sonny Bravo, and trombonist Leopoldo Pineda began to attract influential onlookers and musicians. The band, which would eventually be called Típica '73, recruited several members of the Ray Barretto Band, which in 1972 had scored a solid Fania hit called *Message*. Trumpeter René López, percussionist Orestes Vilato, bassist Dave Pérez, and vocalist Adalberto Santiago defected from Barretto's band, much to that bandleader's dismay. Típica '73's sound focused more on traditional Cuban son and gradually incorporated more Cuban instrumentation. On the band's second album, *Típica '73* (its first two albums are both named *Típica '73*), it brought in a tres player, Nelson González, and on 1975's *La Candela*, the band began a series of musical exchanges with musicians living in revolutionary Cuba, such as Los Van Van's Juan Formell. Synthesizers and distortion pedals (used by tres player González) mirrored the experimentation going on in Cuba and made Típica '73 a remarkable fusion between old-style and new-style Cuban music, all the while grounded in Fania-style funkiness.

In the mid-1970s vocalist Adalberto Santiago, percussionist Vilato, and guitarist González all left Típica '73 to start new bands. A group of new players would take their places, most notably violinist Alfredo de la Fe, who grounded the group in the charanga sound. *The Two Sides of Típica '73*, released in 1977, showed the band flexing its varied musical directions, flowing seamlessly through Cuban son, Latin jazz, Fania salsa, and the latest electric-oriented sound from Cuba, the songo. Later that year, José "El Canario" Alberto became the band's lead singer, and the band embarked on its most controversial period. In 1979 it would participate in the first informal residency of a New York salsa band in Cuba. Fleshed out by conga master Angel "Cachete" Maldonado and saxophonist Mario Rivera, the band recorded *Típico '73 in Cuba, Intercambio Cultural*. Cuban guest artists included the conga player Tata Güines, the tres player Niño Rivera, and trumpeter

Felix Chappotín, among the best contemporary Cuban musicians at the time.

But by the time the group recorded *Charangueando con la Típica '73* in 1980, a backlash, caused by anti-Castro sentiments, began to set in. New York club owners with ties to the Cuban-American community began to blackball the group, refusing to book them. By 1982 Sonny Bravo and Johnny Rodríguez dissolved the band, but many of its players continued to be influential on the New York scene. Típica '73 reunited for some live shows in 1994 and 1999, and Sony released *Live Concert Series* in 2003, culled from some of those dates.

During a time when salsa was beginning to move toward a stage where the singer's star appeal became more important than musicianship, Típica '73 remained dedicated to the high standards of an Afro-Cuban dance orchestra. But the band was never trapped in the mold of being a nostalgia group—it continued to evolve and seek inspiration from Cuba when interaction between New York and Havana was at a nadir.

Celia Cruz

Celia Cruz is the most recognizable and most powerful voice in contemporary Latin music. Though she has been recording and performing from a New York base since the early 1960s, she represents the last gasp of Cuban influence on what would informally become known as the New York school. Born in Havana in 1924, she performed in various talent shows, finally enrolling in Cuba's Conservatory of Music in 1947.

Cruz was a devotee of Paulina Álvarez, a vocalist with Orquesta Antonio María Romeu, but in 1950 latched on to the extremely important band Sonora Matancera, which took its name from the town of Matanzas, Cuba. Formed in 1924, the band was led by guitarist/singer Regelio Martínez. Matancera was an institution in

Cuba and over the years featured close to one hundred vocalists from the Caribbean and Mexico, including Puerto Rican legend Daniel Santos. Cruz replaced Puerto Rican singer Myrta Silva, who began her career in New York in the 1930s with Rafael Hernández's Cuarteto Victoria (see Chapter 5). This was the start of Cruz's classic period from about 1950–1960, when she was cementing her reputation as the most popular female singer in Cuba.

Cruz appeared in several clubs and hotels and on the radio and sang typical fare like *Ritmo Pilón* and the more esoteric, Santería-related *Mata Siguaraya*. She also played with several other groups (Sonora Cubana, Armando Romeu, and Sonora Caracas, to name a few). During her tenure with Sonora Matancera, Cruz and the band left Cuba for a tour that never made it back to their homeland, applying for residency in the United States, where they were able to secure a long-term gig at the Hollywood Palladium. In 1962, Cruz moved to New York and married Pedro Knight, the trumpeter of Sonora Matancera, who eventually became her manager, and the couple made it clear they were political exiles from Cuba.

In 1965 Cruz left Sonora Matancera—which continued on until at least 2003, making it one of the longest-lasting groups in Latin music history—and began to record with Tito Puente. With Puente she recorded *Cuba y Puerto Rico Son*, *Quimbo Quimbumbia*, and *Etc., Etc., Etc.*, between 1965 and 1970, but she also released albums with Orquesta de Memo Salamanca (with which she had earlier recorded *Cuando Salí de Cuba*, the exile anthem), and the Alegre All-Stars, a South Bronx band lead by Al Santiago and featuring both Palmieris on keyboards.

Cruz had the visual impact of a Hotel Tropicana show dancer but her inimitable voice had such power that, like the great jazz divas, she held even the most difficult audiences in the palm of her hand with her biting alto. She brought the funky Cuban essence when she appeared, often dressed in fire-engine red, snapped her fingers and shouted *¡Azucar!* (sugar) in the manner of Beny Moré or countless Cuban vocalists. Her flight from the Cuban revolution was a major contradiction of the notion that Castro's plan liberated Cubans of African ancestry; her decision to become an exile placed her alongside the predominantly white bourgeoisie who left the island in the first exodus.

Cruz's effect on New York salsa as an Afro-Cuban woman, in a field dominated by light-skinned Puerto Rican men, was considerable. Her ability to epitomize the Afro-Cuban experience allowed her to forge ties with Tito Puente, a devotee of Cuban music despite his Nuyorican innovations. Together, they were Latin music's one-two punch before and after the 1970s Fania Records era. In 1966 alone Cruz and Puente recorded eight albums, many of which are now out of print. Her collaborations with Larry Harlow, who wrote one of her signature tunes, *Gracia Divina*, and Willie Colón, with whom she performed the electric *Usted Abusó*, are among the best records of the peak Fania years. Harlow, a veteran of the Palladium days, and Colón, linchpin of the Fania sound, provided her with exhilarating arrangements and excellent session players.

Cruz's ability to translate the culmination of the Afro-Cuban style into the harder, edgier rhythms of New York salsa made for music that was authentic to both tastes. In the 1980s and 1990s, she exploited her position as one of the few female salsa vocalists of note. Her appearance in the movie *The Mambo Kings*, based on the Oscar Hijuelos book, gave her an Ella Fitzgerald-like appeal to the mainstream. In fact, her singing style is very much centered on her ability to unite virtuoso scat techniques in the manner of Fitzgerald with the improvisational style of salsa singing. At the turn of the century, Cruz remained enormously successful as a recording artist and performer, first with Sony and then for Ralph Mercado's RMM label, which was bought out by Universal in 2001. The most interesting of these were *Azucar Negra*, released in 1993 and featuring input from Miami singers Gloria Estefan and Jon Secada, and 1997's *Duets*, which ventured outside of salsa through duets with Brazilian singer Caetano Veloso and Argentine rockers Los Fabulosos Cadillacs, as well as two members of RMM's stable, José Alberto and La India. In 2002, Cruz won a Grammy for *La Negra Tiene Tumbao*, which featured state-of-the-art arrangements, an indefatigable sense of swing, and nods to club music like house and hip-hop—it's a rare late-career album that demonstrated growth and a feeling that Cruz was still peaking as an artist.

Enshrined in the Smithsonian and having received an honorary doctorate from Yale, Cruz is a symbolic cornerstone of salsa music, primarily because of her technically and aesthetically superior voice. Her career as a lead singer with Sonora Matancera and as a collaborator with salsa's key artists (Colón, Pacheco, Puente, and Harlow) put her at the center of the genre's history, at once an innovative performer and an extremely talented perfectionist.

Eddie Palmieri

After the breakup of La Perfecta in 1968, pianist Eddie Palmieri began playing with the Fania All Stars, a lesser-known label group called the Tico All-Stars, and with singers like Justo Betancourt. While Palmieri was disappointed with the end of the Palladium era and the battle-of-the-bands atmosphere surrounding it, he continued to perform in what was known as the *cuchifrito* circuit, an analog of the African-American chitlin' circuit. During this relentless period of touring he made *The Sun of Latin Music*, an album that contained high-concept salsa highlighting Palmieri's virtuosity, and won the first Latin Grammy award in 1974. *The Sun of Latin Music* featured an all-star lineup along with classic compositions and virtuoso performances by Palmieri. The playing was crisp and loose while maintaining a discipline even during the improvisational sequences. Palmieri lead the band with his eccentric pummeling of the piano, using an extraordinarily rhythmic and harmonically textured technique. The idiosyncratic plucking of legendary charanga violinist Alfredo de la Fe only hinted at the driving ecstasy of Palmieri's improvisation in *Nunca Contigo*. The percussion section of Tommy López Jr. on bongó, Eladio Pérez on conga, and Nicky Marrero on timbales fueled the album's many dance-friendly moments. And Palmieri's nine-minute Debussy-ish passage introducing into *Un Dia Bonito* was a journey into a new salsa universe only he could navigate.

Sun of Latin Music also features the stunningly impressive debut of sonero Lalo Rodríguez, who also appeared on 1974's *Unfinished Masterpiece*. Palmieri had originally wanted to use Andy Montañez, then the lead singer of the influential Puerto Rican salsa group El Gran Combo, but the band only agreed to release the singer to do one or two tracks, and Palmieri wanted one vocalist for the whole album. Contacts in Puerto Rico led him to the sixteen-year-old Rodríguez. Strongly influenced by Hector Lavoe, Rodríguez's tenor is stridently nasal, meshing perfectly with the disciplined drumming, the howling horns of Ronnie Cuber and Mario Rivera, the soulful backup vocals of bugaloo king Jimmy Sabater, and Palmieri's provocative piano. *Mi Cumbia* was perhaps the most avant-garde evocation of authentic Colombian cumbia recorded at that time. And there may never have been as elegant a Spanish re-make of a Beatles' song as *Una Rosa Española*, which re-imagines *You Never Give Me Your Number* from *Abbey Road* as a danzón in Havana's Hotel Tropicana.

Palmieri's 1978 release *Lucumí, Macumba, Voodoo* placed the various African syncretic religions of the Caribbean in the forefront and featured Palmieri's typically eccentric big band salsa flourishes, while also containing some less interesting jazz-fusion vocal experiments. *La Verdad/The Truth*, released nine years later, was his fifth Grammy-award winner, with a more fulfilled repertoire of jazz-fusion and African-inflected salsa (*Congo Yambumba* is a standout jam). Of his uneven mid-1980s releases, 1982's *Sueño*, produced by Kip Hanrahan, an avant-garde jazz-Latin bandleader, is the most memorable, particularly for its revised version of the Palmieri classic *Azucar*. As of 2003, Palmieri still toured occasionally and played a major part in New York's Latin music scene—his collaboration with salsa vocalist La India helped bring a legion of younger Latinos into the salsa fold and played a big part in the music's late-1990s revival. Surviving members of La Perfecta were reunited in 2002 and were joined by younger players like trumpeter Brian Lynch, flutist Dave Valentín, and percussionist Richie Flores for *La Perfecta II* (Concord Jazz).

The Fania label's fortunes began to decline in the mid-1980s, partially because of the ascension of a new, slicker style of salsa that focused on the star potential of the lead singer, and partially because of owner Jerry Masucci's failing health. In 1995 Masucci shut down the label after more than fifteen years of success, in which it was compared to labels such as Blue Note and Motown in terms of sustained excellence. The shutdown of Fania, which was revived shortly before Masucci's death in 1997, signaled the end of the golden age of salsa.

Meanwhile, Back in Puerto Rico

In the period between the 1960s and 1980s, at the same time that, in New York, salsa was reaching its peak, significant musical developments were occurring in Puerto Rico that eventually influenced what was going on in New York. On its own terms, the music being played in Puerto Rico could stake a claim as being as modern as New York salsa. There was continual exchange of musical knowledge and influences facilitated by the migration of musicians from the island to New York, as well as the relatively easy flow of information between Puerto Rico, the Caribbean, and the rest of Latin America.

During the mambo explosion of the post-World War II era, many Cuban bands played in Puerto Rico, and local orchestras playing mambo, bolero, and various Afro-Cuban fusions influenced by local music and what was going on in New York made for a lively scene. Standouts included bands led by trumpeter César Concepción (playing orchestra-arranged plenas), Lito Peña (Orquesta Panamericana, which featured a young Ismael Rivera on vocals), and trumpeter Miguelito Miranda. They all began to play at a San Juan beachside club called El Escambrón, which was located at the Caribe Hilton Hotel. Puerto Rico's hotel scene was on a smaller scale than Havana's, but it provided a platform for bands like that of pianist Noro Morales into the 1960s.

A reaction to the bourgeois hotel scene came from newer acts, which called for a return to funky nativism. At the forefront of modernizing the street-derived sounds of Puerto Rican bomba and plena, two musical traditions roughly analogous to Cuban rumba, was congero Rafael Cortijo's combo. From the early '60s to the '80s, Cortijo fulfilled the theory of Luís Rafael Sánchez, a Puerto Rican novelist, that the people's music should be traditional, avant garde, and popular at the same time. Cortijo, who began his musical career in 1954, traveled to New York in 1961 and had a strong influence on that city's Latin music throughout the decade. Cortijo's songs reflected a black perspective that was less filtered by European influences such as the danzón-like underpinnings of the Cuban orchestra repertoire.

His bands, often fronted by one of the all-time great soneros, Ismael Rivera, were innovative by modernizing the bomba and to a lesser extent the plena, homegrown Puerto Rican rhythms, giving them an almost urban feel. Songs like *María Teresa* and *Micaela*, both from the 1960 release *Cortijo y su Combo*, epitomize the fusion of storytelling lyrics typical of bomba with the dance's swirling, bouncy rhythms. The bomba is less restricted than Afro-Cuban dance music, with perhaps more in common with Colombia's cumbia and Brazil's samba. Cortijo was also very inspired by Brazilian samba and by the Colombian hybrid rhythm, the merecumbé, invented by Colombian bandleader Pacho Galán as a fusion of merengue and cumbia. The infusion of Cortijo's bomba and plena innovations into the salsa sound is one of the important characteristics that distinguish salsa from Cuban popular music.

In a self-conscious attempt to bring the music closer to its African origin, Cortijo stripped down the Afro-Cuban orchestra format to the "combo" or conjunto, a move that paralleled the innovations of Cuban tres player Arsenio Rodríguez, by lessening the number of horn and string players in his band. His music reflected the tight, aggressive feel that an emphasis on the rhythm section and more popular themes bring about. Cortijo had a major influence on the developments in merengue in the Dominican Republic, during the emergence of that country from the reign of dictator Rafael Trujillo in the early 1960s.

One of the most significant spinoffs from Cortijo's bands was El Gran Combo, formed in 1962 by ex-Cortijo pianist Rafael Ithier. Ithier didn't create a stripped down bomba and plena unit but returned to the orchestra format, retaining a strong percussion focus. El Gran Combo became Puerto Rico's house band in the way that the Grateful Dead became the house band for the San Francisco counterculture in the late 1960s. For Ithier and his band, more is more—he used two pianists, two saxophonists, two trumpeters, and three lead vocalists, amounting to a thirteen-piece dance orchestra. Perhaps by staying on the island and not becoming part of the Nuyorican scene, El Gran Combo escaped the phasing out of the big bands in New York. Ithier used a massive number of instruments to keep the rhythms traditional, with little room for lengthy improvisation. Sticking to less improvisational call and response, El Gran Combo kept out the edgier, jazz-and-rock influenced arrangements of the Fania posse, who, through local pianist Papo Lucca, were well-known on the island. The most notable vocalist to emerge from El Gran Combo was Andy Montañez, but his partners Elliot Romero and Charlie Aponte formed a harmonic barrage that cut through vast concert rooms as well as intimate dance floors.

Founded in 1954 by pianist Enrique Lucca, La Sonora Ponceña was, with El Gran Combo, one of Puerto Rico's two most important continually performing bands over almost forty years. Hailing from Puerto Rico's second largest city, Ponce, La Sonora Ponceña featured a two-piano attack (Lucca's son Papo, one of the most talented salsa pianists of his generation, and Rafael Ithier); a barrage of lead trumpets; and the well-balanced harmonies of a trio of singers, at one time including a woman, Yolande Rivera—besides Myrta Silva and Celia Cruz, a rarity. Papo Lucca eventually became the group's leader in 1968 at the age of twenty-two, and his father, Enrique, became more of an arranger/musical director.

After their label, Inca, was purchased by Fania in the late 1960s, La Sonora Ponceña began to get far more international exposure. The band recorded Arsenio Rodríguez classics, *Hachero Pa' Un Palo* and *Fuego En El 23*, which became immensely popular. Larry Harlow produced albums like 1972's *Desde Puerto Rico a Nueva York*, 1974's *Sabor Sureño*, and 1975's *Tiene Pimienta*. The lead vocalists were Luís "Luigi" Texidor and Tito Gómez, who provided a grittier, more nasal style that was opposed to the smooth, often bolero-fixated vocalists of the hotel circuit.

With La Sonora Ponceña, Papo Lucca recorded over thirty albums, of which the recognized standout is 1988's *On the Right Track*. One of the greatest straight-ahead salsa records ever made, *On the Right Track* is a relentless assault on the senses. Although it sometimes sounds as if it were recorded in an echo chamber, the extremely high level of playing—especially the keyboard improvisation by Papo Lucca and Rafael Ithier—and the inventive arrangements make this a salsa classic. The often-overlooked trio of vocalists who worked with the band in the 1980s—Hector "Pichy" Pérez, Manuel "Manix" Roldan, and Daniel "Danny" Davila—are at their peak here.

In addition to original material written by Lucca, Ponceña drew from an astute variety of sources for its songs, from Cuban nueva trova composer Pablo Milanés (*Pensando en Ti*) to fusion jazz pianist Chick Corea (*Capuccino*). Milanés's song was given a lilting swing-salsa treatment, replete with singalong chorus, while the version of *Capuccino* drew out the Latin piano elements in Corea's original version in an eminently danceable way.

Like Eddie Palmieri, Lucca demonstrated a profound affection for Colombia's musical traditions, dedicating *A Cali* to Cali, the Colombian city where salsa is most popular (albeit while dabbling in a little cumbia). But perhaps the most powerful track on this album is Danny Rivera's *Jíbaro en Nueva York*, the classic narrative, written in décima form, of the Puerto Rican immigrant experience. The lyrics are declaimed in the traditional décima style, setting off a frenzy of improvisation by the monster band. If that weren't enough, *On the Right Track* concludes with another burst of raw energy, with the band giving the full orchestral treatment to a quintessential Cuban son, Adalberto Alvarez's *La Rumba Soy Yo*.

In 1978, Lucca replaced Larry Harlow as pianist of the Fania All Stars, playing on *Rhythm Machine*, *California Jam*, *Tribute to Tito Rodríguez*, and *Guasasa*, while continuing to perform with La Sonora Ponceña. In 1993 he recorded a cult favorite, *Latin Jazz*, in which, like Tito Rodríguez before him, he demonstrated his considerable abilities as a jazz composer and arranger. Influenced by Harlow's hard-edged style (sometimes known as *salsa dura* or "hard salsa") Lucca added a rich body of work to salsa's electronic keyboard repertoire. His technique was also extraordinarily rhythmic—Lucca's tumbaos were staccato bursts of energy, and he was free to improvise, exploiting the keyboard's percussive potential. As a soloist and arranger he appeared on Albita's *Mujer Como Yo* (1997), Willie Colón's *Hecho en Puerto Rico* (1993), and Celia Cruz's *La Ceiba* (1992). Although La Sonora Ponceña continued to tour Europe, and occasionally the United States on the strength of its authentic salsero status, its last major release was 1998's *On Target*. Lucca remains a legend and was frequently invited to guest in all-star lineups in concerts in New York and Puerto Rico.

Another important and overlooked figure of Puerto Rican salsa is percussionist Willie Rosario, born in 1930 in Coamo, Puerto Rico. As a teenager in 1948 he visited New York and took in all the energy of the mambo era, particularly inspired by Tito Puente. After his solo recording career began in the 1960s, Rosario crafted a music based on the innovations in New York rather than the traditional Afro-Cuban orchestras. In her essay "Is Salsa Music a Genre?" author Marisol Berríos-Miranda made a case that Rosario's orchestras epitomized the genre of salsa because the rhythms played by both the percussion and melodic instruments were "locked" together (sometimes known by the term *afinque*). By opposing this characteristic to the Afro-Cuban orchestra's ability to play with less constraint, Berríos-Miranda distinguished salsa from its precursor. Rosario, who released close to fifty albums, put out one of the genre's most electric releases of 2002, *The Master of Rhythm and Swing: Live in Puerto Rico*, which more than amply demonstrates the timbál player's ability to re-create the jazz/salsa excitement of Tito Puente.

Salsa Romantica and the Hegemony of the Sonero

The period of conservative retrenchment throughout North America in the 1980s, largely inspired by the installation of a conservative presidential administration in the United States, created a strong ripple effect throughout Latin America. The increased role of the United States in political conflicts in Central America during the 1980s may have inspired Rubén Blades in 1981 to write the song *Tiburón*, which has lyrics that are a thinly veiled reference to U.S. intervention in Honduras, El Salvador, and Nicaragua. Blades's collaborative effort with Willie Colón turned out to be one of the last gasps of politically conscious salsa. Just as American cinema turned away from the rough-featured antiheroes of the

1970s toward the teen idols of John Hughes movies, mainstream salsa began to promote baby-faced soneros. Though this phenomenon would be criticized for its deleterious effect on salsa's aesthetic, it gave salsa expanded sales and influence unprecedented in the history of Latin music.

According to Christopher Washburne's essay "Salsa Romantica: An Analysis of Style," salsa romantica emerged as the Fania empire collapsed (at one point it owned several smaller labels like Tico, Alegre, and Inca, and controlled most live performance venues) and Dominican merengue began to make inroads on New York Latin music listeners and dancers. Two records released in 1982 and 1983 on K-Tel, called *Noche Caliente 1 & 2*, produced by Louie Rivera, and featuring young singers José Alberto, Tito Allen, Johnny Rivera, and Ray de la Paz, were credited with inaugurating the genre of salsa romantica. "Tempos were slower . . . vocals were sung in a smooth, crooning style," Washburne suggested, and of course, the lyrics were about love, not struggle. In addition, standard pop and lite-jazz chords were substituted for "hard" salsa's "harmonic tension." A young assistant producer, Sergio George, who first appears on *Noche Caliente 2*, is also credited with introducing North American pop music conventions to the new style.

Puerto Rican studio recordings followed suit. Oddly enough, probably the first star of what became known as "salsa romantica" or "salsa sensual" was Lalo Rodríguez, a vocalist who made his debut on two of Eddie Palmieri's peak golden age recordings in the 1970s, *The Sun of Latin Music* and *Unfinished Masterpiece*. Palmieri, who liked to maintain the high standards of Palladium-era bands, became one of salsa romantica's leading critics. Rodríguez had slipped into relative obscurity after leaving Palmieri after 1974, performing with the Puerto Rico All-Stars and avoiding the end-of-Fania malaise. His breezy tenor was lighter than the prototypical Fania singers, but meshed well with Palmieri's classically influenced, painterly improvisations.

The remarkable success of Julio Iglesias during the Reagan years, which helped establish Latin pop as a genre, also had an effect on the marketing of salsa. Iglesias, a Spaniard, used a simple format—he compiled many of Latin America's favorite traditional ballads and created a kind of pan Latino format that had a broad appeal. While salsa romantica didn't follow Iglesias's methodology, the Latin music industry couldn't help but notice the way he brought back the pretty-boy central figure to the music world, and the resulting spike in sales, especially from women listeners.

In 1986, Lalo Rodríguez resurfaced with a song that has become *the* standard of salsa romantica, *Ven, Devórame Otra Vez*, which appeared on the album *Un Nuevo Despertar.* The song establishes the basic narrative strategy of the salsa romantica sonero: I am incapable of resisting a beautiful woman, and I hope that she will give herself to me, because otherwise I just might die right here and now. Though Rodríguez never produced another song that equaled the enormous international popularity of *Ven, Devórame Otra Vez*, he inspired a string of vocalists who held sway on the salsa scene for more than fifteen years, including Pupy Santiago, Tommy Olivencia, Frankie Ruiz, Jerry Rivera, Frankie Negrón, and Eddie Santiago. The songs followed a strict formula of introductory verses, instrumental break, and a coro section with limited improvisation on the vocalist's part. While increased production values made salsa romantica recordings burst from the speakers, eliminating any trace of tinniness or imperfection from the golden age, and the arrangements allowed for some improvisation, the overall effect of this style was to diminish the intensity of salsa.

Salsa romantica also signaled a vast change in the center of production of salsa music, from New York to San Juan and Miami. Most of the bright lights of salsa romantica were from Puerto Rico, although Miami's Cuban exile community were big players in making the careers of singers Willy Chirino, Pupy Santiago, and a Nicaraguan transplant, Luís Enrique. Perhaps because he was from a country where salsa orchestras are rare, Enrique's orchestra was less processed, creating a kind of 1950s Cuban feel in appearance (their suits) and instrumentation (horns and percussion upfront). Although he scored with romantica hits like *San Juan Sin Tí*, from 1989's *Mi Mundo* and *Desesperado*, from the 1990 follow-up *Amor y Alegría*, Enrique managed to fit more vocal improvisation into the formula, as if to prove that a Central American could throw down with the best that the Caribbean had to offer. Enrique's position on the charts slipped after his initial success. But he did put out the innovative *Timbaleye* in 1999, which featured pop songs and attempts to mine folkloric Afro-Caribbean rhythms, and in 2002, *Evolución*, a mannered collection of salsa and ballads that still didn't recapture the excitement of his impressive beginnings.

The Ralph Mercado Period

The conservative 1980s slowly took hold in New York, where allegiance to salsa's Golden Age reluctantly eroded. Stepping into the vacuum created by the demise of the Fania empire, another promoter, Ralph Mercado, worked to stockpile the remaining big names in salsa music in New York, forming a parallel empire that controlled the city's Latin scene from the mid-1980s on.

A native of the Dominican Republic, Mercado had been promoting concerts on the cuchifrito circuit beginning in the 1970s. By the late 1980s it was almost impossible to get a quality club date without Mercado's involvement. His enormous influence seemed to hold sway at every major venue for Latin music in the city. At one point in the early 1990s, Mercado had in his stable Tito Puente, Celia Cruz, Eddie Palmieri, Venezuelan sonero Oscar D'León, Cruz's heir apparent La India, the surprisingly competent Japanese band Orchesta de la Luz, Hector Lavoe, Johnny Pacheco, former *Típica '73* vocalist José Alberto, bugaloo-salsa revivalist Tito Nieves, and most of the surviving Fania All-Stars. Of the major salsa figures only Rubén Blades, who had diversified his career, Ray Barretto, who had restructured his career as a Latin jazz artist, and Willie Colón could operate independently. The Mercado hegemony was at its peak when the producers of the *Mambo Kings* movie featured his stable of musicians in the film. The appearances by Tito Puente and Celia Cruz—whose version of "Guantanamera" was epic—signaled a new momentum for Latin music in the '90s.

Mercado clearly played a key role in steering New York salsa towards its renaissance in the 1990s. He tirelessly promoted his acts in venues like the Palladium (not the one from the '50s, but a post-Studio 54 "Downtown/New Wave" lair on East Four-teenth Street), the Copacabana, and the Latin Quarter. With Jack Hooke, a former associate of famous DJ Symphony Sid (who em-ceed radio broadcasts and stage introductions of everything from the bebop era on Fifty-Second Street to the Fania All-Stars' stand at the Cheetah Club), Mercado was a partner in the long-running Salsa Meets Jazz series at the Village Gate. The series teamed up quality salsa orchestras with guest soloists from the jazz world and kept salsa music's reputation as "serious" music intact.

The shows at the Palladium were crucial in keeping a younger crowd of Latinos involved with salsa. They also provided the im-petus for the newest generation of salseros, by creating space for old and new elements to mix in a club context. Two groups, one usually a salsa romantica group, would play a show, but between sets, the DJ would mix in mostly house and R&B dance music to keep the kids interested. It was during this Palladium period that Hector Lavoe made one of his last appearances onstage. Trou-bled by continuing problems with drugs, which had prompted a suicide attempt from a hotel balcony in 1988, Lavoe tried to keep performing in the early 1990s, even if it meant being es-corted to the microphone in a wheelchair. On a Valentine's Day showcase, Lavoe appeared with a Puerto Rican flag draped over his legs and sang *Mi Gente* one last time.

The establishment of Tito Puente as the living legend of Latin music was largely Mercado's doing. After the end of the old mambo/Palladium era, Puente had been relegated to a long string of Latin jazz releases on the California-based Concord Jazz label. In the late 1980s, he began to play more shows to a new crowd of adoring fans—his new alliance with Ralph Mercado made him the grandfather of salsa in way similar to Neil Young's mid-career resurrection as an antecedent to punk rock. In an attempt to build on this new generation of fans, Mercado enlisted house DJ Little Louie Vega, who was married to an up-and-coming salsa singer, La India, to produce a new version of Puente's *Ran Kan Kan*. A little-known young sonero, Marc Anthony, contributed vocals. Anthony, like La India, had cut a few records as a Latin hip-hop/freestyle singer, but neither had had much success. Eager to expand his fan base and take advantage of an opportunity to return to his musical roots, Anthony used the Puente collaboration to launch a new career as a sonero, while Puente used it to stay relevant to young people. Mercado expanded his power and influence with this revival, adding Marc Anthony and La India to his roster, and also capitalized on a revival of Celia Cruz's popularity.

Salsa's New Wave

Marc Anthony is at the forefront of the new generation of Latin musicians who want to celebrate their roots even as they flaunt their savvy American-ness. Born in 1969 in Manhattan and named after Marco Antonio Muñiz, a famous Mexican singer who became popular as a balladeer in Puerto Rico, Anthony was raised in East Harlem. He had a typical Nuyorican upbringing, speaking both English and Spanish and listening to both salsa and soul music. He began his career in the mid-1980s singing house music in local New York clubs, often accompanied only by a DAT rhythm track. Anthony was singing backup vocals for a Backstreet Boys-like group called the Latin Rascals when Little Louie Vega, acting as the band's producer, decided to feature him on some of his dance tracks, including the widely heard *Rebel*. When Tito Puente had the Vega-Anthony act open for him at Madison Square Garden in 1992, Anthony was so impressed by the crowd and its reaction that he decided it might be time to return to his roots and sing salsa music in Spanish. As Anthony tells it, one day while he was driving around he heard Mexican crooner Juan Gabriel's version of the ballad *Hasta Que te Conocí* on the radio, something clicked in his mind, and he decided to record in Spanish. Anthony shot to the top of the new wave of salsa in the late 1990s, recording six albums for Sony, *Otra Nota, Todo a Su Tiempo, Contra la Corriente, Libre,* and two fairly successful English-language albums, *Marc Anthony* and *Mended*. The keys to his success were a spectacular, wide-ranging tenor; a key collaboration with Sergio George, a new wave salsa keyboardist and producer whose dynamic keyboard style and electrified percussion arrangements helped create a new salsa sound; and Anthony's ability to bring some of the techniques he acquired singing soul and R&B into the salsa vocabulary, enabling city kids who felt a strong connection with African-American culture to return to their salsa roots.

With its remarkably clean, brilliant sound, expert arrangements, and powerful, melodic tunes, 1995's *Todo a su Tiempo* is one of the best examples of the new wave of salsa. George anchored the album with premium salsa sessionists including bassist Rubén Rodríguez, percussionists Marc Quiñones and Bobby Allende, trombonist William Cepeda, and trumpeter Angel Fernández—Anthony's voice was pushed to its astonishing limits. Songs like *Te Conozco Bien, Te Amaré,* and *Y Sigues Siendo* have become show-stoppers in Anthony's ecstatic live appearances. While these songs echo the post-Fania salsa romantica style in their concern with lost loves and frustrating lonely nights, the conviction of Anthony's singing and the powerful, sharply percussive, R&B-influenced arrangements make his music revelatory. Instead of the rapid-fire syllable-straining vocal improvisation that marked Fania-era salsa, Anthony riffed on his powerful voice, to create Whitney Houston-esque moments of splendor.

Marc Anthony's 1999 eponymous album, with most of the songs in English, was the culmination of several steps calculated to promote him as a major entertainment figure transcending his salsa niche. Also part of that campaign were his acting career in movies and on Broadway, starring opposite Rubén Blades in *The Capeman*; publicity campaigns that painted him in the same light as Frank Sinatra; and his duet with Jennifer Lopez on her debut solo album, *On the 6*. The arrangements and style of the songs on *Marc Anthony* were not at all like salsa—they were conceived as the kind of lite Latin pop that Ricky Martin and Enrique Iglesias pioneered. Although Anthony's record had a bit more funk and creativity than his Latin-pop contemporaries, it was clear that the salsa romantica style had come full circle. After almost a decade of salsa's attempt to slowly return to its roots, Marc Anthony had made a record that brought the Latin sensibility fully into the contemporary world.

While *Marc Anthony* got fairly good critical notices, and its single, *I Need to Know*, became almost as much a part of the zeitgeist as Ricky Martin's *Livin' La Vida Loca*, 2002's follow-up, *Mended* was roundly panned as flaccid and unimaginative. Anthony, who delighted in working with mainstream producers and, like many Latinos of his generation, was very influenced by North American pop, did not see his English work as a novelty, but needed to work harder to stay in that arena. The resounding success of 2001's Spanish-language *Libre*, in which his salsa became increasingly sophisticated, incorporating influences like Colombian vallenato and Peruvian charango, indicated that his strength and fan base was largest in the world of the Latin beat.

Gilberto Santa Rosa

Too young to be part of the older generation of Fania classic
soneros and too accomplished to be compared with salsa romantica contemporaries like Eddie Santiago and Tony Vega, Gilberto
Santa Rosa quietly took the salsa spotlight from New York City
and brought it to Puerto Rico. Although his lyrics and arrangements were farmed out to guest collaborators, and the songs were
all about *cositas de amor*, Santa Rosa maintained a dignity over his
twelve years of recording that helped save the genre from pop
tackiness.

Santa Rosa began his career in 1979 as a member of the Puerto
Rico All-Stars (a collective of emerging singers and veteran players
that goes back to the 1970s). He had a two-year stint with the
Tommy Olivencia Orchestra, then went solo in 1986 on the
Combo label. But he really made his mark with his second album
for Sony, 1991's *Perspectiva*, which featured arrangements and
guest trombone appearances by Luís "Perico" Ortiz, who made albums that were island equivalents to the Fania scene in the '70s.
Perspectiva's songwriting was unusually good for its time, one of increasing vapidity. "My love is like a time bomb," he insisted on
Bomba de Tiempo. The song has a double entendre in that the
rhythm it traffics is a variation of the Puerto Rican bomba, but it
features salsa-like baritone sax riffs engaging in call and response
with a barrage of high-register trumpets.

Santa Rosa's excellent tenor compared favorably with that of
the Venezuelan salsa singer Oscar D'León (another member of
Ralph Mercado's stable in the '80s and '90s). This helped bring
back a focus on Puerto Rican salsa when South American bands
like D'León's, Joe Arroyo's and Grupo Niche (see Chapter 8) began to revive Golden Age salsa values in the late '80s. Santa Rosa
often chose brooding, self-reflective songs, like *A quien? A Mi?*
(Who, Me?), in which he narrates a character "disoriented, trying
to find myself." On *Perspectiva*'s *Concienca*, he wrestles with the

ambiguity of loving someone he probably shouldn't, and on *Se Supone*, where he laments impending rejection, he engages in an affecting, artful conversation with the listener.

Through the 1990s, Santa Rosa was the most important sonero in salsa, regardless of point of origin. Though he stuck to the same formulas on albums like *Escencia* (1996), *De Corazón* (1997), *Intenso* (2001), and *Viceversa* (2002), his voice continued to mature. Santa Rosa's side projects, working with string orchestras and staging major theatrical revues in Puerto Rico, made him a kind of renaissance salsero. He was also a mentor to rising talents like Domingo Quiñones, who starred in the successful stage play *Quien Mató a Hector Lavoe?* (Who Killed Hector Lavoe?), and like Victor Manuelle, one of the best new singers of the early 2000s.

Victor Manuelle

While Puerto Rican vocalist Victor Manuelle is yet another pretty face emerging from contemporary salsa's hit factory, he possesses a formidable tenor. At times sounding like progenitors Rubén Blades and Gilberto Santa Rosa, his music trades on the anguished love-lost laments that pushed Marc Anthony to the top. His band draws from some of Puerto Rico's best sessionists, New York school cohorts like producer Sergio George on keyboards and drummer Marc Quiñones, and is anchored by the ubiquitous bassist Ruben Rodriguez. They do a stellar job setting up Manuelle for the mid-song improvisational scatting that makes or breaks top soneros.

The thirtyish Manuelle, who was born in New York but grew up in Puerto Rico, began his career in storybook fashion when he spontaneously leapt onto the stage while Gilberto Santa Rosa was singing in Puerto Rico in 1986. Santa Rosa was so impressed with Manuelle that he signed him to sing background choruses in his band, and he has mentored him ever since. Manuelle has

since released eight CDs as a soloist on Sony Discos, and he is
the standout figure among the current crop of young singers
promoted in the salsa romantica star system.

On his 1999 release, *Ironias*, Manuelle waded through a litany
of heartbreak with a confident swing, not stretching beyond the
capabilities of his range. He frequently returned to a signature
yelp that sounds like a cowboy kicking his horse into high gear.
His second album, *Inconfundible*, released in 1999, retained the
throbbing sensuality of the kiss-and-tell style while going back to
the harder and heavier Fania years for inspiration. For sheer
dance-floor appeal, *Pero Dile*'s manic momentum makes the heart
race and *Como Duele* edgily delivers on the promise of jazz-
influenced salsa. In *Si por ti Fuera*, Manuelle rode the rolling
cumbia beat into a standard salsa format, delivering one of his sim-
plest and most satisfying flights of romantic fantasy. With *Le Pre-
guntaba a la Luna*, released in 2002, Manuelle made the transition
between emerging talent and star. On his most polished releases,
he evoked the power of a maturing Rubén Blades. His status as
salsa's ultimate ladies' man was solidified with tunes like *De-
vuélveme*, and *El Tonto que No te Olvidó*, and the sheer swing in the
horn section in a song like *Tengo* does bring back memories of the
1970s Fania era.

What's most impressive about Manuelle (besides his good looks
and charismatic presence) is his ability to improvise. After Puerto
Rico's forty-year history of interplay between hotel-style bolero
singers and rustic-roots innovators like Rafael Cortijo, Manuelle,
and to a degree his contemporary Domingo Quiñones, fused the
smooth melodic lines demanded by commercial salsa with the
edgy, scat shouts of a more primal source.

As of 2003, salsa music is still immensely popular despite a number
of controversies and contradictions. In 2002, old guard musicians
like Larry Harlow and Eddie Palmieri made public pronounce-

ments over what they called *salsa monga* (lazy salsa), their term for salsa romantica, even as younger musicians like Sergio George continued to innovate by bringing in more R&B and hip-hop influence to recordings from Marc Anthony to Celia Cruz. In the late 1990s to the early part of the new century, there was renewed interest in "serious" salsa. Trombonist Jimmy Bosch and percussionist Ralph Irizarry developed followings in New York for playing music that was truer to the Afro-Cuban and jazz roots of the Cuban dance orchestra, and in 2002, Oscar Hernández, a longtime Rubén Blades collaborator, released the debut of the Spanish Harlem Orchestra, *Un Gran Día en el Barrio*, reviving classic 1970s salsa tunes.

Statistics from the Recording Industry Association of America showed that sales of "tropical" music, which includes merengue, were down in the United States, and sales of Mexican regional music was up, but salsa radio stations on the East Coast continued their dominance in Nielsen ratings, and salsa dance classes continued to expand. Latin pop and rock continued to gain in popularity, but these genres' vitality often seemed to increase as a function of their ability to include Afro-Caribbean rhythms.

Salsa began as, and will always be, a hybrid, urban music. As new hybrids of Latin music appear, salsa may continue to evolve, but like jazz, it always evokes a special time and place. In the end salsa belongs to a moment when Latin American identity in the United States crystallized, and it created a ripple effect felt everywhere in the world.

4

Contemporary
Cuban Music

Cuba immediately before and after its revolution was a country in cultural ferment. In October 1960, after the revolutionary government started confiscating properties and businesses owned by Americans, the United States declared a trade embargo, which ended all economic activity between the countries except for food and medicine. The Organization of American States, which includes the United States and the countries of Latin America, expelled Cuba, isolating the revolutionary government from most countries outside the Soviet bloc.

But until then, the prevailing musical trends continued to be picked up by Latin music groups in New York, Puerto Rico, and Cuba's Caribbean-neighbors. The charanga genre continued to dominate in those areas, and the pachanga dance fad, almost always associated with the charanga orchestra, also held sway. In Cuba, influences from North America, like rock and jazz, continued to change Cuban music in the 1950s. From the '40s all the way up to the years immediately before the revolution, the informal descargas that Cachao López helped to institute (with the involvement of pianists Bebo Valdés, who recorded the first descarga in 1952, pianist Peruchín, and bandleaders like Antonio

Romeu) in Havana nightclubs such as the Montmartre or Sans Souci produced a new experimental instrumental music. They also engendered a jazz-influenced vocal Cuban music called "filin" (borrowed from the English "feeling," it was said to have come from a song by jazz singer Maxine Sullivan called *I Got a Feeling*).

The new musical energy generated by filin and descarga reflected an increase in cross-pollination between north and south, almost as if they were the flip side to the mambo's impact in the United States. Filin was eventually exported to New York by singer Marcelino Guerra (see Chapter 5), a veteran of the son-oriented Septeto Nacional. His appearances at the Palladium with Machito's big band were the stuff of legend. In general filin represented Havana's continuing sophistication through the influence of outside movements like jazz, Brazilian music, and French singers like Edith Piaf.

Although at first greatly repressed, outside influences, including those from the United States, were eventually welcomed in the early years of the revolution, reflecting Fidel Castro's idea of the new Cuban man. Cuban culture and society was bent on reaching and surpassing the state of the art in several fields, including music, architecture, and film. The idea of constant modernization was part of an ideology that was put in place to avoid nostalgia for pre-revolutionary Cuba. Still, non-revolutionary music came to Cuba through radio broadcasts from Miami (including the anti-Castro Radio Martí), records and ultimately cassettes smuggled in through Europe and the Soviet Union, and relatives from the United States. So while old-style bands like Orquesta Riverside, Orquesta Revé, and Chapottín y sus Estrellas (the latter featuring members of the old Arsenio Rodríguez conjunto) were still popular, the 1960s and 1970s saw the beginnings of a new wave.

Walking a fine line between a government that urged the creation of new art and one seeking aesthetic control, musicians in Cuba began to try new approaches. The vocal group Los Zafiros took a cue from doo-wop and bossa nova in songs like *Rumba como*

Quiera. Bands like Los Van Van and Irakere began adding new, funk-tinged grooves to their music, creating styles ultimately called songo, sandunga, and timba.

Irakere

Irakere and Los Van Van were the two bands that defined the era and its ultimate avant-garde jazz-fusion salsa dance bands. Both of these groups went through a staggering amount of genre experimentation, sometimes sounding like rock and roll, bugaloo, or the reigning fusion supergroups like Weather Report, and Chick Corea's Return to Forever. Formed in 1973 by Chucho Valdés with the best soloists from the Modern Cuban Orchestra, a government-funded institution featuring top conservatory-trained players, Irakere had an instant hit with *Bacalao con Pan*, a much-covered contemporary Cuban standard.

Irakere never retained a vocalist that personified the band, and the band's instrumental virtuosity produced long descargas with cacophonous displays of each member's inimitable soloing ability. The band emulated the contemporary electronic sound using lead guitars and played classic Cuban dance numbers with the bass guitars in front. But Irakere was also key in reviving traditional instruments like the batá drums. Valdés, whose father was Bebo Valdés, the director of musical entertainment at the Hotel Tropicana, the most influential spot for Cuban musicians to play in the 1950s, was also an African religion devotee and was well suited to investigating previously unexplored traditional roots. Irakere was the first group to mix older African diasporic styles with the more evolved Afro-Cuban styles, laying the groundwork for a hybrid that came to be known as timba. In some way timba can be understood as Cuba's incorporation of contemporary salsa, and in its late 1980s–early '90s heyday, it reflected a new era created by the opening of Havana to tourism.

Irakere epitomized the varied interests of the contemporary Cuban musician—it was a major force in Latin jazz, but it also incorporated influences from North American R&B groups like Earth, Wind and Fire to create an exciting brand of dance music. Irakere is remembered for danceable tunes like the aforementioned *Bacalao con Pan*, included on 1989's *Homenaje a Beny Moré*; lush orchestral covers of Arsenio Rodríguez's *La Vida es Sueño*; uptempo funk remakes of danzón composer Ernesto Lecuona's *La Comparsa* (both available on *La Colección Cubana*, an anthology on the 1998 Cuba Libre Music club label from the United Kingdom); and a straight cover of the adagio from Mozart's Concert for Flute, which originally appeared on a live album of appearances in New York and Montreaux released by Columbia in 1979.

Cuba's seminal contemporary band, often referred to as Fidel Castro's house musicians, Los Van Van was formed by song writer/bassist Juan Formell in 1969 after he spent a year with renowned bandleader Elio Revé, leader of Orquesta Revé. Often credited with the invention of songo, a post-revolutionary Cuban genre influenced by rock, jazz, and Brazilian genres like samba, Formell guided Los Van Van as it became one of the island's most influential and progressive dance bands. While songo's beat is essentially an electrified Afro-Cuban son, it also uses the violin and flute sound of charanga, something that made Los Van Van's sound one of the most sophisticated in salsa. Despite these airs, Los Van Van is profoundly anti-elitist—its shows are always dance parties, and its songs tell the stories of the everyday Cuban citizen.

It was in the late-1970s atmosphere where the old orchestras coexisted with new pop- and jazz-influenced electric bands that Bruce Lundvall's Havana Jam was conceived. In late winter of 1979, Cuba was still a very closed society, and the Cold War was about to heat up into Reaganite proportions. With the help of some sympathetic Jimmy Carter cabinet officials, CBS record executive Lundvall devised a plan to bring North American musicians to Havana to play at the Karl Marx Theater in March 1979.

Lundvall had made a career out of discovering talent, like legendary jazz fusion bassist Stanley Clarke, and he realized that there was a wealth of undiscovered brilliance in the forbidden Communist island.

The concert was a major cultural event that had long-lasting repercussions. For the first time, many of the musicians whom Cubans could only hear on the radio would play live in their country. The original Weather Report, featuring the Cuban-influenced bass playing of Jaco Pastorious, the Fania All-Stars featuring Rubén Blades, Johnny Pacheco, and Hector Lavoe, the CBS Jazz All-Stars, featuring Dexter Gordon, Stan Getz, Hubert Laws, and Willie Bobo, even rockers Steve Stills, Billy Joel, and Kris Kristofferson all played.

The concert was not just an American affair; it also featured the best musicians of Cuba, including Orquesta Aragón and Irakere. For Irakere leader, Chucho Valdés, as well as his contemporaries, the Havana Jam was an incredible experience, an opportunity to see players they had only imagined. The converse effect was that for the first time, contemporary Cuban music became known to U.S. listeners. In late 1979, Columbia Records released *Irakere*, the American debut of the supergroup, featuring Valdés on piano, trumpeter Arturo Sandovál, and saxophonist Paquito D'Rivera.

The socialist government's support of artists like Los Van Van and Irakere allowed them to take avant-garde chances and experiment with rock and jazz fusion trends to produce music of an originality unheard of in most of the Latin music scene. The intensely experimental period in the 1970s, during which Cuban groups engaged in a psychedelic, jazz-funk expansion of traditional Afro-Cuban style, produced some of the most sophisticated rhythmic music of the century.

There is a downside to being a professional musician in socialist Cuba. It is especially anomalous that the unbridled nature of Latin

music is controlled by the strict rules of the planned Cuban economy. In some senses, Cuban musicians, like certain members of
the military, athletes, or privileged members of the ruling party's
inner circle, form part of the elite of Cuban society. Musicians
earn a modest state salary, but can also cut their own deals for performances and recordings. When internationally known groups
like NG La Banda or Bamboleo play major venues in Havana, the
musicians can command a percentage of the gate. But income is
subject to taxation, and since personal income is strictly limited in
the Cuban system, what they take home doesn't amount to much.

Since Cuban orchestras are large enterprises, sometimes containing up to fifteen pieces, the money from the box office receipts
at a club like Casa de la Música in the relatively upscale Vedado
section of Havana, divided among its members, is meager. The
cover standard for "tourist shows" is fifteen dollars a person.
Shows for local Cubans charge the much less valuable Cuban currency, and an individual musician can go home with as little as ten
dollars for a night's work. Of course that figure compares favorably with many respected occupations in Cuba because of the relatively low value of the national currency. Recording contracts with
the national label, Egrem, work along roughly the same dynamic.

Whatever type of music they play, many musicians in Cuba are
products of the Escuela Nacional del Arte (National Arts School)
system, which culminates in study at a conservatory, the most presti-
gious being the Conservatory of Music in Havana. Recent stars of
Cuban music, like Bamboleo's musical director Moisés Valdés,
Cubanismo leader Jesús Alemañy, the Los Terry family of musicians, and jazz pianist Gonzalo Rubalcaba, were trained in this rigorous system, as were the members of Irakere. The best students go
to the Instituto Superior del Arte (Superior Institute of the Arts),
part of the national university system, which occupies grounds once
used by an exclusive country club in the pre-Castro days. While the
musicians are well schooled in classical theory, the conservatories
perform a function unique in the world—they instill an almost

scholarly approach to what is essentially popular dance music. In this way the Cuban tradition is protected more than almost any popular music tradition in the world.

Once music students finish their training, their careers are inexorably linked to governmental channels. Government officials say they act more like an agent for the musicians than anything else, but the power relationship is not at all the same. In the United States and Europe agents work for the artist, while Cuba still has not entirely let go of the idea that the artist is a government employee. Musicians without steady gigs or the clout to demand private payment from club owners are left with their state salaries, which can amount to as little as twenty dollars a month.

Although Cuban artists had played places like Spain and Africa in the 1970s and Irakere and Orquesta Aragón had a few gigs in the United States at decade's end, a new era dawned in the early 1990s. After Castro's reforms of the early '90s, which allowed limited forms of private enterprise and legalized the use of the dollar, the strict U.S. enforcement of laws regarding cultural exchange concerts by Cuban musicians were relaxed, and many groups took advantage. Cuban musicians cannot be paid a direct fee for performances in the United States because of the U.S. economic embargo, and tend to perform as part of a cultural exchange program. This form of compensation only covers travel and accommodations, as well as a per diem and health insurance. Like U.S. travelers who avoid the laws against tourism in Cuba by traveling through a third country, Cuban musicians have been known to receive payments routed through another country, like the Bahamas.

Arturo Sandovál and Paquito D'Rivera defected from Cuba to the United States in 1984 and 1989, respectively, leaving Valdés to carry on the project of Irakere. These powerful instrumental forces were replaced by saxophonist Germán Velazco Urdeliz and a charismatic flute player named José Luís Cortés. Valdés then moved the group further toward esoteric African music, like 1998's *Babulú Ayé*. Once Valdés established himself as a major solo

Latin jazz artist, Irakere became only a part-time occupation of his, although he remained its artistic director. Valdés also became director of the Havana Jazz Festival, which has become one of the most influential jazz festivals in the world and spawned jazz trumpeter Roy Hargrove's enormously successful *Crisól* album and traveling band.

As of 2003, Irakere still existed, but it was largely in remission in favor of Valdés's ability to pursue solo projects. Recent recordings included the band's usually mixed fare, from 1999's *Yemayá*, which is mostly jazz, to *Live in Cuba: Ivan Lins, Chucho Valdés and Irakere*, in which Valdés is paired with Brazilian singer Lins in an entirely eclectic affair. In the end Irakere's legacy has become Valdés's, a tribute to his quest for excellence in various Cuban music traditions.

Los Van Van

Los Van Van has remained Cuba's official dance party band, and Juan Formell retained the dual roles of articulator of Cuban culture under the revolution and voice of the new Cuban man. For this reason, Los Van Van's appearances in South Florida are often met with loud vocal opposition—it was the response to Los Van Van's 1999 show in Miami that made the Latin Grammy organizers move the 2001 awards at the last minute from Miami to Los Angeles.

The most important change the band brought to Cuban music was electrification, led by use of jazz-fusion-style bass guitars and synthesizers and the introduction of the drum kit by José Luís Quintana (Changuito), which paved the way for the development of the songo and timba styles. In the late '70s, Los Van Van pioneered hybrid forms of salsa that were influenced by R&B and urban-tropical hybrids. This kind of experimentation strongly influenced the New York-based producer Sergio George, who revitalized that salsa-hotbed sound through his work with Marc

Anthony and groups like DLG. Nearly thirty years after it began, the band featured Formell; jazz-influenced, timbales-obsessed percussionist Changuito Quintana; the innovative ex-Orquesta Revé pianist César Pedroso; the fedora-sporting baritone Pedro Calvo; and the dreadlocked Mario "Mayito" Rivera, and the chemistry between them is still remarkable. Most of the band's catalogue is on the state-owned Egrem label, and it continued to tour in the early 2000s.

In recent years, more of Los Van Van's work has been released outside Cuba, including a self-titled record for Island and CDs on Xenophile (*Azúcar*) and Atlantic Records' Caliente label (*Llegó Los Van Van*). Much of the group's amazingly innovative work from the 1970s and 1980s is captured on anthologies compiled by David Byrne for his Luaka Bop label and by Ned Sublette on his Qbadisc label.

Island Records' *Songo*, released in 1980, was an attempt to announce a music that had been brewing in Cuba for several years. When news of the furor created by songo's popularity hit U.S. shores, it set off a rush among New York Latin musicians to duplicate the style. Rubén Blades toured with a cover of *Songo*'s signature, anthemic tune, *Muévete*. By laying funky, 4/4 rhythms over 6/8 syncopation, Los Van Van made it possible to dance to its music freestyle, with no knowledge of mambo footwork nor frantic partner-spinning necessary. Co-produced by bandleader Juan Formell and *Siembra*-era Blades engineer Jon Fausty, *Songo*'s songs are lush re-recordings of time-tested hits. The funk bassline of *Que Palo Es Ese* is augmented by velvety synth and string lines; *Sanduguera (Por Encima del Nivel)* praises the typical Cuban femme fatale while allowing pianist César Pedroso to showcase his percussive Palmieri-isms.

In 1993, World Pacific released the compilation *Bailando Mojao* (Dancing While Wet) a collection of some of the band's best recordings. All of Van Van's essential elements—impeccable swing, innovative arrangements, use of hybrid styles and in-your-face lyrics—are here in abundance. From the sweaty upbeat "merengue son" of the title track to the "rap songo" of *Deja La Bobería*, *Bailando Mojao* is a kinetic frenzy of modern dance music. *El Buena Gente* is a relentlessly driving songo that is a parable about a man whose generosity is made necessary by the hard times Cuba, and its revolutionary experiment, are continually facing. As the 1990s drew to a close, Los Van Van released several strong studio and live albums, most notably 1996's *Ay Dios, Ampárame* and 1997's *Te Pone la Cabeza Mala*, both on the Caribe label. The Formell-Pedroso duo was still functioning at top form, with Mario "Mayito" Rivera beginning to steal the show from Pedro Calvo. In 2003, the band released the mesmerizing *En el Malecón de la Habana*, a live album that did not feature Pedroso or Calvo. But Los Van Van made a triumphant appearance that year at New York's Carnegie Hall with both members back, plus the addition of a new revelation, vocalist Yenisel Valdés.

NG La Banda

NG La Banda ushered in the new sound of timba, taking the reins of dance band popularity from Los Van Van and Irakere in the late 1980s at the dawn of Cuba's "Special Period," the years that followed the fall of the Soviet Union, which resulted in an economic catastrophe the island is still living through. Timba was associated with the fast living brought on by the increase of tourism and prostitution in the early 1990s, a period that brought a sudden materialism to Cuban youth. The band's hugely successful 1990 hit, *La Expresiva*, made NG La Banda's original lead singer, Isaac Delgado, a cult figure outside of Cuba. *La Expresiva* seemed to return to the salsa values of New York's Fania era, with its familiar Van Van-style electric keyboard sounds and vaguely songo-ish beats. But the song is actually a "bomba-son," a hybrid of the Puerto Rican bomba rhythm and the Cuban son, and there is a lighter-than-air charanga-style flute solo that anchors the song's improvisational section. The song celebrates Havana with its litany of shout-outs to neighborhoods like Cayo Hueso, Buenavista (the same one where the "social club" is located), and Vieja Habana. *La Expresiva*, as well as *Un Tipo Como Yo* and *Que Yo Gozo*, can be found on NG La Banda's *En La Calle* release on Qbadisc.

The NG sound is a little heavier on the accelerator pedal than its predecessors. Timba is basically a more aggressive version of songo, with an expanded number of instrumental and stylistic influences, mostly from African-American funk and jazz fusion. Delgado's mid-range tenor, with a haunting ebb and flow, similar to Puerto Rico's Cheo Feliciano, anchored the band. Delgado eventually went on to a solo career in Cuba in 1995, releasing two albums on Qbadisc. On 1996's *Con Ganas*, Delgado covered Pablo Milanés's *Son de Cuba a Puerto Rico*, a song that celebrates Puerto Rican and Cuban unity by likening the relationship between the countries as being two wings of the same bird. The song seemed to predict his signing with the Ralph Mercado-owned RMM Records in 1997, when he traveled to New York to record *Otra Idea* with Puerto Rican session players. RMM released two more albums, *Rarities*, a '90s compilation, and *La Primera Noche, Desde Europa Con Sabor*, which featured duets with Cheo Feliciano and Ana Belen, in 1998. His 2002 album, *Versos en el Cielo* (BIS), was an ambitious fusion between nueva trova styles, pop, and timba.

By the late 1990s, with Delgado gone, NG La Banda had eschewed emphasis on electric keyboards for a more traditional piano sound. José Luís Cortés ("El Tosco," or "The Coarse One") had moved from flute to lead vocalist and main songwriter. Darker-skinned and less of a matinee idol than Delgado, Cortés brought a more defiant presence to the band, pacing around the stage, offering a stream of harangues and blessings designed to evoke the contemporary Cuban attitude: busy, aggressive, and in love with the music of the people. When he arrived onstage he was looking to take an emotional inventory, assess the room's spiritual needs, and deliver a spiritual cleansing. When his band made the room shake with the opening chords of *Santa Palabra* (The Holy Word) Cortés shook his body madly, introducing the chorus: *Despójate/Quítate lo malo* (Divest yourself/Shake off the bad stuff).

NG La Banda returned pure funkiness to dance music that was beginning to collapse under the weight of its experimental tendencies. Shifting almost effortlessly between all manner of guaguancó, rumba, bebop, jump blues, jazz fusion, and cumbia, NG is the master of all grooves. The band members attack Beny Moré boleros, make love to classic mambos, elevate and refurbish Chick Corea jams, and even embrace a boogie-woogie Cab Calloway would have felt at home with. The cascading intensity of NG's horn section kicks directly from the unerring precision of its rhythm crew, making for a dizzying swell of syncopation and swing. The band's willingness to incorporate a broader range of African diaspora styles, like West Indian steel drums and soca beats, while retaining a strong connection to the Havana faithful, made it perhaps Cuba's most significant group of the 1990s. On the 2001 *Baila Conmigo*, however, NG La Banda seemed to have abandoned its harder sound in favor of more traditional mambos, guaguancós, boleros, and even merengue.

Bamboleo

At the same time, many followers of Cuban music in and outside of Cuba were looking to a younger group of musicians who were taking the momentum created by timba and taking it further. Bamboleo, formed in 1995, has become one of the primary proponents of timba brava, a timba with no holds barred, one that tries to go where no salsero has gone before. Timba brava reflects Cuba's constant awareness at what is going on in the music world outside, where hip-hop and new jack R&B continue to innovate in the attempt to create a proper soundtrack for the constantly evolving African diaspora. Led by pianist Lázaro Valdés, songwriter and arranger, Bamboleo's early years were marked by two stunningly tall and talented lead singers, Vannia Borges and Haila Mompié. Borges, who studied at a conservatory in the 1970s, established Bamboleo after spending time performing with Bobby Carcasses and Hector Tellez. Many members of the fourteen-piece band had trained at Havana's National School of the Arts.

Opening Estudio 10, the first song on Bamboleo's 1997 album *Yo No Me Parezco a Nadie*, is a stunning trumpet-led reconfiguration of the guaguancó, with a swing punctuated by bursts of saxophone and a chanted chorus that demands the listener to get on the dance floor. A languid wah-wah electric guitar figure gives the song an almost blaxploitation soundtrack feel while hypnotic tumbaos played by Valdés create an air of anticipation—something new and exciting had arrived. In both live performances and on record, Bamboleo is constantly switching tempos. The title track is a celebration of millennium era Cuban solidarity with trumpet patterns recalling the height of NG La Banda. On subsequent tunes like *Tú y Yo, Una Misma Cosa* and *Miranda al Cielo*, funk and blues-derived basslines make a sudden transition to standard 4/4 rhythm patterns and, in a concession to modern pop, the syncopated clave is temporarily discarded. On *Si No Hablaras Tanto*, hip-hop becomes the matrix for an "answer song," like the work of New York's Roxanne Shanté, about a lover no longer deserving of Borges and Mompié's affection.

Bamboleo underwent changes in personnel in 1999, and Haila Mompié went off to front Azúcar Negra, whose sound is a bit of an evolution. The new group still has the crashing piano tumbaos, hooked together with a brass attack over a frenetic timbo beat. Instead of two female vocalists, Azúcar Negra has a chorus of male voices doing a call and response with Haila. The groove is a bit streamlined, and the performers set the stage for Haila Mompié to go solo.

Mompié's solo release of 2001, *Haila*, was one of the year's best tropical/salsa recordings anywhere. A tribute to the music of salsa diva Celia Cruz, *Haila* (BIS Music) is a stunning piece of

Afro-Cuban artistry, featuring crisp, highly expert playing, exhilaratingly complex arrangements, and the coming of age of one of the genre's brightest voices. The barrage of trumpets that frame Mompié's riveting duet with Los Van Van's singer Mayito Rivera sets the heart racing; her sensual treatment of the bolero *La Rosa* is as effortless as it is enchanting. Produced by Isaac Delgado, the album's Cruz covers like *Usted Abusó* and *Químbara* swing with all the energy of the originals, and more.

Cubanismo

A drummer, songwriter, arranger, and bandleader, Giraldo Piloto played pivotal roles in the development of four of the most important groups in contemporary Cuban music. He was the first drummer for NG La Banda, for whom he wrote *Te Confunde Ser Esa Mujer*. Then he was drummer and musical director of the group Isaac Delgado formed to support his solo efforts after leaving NG, and co-wrote Delgado's classic *Por Qué Paró?*, as well as what some consider the essential introduction to timba, *No Me Mires a los Ojos*. Piloto also collaborated with La Charanga Habanera, writing the band's first big hit, *Fiebre de Amor*. *Fiebre* helped the band modernize its traditional charanga sound and join the ranks of the timba revolution.

In 1995, Piloto formed his own group, Klímax, which soon was at the center of the music scene in Havana as well as playing major clubs and Europe. Klimax's 2000 release, *Oye Como Va*, coincidentally came right before Tito Puente's death, and the title track functioned as an update of the classic as well as a tribute.

The conservatory-trained Piloto served an important apprenticeship with the Hotel Tropicana Orchestra between 1980 and 1987 and played with another extremely influential musician, trumpeter Jesús Alemañy, who founded Cubanismo in 1995. Alemañy's *Preguntón* from the Cubanismo album, *Malembe*, is a gentle re-proaching of the Latin American sport of carping about your neighbors. His trumpet does the main musical narration, setting off a series of flute and piano solos that cohere in a seamless collage of son, guaracha, changüí, and charanga. But the chorus at *Preguntón*'s heart is a friendly taunt: "You pass your life talking about people/What do you want to know?/What are they asking you?"

A charismatic trumpeter with the regal bearing of Miles Davis and the funky, precise flow of Fats Navarro, Alemañy took as his role models obscure-in-the-North Cuban stylists like Felix Chapotín and Lázaro Herrera (of the Ignacio Piñeiro Septet). The hot property of the U.S.-based Hannibal Records, Alemañy's crew exploded onto the U.S. scene in 1986 with a simultaneous release by featured pianist Alfredo Rodríguez, *Cuba Linda*. In live performance, Cubanismo stuck to its essential format of descarga—a series of improvised solos by Alemañy, Rodríguez, alto saxophonist Yosvany Terry Cabrera, and tres player Efraín Rios evolving from stately cha-chas and slinky guaguancós. The timba variation rhythms of *Salsa Pilón* are introduced by a crisp timbál riff and embellished by Rodríguez's undulating tumbao. Cubanismo was fronted by a neatly coiffed, long-haired lead singer named Rojitas, who played the role of the seductive sonero as well as any salsa sensual star.

Cubanismo is one of the best examples of a modernist popular avant-gardism that had flourished under Castro's cloak. Rodríguez's groundbreaking Satie-meets-Santería fusion is yet another demonstration that dance music can be intelligent, and intelligent people can dance.

Buena Vista Social Club

In the first decades after the revolution Cuba was so concerned with progress that it didn't revel much in its classic music from the 1930s to the 1950s. That changed when the Buena Vista Social

Club drew massive international attention in 1999. Formed by North American blues-rocker Ry Cooder, with the help of Sierra Maestra leader Juan de Marcos González in 1997, the Buena Vista Social Club became a major force in revitalizing interest in traditional Cuban music around the world and in Cuba in the late 1990s. The Buena Vista Social Club is actually a super group made up of some of the greatest Cuban popular musicians from the '40s and '50s, brought together in their later years for a last hurrah. While there has been debate whether Cooder's slide-guitar playing on the album is superfluous or genuine collaboration, his injection of new (or rather, "old") life into Cuba's music scene has left a lasting impact on Latin music fans everywhere.

The music of Buena Vista strikes a deep chord because the Cuban boleros and sons of the early to mid-twentieth century are in many ways the basis of popular music in all of Latin America. They are deeply nostalgic to an entire generation of Latin American immigrants in North America because it was the last music they heard before they came north.

The oldest musician on the album, guitarist and vocalist Compay Segundo, combines country roots of "guajiro," or peasant music, with old-style boleros. Vocalist Ibrahim Ferrer once sang backup vocals for the legendary Beny Moré, and also had a few hits of his own. The great bolero singer Omara Portuondo, sometimes known as the Edith Piaf of Cuba, brings a haunting soprano. Eliades Ochoa, the youngest of the group, is an engaging singer in the country guajiro style. Pianist Rubén González, veteran of Arsenio Rodríguez's early 1940s band, is the last of the great Cuban pianists of the past, like the legendary Peruchín.

Cooder, who plays electric slide guitar on many of the songs Buena Vista has recorded and played in concert, had been interested in Cuban music for many years and finally saw the opportunity in the late 1990s to bring together a group of musicians that were all but forgotten. Cooder had visited Cuba clandestinely in the 1970s after a friend had given him a tape of post-revolutionary

music. Twenty or so years later, he contracted with English producer Nick Gold to record an album with some Cuban musicians
and a West African group. When the Africans were hopelessly de-
tained in France, Gold and Cooder decided to go ahead with the
project with whomever they could find. Musical director Juan de
Marcos González had been gathering older musicians for his
Sierra Maestra project, including bassist Cachaíto López (Cachao's
nephew) and much of the band's rhythm section.

But some of the musicians were brought in through word of
mouth: The then penniless vocalist Ibrahim Ferrer was sum-
moned by an impromptu phone call; González had retired because of arthritis and did not even own a piano. Following the
release of the album, the group toured extensively in the United
States and Europe, and some of those concerts, plus the sessions
for Ibrahim Ferrer's solo record, were the subject of an Oscar-
nominated documentary by German filmmaker Wim Wenders in
1998. But just as the Buena Vista Social Club was crucial in
reawakening the public's appetite for the classics of Cuban music,
it is completely out of context with the developments in post-
revolutionary Cuban music. Cooder and Gold's project was a
happy accident—the mining of great, forgotten talent from a politically frozen cultural zone was something easily accomplished
by capitalist means, but a minor miracle in Cuba's restrictive
economy. The band inspired an entirely new fad previously unheard of in forward-thinking Cuba: a wave of nostalgia for music
that was popular in the era before Castro's revolution.

One of the most remarkable Latin music albums ever made,
Buena Vista Social Club at once culminates a century of Cuban music while driving it into the future. The Buena Vista Social Club
re-creates the elemental form of the son. Like a blues album revealing the secrets of its offspring, rock and roll, *Buena Vista* brilliantly uncovers the essence of popular dance forms like rumba,
mambo, cha cha, and salsa. Each song allows riveting solo turns by
Ferrer, Portuondo, González, Segundo, and Ochoa. *Chan Chan* is

in many ways the signature song of *Buena Vista*, in the way it introduces a pure version of son whose lyrics are based in the simple circumstances of the countryside. Its rhythmic title follows a tradition in Latin music—onomatopoetic phrases become the voice of percussive patterns that underpin the music itself. *Chan Chan* is a timeless lyrical phrase that stays in the mind long after the song finishes playing. *Pueblo Nuevo* has the function of reclaiming the elegance of the danzón, and the driving son-tumbao *Candela* is elemental in the way it presents the almost obvious device of sexual double-meanings. Although the rustic Cuban son as performed by this group does have many similarities to American country music, Ry Cooder, to his credit, rarely lets his slide-guitar playing become the center of attention. The *Buena Vista Social Club* instead focuses on the purity of Cuban rhythms and harmonies, allowing the musicians to coax the most transcendent moments out of their acoustic instruments.

Ibrahim Ferrer, who has been called the Nat King Cole of Cuban music, was born to sing—his mother gave birth to him in 1927 in the middle of a social club dance in the city of Santiago. Ferrer found his passion for music at age twelve, when, during a singing contest in Santiago, he performed *Charlemos*, a song by Argentine singer Alberto Gómez, and won a free ticket to see a Tom Mix movie. He went to sing with Santiago's finest orchestra, Chepín-Chovén; with Los Bucocos, a Havana band that toured internationally; and as a chorus singer for Beny Moré in the 1940s and 1950s. During a twenty-year span from the '50s to the '70s, he had hits like *El Platanal de Bartolo*, *Cuando me Toca a Mi*, and *Que me Digan Feo*, with Los Bocucos, led by Pacho Alonso.

Ferrer picked up several different skills as a chorus singer for Beny Moré. The chorus singer often needs a more developed sense of the rhythm than the lead vocalist, and the chorus can be more complicated than the standard verse. On Moré's classic,

Como Fue, from his solo album, Ferrer acts as both lead and chorus singer, changing registers as only someone who knew both parts could. Ferrer's climactic duet with Omara Portuondo in Rafael Hernández's *Silencio* was one of the most emotional of many such moments in Wim Wenders's documentary on Buena Vista, and he is perhaps the group's charismatic center. His status as a second-string singer who never made it lends an emotional urgency to the music, as well as proof that Cuba's musical talent runs so deep that its secondary stars are spellbinding when finally given center stage, even at more than seventy years of age.

Originally a dancer at the timeless Tropicana, Omara Portuondo, born in Havana in 1930, was a key vocalist during the Havana era that coincided with the emergence of the descarga and the informal rise of the genre called filin, playing in places like El Gato Tuerto alongside legends like Elena Burke. Filin was a genre that had absorbed influences from North American jazz, and eventually rhythm and blues and soul. So in a sense, Portuondo has a little bit of Ella Fitzgerald and Sarah Vaughan in her, although her repertory is mostly Cuban in origin. Her understated, yet sinfully rich contralto makes her a jazz alternative to Celia Cruz—and she even covers Gershwin.

Rubén González displays the technique that is standard among the best Afro-Cuban pianists. González was born in 1920 in the town of Santa Clara and migrated to Havana in 1941 after attending a conservatory in the town of Cienfuegos and briefly enrolling in medical school. His most important gig was playing with the Arsenio Rodríguez conjunto before the bandleader left for New York in the 1950s. He also played in Orquesta de los Hermanos, which at one time featured Mongo Santamaría, and in the 1970s played in Argentina with tango groups.

González roams the keyboard effortlessly, squeezing every subtlety out of his arpeggios, echoing Bud Powell or even Thelonious Monk. Together with his contemporary, Peruchín, his playing is a strong influence on Eddie Palmieri—the elemental tumbao figure that is standard for Latin music pianists is elevated to an uncommon form of artistry. *Puerto Nuevo*, the song he contributed to the Buena Vista Social Club album, is a time capsule of the style of the 1940s, when he was playing with Arsenio Rodríguez. He begins playing in danzón rhythm, then improvises in a mambo, or montuno section. His accompaniment of Ibrahim Ferrer on *Murmullo* evokes jazz pianist Erroll Garner, while remaining true to the delicate bolero pacing.

Perhaps the most charismatic member of the Buena Vista Social Club, Compay Segundo is a master of the son tradition. Born in 1907 in mountainous Siboney (González plays a version of Lecuona's *Siboney* on his first solo album), Segundo moved at an early age to Santiago, where the son grew into maturity in the early part of the century. He soon learned to play the tres and guitar and began composing at the age of fifteen. He invented his own instrument, called the armónico, an alternate name for a trilina, which is a cross between a guitar and a tres, using seven strings, with the middle string doubled. He traveled in Mexico with the singer Justa García's Cuarteto Hatuey in 1938, and in 1942 he started a duo called Los Compadres with Lorenzo Hierrezuelo. In this duo, he sang bass harmonies, a talent for which he was given the nickname "Compay Segundo," or "second voice."

But after forming Compay Segundo y sus Muchachos in 1956, and having a degree of success, he soon faded into obscurity, only to be rescued in 1989 by the Smithsonian Institution, where he performed a series of concerts. This resuscitation of his career led to a residency in Spain in the mid-1990s, which produced *Lo Mejor de la Vida*, released almost simultaneously with the first Buena Vista album in 1998. Tributes to poet Federico García Lorca and Cuban folk singer Silvio Rodríguez anchor the "trio" feeling of his recordings (see discussion of "trio" in Chapter 5). Segundo's follow-up efforts, *Calle Salud* (1999) and *Flores de la Vida* (2001), sold well in the wake of Buena Vista's enormous popularity. Segundo's 2002 release, *Duetos*, features duets with Cuban giants like Pablo

Milanés and Silvio Rodríguez, Algerian singer Khaled, and some unusual collaborators with French singer Charles Aznavour, actor Antonio Banderas, and *Mambo No. 5* novelty singer Lou Bega.

While the Buena Vista Social Club has released only one album, the numerous solo efforts by its members have created a small catalogue of albums. The Afro-Cuban All-Stars, which features virtually the same lineup, adding some percussion players, issued *A Todo Cuba le Gusta* in 1997 and *Distinto, Diferente* in 1999. Compay Segundo issued three albums; Rubén González released a self-titled album in 1997 and *Chanchullo* in 2000; Ibrahim Ferrer, Omara Portuondo, Orlando "Cachaíto" López, Barbarito Torres, and Eliades Ochoa all issued solo records. In 2003, Ry Cooder released *Mambo Sinuendo*, an adventurous collaboration with Zafiros guitarist Manuel Galbán, and Ibrahim came out with his second solo album, *Buenos Hermanos*.

The Buena Vista Aftermath

Most Latin music fans agreed that the Buena Vista Social Club albums and side projects were brilliant evocations of a classic style of Cuban music that moved us heart and soul. But after five or six albums of these elegant, hauntingly played songs, these perfect son, danzón, and bolero epiphanies, had they had enough? Then came *Cachaíto*, the self-titled debut of acoustic bassist Orlando "Cachaíto" López, the rhythmic core behind the Buena Vistas, and suddenly Cuban nostalgia was transformed into the new avant-garde. Enlisting an eclectic lineup featuring Aswad's Hammond organist Bigga Morrison, James Brown's former tenor saxophonist Pee Wee Ellis, South African flugelhorn legend Hugh Masekela, and French hip-hop pioneer DJ Dee Nasty, Cachaíto put out one of the best Latin albums of 2001. *Cachaíto* includes forays into Jamaican dub, orchestral jazz, and, on the track *Cachaíto in Laboratory*, two turntables scratching and sampling.

While most listeners are entranced by Buena Vista's melodic narratives and harmonic journeys, the motor that drove this vintage Cuban vehicle was Cachaíto's dialogue with various sources of percussion. On *Cachaíto*, the classic songs and yearning vocals of *The Buena Vista Social Club* are gone—all that is left are López and conga player Miguel "Angá" Díaz working out basic Cuban bass tumbaos, while the rest of the musicians find a way to embellish the groove.

López was born in 1933 in Havana and had a unique training ground, accompanying his father Orestes to rehearsals at the Havana Symphony and to various recording sessions with the Arcaño orchestra. He grew up watching and listening to Orestes, and his uncle, Israel "Cachao" López, one of the inventors of the mambo. During his lengthy career he played with Arsenio Rodríguez, Chucho Valdés, and Paquito D'Rivera, among many others.

While the music he played with this variety of great Cuban musicians covered many different genres, for Cachaíto, the operative word is descarga. In the 1950s, he would go out and play in a descarga, every night. He, like his fellow collaborators, took the word literally, and the jam sessions were meant to discharge all the creative energy built up during the day.

For these new-school descargas López introduced atypical instrumentation. Throughout, Morrison's Hammond organ creates a Jamaican dance-hall feel; on *Wahira*, Juan de Marcos González plays a traditional Cuban folk guajira tune on a tres equipped with a wah-wah pedal; and on *Conversación*, flute player "Polo" Tamayo and guitarist/musical director Manuel Galbán create a jazzy, avant-garde feel. Díaz, who played on 2000's breakthrough album by Cuban rappers Orishas, is key to *Cachaíto*'s hip-hop sensibility.

The music scene in Havana in the early twenty-first century is as vibrant as ever. U.S. rock and hip-hop and other North American styles of music are constantly available through radio and imported tapes and CDs. It's just as easy to hear Eminem wafting from a rooftop as it is for a cab driver to pop in a cassette of Air Supply. Hip-hop continues to be the strongest trend, especially with the recent success of Orishas, who emigrated from Cuba to Europe in the late 1990s. Groups of conservatory-trained musicians continue to play the limited club and bar circuit and put out albums on state-owned record labels. Most notable among these is Charanga Habanera, which, despite its allusion to a pre-revolutionary style, is very much a contemporary orchestra, albeit a little less electronic than Los Van Van. Carlos Manuel, who defected in June 2003, and Manuel Hernández, the medical student better known as *Manolín El Médico de la Salsa* (The Salsa Doctor) who moved to Miami and then San Francisco in 2000, both retain the folkloric son feel in their contemporary salsa songcraft. Vocal Sampling could be considered something of a novelty act since its members sing a capella, much like American recording artists Take 6 or Manhattan Transfer. But their dedication to the artistry in the Cuban son and bolero, as well as an almost hip-hop edginess, make their music compelling. Vocal Sampling released *Cambio de Tiempo* in 2001, and Manolín the pop-flavored *Giro Total* on BMG in 2003.

Perhaps one of contemporary Cuba's most surprising success stories is Orquesta Aragón, a dance orchestra that was founded in 1939. Having evolved through many of the styles of the mambo-típica era, including cha-cha, and of course the charanga, Aragón survived several lineup changes and in 2001 put out one of its best efforts ever, *En Route*. The album, which was nominated for a Grammy in 2002, has some of the most high-intensity, revved-up violin-charged charanga ever recorded. Aragón also pays tribute to rock and roll and rap, as in the tune *Guasabeando el Rock and Roll* and the hip-hop-flavored "rap-cha" of *Cha Cuba*. Aragón proves that sticking to their roots and a commitment to high-level playing produces an immortal brand of Cuban music.

Music in Cuba today continues to thrive on contradiction. On the one hand, hundreds of talented, well-trained musicians are drawing from one of the most dynamic musical cultures in the world. But economic and sometimes political restrictions force much of the music underground and away from listeners in the rest of the world. More Cuban musicians are working out deals to live and play in different parts of the world without defecting, and even those who do, like hip-hop stars Orishas or pop singer Amaury Gutiérrez, are less hostile to Cuba and merely cite lack of opportunity as their reason for leaving. Hip-hop and jazz retain a strong cultural trendiness, but traditional son and bolero continue in the cafes of the major cities, and every Sunday there is a raucous rumba at the Callejón de Hamel, where tourist throngs mingle with everyday Cubans.

5

The Latin Ballad from the Bolero to the New Latin Pop

When Latin Americans get together, they are as likely to burst out into a rendition of a classic bolero as they are to start dancing to a tropical beat. It is as if the bolero captures a slower, more sentimental moment in the Latin psyche, letting dance partners catch their breath, and lyric lovers lose themselves in a story. When bolero enthusiasts break into song, they are imagining themselves as the singer, who has come to play the role of the pop idol, the apex of the orchestra, the heartthrob, the golden voice. Contained in that voice are painful cries of the flamenco singer, the Cuban trovador, the fifteenth century Spanish troubadour.

The Cuban Bolero

The Cuban bolero is sometimes misunderstood because its name derives from a folkloric, flamenco-rooted eighteenth century dance in southern Spain, performed in a 3/4 rhythm. Said to be a merging of the family of dances known as sevillanas and the Span-ish contradanza, the bolero has an association with gypsy culture and strutting displays of sexuality that were tempered by a kind of classical ballet formalism, evident in Maurice Ravel's composition of the same name. The song forms that accompanied the bolero dances of Spain had four-line verses of five and seven syllables. In the process of the continuing exchange of dance and song forms between Spain, the rest of Europe, and Cuba, bolero the dance gradually disappeared in Cuba, and the song form's meter shifted to 2/4 or 4/4. The bolero tradition continues in Spain, for the most part unrelated to what has become the most popular lyric tradition in Latin America.

The ballad form we know today as the Cuban bolero has its roots in traditions that go back to medieval Spain. Despite the fact that the word *ballad* has its etymological origins in the word for dancing, it is a poetic form that grew out of the songs that were sung during performances of the ballad dance. The Spanish tradi-tion diverged from the rest of Europe because of its emphasis on epic narrative. The Spanish ballad employs the octosyllabic line format with the décima, and evolved in Europe from its oral stages to the seventeenth century heights of the Spanish empire, when educated writers were adding their gloss to what began as a peo-ple's art form.

The ballad was made popular by the troubadours who origi-nated in southern France and became popular in neighboring Spain—the troubadour tradition was translated into various Ro-mance languages. The troubadour's wandering lifestyle and dedi-cation to telling stories that constituted both legends and the "news" would have a lasting resonance. *The Poem of El Cid*, which tells the story of the legendary king of the eleventh century, is often referred to as the seminal influence of Spanish literature, and many ballads based on this poem also exemplify the epic, story-telling characteristic of the Spanish ballad that would ultimately show up in Cuba in the nineteenth century.

The Cuban form of bolero was developed in Santiago in the late nineteenth century, when the tradition of trova, (derived from *trovador*, Spanish for troubadour) or *canción* (song), a kind of urban storytelling tradition sung by traveling singers, began interacting with the explosion of musical styles on the island. Like most of nineteenth century Cuban music, the trova was influenced by French romantic styles, the Neapolitan tradition of farcical musical comedies, and of course opera—popular music forms despite their seemingly aristocratic pedigree. Performed by mostly unrecognized singers wielding a guitar and playing in small bars and on the street, the trova was closer to its early Spanish origins as a folk music. The lush countryside and more laid-back pace of the Oriente province, where Santiago was situated, removed from the comparatively cosmopolitan Havana, was a perfect breeding ground for trova.

Although some authors say it dates to the early nineteenth century, the modern Cuban bolero dates from the work of José Pepe Sánchez, whose *Tristeza*, written in 1885, was considered the first classic in the genre and popularized the use of the term bolero. Sánchez grafted the trovador tradition onto styles like the danzón, danza, habanera, and son, with the cinquillo rhythm playing an important role in its juxtaposition to often décima-derived lyrics. Sánchez followed the trova's tradition alluding to the sentiments of the people by creating a nationalist political tone in his songs, which included *La Cubana* and *Cuba, mi Patria Querida*. Sánchez has been credited with teaching the guitar to early trovadores Rosendo Ruiz, Alberto Villalón, Manuel Corona, Ñico Saquito, and, the most famous of the bunch, Sindo Garay.

Sánchez and his contemporaries took the traditional Cuban trova and incorporated more improvisational musical passages (inspired by the montuno breaks in son) in the middle of the song, almost like the rhythm-and-blues bridge. In the early twentieth century, the bolero developed in parallel fashion to the Cuban son in the way it reconciled Spanish guitar melodies, lyrics, and 4/4 rhythms with the Cuban cinquillo rhythm. But while the formal aspects of Cuban music were central to the origins of the bolero, its greatest evolutionary leaps were made possible by the turn-of-the-century nationalism and new urban styles coming out of the streets and house parties of Santiago.

Sindo Garay continued Sánchez's political bent by re-writing *La Bayamesa*, originally a poem by Carlos Manuel de Céspedes, which encouraged a war of independence against Spain in the late nineteenth century, and paying homage to martyred nationalist poet and essayist José Martí in another song. The Cuban bolero is notable for its ability to include the verses of well-known poets in the lyrics. As previously mentioned, the poet Adolfo Utrera's were included by composer Nilo Menéndez in the famous bolero, *Aquellos Ojos Verdes* (Those Green Eyes). *Aquellos Ojos Verdes* was recorded by innumerable bands—some of the more offbeat versions include a grunt-filled Pérez Prado mambo and one of Nat King Cole's heavily accented Spanish recordings. *Guajira Guantanamera*, a song written by bolerista Joseito Fernández in 1928, was remade into perhaps the most famous Cuban bolero ever when in the 1950s, Jose Martí's *Versos Sinceros* were added: *Yo soy un hombre sincero/De donde crece la palma/Y antes de morir quiero/Echar mis versos del alma.* (I am a sincere man/From the land where palm trees grow/And before I die I want to/Express the verses from my soul.) Note how this quintessential bolero conforms to the octosyllabic structure of the décima, although the ten lines are shortened to eight, as is often the case.

The trova, as a descendant of the Spanish ballad, is one of many manifestations of that form that existed in various parts of Latin America—in Puerto Rico, it existed as the pregón, in Mexico, the corrido. But the trova was destined to evolve. The rustic trova was transformed in the sophisticated urban milieu of Havana when Pepe Sánchez's circle of trovadores began to play as intermission acts at theaters where plays and musical revues were performed. It influenced the Mexican romantic song in the early part of the twentieth century, creating both an urban bolero movement and a rural bolero that ultimately became known as the ranchera.

When one of the last of the old-style trovadores, Eusebio Delfín, scored an international hit in 1924 with *Y Tú Que Has Hecho*, a new period of evolution began. Bolero hybrids like the bolero-son, invented by Miguel Matamoros, began to be performed by artists like Arsenio Rodríguez and Beny Moré. In the '30s, bolero also mutated into different styles like bolero beguine (derived from the "beguine" beat in the rhumba ballroom version of a syncopated dance beat that originated on the island of Martinique), bolero montuno, and bolero mambo, which were played with a subtly different rhythmic patterns. (The story of trova doesn't end here, however: it would be revised by the nueva trova movement, which spotlighted artists like Pablo Milanés and Silvio Rodríguez singing songs in praise of the Cuban revolution, andrevived by artists like the Buena Vista Social Club's Compay Segundo.)

If you've ever been in a Latin American country, particularly Mexico (or if you have braved the embargo-laden Havana to sit in the garden restaurant at the Hotel Tropicana), you'll notice that the most ubiquitous format for boleros is the trio, which usually consists of three guitarist-vocalists, or two guitars and one percussionist. The lead guitar is usually a requinto, a kind of smaller guitar with a higher-pitched string on top. When three guitars are used, one is often in a lead position, with the other two playing rhythmic or improvisational lines. The first and second voice roles were originally popularized by the Sindo Garay/Pepe Sánchez circle.

The bolero and trova song forms of Santiago were necessary antecedents to the modern tropical music styles like salsa, but the bolero also kept evolving on its own, in parallel to the son, in terms of opening up space for improvisation. In the 1940s and 1950s, bolero became something of the standard pop music form for all of Latin America. As a Latin American musical style, the bolero is nothing if not a crucible of romantic sentimentality—it often has no impact unless it is performed with wild, almost excessive emotion, and the growing penchant for improvisation showcased the singer's display of feeling. The bolero's internationalization began at the end of the nineteenth century, when it spread to the Yucatán Peninsula of Mexico through Spanish colonialists and Cuban independence activists, both escaping the aftermath of the Spanish-American War, when the United States took control. Guitarist/composer Alberto Villalón visited the Yucatán in 1908, and the first hit Mexican bolero was written by Yucatán native and singer/songwriter Guty Cárdenas in 1928. Probably because of the work of Mexico's Agustín Lara, one of the preeminent songwriters of the twentieth century, boleros were especially popular in that country, where most norteño and mariachi groups still sing them, and even groups of young people more affiliated with rock can perform them from memory. In Argentina, performer Carlos Gardel helped to shape the twentieth century ballad by merging elements of the Cuban bolero with the tango, itself based on the habanera rhythm, and became one of Latin America's most popular singers.

Carlos Gardel and the Tango

Carlos Gardel began singing tangos in the early part of the twentieth century; he revolutionized the tango experience by making vocals important and reinvented the ballad/bolero tradition while he was at it.

Born in 1890 in Toulouse, France, Gardel was brought up in Buenos Aires, where he arrived at age two. As a teenager, he quickly gravitated to the clubs and cafes of popular barrios. He began his singing career in a duo with a Uruguayan singer named

José Razzano, but his decision to sing tangos in the early 1920s changed his career. In the mid-'20s, his partnership with Razzano dissolved and Gardel made his way to Madrid and Paris, where he met composer Alfredo Lepera, who would write most of the lyrics for his tangos. In the '30s Gardel made it to New York, where he appeared in a few films shot at the Astoria Paramount studios. Some of the songs he is most famous for are *Tango Bar*, *Mano a Mano*, *Luces de Buenos Aires*, and *Melodía de Arrabal*. His career was cut short: He died in a plane crash just outside Medellín, Colombia, in 1935.

While most tango singers remain relatively obscure and appreciated mainly by Argentineans or tango aficionados, Carlos Gardel's voice captured listeners worldwide, and its quavering emotion stirred fans all across Latin America. Although Latin Americans struck a defiant pose of independence from Spain, they were vulnerable to nostalgia for it. Argentina had been "invaded" by numerous Italian immigrants in the early twentieth century, and Italy's popular music and opera were already influential. The celebrated tenor Enrique Caruso was a major inspiration for Gardel. And the habanera rhythm embedded in the tango, along with other sublime African influences, helped his music enchant the Latin world from Mexico City to Havana to Bogotá.

Gardel became more affected by bolero as his career got bigger. He was exposed to bolero and bolero-son instrumentation during his travels, and the parallels between tango as a fusion music and these Cuban fusion styles made a connection inevitable. One of Gardel's most famous songs, 1932's *El Día Que Me Quieras* (The Day That You Want Me) provides an interesting glimpse into how this happened. The song, written by Lepera, is thought by some scholars to have been a response to a 1915 poem by Mexican poet Amado Nervo called *El Arquero Divino*. Gardel's recording includes a break in which he recites the song as poetry (true to the décima structure), which in turn introduces a rhythmic break that mirrors the developments in Cuban bolero at the time.

Gardel also influenced bolero singers around Latin America because he was able to fly into a musical space few listeners had experienced and told a story at the same time. The pathos of tango—typically embellished by a mournful-sounding brass and string section—was also something very palpable to the rest of Latin America. And Gardel's popularity in France gave him further cachet in countries like Mexico and Cuba, whose Francophilia is well-documented—both Mexico and Havana considered themselves competitors as Latin America's version of Paris. Gardel's work is still part of country and urban lore in most of the countries of South America, and the tinny sound of his recordings float up airshafts in every major city—sometimes even in New York.

Argentina's economy was the most developed in Latin America in the early part of the twentieth century—it was ahead of countries like Japan and Italy, for instance–and Gardel's work was heard far and wide in Latin America because of Argentina's superior recording and distribution systems. He became one of the first international Spanish-language recording stars. The tango didn't use heavy percussion, as in Afro-Cuban dance music—although it is quite rhythmic, the percussion is transmitted by the accordion-like bandoneón or the piano. The fact that it was a relatively difficult dance encouraged listeners not necessarily in the center of the Buenos Aires tango bar universe to sit back and listen. Gardel's similarities and conceptual links to the Italian opera singers of the late nineteenth century, who became pop recording stars in their own right, made him a forerunner of Latin stars later in the twentieth century.

Agustín Lara and the Mexican Bolero

Mexico's enchantment by the bolero in the '30s and '40s was crucial to the bolero's international development, because it was integrated with and modified by national styles like ranchera, mariachi, conjunto, and corrido. The regional inflections in these folkloric styles gave bolero a different flavor from its predecessors in Cuba and Argentina. Perhaps Mexico's most important bolero artists were Trío Los Panchos and Agustín Lara. The trio, which combined poignant, rapid-picking guitar licks on their Mexican-style tres instruments with sentimental harmonies, spawned a huge legion of imitators, even to the current day Los Tri-O, a Colombian group that combines youthful appearance with the older traditional style.

Long after his death in 1970, Agustín Lara is something of an institution in Mexico, where he wrote songs that captured the spirit of a country that was creating a post-revolutionary society at the same time that it was joining the modern world. Lara was expert at synthesizing various outside influences and creating a sophisticated, urban bolero—his marriage to movie star María Felix, which was memorialized in his signature song *María Bonita*, also helped to introduce Mexico to the modern world of celebrity couples. Every year there is an international festival of music in his honor, with events held in Veracruz, Mexico City, Havana, two cities in France, four in Spain, and Buenos Aires. Along with his contemporary, vocalist Chavela Vargas, he is remembered through the Latin alternative band Café Tacuba, who recorded a tribute to his style, *Esta Noche* on the 1993 album *Re*. His songs still send shudders through any true Mexican national.

One of Mexico's seminal songwriters during the pre-World War II era, Lara wrote many of the standards of the twentieth century Latin ballad, including *Granada*, *Solamente una Vez*, *María Bonita*, *Farolito*, and *Palabras de Mujer*. Although primarily known for his ability to write instant bolero standards, he was equally adept at a number of other song styles, including ranchera, son, and the tango.

Lara was born in 1897 in the Caribbean port of Veracruz, but his parents soon relocated to Mexico City. Lara took piano lessons and wound up playing in a bordello until his father sent him to military school. After his military stint, he came back to Mexico City and, in 1928, began composing songs on the piano. That year he recorded his first song, *Imposible*, with Adelaido Castellada's Orchestra.

Lara was an almost-overnight success—his songs were premiered on the radio in the early 1930s by legendary vocalists Toña la Negra and Ana María Fernández, and he became a huge radio star during an era when radio was the most important medium. Lara also composed for the golden era Mexican films of the 1940s. During the '50s and early '60s, Lara cemented his international star status by touring Europe. He became an icon for the bolero, with his songs recorded by the pivotal figures of the era, from Latin trailblazers like Xavier Cugat and Desi Arnaz to mainstream singers like Nat King Cole and Bing Crosby. He was further canonized when, in honor of the centenary of his birth, Plácido Domingo recorded an entire album of his compositions, *Bajo el Cielo Español*.

Despite his Mexico City veneer and worldly pedigree, Lara may have owed his musical genius to the coastal region of his birth. "I was born with the heart of a pirate," he said in *Veracruz*, and Lara had the hot rhythms and the wandering spirit of the Caribbean in him—there is even some speculation among scholars as to whether he had some African lineage. Veracruz culture is decidedly different from much of the rest of Mexico—although ostensibly celebratory of its indigenous culture, Mexico tends to marginalize its African diaspora. Veracruz was part of an African-influenced culture that was replenished by contact from sister cities like Havana, New Orleans, Tampa, Santo Domingo, Cartagena, and San Juan.

On the printed page, Lara's lyrics work as simple poetry, at times recalling the lovelorn verse of Pablo Neruda. Compare these lines from a passage in *María Bonita*, written about his wife, María Félix, with a passage from *La Infinita*, a poem Neruda wrote about his longtime wife, Matilda Urrutia:

Acuérdate, que en la playa/Con tus manitas las estrellitas/
  Las enjuagabas
(Remember how at the beach/With your hands you washed/The stars)
                                                                    María Bonita

Vea estas manos? Han medido/la tierra, han seperado/Los minerales y
  cereales"
(See these hands? They have measured/the earth, have separated/
  Minerals and grains)
                                                                    La Infinita

Working at almost the same time as Lara was Puerto Rican-born Rafael Hernández, whose career took him from a small island town to metropolitan San Juan and finally to New York, where he was pivotal in the development of Latin music in the United States. Ironically, Hernández achieved his largest fame while in Mexico. Although he has always been associated with his native Puerto Rico and his enormously influential tenure in New York, in some ways Hernández was a central figure in Mexican music history.

Born in 1891 in the town of Aguadilla, Hernández studied with music professors, learning violin, trombone, guitar, and the piano in his childhood years. As a Caribbean port in constant cultural conversation with Havana, San Juan was a point of entry for Afro-Cuban music onto the island. But like most Caribbean nations, Puerto Rico had its own development of Latin music roughly parallel to what was going on in Cuba. Folk genres, developed in the countryside, included the décima (a literal term for the adaptation of the décima to music), seis, aguinaldo, the latter a typical Christmas song; and the danza a variant of the Afro-Cuban contradanza. The bomba was a more pure African dance, similar to the Afro-Cuban rumba, and the plena was a trova-like music that announced the news of the day as well as providing epic-like stories of local heroes, continuing the tradition of the Spanish romances. The décima-based genres used instrumental lineups that resembled early Cuban sextetos, with an emphasis on the cuatro, the Puerto Rican analog to the Cuban tres; bomba and plena instrumentation was more like Arsenio Rodríguez's conjunto.

As an adolescent Rafael Hernández moved to San Juan, where he played with the Municipal Orchestra under the direction of Manuel Tizól. In 1912, he composed his first song, a danza called *María and Victoria*. With the arrival of World War I, the young Hernández was drafted into the U.S. Army, where he played in the Army band. When he moved to New York for more recording opportunities in 1926, he established the Trío Borinquen, a three-piece group that sang patriotic and romantic songs accompanied by guitars and incidental percussion like maracas and used intricate three-part harmonies. The more sophisticated electronic recording studios that came into existence in New York at this time encouraged the development of tríos and quartets, because the sound on the recordings could be significantly amplified and augmented with additional string, brass and percussive instruments. Along with Trío Matamoros, a vocal group almost as popular as the Ignacio Piñeiro Orchestra, which was founded almost simultaneously in Cuba, Trío Borinquen became enormously influential. It helped set the stage for Trío Los Panchos, which would form in Mexico in 1944 and whose story is told below.

Rafael Hernández's formal impact on the development of the bolero stemmed mostly from the access he had to sophisticated recording techniques, his careful attention to jazz arrangements à la Duke Ellington, and the fact that he was informed by Puerto Rican traditional music as well as Afro-Cuban. It can be said that the danza and seis styles were relatively less evolved in instrumentation and execution than their Cuban equivalents, giving them a more rustic flavor. At the same time, Hernández was purportedly concerned about being stereotyped as a black Latin musician, and he did not tolerate as much improvisation as his Cuban counterparts, thereby creating a form of bolero that was simplified. This aided its internationalization, something his popularity in Mexico seemed to bear out. He insisted that his songs and musicians obeyed tight linear structures that maintained the Afro-Caribbean tradition of complex harmonies meshed with syncopated rhythms.

Hernández formed the Cuarteto Victoria in New York a few years later, and the expanded lineup allowed him to play up-tempo guaracha and son styles from Cuba. But it was his compositional ability, not his extremely competent dance band, that made Hernández immortal in the annals of Latin music. Hernández, who composed Puerto Rico's unofficial national anthem, *Lamento Borincano*, as well as classics like *Silencio* (recorded by the Buena Vista Social Club on its 1998 album), *Cumbanchero*, and *Capullito de Alelí*, immediately attained extraordinary acclaim as a composer and bandleader. Having immersed himself in the tropical swing of the day, and heavily influenced by both North American jazz and Afro-Cuban music, Hernández had a seemingly boundless musical range and was a singular presence.

Hernández was a prolific composer, and the subjects of his songs ranged from patriotic fervor about Puerto Rico to the dominant subject of bolero—romantic love. Hernández lived in a self-created world of fascinating contradiction—he acquired the image of a countrified peasant because of his songs when in fact he was raised in urban San Juan and became a globetrotting Latin American musical giant. One of his songs, *Linda Quisqueya*, a tribute to the Dominican Republic, was originally *Linda Borinquen*, a tribute to Puerto Rico. His songs contained an anti-U.S. edge but he made few public statements expressing his Puerto Rican nationalism. In fact the story behind his most famous composition, *Lamento Borincano*, is key to understanding the transition Latin music underwent in North America.

Lamento Borincano was performed by Manuel Canario Jiménez, a classic trío vocalist who would ultimately dedicate himself to the traditional Puerto Rican plena but got his start in Hernández's Trío Borinquen and helped establish the trío in the New York Latin music scene. Known as perhaps Latin America's first protest song, *Lamento Borincano* tells the story of a Puerto Rican peasant farmer during the years of the Depression. He gathers his humble crop harvested from his even more humble piece of land, goes to the local town to sell it so he can buy his wife a dress, but then finds that there are no buyers because of the economic devastation. The song, which so poetically conveys the state of mind of the average Puerto Rican in the first half of the twentieth century, was entirely composed in New York while Hernández was experiencing the difficulties of a black Puerto Rican musician succeeding in the cold North. He had moved there to join a growing community of Puerto Rican and other Latin American musicians, taking part in a northward migration that was made easier by his island's status as a U.S. territory, which granted all Puerto Ricans U.S. citizenship. With one song, Hernández managed to convey not only the plight of underdeveloped Latin America but the early experiences of the immigrant flight, a phenomenon that continues unabated to this day.

Hernández also was greatly influenced by his stays in Cuba and especially in Mexico. In the 1920s, he lived in Havana for four years before returning to New York, and he went into a flurry of writing that produced a number of danzóns and danzas, as well as more formal waltzes. During this period he wrote *Cachita*, a song so steeped in Afro-Cuban style it is often assumed to be written by a Cuban.

In 1932 Hernández moved to Mexico, intending to stay just for a month to play some shows. He wound up staying fifteen years. There he wrote several of his most famous songs and became a national figure, composing another anthem, this time in honor of Mexico. He served a long tenure in the Mexican film industry, where he wrote music for classic films like *Perfídia* and *Águila o Sol*. During his stay in Mexico he became strongly identified with *Cumbanchero*, an upbeat, mambo-ish tune that gained him international fame as "Mr. Cumbanchero," an epithet reportedly used by President John Kennedy during Hernández's visit to Washington,

D.C. in the early 1960s. Hernández's career may not be as celebrated as the great Afro-Cuban bandleaders and bolero singers of his time, because of his proficiency in several genres and areas of music, but his impact on the bolero is essential to understanding its popularity in Latin America.

Influenced by Hernández and Cuba's Trío Matamoros, Mexico's Trío Los Panchos pioneered and made trío music popular worldwide. The trío style the group perfected brought soaring harmonies, a return to folkier instruments (three guitars), and a renewed sense of romanticism to the bolero. Trío Los Panchos has one of the most recognizable sounds in any Latin music genre—the trío, consisting of three guitarists who sing elaborate harmonies, impacts the listener in an entirely different way from the solitary singer or a larger chorus. It is as if the high-pitched chorus of a charanga band became the primary focus, with soaring harmony providing earnestness the way a trilling vocal solo would.

Trío Los Panchos was formed in 1944 by lead singer Hernando Áviles, who teamed up with Chucho Navarro (mainly a second voice) and Alfredo Gil, who played a modified Cuban tres, known in Mexico as the requinto. The lineup went through several changes over its thirty-seven-year reign, most notably the departure and return of Áviles. The most significant new voice in the group was the Puerto Rican singer Johnny Albino, who arrived in 1958 and later garnered considerable fame as a solo performer. Said to have taken their name from Mexican revolutionary Pancho Villa, the group's members drew on traditional Mexican music such as ranchera, mariachi, and corrido. But they also absorbed influences as varied as the Argentine tango and the Colombian cumbia, styles which, along with other Colombian forms like the bambuco and pasillo, were spread by musicians traveling from their home countries. It was Los Panchos's adaptation of the bolero that made them international stars.

Some sources point to the influence of Argentine composer and musical director Terig Tucci in Los Panchos's development. Although early recordings and performances stuck almost entirely to Mexican ranchera and trío traditions, Tucci provoked a change in Los Panchos's harmonizing style and the composition of new tunes to reflect those influences. A pianist who became a major orchestral leader and musical director for radio and film in New York and Los Angeles, Tucci had worked with Carlos Gardel for years, arranging on songs like *El Día Que Me Quieras*. His ability to employ the most sophisticated recording techniques and his central role in the increasing internationalization of Latin music made him an excellent collaborator in Los Panchos's worldwide success.

Los Panchos's songs feature characteristically lilting melodies with lyrics that are focused on the historical concerns of the bolerista: lost love, love that almost was, forbidden love, longed-for love. "Golden Age" Panchos material from the middle to late 1940s reflected the Gardel melancholy, particularly songs like *Me Castiga Dios*, *Perdida*, and their signature classic, *Sin Tí*. Alfredo Gil was one of the primary composers, although Chucho Navarro was responsible for *Perdida* and *Sin Remedio*. Their strong Cuban influence was shown by their fondness for Mercedes Valdés's *Me Voy Pa'l Pueblo*, which represented a fusion between secular and religious Yoruba music, as well as son. Rafael Hernández was also a source Los Panchos drew from, covering songs of his like *Silencio* and *Capullito de Alhelí*, collected on the 1990 Sony release *Love Songs of the Tropics*.

Trio Los Panchos's signature style owes most to its high-range harmonies and its pioneering of the high-pitched requinto guitar. The members' singing of such notes is so flawless that it is impossible to call it falsetto, and their very emotional power comes from their resonating choruses. While their songs are not written as décimas in a strict formal sense, the lyrics occasionally settle into an octosyllabic flow, a kind of attenuation of the original form that continued with the popularization of the bolero. Their carrying forward of the mariachi, ranchera, and corrido styles did much to popularize the forms internationally, although their success was mostly due to their mainstreaming of these regional genres. From the 1980s on, Trío Los Panchos has become the essence of nostalgia in Latin American radio programming, bursting onto the airwaves without fail when pop music shows give way to "nostalgia" shows, usually broadcast on Sundays in Latin America. The group spawned a host of imitators, and their spirit is kept alive by the contemporary Colombian group, Los Tri-O.

The Mexican ranchera and mariachi styles were central influences on the development of the bolero in Mexico. The ranchera is a musical genre, literally a song that is sung on a Mexican ranch, originated in the era immediately preceding the Mexican Revolution. Characterized by vocal trilling and straightforward lyrics often expressing nationalistic and/or regional pride, a ranchera can be sung to a variety of rhythms that have been popular in Mexico in the twentieth century, from Cuban/Mexican bolero to German waltz and polka. Mariachi refers more to a collection of musical styles played by orchestras that evolved over many centuries. The typical contemporary group features six to eight violins, two trumpets, the vihuela and guitarro, two guitars of different pitch, and Mexican folk harp. In the late nineteenth century mariachi bands were playing various forms of the Mexican son, which were similar to the Cuban son, but incorporated more local and indigenous influences. The various sons included son jalisco, son huatesco (a.k.a. juapango), and the son jarrocho (a.k.a. son veracruzano), which all reflected the regions they were named after. The mariachi that became popular in the twentieth century in the state of Jalisco is a slowed-down version of son jarrocho, which is a dance form that incorporates African and indigenous influences.

In 1934, the band known as Mariachi Vargas became essential in standardizing the arrangements of traditional son and other genres, setting the stage for stars like Pedro Infante and Lola Beltrán, who would emerge in the 1940s. Mariachi singers also sang rancheras, corridos, boleros, and other forms of popular songs. The characteristic glissando and stretching out of the last line in ranchera has also become associated with mariachi in general—meant to convey emotion, these attributes sometimes evoke Mexican stereotypes.

The corrido, which is more explicitly derived from the Spanish ballad and décima tradition than the ranchera, was strongly associated with political themes during the revolution, and especially with the ethnic tension in Mexico in the nineteenth century following U.S. incorporation of formerly Mexican territories. Having developed outside of the context of the bolero influence, the two genres, while sharing the décima's poetic structure, were not related. José Alfredo Jiménez was Mexican bolero's great innovator, bringing together traditional forms like ranchera and corrido into a more standardized pop format. He took the emotion of the ranchera and the folksy newsiness of the corrido and created a new kind of Mexican popular voice strongly identified with ranchera, ironically developing in the urban areas of Mexico during the 1950s and '60s. Jiménez had his own trio, but was perhaps most noticed when he collaborated with singers like Jorge Negrete and Pedro Infante. His best known songs include *Ella*, *Cuatro Caminos*, *La Que Se Fue*, and *Guitarras De Media Noche*. Contemporary ranchera and mariachi star Vicente Fernández has used Jiménez as a muse, recording a slew of albums of Jiménez's compositions. But as significant as Jiménez's contributions were, his fame pales in comparison to that of Pedro Infante, whose ubiquity in the movies made him an unforgettable icon.

Born in the northern Mexican city of Guamúchil, Sinaloa, in 1917, Infante used carpentering skills to make his own guitar. He began singing professionally at age twenty and wound up moving to Mexico City in the late 1930s to sing on radio stations and perform in concert halls. His recording and acting careers began almost simultaneously in the early '40s. Infante starred in fifty-five movies made in Mexico and recorded 366 songs between 1943 and 1956. Acting in a wide range of movies jumping between comedy and arte-povera-inspired "films of bittersweet poverty," Infante embodied the hopes and frustrations of the Mexican lower classes in a way similar to the comedian Cantinflas, a popular comedic film star who championed the poor with sarcasm and subservisive-ness. Instead of the latter's sarcastic rebel, the pachuco, Infante played a more naïve dreamer who was also a womanizer. Infante was rivaled by fellow singer/actor Jorge Negrete, and in the early 1950s actually appeared with him in a movie about motorcycle cops (an unacknowledged predecessor to Erik Estrada's *CHiPs*, perhaps) called *El Gallo Giro*.

But tragedy was in the cards for Infante, who first watched Negrete die of hepatitis, then was involved in two airplane accidents before a third one, in 1957, took his life. His death, like that of 1990s star Selena, came just before he was about to break through to mainstream America, since he had already made plans to star in movies with actors like Marlon Brando, John Wayne, and Joan Crawford.

Infante lived on for years through the endless replaying of his movies on Mexican TV and Spanish-language television in the United States. His greatest influence was popularizing the fusion of ranchera with bolero on songs like Lara's *Mujer* and Portillo de la Luz's *Contigo en La Distancia*, paving the way for later singers like Javier Solís and Marco Antonio Muñiz.

According to legend, on the day of Pedro Infante's death in 1957, a young Javier Solís stood before a crowd in Puebla and sang a tribute to Infante with his song *Grito Prisionero* (Prisoner's Shout). Weighed down for ten years with the stigma of being an Infante imitator, Solís was finally able, with the intervention of composer Gabriel Carrión, to develop his own style, an advance of the bolero ranchero style, particularly with his 1949 recording of *Amorcito Corazón*. Solís also had a movie career, appearing in thirty-three films, which showed off a spectacular singing range, if not Infante's skills on the big screen. His most famous song was probably *Payaso*, although the Latin Grammy Hall of Fame inducted his version of *Sabor a Mi* in 2001.

A number of artists dominated the vocal scene, most of them coming from Cuba, Puerto Rico, and Mexico, as the Latin bolero entered the 1950s. In much the same way they were for pop and jazz singers in the United States, the bolero recording style and orchestra became standardized across the Spanish-speaking world. Among the era's hits were the Cuban diva Olga Guillót's *La Dueña del Bolero*, Mexican singer Armando Manzanero's *Somos Novios*, the work of Mexican bolerista Chavela Vargas, and two Puerto Rican classics, Daniel Santos's *El Inquieto Anacobero* and Tito Rodríguez's *El Inolvidable*.

With a career that began in 1945 in Havana's exclusive Zombie Club, Olga Guillót became the reigning queen of the Cuban bolero. Born in 1925 in Santiago, she moved to Havana at age nine and as a teen sang briefly with her sister in a duo. Her earliest hit and claim to fame was *Llúvia Gris* (Gray Rain), her translation of *Stormy Weather*, in 1943. Perhaps because of her enormous popularity with Cuban exiles, in 1964 she was the first Latin act to perform at Carnegie Hall. Forty years later, still possessing a flawless soprano that trilled with emotion, albeit less dramatically than her successor, La Lupe, Guillót was an almost forgotten gem from the past, but was still recording. On her recent album *Faltaba Yo*, she scored with versions of Armando Manzaneros's *No Sigas Por Favor* and Puerto Rican singer Sylvia Rexach's *Alma Adentro*. Backed by impeccable jazz-orchestra arrangements featuring guest appearances by trumpeter Arturo Sandovál and legendary bassist Israel "Cachao" López, she whispered furtively, coaxing every bit of sentiment from the songs.

Guillót's work reinforced the fact that probably the most important innovation during this period came from Cuba. It was called filin, a Hispanicized version of the word "feeling." Inspired by jazz,

R&B and other African-American forms that were filtering into Havana from the United States via the American-conscious Cuban public, filin added a dramatic and sensual element to bolero delivery. Marcelino Guerra, who sang with son groups like Ignacio Piñeiro's Septeto Nacionál, is often credited with providing the basis for filin in Cuba. His interest in the sophisticated harmonics of jazz seeped into his son and bolero compositions. He moved to New York in 1944 and sang with Xavier Cugat, and more importantly, Machito's Afro-Cuban orchestra. But even though he never moved back, his influence on Cuban musicians helped to incubate filin.

Composers like César Portillo de la Luz (*Contigo en la Distancia*), Rosendo Ruiz, and the songwriting team of Giraldo Piloto and Alberto Vera picked up on Guerra's innovations and created a new format for the boleros that would become famous in the filin movement. Singers like Elena Burke and Toña la Negra infused the style with a deep soulfulness. According to Cuban music historian René López, the breakthrough performer of filin was singer Roberto Faz in the early 1950s, through his recordings with the Conjunto Casino and his performances on television. One of the most famous of those singers, Omara Portuondo (featured in the Buena Vista Social Club), was still alive in 2003. The influence of the filin style spread among bolero singers throughout Latin America in the '50s, but is noticeable only in subtle ways, as in the way you might hear Billie Holiday in Frank Sinatra's style.

In Puerto Rico, the bolero was promulgated by almost all of the island's singers not involved in mambo or folkloric bomba and plena. Pedro Flores, who had been a contemporary of Rafael Hernández in New York, had returned home and recorded *Perdón* and *Obsesión*. One of the most enduring of Puerto Rico's boleristas was Tito Rodríguez, whose career had peaked in New York as one of the big three leaders of mambo orchestras. Rodríguez, who turned to bolero when the mambo era died in New York, continued the string orchestra format, but like many of his contemporaries in

Puerto Rico, he began to include some rock instrumentation, such as the electric guitar. This trend was continued with Daniel Santos, who affected a somewhat melodramatic tone with hits like *Linda*, *Despedida*, and *Jugando, Mamá, Jugando*. His early career, singing tunes written by Pedro Flores in the 1940s, made him extremely influential. But Santos was ultimately eclipsed by singers like Felipe Rodríguez, whose nickname, "La Voz," inspired Hector Lavoe to rename himself in the 1960s, and Bobby Capó, the writer and singer of one of the world's most famous boleros, *Piel Canela*.

Capó, an Afro-Puerto Rican, left a mark on Puerto Rican music and the bolero that seems to increase in importance with the passage of time. Born in 1922 in Coamo, Puerto Rico, he moved to New York in the '40s to play with Cuarteto Victoria, Cugat's orchestra, and Machito's Afro-Cubans. His '50s classic *Piel Canela* (Cinnamon Skin) was an overt reference to an aesthetic blackness, the title drawing attention to a theme sometimes buried by the song's refrain, *Tu y tu y tu y nadie mas que tu* (You and you and you and no one else but you), which is what everyone remembers about the song. Capó recorded a number of songs with bizarre wah-wah guitar effects along with syrupy strings. His homage to negritude influenced another rock-inspired ballad singer, Lucecita Benítez, who at one point grew a flamboyant Afro to prove her point. But even though Capó took part in the musical experimentation of the '60s, his voice had such a high quality that it must be considered among the best of Latin American boleristas. Capó's work was resurrected in 1999 by Latin jazz saxophonist David Sánchez, who has recorded a number of Capó's songs on his albums.

Nueva Trova, Nueva Canción

A strange thing happened in Latin America on its way to the '60s: Rock music was often rejected, changed into something else, watered down, or completely mutated into unrecognizability when it came into contact with the bolero. Some credit Bobby Capó with mixing in certain forms of the rock beat, particularly one known as the beguine beat, to create a rock-like music palatable for Puerto Ricans. In Mexico, rock was repressed actively by the government once it manifested itself (see Chapter 10). In Cuba, the innovations made by filin allowed for the creation of a new kind of folk music just in time for the needs of the fledgling Castro revolution.

At the center of this sea change was Pablo Milanés, who was born in 1943 in the town of Bayamo, Cuba, and studied under the Cuban master Leo Brouwer. Milanes began his career as a filin singer and wound up becoming one of the essential artists in a new rock- and soul-inspired song form that became known as the Cuban nueva trova. Having begun his career in the 1960s with vocal quartets that sang an R&B and gospel-influenced music, Pablo Milanés first got attention with his 1965 composition *Mis 22 Años*, which was recorded by filin diva Elena Burke. The nueva trova movement, which recalled the early twentieth century trovadores' nationalism combined with the folk protest genres developing in the United States, Argentina, and Chile, blossomed in venues like El Rincón del Feeling in Havana. It celebrated the plight of the Latin American worker and iconic heroes like Che Guevara. In 1967 Milanés was sent to a prison camp for undesirables by suspicious Castro authorities. After being "rehabilitated" he was liberated from the camp by Haydée Santamaría, a heroine of the Revolution.

Santamaría was in charge of one of Havana's central cultural institutions, Casa de las Américas, from within which she organized the Centro de la Canción Protesta (The Protest Song Center), which helped to establish la nueva trova. The ideologically reformed Milanés became a strong supporter of the revolution, in spite of his stint in prison, and wrote many songs in the new genre.

The protest aspect of la nueva trova gave it several ready-made audiences who made Milanés a superstar in Latin America. In the '70s, Mexico's left-leaning government pushed trova as an antidote to the frightening rock and roll from the United States. In southern cone countries like Chile and Argentina, nueva canción, which preceded nueva trova, was popular with leftist college students still reeling from the murder of protest singer Victor Jara by the Chilean national police. Milanés's music had enough Afro-Cuban elements to appeal to anyone who was a fan of Latin music. His songs followed a predictable dichotomy between romantic love and social protest. While pro-revolutionary songs like *Amo Esta Isla* (1981) and *Identidad* (1993) are stirring, Milanés is probably best known for *Yolanda* (1981), as sappy a love song as they come. Milanés is the kind of singer whom hippies and liberation theologians (Marxist Christians) would like, but he has little appeal to punk types.

"I'll join your street-style madness," said Milanés in *Identidad*. "Your refusal to accept the way things are/And forever just like you I'll stick my chest out." Perhaps more than any other Cuban singer, he captured the brave and sexy risk of the revolution, during a time when very few from the outside world knew exactly what was going on there. Milanés also has a voice that transcends genre—it is extraordinarily light, but still possesses a kind of profound, thunderous authority. Milanés, like the rest of the nueva trova singers, used a kind of trill in his voice that was used later by jet set pop singer Julio Iglesias. But the Milanés trill, as well as that of his contemporary, the singer Silvio Rodríguez, seemed to project a depth of emotion that only a revolutionary could feel, apart from the experience of a capitalist bolerista. Of course, to some the nueva trova style may seem overdramatic to the point of grating on the listener, and the tinny, harpsichord-like '70s keyboards these singers preferred sounded like a telenovela soundtrack.

Still, there's no overlooking the strong African roots in Milanés's music. On a song like *Homenaje* (Homage) in 1987, which appears on David Byrne's Luaka Bop collection *Diablo al Infierno*, the keyboard plays classic son tumbaos, a chorus of voices evokes Yoruban rumba, and the bass jumps along with Los Van Van aplomb. Milanés also collaborated with Buena Vista Social Club member Compay

Segundo on a version of *Chan Chan* that appeared in 1994, years before the Social Club album was released.

Despite the apparent pitfalls of nueva trova, few things are more stirring to the Latin music listener than the work of Silvio Rodríguez. Barely a teenager when the Cuban revolution came, Rodríguez was recruited by Haydée Santamaría at Casa las Americas and became a colleague of Milanés. He worked with jazz-influenced pianist Emiliano Hernández and composed primarily on the guitar, as opposed to Milanés, who was a pianist.

Rodríguez's classic *Días y Flores* (1975) was released the same year as Bob Dylan's *Blood on the Tracks*, but it is the *Bringing It All Back Home* of nueva trova. Comparisons with Dylan are apt here: Rodríguez's plaintive, slightly off-key voice is all about keeping the revolutionary spirit alive in Cuba just as it was dying up north. The performances by the musicians, the quality of the songs, and the crackling experimentalism evoke the feeling that something was in the air, that this was a time of change and innovation. Rodríguez's high-pitched, piercing vocals are surrounded by ethereal organ sounds, Francisco Arnat's twangy guitar riffs, and the expertly understated percussion of Ignacio Berroa, one of Cuba's greatest drummers.

Rodríguez's version of nueva trova is probably the most familiar around the world and it represents another turn in Cuban music toward the European or North American. In its folkiness the music sounds like Crosby, Stills, Nash, and Young or Joni Mitchell; the Afro-Cuban accent, despite the presence of Ignacio Berroa, is muted. Still, as folk rock, it is a decidedly Latin-influenced one— the sound of the Cuban tres gives it a guajira-ish folkloric feel and Rodriguez's poetry ranks with that of the better bolero composers. "This song is more than a song," he says in *Esta Canción*, from *Días y Flores*. "This song is my necessity/to tie myself finally to the earth/to have you see yourself in me/and me in you."

While aspects of nueva trova grew out of developments in Cuban bolero and trova, an important predecessor to this genre was Chilean nueva canción, which was spearheaded by singers like Mercedes Sosa, Violeta Parra, and Victor Jara. Sosa, who was born in Tucamán, Argentina, a week before the plane crash that took Carlos Gardel's life in 1935, sang songs of protest and in defense of indigenous rights in the 1960s. Her work is inspired by the traditions of Spanish décima and ballad as well as the folkloric traditions of rural Argentina—her music was characterized by her use of the guitar and Andean flute and percussion. Best known for her interpretations of works by her contemporaries, Sosa has immortalized songs written by Parra, Jara, Milanés, fellow countryman Atahualpa Yupanqui, and the Brazilian singer Milton Nascimento.

Violeta Parra, who was born in San Carlos Chillán, Chile, to a family of musicians, began writing and recording in the mid-'50s, moving back and forth between Santiago, Chile, and Paris. Like Sosa, Parra used her haunting alto to tell the stories of the disenfranchised. The nueva canción movement was strongly connected to Pablo Neruda, part of the Chilean intelligentsia that was repressed during the CIA-sponsored coup in 1973, and Parra's songs owe debts to the Latin American literary tradition.

One of the most charismatic folksingers of any stripe, Victor Jara was born in 1932 in a small town outside the capital city of Santiago. He grew up in poverty, becoming a staunch leftist. He came under Parra's wing when he moved to Santiago in the mid-'60s. Jara's most famous song, played in classic folk-rock style with an acoustic guitar, is *Te Recuerdo Amanda*, which tells the story of a woman in love with a factory worker repressed by police. Jara used the names of his parents, Amanda and Manuel, to tell the story.

Jara also wrote songs like *El Derecho de Vivir en Paz* (The Right to Live in Peace) and *A Cuba*, in which he encouraged the listener to go to Cuba, join the revolution, and drink "rum *without* Coca-Cola." Jara lived his ideals right up to his death, when he was brought to Santiago's National Football Stadium and machine-gunned to death by the Chilean military after his hands had been smashed and he refused to stop singing.

From Bolero to Rock and Pop

The bolero, like the North American ballad, fell under the influence of rock music just before the development of nueva canción and nueva trova. While it continued to be sung with traditional orchestras, variants of bolero began appearing in which singers adopted rock instrumentation. The adherence to the décima structure lessened, and the 4/4 tempos of pop began to replace bolero's syncopated clave. It was a meeting of two strands of international pop music, both evolving by absorbing hybrid influences. The way that bolero was transformed by its contact with 1960s and 1970s pop conventions virtually created the genre of Latin pop, which is still evolving today.

As mentioned, rock and roll began to make an impact on Latin American pop in the late '50s and early '60s, influencing vocalists in countries from Mexico all the way to Argentina. While the earliest evidence of rock en Español appear to be in mid-1950s Mexico, setting off an era that climaxed in 1961 with the reign of the teenybopperish Los Teen Tops, rock didn't begin to affect bolero-oriented Latin pop until later. In the early 1960s Puerto Rican boleristas like Bobby Capó, Danny Rivera, and Chucho Avallanet began to alter their styles slightly with the use of rock instrumentation (electric guitar, bass, trap drums, and ultimately electric keyboards and synthesizers) and 4/4 rock rhythms that sometimes supplemented and sometimes supplanted the syncopated Cuban bolero format. American counterparts to these singers were Bobby Darin and Paul Anka (who was of Lebanese descent and took advantage of his Mediterranean looks to become a major star in Latin countries like Puerto Rico). The singer Lucecita Benítez also teamed up with Avallanet, Daniel Santos, and Danny Rivera to form what was called la nueva ola portoricensis (the Puerto Rican New Wave) during the mid-1960s, fueled by the advent of television, where they appeared regularly. Benítez, who with Rivera became active in the Puerto Rican independence movement, displayed an early sympathy for the Castro regime that permanently drew the wrath of anti-Castro Cubans. She was a fascinating symbol of this era. Although a relatively light-skinned, "white" Puerto Rican, she actually teased out her hair into an Afro to make a statement about her identification with her African self.

Coinciding with the Puerto Rican bolero/rock movement was the enormous popularity of Sandro (born Roberto Sánchez), an Argentine singer whose style was so emotional that it became a signature as well as a derided aspect of his performance. Argentina's European orientation as well as a love-hate relationship with England, which in the late nineteenth century had almost imperial power there, spurred an interest in rock music. Sandro's influences ranged from Elvis Presley, whom he enjoyed imitating, to the Beatles. Like almost all prominent Argentine singers after Gardel, Sandro was influenced by and reinterpreted Gardel's dramatic style. With songs like *El Trigo*, *Penumbra*, and *Penas*, Sandro, who co-wrote his songs, trilled his way to the hearts of all Latin America, even coming to New York for a sold-out show in Madison Square Garden in 1969. Sandro originally sang for a rock band called Trío Azúl and continued to feature the guitar prominently in his songs, which made them popular as soundtracks in the kind of James Bond knock-off movies that proliferated throughout Latin America in the late '60s. Both Sandro and his Mexican counterpart José José, whose career had spanned over thirty years starting in the mid-'60s, were the subject of tribute albums in the late 1990s. On them, Latin alternative stars such as Aterciopelados and Julieta Venegas acknowledged Sandro's influence on their music.

La Lupe

Born in Santiago, Cuba in 1939, La Lupe (Guadalupe Yolí) was an extraordinary singer who rose from humble beginnings to enormous stardom in New York in the late '60s. The daughter of a singer, La Lupe began her career when her family moved to Havana in 1955, and she became famous for singing boleros like Facundo Rivero's *No Me Quieres Así.* In 1963, after the Cuban revolution, she moved to New York and collaborated with Mongo Santamaría and Rafael Cortijo. While she excelled as vocalist for the Tito Puente Orchestra and she holds a place in the great salsa pantheon, La Lupe was primarily a bolero singer, a kind of juiced-up version of Olga Guillot transferred to the Big Apple as it was going through economic and political convulsions.

As a native Cuban who thrived in the midst of New York's soul, jazz, and rock-influenced pop scene, she was a ready-made filin artist, even though she had no connection to that Havana scene. Her presentation was famous for being extremely passionate—she could turn bolero into a harrowing exercise of emotion.

La Lupe did not so much transform bolero as end its innocence with her wild displays. Her classic songs, *La Tirana* and *Que te Pedí*, recorded in the early 1970s, were demanding female pleas for respect that made her a feminist icon as well as the role model for every Latino transvestite. She performed with frantic, sensual dance steps, calling on every agonizing breath to produce an inimitable phrasing that became her trademark. She would take her false eyelashes and wig and shoes off and throw them at the crowd, throw them at the band. She would even confront Tito Puente himself and tell him his band was playing out of rhythm. Inspired by Judy Garland, Brenda Lee, and Eartha Kitt, La Lupe was also a Santería devotee, and each performance seemed like the enactment of a possession ritual.

Although she is mostly remembered by hardcore salsa fans who made the club scene in the '60s and early '70s, La Lupe was a crossover success in her day, appearing as a guest on late night TV shows hosted by the likes of Dick Cavett and Merv Griffin. Her bilingual song *Once We Loved/Se Acabó*, performed on the Cavett show, is the kind of astonishingly passionate, yet campy performance that pegged her as ahead of her time. Perhaps embittered by the sexism of the Latin music business, and addled by psychological problems, she both felt deeply and lampooned the pathos of the bolero. This strange contradiction in her performance, this over-the-top portrayal of a woman in distress, makes her the favorite of many contemporary drag queen performances.

La Lupe's meteoric rise to the top of Latin music was followed by a tragic fall—as it was prophesied by a Santería seer, La Lupe lost her fame (her spot as Tito Puente's singer/collaborator) and fortune (a mansion in New Jersey, three cars, and a closet full of furs). Many accounts of her life imply that La Lupe's fate was at least partially determined by her uncompromising behavior—she was somewhat of a tyrant in rehearsal and provoked male musicians who expected her to take a more passive attitude about the performance of a song. In the end, it seemed impossible to separate her artistry from her rocky personal life. La Lupe died penniless due to complications from AIDS—most likely brought on by intravenous drug use—in 1982, at the age of forty-three. Her songs have been revived in an album by Puerto Rican singer Yolanda Duke, as well as in a cover version of *Que te Pedí* (written by Puerto Rican songwriter Tite Curét Alonso) by Nuyorican salsera La India.

In 1970s Puerto Rico, and to a lesser extent Caribbean countries like the Dominican Republic, the rock- and pop-influenced bolero became less important because of the onset of salsa romantica and merengue. Rock became more popular in Mexico, until it was virtually outlawed by the Mexican government after a disastrous 1971 concert at Avándaro, in which the audience was attacked by Mexican police, enforcing the government's idea that rock was dangerously subversive. (Soon after, the cast of *Hair*, on their first Latin American tour, were thrown out of the country after just one performance in Acapulco because of the play's countercultural scandalousness.) Mexican artists like José José and Juan Gabriel thrived singing popular versions of ranchera and bolero while sometimes incorporating rock instrumentation, filling the vacuum caused by the repression of Mexican rock music.

Pop versions of bolero and tango were a staple of the Argentine musical diet, but a new era of 1970s-1980s style rock was fueled by the Falklands War, which limited English imports to the country. The temporary boycott of English influence increased the demand for Argentina to produce its own rock groups, which would become one of the first waves of modern Latin alternative.

The climate was different in North America, where a new center for the creation and marketing of Latin music began to emerge in Miami. A steady stream of exiles from the Cuban revolution of 1959 had transformed that Florida city into the North American capital of Latin America. Although Miami Cuban exiles held tightly onto their traditions, they also had a great motivation to put their past behind them and construct an Americanized, internationalized idea of Cuban culture. By continuing to incorporate rhythmic and formal influences from North American pop, bolero mutated again and became something new, largely because of the efforts and success of one singer from Spain.

Julio Iglesias

Loved by millions, but a symbol of pop fluff for many others, Julio Iglesias almost singlehandedly kept the bolero alive in 1970s and 1980s. Not incidentally, he kept alive the Latin recording industry as well, selling over 100 million albums around the world. His sensual, low-key, trilling voice was seductive enough to win the hearts of almost every Latin American woman and the men who wanted to know how he did it.

The story of Iglesias's rise is well-known: Born in Madrid in 1943, at first he wanted to be a lawyer, and while in school he was a star goaltender for the Real Madrid soccer team. His career as an athlete was cut short after a scary car accident in the mid-1960s.

While he was recovering, Iglesias began playing guitar and writing songs. After getting his law degree from Cambridge University (while in England he sang in lounges covering the Beatles and Tom Jones), he entered the 1968 Spanish Song Festival. His song, the pop bolero *La Vida Sigue Igual* (Life Goes On) won first prize along with a record contract with Discos Columbia, a Spanish independent record label.

Although Iglesias made his initial success through songwriting, he became a megastar by covering various styles. His music echoed popular forms of Spain such as flamenco and incorporated Afro-Cuban bolero, Argentine milonga, and Andean rhythms, while also reflecting the international pop performed by singers such as Charles Aznavour and Englebert Humperdinck. While he had many songwriting collaborators, he did a substantial amount of writing. The songs he chose ranged from established classics to popular folk songs and of course, romantic ballads. His biggest breakthrough came by appealing to the Spanish-speaking Latin American world, particularly with an album like 1976's *América*, on which he covered classics like *Guantanemera*, *Historia de un Amor*, *Vaya Con Dios*, and *Moliendo Café*.

During Iglesias's tour of Europe and Latin America in the 1970s, he gained a large fan base with hits like *Manuela* (1975). He signed a contract with CBS in 1978 and put out a series of albums including *A Flor de Piel*, *América*, *Emociones*, *and Hey!*. On these he reinterpreted old Latin American bolero standards (like Pedro Flores's *Obsesión*) and included some original material, making him the darling of the traditional sector of Latin American and U.S. Latino culture, which rejected both salsa and rock. Songs like *Hey!*, *Ni te Tengo ni te Olvido*, and *Milonga*, delivered in his inimitable style, made him a symbol of traditional Latino aesthetic. In 1982 Iglesias began to sing in English on his release *Moments*, and he achieved major crossover success in 1984 with *1100 Bel Air Place*, which included the duets *To All the Girls I've Loved Before*, with Willie Nelson, and *All of You* with Diana Ross.

Although Iglesias's voice was formidable, his importance had more to do with marketing than with anything he brought to the music. He proved that a star Latin singer could sell massive amounts of records when receiving the right studio treatment and publicity machine. Even more important to his persona than his pop recontextualization of the troubadour was his guise as an unstoppable sex machine and his ability to play the loser at love and the incorrigible ravisher with equal relish.

While Iglesias's best work tends to fade into the tinny soundtrack of a cheap affair, he remains a classic voice with an arsenal of songs that carry all the emotional power and rewards of the Latin bolero. His only rival for the period that he dominated was Roberto Carlos (see Chapter 7), a Brazilian singer who was pivotal in the development of that country's rock scene and became a Spanish-language bolero singer in the 1980s.

Gloria and Emilio Estefan and the Miami Sound Machine

In the mid-1980s, when salsa made major concessions to pop, merengue was emerging, and Julio Iglesias reigned supreme in the world of Latin pop, the famously married Emilio and Gloria Estefan's Miami Sound Machine broke through with several mainstream hits. Both Emilio and Gloria were born in Cuba, but had been forced to emigrate to Miami in the early 1960s by the Castro revolution. In 1975, Gloria auditioned for a gig with the Miami Latin Boys, who were led by Emilio and worked mostly at weddings. Four years later, the Estefans were married, and the band changed its name to the Miami Sound Machine.

Miami Sound Machine was one of the most important Latin music bands of the 1980s. It picked up on the increasing ties between ballad singing and Latin pop, which had developed through Iglesias's career, and combined those with post-disco pop mainstream

influences. Using a Santana-like lineup that combined electric guitar and bass, trap drums, and electric keyboards with a substantial
Latin percussion section, Miami Sound Machine went a step further, incorporating elements of disco, funk, and R&B. The group's
second hit, *Conga*, is probably the most significant Latin hit since
Santana's rock remake of Tito Puente's *Oye Como Va*, if only because
it successfully rhymes "conga" with "longer." *Conga*, like MSM's
other hits, *The Rhythm Is Going to Get You*, and *Doctor Beat*, manages
to incorporate a Latin percussion section (including congas and
timbales) with the electric bass beats of the post-disco era. The band
went through several stages in terms of who was writing the music.
Doctor Beat, as well as much of the music on the first album, *Eyes of
Innocence* (1984), was written by drummer Enrique "Kiki" García.
Conga, *Bad Boys*, and all the songs on 1986's *Primitive Love* were
written by arranger Lawrence Dermer. *The Rhythm Is Going to Get
You* on *Let It Loose* (1988, with the group billed as "Gloria Estefan
and Miami Sound Machine) marked the arrival of the Estefans as
songwriters.

The unavailability of music from Castro's Cuba had two effects
on Latin music. There was no longer an experimental Latin music
to drive tropical dance music, and Miami had a wide-open field for
establishing a new aesthetic. Miami Sound Machine made itself
central to the idea of what Latin music was becoming, and its use of
Afro-Cuban percussion, combined with Gloria's passable sexual
appeal and adequate voice, made it a monster. Miami Sound Machine and the Estefans' success turned Miami into a music capital
and fostered the star-making machinery by focusing on the singer,
something that turned salsa into a formulaic genre. The Estefans
co-produced a spin-off act, an R&B-inspired singer, Jon Secada,
and jettisoned MSM member Willie Chirino, who made a series of
mildly important salsa-pop records in the early 1990s. Chirino later
became one of the few Cuban-American artists to consciously pay
homage to the music being played in Castro's Cuba, and his records
Cuba Libre, *Soy*, and *Afro-disiac* were geared toward purist taste.

In the early 1990s, Gloria Estefan became a solo performer, and the Estefans tried to capitalize on the nostalgia felt by the first generation of Miami-bred Cubans. With the release of *Mi Tierra*, their first all-Spanish language recording, Gloria Estefan succeeded in transforming the particular poignancy of Cuban nostalgia into a roots-rock party, as well as transcending her somewhat bland pop image. Rather than do an album of standards from the rich history of Cuban music, Estefan chose to write new songs that conformed to traditional Cuban styles. The strongest tunes on *Mi Tierra* are the full-force sones, guaguancós, and danzóns, which make the best use of distinguished guest musicians like flutist Nestor Torres, percussionist Luís Enrique, pianist Paquito Hechavarría, bassist Israel "Cachao" López, saxophonist Paquito D'Rivera, trumpeter Arturo Sandoval, and timbalero Tito Puente.

Cachao is magnificent throughout, particularly in *No Hay Mal Que Por Bien No Venga*, a perfectly realized neo-danzón that he wrote the music for. Similarly ecstatic heights are reached in the title track, a straightforward hard-montuno strut celebrating love and longing for the old country; the loping traditional son, *Si Señor!*; and the record's stunning finale, *Tradición*, which uses the guaguancó as a rhythmic matrix for the inspired outbursts from D'Rivera on sax, Sandoval on trumpet, and Puente on timbales. Unfortunately, boleros like *Mi Buen Amor* and *Volverás* can be somewhat droopy. The record's too-perfect pop production sheen is its only other flaw. Something about using the London Symphony Orchestra's string section seems at odds with tropical swing.

Despite the Estefan's often-expressed right-wing positions, *Mi Tierra*'s only overtly political statement is not a knee-jerk Miami anti-Castro diatribe. In *Hablemos La Misma Lengua*, Estefan proposes that Cubans, Puerto Ricans, Mexicans, Colombians, Dominicans, and so on, bury their differences.

In 1995, Gloria Estefan scored again with *Abriendo Puertas*, an album in which Colombian producer/songwriter Kike Santander figured heavily. Taking the cue from the inroads made by Colombian pop star Carlos Vives (see Chapter 8), who updated vallenato, a traditional Colombian style, into pop, the Estefans once again reinvented themselves. They also moved into a period in which they would seemingly appear at almost every music business award ceremony and Gloria would attain the status (if not musical stature) of divas like Whitney Houston, Aretha Franklin, and Chaka Khan. The Estefan style, as perfected in Emilio's Crescent Moon studios, which he constructed in Miami in 1998, dominated the production of Latin pop, and most of the big names clamored to be recorded there.

As the 1990s gave way to a new century, the Estefans faced a little adversity. They were abandoned by one of their big projects of the future, Shakira, and they faced lawsuits from former collaborators Willie Chirino and Kike Santander for allegedly stealing their songs by taking a writing credit or even a production credit when not applicable. They also announced a boycott of the 2001 Latin Grammy Awards (which were ultimately canceled because of the World Trade Center Attacks) when the show moved out of Miami to Los Angeles at the last minute. But by 2002, the suits had been settled out of court, a new album by their protégé Jon Secada was selling well, and Gloria served as co-host of the 2002 Latin Grammys.

Luís Miguel

Mexican pop had long been dominated by singers who in some way referenced regional ranchera/mariachi traditions, like Vicente Fernández, Juan Gabriel, and Rocio Durcál. Seemingly always dressed in ranch-style attire, Fernández, along with his son Alejandro, is the central figure in popular ranchera. Rocio Durcál leans more toward boleros but is most fondly remembered for traditional rancheras, and Juan Gabriel is a kind of Renaissance man who combines many Latin pop genres. But the new, Miami Latin pop scene that was in large part created by Cuban exiles, especially the Estefans, created an ambience and an infrastructure—major labels set up offices there—for the emergence of a megastar like Mexico's Luís Miguel.

Miguel by 2003 was the most powerful long-reigning Mexican pop star, sporting good looks and possessing a strong enough voice to entrance large crowds. Though most of his records recycle up-tempo lounge tunes and lush ballads, Miguel's move in 1991 to collaborate with the master composer of modern bolero, the Mexican Armando Manzanero, on the CD *Romance* almost singlehandedly revived interest in the bolero. Beyond merely being a revival, *Romance* and its 1994 follow-up, *Segundo Romance*, was a significant update of the genre, using the high-production values established by the Miami renaissance. In addition to Manzanero classics like *Te Extraño* and *Somos Novios*, the *Romance* series of CDs (including 1997's *Romances* and 2001's *Mis Romances*) featured a series of classic boleros. These included *Inolvidable* by Julio Gutiérrez, a Cuban; *Contigo en la Distancia*, by César Portillo de la Luz, another Cuban; and the Mexican bolerista Luís Demetrio's *La Puerta*.

Miguel's revival of Armando Manzanero brought to light an overlooked master of the genre. Born in Mérida, Mexico, in 1935, Manzanero studied at the Bellas Artes conservatory of his home town. After moving to Mexico City in 1957, he became the pianist for artists like Chilean bolero master Lucho Gática and the Mexican singer/composer Luís Demetrio, and he also worked with Bobby Capó. Over his forty-year career he wrote more than 400 songs, most famously *Somos Novios*, which was remade in English as *Impossible* by American crooner Perry Como.

Miguel's main rivals for international Latin pop stardom are the Venezuelan-born Alejandro Montaner and Alejandro Sanz from Spain. Born in Argentina in 1957, Montaner was raised in Caracas, Venezuela, where he sang in a church choir and became a drummer in a rock group called Scala. Montaner sings in a light tenor and uses standard pop instrumentation, often employing a string section to heighten his emotional impact. He brings a kind of country-ish feel to his singing, maintaining a posture of innocence rather than adopting Miguel's winner-take-all strategy. He first rose to prominence in the early 1990s with a series of albums for Polygram, and he won a major award at Chile's Viña del Mar festival, a major event in the world of Latin pop. In 1999, he put out *Con la Metropolitan London Orchestra*, but Montaner tends to stick to simplicity. His 2002 *Suma*, a collaboration with pianist/arranger Bebu Silvetti, is a tribute to the bolero style with all original songs, a landmark in the bolero revival that Luís Miguel began.

As the end of the 1990s approached, the Latin pop scene was dominated by a style that had been steadily incorporating American and European influences—more and more non-Spanish-speaking singers like the Italian Eros Ramazotti and the French Canadian Celine Dion were recording in Spanish, since their song formulas easily translated into the Latin market.

Spain's Alejandro Sanz is one of the few vocalists on the Latin pop scene who can claim the integrity of a singer/songwriter. While his arrangements are typically pop lite, and he appeals to Latin pop tastes, his songs have more impact because he composes them himself. Not surprisingly, there is a strong flamenco undercurrent in his work. Sanz was born in Madrid in 1968 to parents from Cádiz, the Andalusian capital, which is a major center for flamenco. He began composing at age ten, and, a rebellious child, he was singing on the streets by the time he was a teenager. His education in the school of hard knocks of Madrid's flamenco scene was augmented by tutelage under guitarist Miguel Angel Ardenas.

Sanz uses a more sophisticated instrumentation than many of his peers, incorporating the jazz-rock flair of fellow Spaniard Presuntos Implicados. His breakthrough album, *Más* (released in 1997, his fourth for WEA Latina), established Sanz's brand of pop, in which flamenco, although not conspicuously, is lurking in the soul of the synthesizers. Songs like *Y Si Fuera Ella?* and *Corazón Partido* transmitted the usual bolero sentiment of love out of man's control.

Using revved-up electric guitar solos, Sanz has always included a touch of hard-rock kick in his songs, giving him further youth credibility. His follow-up album of 2001, *El Alma al Aire*, lacked *Más*'s instant classic feeling, but his raspy, emotive voice was still in top form, and his backing band was as clean and crisp as ever. By 2002, with his *MTV Unplugged* album sweeping the Latin Grammy awards, Sanz stood as the most powerful artist in Latin pop. His duet with R&B group Destiny's Child, broadcast on the 2002 Grammys, was a testament to his growing popularity and influence.

The Latin Pop Explosion

In the mid-1990s in the United States, young pop idols like Enrique Iglesias, Ricky Martin, and Puerto Rican pop singer Chayanne, as well as some Mexican regional stars like the late Selena and La Mafia, were building up huge followings. The Latin music world was focused around Miami, where most of the major labels set up offices, and where the Estefans were waiting and ready to serve as power brokers and executive producers for a new crop of stars who would appeal to a mainstream audience. In 1998, Ricky Martin, who had been building momentum both abroad and in the United States with a series of international hits and appearances on U.S. soap operas and the Broadway stage, broke through with a memorable performance during the telecast of the mainstream Grammy awards.

Martin rose to the top of his profession despite the fact that for most of his career, his biggest fans were Latin American teeny boppers who didn't constitute the bread and butter of the Latin music industry. Born Enrique Martin Morales in 1971 and raised in middle-class, suburban San Juan, Puerto Rico, Martin became a child star in Menudo, a group of teen pop singers that predated U.S. groups like New Edition and New Kids on the Block.

Slightly younger and smaller than the rest of his Menudo com-
pañeros, he was a kind of Michael Jackson figure, dominating the
group with star presence. With Menudo, he was able to tour the
world and learn about the fast life and treachery of show business.
The group had a strong run during Martin's tenure, but following
Martin's departure, it was plagued by rumors of sexual molestation
of group members by a Menudo manager, Edgardo Díaz. This
scandal would become the root of the constant obsession by the
media about Martin's sexual preference.

Perhaps the most important thing Martin got from those years
with Menudo was his friendship with fellow singer Robi Rosa.
Rosa was raised mostly in a New York suburb on Long Island, but
he moved to Puerto Rico in early adolescence and pestered his
way into a writing and arranging role with Menudo, ultimately becoming one of its most popular members. Rosa grew up to star in
a shlocky *Dirty Dancing* remake about Latin dancing called *Salsa*—
his dancing was so good he seemed destined for a career like rival
boy-band leader Chayanne. But Rosa desperately wanted to be a
rock star in the mode of Jimi Hendrix or Lenny Kravitz. He covered his body with tattoos, became a heroin addict, and wrote incredibly dark, goth-laced songs based on Rimbaud poems. When
Ricky Martin went through his Broadway-play, then soap-opera
internship (*Les Miserables, General Hospital*) in New York and was
ready to start a new recording career, he called Robi Rosa.

Although he's often criticized for being a typical lite-pop Latin
singer, Martin, with the help of his songwriter and co-producer
Rosa (often credited as Ian Blake), actually explored the flamenco-
based rhythms that have livened the pop-bolero genre. He also experimented with harder rock sounds. His albums *Me Amarás* (You
Will Love Me) in 1993, *A Medio Vivir* (Half-Lived) in 1995, and
Vuelve (Return) in 1998 each contributed to his evolving contemporary sound. The albums perfected his formula of increasingly
incorporating rock embellishments, while Rosa's composing ability added power to his ballads. Still, the root of Martin's success

was Rosa's constant reworking of similar musical themes in his hit songs. *María* on *A Medio Vivir* begat *The Cup of Life* on *Vuelve*, culminating in his English/Spanish crossover breakthrough *Livin' La Vida Loca* in May 1999.

The self-titled English-language debut album was a lot more than just *Livin' La Vida Loca*—it featured some further examples of flamenco pop, such as *Spanish Eyes*. *Be Careful*, the duet with Madonna, could legitimately be considered edgy, largely because of Rosa's quirky pop and rockabilly/funk arrangements. The title song itself perfectly captured the natural Latin rock affinity for ska, the upbeat style of calypso music born in Jamaica in the 1960s and adopted by British punk rockers in the late 1970s, as well as a kind of polished adolescent idea of sexual adventurism. The double message of the song is implied because of the popular usage of the word *loca* in Latino slang for gay man (literally means "crazy woman").

Perhaps because of the rush to put Martin's follow-up album out, and perhaps because of Rosa's diminishing participation in the studio, *Sound Loaded* (2000) was a classic example of rehash. It may be that Ricky Martin will be a flash in the pan in English, but he is a formidable live musician who, unlike many of his Latin pop contemporaries, insists on using heavy African beats (like Brazilian samba) and traditional Puerto Rican bomba and plena in his live performances. Behind the apparent bland superficiality, Martin's music moves forward both the Latin ballad and the world pop sound.

In 2003, Martin returned with the Spanish-language *Alma del Silencio*. As was widely reported, Martin had already recorded over thirty songs in English for a new album but suddenly decided that he had to go back to his roots. *Almas del Silencio* consistently displayed a preoccupation with Afro-Caribbean rhythms and the prominent use of folkloric drums, whether on the pseudo-vallenato of *Besos de Fuego*, the bomba and plena of *Raza de Mil Colores*, or the mutant samba of *Si Ya No Estás Aquí*. Martin's ballads proved that sentimental froth makes much more sense in a Romance language. "Maybe I never gave you what you hoped for/And I wasn't there when you needed me," Martin intoned apologetically on *Tal Vez.* "Maybe I forgot that I loved you." With *Almas del Silencio,* a love letter to the language and the culture of the millions of Spanish-speaking fans that first made him a star, Ricky Martin appeared to have made amends.

Enrique Iglesias, son of the world-famous Julio, doesn't have the charisma and vocal depth of his father but he does have the trademark trills, and the Latin-pop ear candy he manufactures is not really based on his father's work. With a little higher pitch to his tenor than Julio, he is influenced more by soul and Euro-pop than bolero. In 1999 he joined the Latin Explosion with his debut English album, *Enrique.* Songs like *Bailamos* and *Rhythm Divine,* while sounding suspiciously alike, nonetheless charmed their way to the top of the charts, and Iglesias struck an appealing pose for MTV, assuring his success.

Born in 1975 in Madrid and raised in Miami, Enrique exemplifies the Latin pop trends that dominate his era, capitalizing on sophisticated recording studio techniques and increased use of disco and Latin rhythms. Like Martin and Marc Anthony, Iglesias labored in front of swarms of Latin American fans (including packed houses of screaming Latinas in arenas across the United States), beginning in the mid-1990s, to build a following.

In a live show at Madison Square Garden in 1999, Iglesias cleverly deflected charges of nepotism, by insisting he was a Cinderella story when introducing *Si Tú Te Vas,* his smash single, which was at first rejected by several know-nothing record companies. His defenders point out that unlike Luís Miguel, Iglesias has written about half of his recorded oeuvre, and his voice does manage to carry rooms as big as the Garden. With 2002's *Quizás,* Iglesias returned to the emotion-wrought style of mainstream Latin pop, albeit continuing to incorporate influences from electronica and trip hop.

Colombian-bred pop-rocker Shakira is blessed with an explosive, emotion-charged voice that expresses the feelings of a new generation of Latin American youth. Her 1998 breakthrough with the album *¿Dónde Están Los Ladrones?* (Where Are the Thieves?) has positioned her to play a major role in the recent renaissance of Latin pop. But compared to the sugary style usually associated with the genre, Shakira is a fiery bird of a different color. She has a harder rock edge, and she writes poetic and philosophical lyrics that dig way below the surface of pop glitter.

Born in 1977 in coastal Barranquilla, Colombia, the daughter of Lebanese parents, Shakira has been bent on conquering the world through music since early childhood, when she entered singing contests in radio and television. Her father, William Mebarak, a jewelry salesman, instilled in her the desire to read (in interviews she lavishes praise on novelist Gabriel García Márquez and New Age guru Brian Weiss), and the cultural drive to perform the ancestral art of *la danza árabe*, an Arabic dance form that gives her performances a Middle Eastern feel. The Mebaraks were part of a small but influential Lebanese community in Barranquilla, which not only retains its Arabic cultural roots but also takes an important role in the city's yearly carnival celebrations. At age thirteen, Shakira signed her first recording contract with Sony Music Colombia, and in 1991 she released her first album *Mágia*, which included songs she had been writing since age eight.

Shakira's effervescence and headstrong persona won the attention of the Colombian public. After graduating from secondary school, she decided to dedicate her life to music, recording *Peligro* (Danger) in 1993 and *Piés Descalzos* (Bare Feet) in 1995. With the latter album, Shakira broke through to Latin America, Spain, and the Spanish-speaking United States by establishing her folky, down-to-earth, neo-hippie style, refusing to dress like a fashion model, and writing songs that reflected idealism rather than shallow love ballads. While there are elements of reggae, Colombian folk music, and the pop ballad in her work, and some of her songs are reminiscent of the Cuban nueva trova era of the 1970s, Shakira is one the first Latin pop stars to market herself primarily as a rocker. The songs on *Piés Descalzos*, co-written by Shakira and Luís Ochoa, are nuggets of wisdom that capture the attitudes of Latin America's student-age youth.

Performing with standard rock instrumentation and relying on simple guitar riffs, Shakira uses her highly flexible vocal range to infuse her melancholic love songs with an unusual power. Songs like *Pienso en Tí* (I Think of You) and *Te Necesito* (I Need You) have a haunting, elegiac quality. *Un Poco de Amor* (A Little Bit of Love) is a rollicking celebration of reggae's reach beyond Jamaica, and the title track brings you into the mental state of idealistic Latin youth: "You belong to an ancient race of barefoot people/And now you just want to be happy." The album sold millions of copies and made Shakira the youngest and most promising Latin-American star of the 1990s.

Shakira's next album, *¿Dónde Están Los Ladrones?* (1998), fulfilled the promise of her earlier works. The album's title refers to the theft of all the sheet music for a CD's worth of songs in Bogotá's airport, which forced Shakira to come up with new material from scratch. Hard-hitting, well-crafted songs like *Ciega, Sordomuda* (Blind, Deaf, and Dumb), *Tú* (You), *Inevitable*, and *Ojos Así* (Eyes Like That)—the latter is sung in Arabic and features Middle Eastern instrumentation—captured the imagination of the international market, producing strong sales in both Latin America and the United States.

Shakira's first English-dominated album, *Laundry Service* (2001) may be the first successful translation of a young Latin American sensibility into viable English-language songs. While Ricky Martin had to rely on Robi Rosa's eccentric pop concoctions, and

Marc Anthony employed bland pop songwriters for his material, Shakira actually learned English well enough to express her idiosyncratic self. On ballads like *Underneath Your Clothes* she proclaimed, "You're a song/written by the hands of God," and on *The One* she intimated, "I have a reason to shave my legs/Each single morning." Shakira's freshness is a welcome departure from Latin pop's mindless staleness, but it remains to be seen whether she can hold her own against the numerous rap and R&B divas who go much further. Despite her Arabic and Latin American background, she also displays a strong preference for 1980s hard rock (even performing Aerosmith and AC/DC covers in her live shows) over more modern rock-rap-pop formats.

While Jennifer Lopez, born in the Bronx in 1970, doesn't make what most would consider Latin music, or Latin pop, she is unapologetic about her Puerto Rican roots, and she recorded a salsa track with Marc Anthony, *No Me Ames* (Don't Love Me), that is more than just competent. With a voice that shows flashes of intensity when it isn't just cooing to state-of-the-art production, Lopez seems to be going for the "just another girl from the block" approach that serves her well as an actor. Lopez's music, as demonstrated on her debut, *On the 6, J-Lo,* and *This Is Me . . . Then* is an eclectic blend of the musical influences she had growing up in the Bronx. R&B, hip-hop, rock, house music, and salsa all seep into Lopez's songs, which are co-written with professional R&B songwriters like Corey Rooney.

By singing mostly in English, Lopez expresses a Nuyorican point of view—she turns to salsa and falls for the romantic innocence of it, as in *No Me Ames,* and she strongly identifies with hip-hop, as on her collaborations with rappers Fat Joe, Ja Rule, and Jadakiss. Lopez created a small controversy by using the word *nigger* on *I'm Real* from *J-Lo,* which drew the ire of some African-Americans, but few commentators acknowledged that being Puerto Rican implies at least partial African ancestry and being Nuyorican often implies African-American socialization. Lopez's music is in many ways no different from the eclectic experiments of Latin alternative musicians. It's just her chosen language and the fact that she can be indistinguishable from a black pop singer that keep her from being identified with her Latino and Latin American peers.

As one of the biggest entertainment stars in the world, Lopez has timed new albums to be released simultaneously with her movies: In 2001, *J-Lo* was released in tandem with *The Wedding Planner*, and in 2002, she released *This is Me . . . Then* in conjunction with the movie *Maid in Manhattan*. Lopez continues working within her formula, mixing ballads (which her voice doesn't carry particularly well) with up-tempo dance numbers and hip-hop duets with famous rappers. *All I Have*, with L. L. Cool J, is not as winning as *Jenny from the Block*, which coincided with a massive publicity campaign about Lopez's going back to her ancestral home of the northeast Bronx. Lopez's strongest suit is selecting songs that reflect her varied tastes, and her presentation is just good enough to keep fans taking her seriously.

With *Mi Reflejo*, released in 2000, teen R&B diva Christina Aguilera conquered the reverse crossover, placing her high on the Billboard Latin Music charts and on video channels in Latin America, endearing herself to Latinas looking northward for soulful inspiration. Born in 1980 in Staten Island, New York, she was raised in Wexford, Pennsylvania, and at age six began performing in talent shows. By the time she was twelve, she was a regular on the Mickey Mouse Club with future teen stars Justin Timberlake and Britney Spears. Aguilera, who is half-Ecuadorian, drew on her Latin roots by recording *Mi Reflejo* (2000), a Spanish-language version of her eponymously titled debut album, just a year after the first album's release. Aguilera draws largely on influences like Mariah Carey and Whitney Houston, but when tackling the bolero, she adds an R&B flavor.

Spanish remakes of Aguilera hits (written by professional song-writers) like *Come on Over*, *I Turn to You*, and *Genie in a Bottle*, seemed to mature in the translation. With the help of heavyweight Latin pop producer Rudy Pérez, Aguilera gives an exhilarating shot in the arm to flamenco ballad on *El Beso del Final*, and com-mands a rousing salsa stomp in *Cuando No Es Contigo*.

Aguilera has a feel for the Spanish language and the rhythms, even the sentimentality, and that should keep her making records in Spanish for the rest of her career. Her incorporation of R&B in-fluences to boleros like *Contigo en la Distancia* and Giraldo Piloto's *Falsas Esperanzas* feels like a revisit to Cuban filin, except instead of Latinos discovering jazz and R&B, it's an R&B singer discovering Latin music.

Latin Pop Rock

Since the 1950s Mexico has been a primary breeding ground for both pop-rock and rock artists. As Chapter 10 will discuss further, Mexico has a strangely contradictory relationship with rock music. Mexico was probably the first Latin American country to have rock bands. Then, in the mid-'70s, rock was virtually banned in Mexico by a conservative government. Perhaps embodying this split between embracing rock and rejecting it is Mexico's current crop of female pop singers who perform a watered-down pop rock and try to pass themselves off as rock artists.

One of the earliest Mexican rock babes is the scandal-ridden Gloria Trevi, who seduced Mexican audiences in the late '80s and early '90s with a transparent imitation of Madonna, replete with ripped stockings and displays of undergarments and cleavage. Alejandra Guzmán followed in Trevi's footsteps, evoking an un-controllably libidinous cantina creature who reflects the lust of tequila-soaked machos. More recently, former Sony executive and Latin pop mogul Tommy Mottola's new wife, Thalía Sodí, has been flirting with Latin dance, pop, and rock stardom. Her 2001 album, *Banda*, gives the regional northern Mexican music banda a superficial nod, while sticking to Euro-disco and rock conventions to smooth her path to the top of the charts. Her 2002 self-titled album featured three English-language tracks, attempting to reach a broader audience, but her collaboration with new pop production whiz Estefano gave the Spanish songs a stronger, more modern appeal.

A more recent contender for the Mexican rock babe throne is the aptly named Paulina Rubio—her last name describes the color of her tinted blonde hair. Rubio, whose vixen-playing is certainly her strength, was a member of the same teen rock band (parallel to the Mickey Mouse Club) called Timbiriche that spawned Thalía. Her self-titled breakthrough album begins with the guitar screeches of *Lo Hare Por Tí*, but she soon decelerates to ballad tempo for *Tal Vez, Quizá*. *Y Yo Sigo Aquí*, her hit single, follows the Europop-inspired vocoder-distorted vocal trend that dominates European music, pulsing along with a Latinized house rhythm. Rubino's voice is pleasant enough, and she does avoid the trashy excesses of her predecessors, but it remains to be seen if she will cross over with English-language albums. In 2002, Rubio released a mostly English-language album, *Border Girl*, which got her a lot of attention but broke little new ground, falling short of the stardom bestowed on Shakira after her *Laundry Service*.

The Mexican band Maná had been around since the beginning of the Mexican rock wave of the early 1990s, having appeared in the United States alongside much more progressive groups like Café Tacuba. Formed in Mexico City in 1985 by lead singer and Guadalajara native Fher and Colombian/Cuban drummer Alex González, Maná began by playing small clubs, and released its first album in 1992. While anchored by a competent rhythm section led by González and the guitar work of Cesar López (now with

Jaguares), Maná came off as Police imitators to the critics, even though it developed a huge fan base. At times Maná's songwriting (mostly done by Fher and González) was inspired, and the group's commitment to the environment, as demonstrated on *Dónde Jugarán Los Niños?* (Where Will the Children Play?), and Fher's earnest vocals endeared them to a considerably large base of fans. *Revolución de Amor*, released in 2002, emphasized more powerful guitar solos from Sergio Vallín, the anthems *Justicia, Tierra, y Libertad* and *Angel de Amor*, as well as guest appearances by Rubén Blades on *Sábanas Frías* and Carlos Santana on *Justícia, Tierra, y Libertád*. The album and subsequent tour proved to be one of the strongest moments of the year for Latin pop rock.

Founded as a five-piece band in Santiago, Chile, in 1988, La Ley—a trio composed, in 2003, of Beto Cuevas on vocals, Mauricio Clavería on percussion, and Pedro Frugone on guitars—became one of Chile's biggest selling bands, staking a place as pioneers of the Latin rock movement. The band relocated to Mexico in the early '90s to take advantage of Mexico City's platform for rock acts, and immediately achieved great success and a Pepsi commercial contract.

The members of La Ley are survivors, managing to stay together despite the tragic death of their former lead guitarist, Andrés Bobe, in a motorcycle accident in 1994. A few years later, they also withstood the untimely desertion over creative differences of their bassist, Luciano Roja, hours before they were to play before a crowd of 30,000 in Mexico City. Strongly influenced by the New Romantic modern rock movement that caught fire in England in the mid-'80s, La Ley makes music with the kind of soaring keyboard lines and electric intensity that marked bands like Duran Duran, Depeche Mode, and the Pet Shop Boys. Bobe's presence was strongly felt on their debut *Doble Opuesto* (1992), but all of 1995's *Invisible* was written by collaborator/producer Alfredo Gática.

On the group's albums *Vertigo* (1998) and *Uno* (2000), La Ley seems to be withdrawing from electronic influences and concentrating more on songwriting, a good idea, since Cuevas can hold his own with a guitar and a microphone. Still, while La Ley is considered by many to be a true Latin alternative band, the turn taken over the last few albums indicates that the music seems better categorized as pop. Firmly establishing the new direction, Beto Cuevas became the band's central force on *La Ley Unplugged*, released in 2001. From the gentle explosion of the first track *Animal*, through *El Duelo*, his haunting duet with special guest, Mexican rocker Ely Guerra, Cuevas gave the performance of his life. The *Unplugged* format seems to help, allowing the well-crafted essence of La Ley to be front and center and not buried in a storm of pompous synthesizers.

The bolero, while not always a strict formal influence in lyrical meter or musical rhythm, survives today as an essential element of the emotional and melodic power in Latin pop. As of this writing there has been no great infusion of new blood in Latin pop since the 1998 pop explosion. Ricky Martin has returned with a strong Spanish-language album; Enrique Iglesias scored considerable success with an English-language crossover, *Escape* (2001), and his return to Spanish in *Quizás* (2002); and newer pop stars like Cristian Castro and Estefan-protégé Alexandre Pires, from Brazil, have made a strong showing. The pop landscape is also dotted by several salsa singers, such as Puerto Ricans Luis Fonsi and Frankie Negrón and Colombian-born Carolina Laó, who have abandoned their dance sound for simpler pop rhythms and greater commercial success. Latin alternative bands like Aterciopelados, from Colombia, and Gustavo Cerati, the lead singer from the legendary Argentine rock band Soda Stereo, have fiddled with a fusion of electronica with the bolero. As long as there is a singer with a feel for the epic romance of Spain and the hot passion of Havana, the bolero will never die.

The Latin alternative field, discussed in Chapter 10, has also produced some compelling songwriters, such as the Tijuana-border product Julieta Venegas, whose ranchera- and bolero-influenced message is a little abstract at times, or Juanes, whose Colombian folkloric rock tells the story of the scary reality of the modern-day Colombian. French/Spanish Manu Chao lives a vagabond existence traveling from Spain to Latin America as a modern-day troubadour, trying to evoke the narrative of the Latin American migrant, as he does in songs like *Clandestino*, which laments the fate of someone without a visa or other documentation.

It will be interesting to see whether Dominican bachata's wild rise in popularity in the last few years becomes the latest form of the Latin ballad. While much of the genre's recent output has gone the pop route, an artist like Zacarías Ferreira makes the case for continuing the tradition's true poetic intentions. The tradition of storytelling remains strong in Latin American music, and the simple presence of a musician performing with just a guitar and a well-crafted song is something that seems essential to the Latin American soul.

•6•

Latin Jazz

When the brilliant Cuban jazzman Mario Bauzá introduced Dizzy Gillespie and Charlie Parker to the syncopated rhythms of his native island, he started a debate that has never been settled. What is Latin jazz? Is it jazz driven by Latin 6/8 rhythms, or can it be Latin music played with jazz arrangements or instrumental technique? Is it a great Latin band, led by the likes of Tito Puente, Eddie Palmieri, or Ray Barretto, improvising as if they were Count Basie? Or is it jazz musicians like the brilliant bassist Charlie Haden or the young saxophonist David Sánchez reinterpreting Latin music from a jazz perspective?

Many Latin jazz musicians dislike the term Latin jazz because they feel it dilutes the fact that they are playing jazz at the highest level. The prefix "Latin," especially in the mass record market, can automatically connote "lite" or "frivolous," or perhaps "danceable." But marketing considerations aside, the Latin inflection, usually taken from son structures or other forms of Afro-Cuban percussion, makes Latin jazz unmistakable. In some ways Latin jazz is more African than African-American—the rhythms, and at times the melodies and harmonies, are closer to the source, less tied to the melodic and rhythmic structure of American popular music. Starting with the collaboration between Dizzy Gillespie and Mario Bauzá in the 1940s, Latin jazz is strongly tied to Latin big band music, which is intended for dancing. Through its dance aspect it is also connected to the popular landscape in a way mainstream jazz isn't anymore.

The stereotypical idea of Latin jazz is jazz top, Latin bottom, referring to the jazz riffing techniques employed by horn players, played over a typically complex Latin percussion arrangement. Over time, the worlds of Latin music and jazz have become so intermeshed that the realm of Latin jazz has grown beyond its previous boundaries—jazz's status as music of the African diaspora has led Latin musicians to explore African influences apart from Cuba, and even the Caribbean.

Most of the central figures of Latin jazz started out playing jazz-influenced Afro-Cuban dance music. The musical skill that enabled them to handle the complexity of that popular music, as well as their admiration for legendary figures of bebop and beyond, drew them to jazz. In the post-big band era, dance music was no longer considered jazz. New York players, such as flutist Dave Valentín, a Tito Puente alumni, pianist Hilton Ruiz, and bassist Andy González searched for other opportunities to play serious music that would be considered on par with the jazz musicians they admired. Others, like saxophonist David Sánchez, pianist Danilo Pérez, and percussionist Giovanni Hidalgo, came to the Northeast from Puerto Rico and the Dominican Republic in the early 1990s to study jazz at places like Rutgers University and the Berklee School of Music and to play with the Dizzy Gillespie Orchestra, taking part in the last historical link to the Bauzá-Gillespie-Parker days. Cuban exiles such as trumpeter Arturo Sandovál and Paquito D'Rivera played a popular music at such a high level that they considered themselves serious musicians before they got to New York, but wanted a chance to play jazz, which was considered capitalist decadence in Cuba.

In *Latin Jazz*, John Storm Roberts documented the absorption, by pianists such as Jelly Roll Morton and Scott Joplin, of what Morton called "The Latin Tinge." This occurred through interchanges they had with Cuban and Mexican musicians in New Orleans in the late nineteenth and early twentieth century. The piano in Latin music acts as a percussive instrument, incorporating the hypnotically repetitive rhythmic figures, or bass patterns, called tumbaos. The Latin jazz pianist, in conjunction with the rhythm section, establishes the Latin rhythmic structure of a song with one hand, and the other hand is free to engage in improvisation. Pianists have always been key players in Latin jazz: Think of Chucho Valdés, Hilton Ruiz, Danilo Pérez, Michel Camilo, Gonzalo Rubalcaba, and salsa/mambo big band crossover artist Eddie Palmieri.

The roots of Latin jazz were firmly planted in New York through a transplanted Cuban bandleader, Don Azpiazu, in 1930 with *El Manicero* (The Peanut Vendor), a song covered by Duke Ellington in 1931, Gonzalo Rubulcaba in 2002, and many others in between. Ellington's jazz reinterpretation of what may have been the first Afro-Cuban popular song in North America was a working model for the essential dynamic of Latin jazz. But the cross-referencing of the two genres didn't become a true hybrid until the genre we have come to know as Latin jazz was "invented" in the 1940s. The Gillespie and Machito Orchestra's instant classics *Afro-Cuban Jazz Suite*, *Tangá*, and *The Manteca Suite* (co-written by Gillespie, Chico O'Farríll, and Chano Pozo), all recorded between 1943 and 1950, may have been dance music, but their incorporation of jazz instrumentation and technique made them Latin jazz. The Gillespie composition *A Night in Tunisia* was the first conventional jazz hit to incorporate Latin melodic themes and percussion, coalescing the idea of the jazz melody strongly influenced by a Latin rhythm section.

Luciano "Chano" Pozo also had a tremendous effect on Machito and Dizzy Gillespie. The man who introduced conga to the jazz orchestra, Pozo was an improvisational genius on his instrument, and also composed a number of songs. Born in 1915 in Havana, he moved to New York in 1946, where he became an indispensable interpreter of the syncopation Gillespie was grasping for in tunes like *A Night in Tunisia*. According to Isabelle Leymaire's *Cuban Fire*, "The Cuban concept of the downbeat differs radically from the jazz one. The strong accent of the clave, called 'bombó' . . . falls on the second quarter note of the second bar, and Cuban percussionists tend to think of this beat, rather than the first one of the first bar of the clave, as the one that really starts the musical phrase." Gillespie felt that Pozo "beeped" instead of "bopping," but eventually Pozo taught Dizzy's band how to attain a true Afro-Cuban feel.

Another bridge from the mainstream to the Latin jazz fields was trumpeter Arturo "Chico" O'Farríll. Originally a Hotel Tropicana musician in Havana, O'Farríll came to New York in 1948 and went on to work with Benny Goodman, Machito, Dizzy Gillespie, and Count Basie. He was commissioned as arranger of the *Afro-Cuban Jazz Suite* and became an integral part of the Machito and Gillespie bands.

While the Machito Orchestra was more identified with the compositional grandeur of Duke Ellington, Tito Puente's was perhaps more analogous to Count Basie's. Riff-oriented, percussion-heavy, Puente's band was more prone to improvisation and to allowing rhythmic progression to determine where the night was going. It may have been Puente's origins as a dancer that solidified his percussive approach—this drawing from the rhythmic impulses of dancing has been referenced again and again by contemporary Latin jazz musicians. While Thelonius Monk was known to stand up from his piano seat, do a little hokey-pokey turn, and sit back down, Puente was envisioning the complex dance pattern of a mambo, guaguancó, or a cha-cha in his head and allowing it to take over the direction of his drumming.

The Tito Puente band had a great impact on the course of Latin jazz during his RCA recording days (from 1949 to 1951 and 1955 to 1960). As deep as Puente's love for traditional Afro-Cuban and even

African music was, he was strongly influenced by, and deeply caught up in, the big band jazz world. The most important thing to remember about Puente's music, a point also essential to understanding Latin jazz, is that his traditional style—the big Latin dance band—was playing "jazz" music, at least the branch of jazz begun by the Cubop fusion of the 1940s. When Puente released albums like *Puente Goes Jazz* and collaborated with "straight" jazz performers like Woody Herman and Stan Kenton, he wasn't changing styles— his big band style is a complementary branch of jazz. Kenton shared a conga player with Puente's band, Cuban émigré Patato Valdez, who would become a legendary figure of the genre.

Sometimes, George Shearing's band, another popular jazz big band on the New York scene after World War II, shared bills with bands like Machito's. According to Roberts' *Latin Jazz*, Shearing's interest in Latin music began when his band played opposite Machito in 1949, but he didn't actually form a Latin jazz group until 1953, when he featured vibraphonist Cal Tjader, as well as percussionists Willie Bobo and Mongo Santamaría. That trio of musicians soon became key players in the birth of the West Coast Latin jazz scene when they moved to Los Angeles in the late 1950s. Tjader united these players with an Italian-American pianist well schooled in the Cuban sound, Vince Guaraldi (perhaps most famous for composing the animated *Peanuts* TV soundtracks), and in 1954 recorded *Ritmo Caliente*, probably the first Latin jazz album from the West Coast. The mellowness of Tjader's vibes not only evoked California but also softened the brass-and-reeds intensity of the mambo orchestras. Tjader's bands had long-lasting impact on a generation of players, but it was above all his congero, Mongo Santamaría, who left an enormous legacy to Latin jazz, not to mention soul, pop, and rhythm and blues.

On talent and performance alone, Mongo Santamaría could be the most important Cuban percussionist of his time. With Cal Tjader, he pioneered the West Coast jazz-Latin fusion that influenced everything in pop music from bossa nova to Santana and the Doors. Born in 1922 in the rumba epicenter of Jesús María, a predominantly Afro-Cuban neighborhood of Havana, Mongo Santamaría began playing drums almost as soon as he could walk. By the time he was a teenager, he had flirted with the violin, but decided to focus entirely on the large, bass-sounding tumbadora, the compact bongó, and the snare-like timbál, all Afro-Cuban drums. His apprenticeship in Cuba was mostly administered at the famous Tropicana Club, under the tutelage of musical director Bebo Valdés. Like Pérez Prado, whom he played with briefly, Santamaría took off for Mexico City, but he came to New York in 1950 and wound up playing with the George Shearing Band and then Tito Puente. After recording six albums with Puente, he embarked on a solo career in 1955 with a record called *Changó*.

In the late 1950s he moved to Los Angeles, and in 1957 he teamed up with fellow percussionist Willie Bobo and Cal Tjader to record *Más Ritmo Caliente*, a follow-up to the already classic *Ritmo Caliente*. In 1959, he jump-started his solo career with a self-titled effort for the San Francisco-based Fantasy label. The album included his most famous composition, *Afro-Blue*, which became a jazz standard that was one of John Coltrane's favorites. Over the next several albums of his career, Santamaría gradually incorporated Yoruban ritual instruments like the chékere and the batá drums into jazz for the first time.

In the early '60s, Santamaría formed a new band that included the young keyboardist Chick Corea and helped make Herbie Hancock's *Watermelon Man* a jazz standard. Mongo Santamaría's opening beats on *Watermelon Man* are as distinctive and awe-inspiring as any laid down by a conga player in the history of recorded music. When he is joined by Hancock's grooving piano and a teasing horn section, you can hear a whole new style coming into being. The Cuban-jazz hybrid that Santamaría pioneered was a little heavier on the blues than its predecessors. The result was an easygoing, R&B/jazz signature that became the soundtrack for countless hipster gatherings and gave a whole new meaning to jazz and Latin.

Mongo also collaborated with the wild bolero singer La Lupe, saxophonists Nat Adderly and Stanley Turrentine, and Israel "Cachao" López. In the '70s he began recording for salsa impresario Jerry Masucci and made several salsa-tinged records. In records for various labels through the 1980s and 1990s, he played with talents like Michel Camilo, Hilton Ruiz, percussionist Poncho Sánchez, and Tito Puente. His 1962 classic *Watermelon Man* typifies Santamaría's straddling of Latin and R&B and was a precursor to bugaloo. On a song like *Bayou Roots* he mixed a bebop saxophone solo with a typical Latin piano figure, with Mongo's percussion section motoring into ecstatic heights. *Yeh, Yeh* has a classic hook that ultimately became a rock-and-roll hit for the '60s British invasion group Georgie Fame and the Blue Flames. The band, which includes trumpeter Marty Sheller, does an updated version of *El Manicero* and fleshes out Santamaría's fusion style on *The Boogie Cha Cha Blues.* Also striking are Rene Martínez's piano solo and appearances on various tracks by legends Willie Bobo on timbales and José "Chombo" Silva on saxophone. On the title track, written by Herbie Hancock, you can hear, if you listen closely, La Lupe giggling, "That's right, baby."

The Brazilian Factor

Latin jazz fusions began to yield new forms as the 1950s morphed into the 1960s, and North American pop music and jazz continued to flourish. Bossa nova, a jazz-influenced update of the Brazilian samba (see Chapter 7) had a central compositional genius, Antonio Carlos Jobim, who was influenced by the songcraft of several styles of North American music, including Cole Porter and Benny Goodman's big band swing. Jobim was particularly influenced by the Gerry Mulligan West Coast school of jazz that flourished parallel to Cal Tjader's efforts in the 1950s. In Mulligan's music, blues shadings distilled from mainstream jazz created a haunting harmonic and melodic effect that strongly affected Jobim's compositional style. Mulligan, who played baritone saxophone, had cut his teeth on Miles Davis's 1949 *Birth of the Cool*, formed his famous quartet featuring trumpeter Chet Baker in 1952, and all but defined West Coast cool jazz. Guitarist Charlie Byrd, who had toured South America extensively in 1961, discovered bossa nova in Brazil. Bossa nova gained international exposure through *Jazz Samba*, a 1962 release featuring Byrd and saxophonist Stan Getz, both West Coast devotees. The genre's first hit, *Desafinado*, written by Antonio Carlos Jobim, appears here, as well *One-Note Samba*. Both songs were present on the Verve sessions of the early 1960s that yielded, among other classics, 1963's *Getz/Gilberto featuring Antonio Carlos Jobim*, an album that also included Brazilian guitarist and vocalist João Gilberto and his wife Astrud's immortal version of *The Girl From Ipanema*. Gilberto, largely credited with inventing the bossa nova style on the guitar (see Chapter 7) and Jobim were central to the development of bossa nova in Brazil. The sound, based on a slowed-down samba rhythm, was quickly embraced by musicians like Herbie Mann and Dizzy Gillespie, who found its African rhythms challenging and its harmonic and melodic sense more developed than Afro-Cuban music.

In the United States, pop bands like Brazilian pianist/bandleader Sergio Mendes's Brasil 66 leaned toward the lighter jazz sound of collaborators Clare Fischer and Hubert Laws. The Brazilian husband-and-wife team of Airto Moreira and Flora Purim were a major influence at the dawn of the jazz fusion era, particularly on *Free*, *Fingers*, and *Virgin Land*, all released in the early 1970s. Also important was their work with Boston-born Portuguese American pianist Chick Corea.

While Brazil has a strong jazz scene unto itself, many of the musicians who emigrated to the North continue to make a strong mark on the New York scene playing both Brazilian-beat influenced as well as mainstream Afro-Cuban jazz style music. These include guitarist Romero Lubambo (who in 2002 appeared on a Grammy-nominated duet album with vocalist Luciana Souza); pianist Elaine Elias, who broke new ground using tape loops and a traditional jazz trio to augment her Brazilian jazz; and trumpeter Claudio Roditi, who has played with Michel Camilo and Paquito D'Rivera.

Many of the central players in what eventually became the New York salsa scene were also major contributors to the Latin jazz scene. This crossover goes back to early 1960s collaborations between Cal Tjader and Eddie Palmieri on *El Sonido Nuevo* (fittingly, The New Sound) and *Bamboléate*. Palmieri, whose influences are as far-flung as Claude Debussy and McCoy Tyner, has always been on the avant-garde side of salsa. Ray Barretto and Tito Puente, who traveled in the same universe, both contracted with the Concord Jazz label to release a string of jazz-oriented records in the 1980s and 1990s.

Salsa Meets Jazz

The intermingling of styles had been a constant in the New York jazz scene as far back as the 1950s. In the '70s and '80s the weekly salsa-meets-jazz shows at the downtown club the Village Gate featured salsa bands and Latin jazz bands playing back to back, with special instrumental guests splitting time between the two. During this series a jazz saxophonist like Chico Freeman would play with a salsa act, both types of groups would swap percussionists like Giovanni Hidalgo, and Willie Colón would sing with jazz pianist Billy Taylor.

Saxophonist Mario Rivera's Salsa Refugees could shift from Miles Davis's cool jazz classic *All Blues* to the Coltrane standard *I Want to Talk About You*, then a funny thing would happen. The band would shift gears into a frantic two-step merengue; suddenly everyone was on the dance floor and the whole band wanted to take a turn on the timbales.

The salsa-meets-jazz series helped create an atmosphere that produced many of the important Latin jazz groups in New York throughout the 1980s, such as Jerry González's Fort Apache Band; Paquito D'Rivera's group, which included Michel Camilo, pianist Hilton Ruiz, and flutist Dave Valentín; and Manny Oquendo's Orchestra Libre. Most of these players did tutelages in the Tito Puente or Ray Barretto bands, and those individual players who didn't go on to front their own bands wound up as essential session players for all kinds of Latin music projects.

Fort Apache follows a simple formula: Take a jazz tune you admire and develop it, or even strengthen it, by grafting on Latin rhythmic ideas. The group's Bronx-born cofounder, Jerry González, grounds the band in a Latin-jazz concept with his doubling on brass and conga. On any given tune you can hear his muted trumpet, an unusually expressive flugelhorn, and some of the best conga playing in the Latin universe. Jerry's brother, Andy González, is a bass virtuoso, anchoring the complex rhythm changes between five-beat clave patterns and conventional-jazz walking bass figures that are the band's signatures. The group's music sounds like the feverish dreams Miles or Monk might have had if shipwrecked in the Spanish-speaking Caribbean.

Under the name of Jerry González and the Fort Apache Band, the group has played together on ten albums, the most highly regarded of which is 1988's *Rumba Para Monk*. On a Thelonius Monk tune like *Evidence*, originally recorded by González on his first solo effort, muscular solos are sandwiched by a quirky six-note bridge, taken from Cuban pianist Frank Emilio, which suits Monk's odd sense of melody. González likes to play on Yoruba themes, as demonstrated by his titling of his next 1988 release,

Obatalá, a reference to one of the gods of the Yoruba pantheon. The band's cover of Miles Davis's *Nefertiti* glides easily between a Yoruban percussion riff, employing the conga and the chékere, a rattling instrument that produces an onomatopoetic sound, and pianist Larry Willis soulfully improvises on saxophonist Wayne Shorter's moody theme. *Obatalá*, dedicated to a Yoruban orisha, is a frenetic rumba, with Andy plucking a melodic bass figure, then adding obligatos to Santería practitioner Milton Cardona's vocals, as Jerry and Héctor Hernández bring their congas to multiple climaxes. Following 1995's *Pensativo*, Fort Apache's last release was 1996's well-received *Fire Dance*, although the group continued to play live with some regularity.

Latin music's long love affair with the flute goes back to Cuba in the early part of the century, and the popularity of Cuban flutist José Fajardo during the charanga fad of the 1960s. Cal Tjader's collaboration with Eddie Palmieri brought the instrument renewed prominence. The career of virtuoso flutist Dave Valentín marks a new chapter in that history. Valentín grew up in the Bronx, where he was born in 1954. He attended the High School of Music and Art, where he took up percussion, but in college he discovered the flute. Although he studied briefly with jazz flutist Hubert Laws, he is primarily self-taught.

Valentín recorded at least eighteen albums, and like Sergio Mendés, he liked to cover popular rock songs as well as jazz classics—but he also composes many of his own songs. On 1988's *Live at the Blue Note* he moved from covering a Beatles song like *Blackbird* to invoking the panpipe sound of the Andes—he plays both Bolivian and Peruvian instruments and carries up to twelve different flutes to his performances. He also drew on Gershwin, covering *Porgy and Bess*, and the Cuban danzón, whose deliberate, melodic flourishes mesh well with Valentín's ethereal effect. His version of Mongo Santamaría's signature *Afro Blue* showcased his improvisation and helped launch the career of percussionist/conguero Giovanni Hidalgo when they engaged in charged duets on *Live at the Blue Note*.

Pianist Hilton Ruiz, who got his name because his mother carried him to term in the shadows of a massive hotel from that chain, grew up in New York and studied under jazz legends Roland Kirk and Mary Lou Williams. A child prodigy who played his first recital at Carnegie Hall at age eight, he made his recording debuts collaborating with Jerry González and Paquito D'Rivera. On a typical night at New York's Salsa Meets Jazz he would duel with Michel Camilo during a re-take of Dizzy Gillespie's *Night in Tunisia*. Ruiz grew up listening to early rock and roll and blues as well as Latin music, and his playing reflects the boogie-woogie stride style of pianists like Jelly Roll Morton. Ruiz does more to invoke the purer jazz aspect of stride piano than most Latin jazz players. He likes to play tumbaos on his left hand, creating a hypnotic effect, while he improvises with his right hand. His peak recordings were *Something Grand* in 1986, *El Camino* in 1988, and *Hands on Percussion* (Ralph Mercado's Tropijazz label) in 1994. Most of his records feature a who's who of New York Latin jazz and dance orchestra, including Andy González on bass, David Sánchez on saxophone, Papo Vásquez on trombone, and Dave Valentín on flute. His greatest hits compilation was released on RMM in 1999.

Two of Cuba's most celebrated jazz musicians, trumpeter Arturo Sandovál and saxophonist Paquito D'Rivera, from Irakere, had defected to the United States by the end of the 1980s. D'Rivera, who arrived in 1981, and Sandovál, who followed in 1990, were quickly signed to major labels and embarked on new careers of playing in a more traditional jazz vein, which both claim they weren't allowed to do by the Cuban government.

Known for a silky-smooth tone and evocative phrasing in the manner of 1960s standout jazz saxophonist Dexter Gordon, Paquito D'Rivera is one of the great alto saxophonists of his era. Sandovál seems to spill his entire soul through his trumpet every time he plays. D'Rivera, whose group once featured the pianist Michel Camilo, plays with Sonny Rollins' clarity, John Coltrane's soul, and Charlie Parker's eagerness to break new ground. His career has been as dramatic as his playing. Born in 1948 in Havana, D'Rivera was the son of a Cuban tenor saxophonist who once played with Benny Goodman. He made his professional debut on soprano when he was all of six years old, and at age twelve, he entered the same music conservatory as his future collaborator and bandmate, pianist Chucho Valdés. In 1970, after a successful showing at the Warsaw Jazz Festival, D'Rivera and Valdes formed the experimental salsa-jazz fusion band Irakere.

In 1980, after his defection, D'Rivera started a group called the Havana/New York ensemble, which produced stars like percussionist Daniel Ponce, pianists Hilton Ruiz, Michel Camilo, and Danilo Pérez, and trumpeter Claudio Roditi. During the 1980s D'Rivera also collaborated with other Cuban expatriates–Israel Cachao López, the legendary bassist often credited with inventing the mambo, and Mario Bauzá. D'Rivera appeared on *My Time Is Now* (1993), Bauzá's next-to-last recording. In the 1990s, D'Rivera worked on various recordings with Chucho's father, the pianist Bebo Valdés, McCoy Tyner, Tito Puente, Astor Piazzolla, and Jerry González, among others. He performed with several groups of his own creation: the Paquito D'Rivera Big Band; the Paquito D'Rivera Quintet, a chamber music group; Triángulo; and an Afro-Caribbean dance band, the Caribbean Jazz Project. He won a Grammy in 1996 for *Portraits of Cuba*, a collection of Cuban classics recorded with a big band including many of New York's best session players under the supervision of the premier Latin jazz arranger Carlos Franzeti.

Portraits of Cuba is like a night at a great concert hall, where the elegance of the Cuban tradition is augmented by an Ellingtonian sense of style. Bouncy numbers that everyone recognizes like *The Peanut Vendor* become elegant exercises in big band ecstasy, the melody teased out like a perfect strand of Cuban history. Tunes like Ernesto Grenét's *Drume Negrita* and René Touzét's *No te Importe Saber* get elaborate string and reed treatments that recall the

Gil Evans–Miles Davis era. Throughout, D'Rivera's playing is restrained and respectful, with occasional bursts of raw jazz emotion. Two D'Rivera compositions, the edgy cha-cha *Portraits of Cuba* and the lament *Song to My Son*, demonstrate his excellent range and command of his instrument. No collection of Cuban classics would be complete without an Ernesto Lecuona waltz, and the wistful *Como Arrullo de Palmas* is captured here with a subtle grace. Still this album's sentimental peak may be the rendition of Marco Rizo's *Theme From 'I Love Lucy.'* D'Rivera's band turns a melody forever associated with a goofy situation comedy into a swinging reminiscence that somehow makes a profound statement about the presence of Cubans in American culture. Ignacio Piñeiro's *Échale Salsita* brings the migration of Cuban music from Havana to New York full circle.

D'Rivera's 2002 release *Habanera*, despite its title, is a fairly straightforward jazz record. That same year D'Rivera also appeared in *Calle 54*, Spanish filmmaker Fernando Trueba's documentary about Latin jazz, and did an album with Cuban pianist Bebo Valdés, *El Arte del Sabor*, a collection of Cuban classics (and *Cumbanchero* by Puerto Rican composer Rafael Hernández). *El Arte del Sabor* was one of the most lyrical Latin jazz releases of that year and was brought about because of the reunion of Bebo and his son Chucho (also of Irakere) triggered by the making of *Calle 54*. In 2002, D'Rivera also released *Brazilian Dreams*, in which he leads a band that includes Brazilian trumpeter Claudio Roditi among others, reinterpreting classics by Antonio Carlos Jobim and Luis Bonfa.

Pianist Michel Camilo's conservatory training in both the Dominican Republic, where he was born in 1954, and the United States and his polished live presentation gave him a different air from many of the other players in the New York Latin jazz scene. Camilo burst onto the scene through a stint with D'Rivera, on his classic *Why Not* (1984). His self-titled U.S. debut album (1988) had, on the surface, a split personality: The first few songs play like conventional jazz while the latter are soaked in Caribbean sweat. The tunes vary from the McCoy Tyneresque hard-bop intensity of *Crossroads* and the acrobatic *Suite Sandrine, Part I* to the moody Keith Jarrett-like *Nostalgia* and *Dreamlight*. Camilo's technical virtuosity is riveting, without obscuring the emotion in the pieces. The fiery percussiveness of his chord play is one overt clue to his identity, but with repeated listening, you can also sense his Latin soul filtering through the Tatum edginess and the studied melodic development.

Pra Voce (For Tania Maria) is a simmering samba that features smashing interplay between Camilo, whose chords hit higher peaks after each verse, and his trap drummer, who seems to be breaking down the door for him. Kenny Dorham's standard *Blue Bossa* is reconceived here as a duet between Camilo and legendary congero Mongo Santamaría—a moving dialogue between an emerging virtuoso and an old master.

Rather than simply merging jazz technique with Latin rhythms, Camilo embraces the attitude and compositional approach of three traditions: jazz, Afro-Cuban, and Dominican. *Yarey* starts out with a funky jazz melody, then progresses to a walking bass line, a samba interlude, and an Afro-Cuban tumbao. The song palpitates with the crescendos that work off each rhythmic style. Fittingly, the name of the tune comes from a central plaza in a Dominican town near the sugar cane fields where all the different stories of the town would be told, hence the litany of rhythmic changes.

Caribe is influenced by the style of Cuban pianist Ernesto Lecuona. Amidst graceful folkloric fingerwork, Camilo inserts expressionist rhythmic interludes, giving *Caribe* a hectic, ironic feeling: Picture a Latin Scott Joplin weaving in and out of midtown traffic. Camilo's work plays with a notion of transplanted roots—it's as if he's asking himself, how can I marry the courtly, mannered tempos of the Cuban danzón sound with life in New York City? In his trios, and again when he uses a five-piece band,

Camilo encourages dialogues between the piano and the rhythm section, either through solos from bass, drums, and/or congas or internal tempo changes.

The most critically acclaimed of Camilo's eight albums was his 1989 sophomore effort, *On Fire*. Recorded with a revolving corps of trios, this album of original songs is perhaps Camilo's strongest argument for fusing classical structure, jazz fusion intensity, and Afro-Cuban beats. He has varied the size and concept of his groups, alternating between his concept of chamber music for jazz musicians and traditional jazz quintets and quartets. Despite the strong jazz influences in his playing, the Latin tinge, particularly the slower, formal danzón tradition of Lecuona, is always present. *Triángulo*, released in 2002, returned to the trio, with long-time bassist Anthony Jackson and young Afro-Cuban drummer Horacio "El Negro" Hernández, who took the New York Latin jazz scene by storm in the late 1990s. Camilo's pyrotechnics in *Triángulo* lean on the jazz style except for the Latin outburst of *Descarga for Tito Puente*.

Trumpeter Arturo Sandovál left Irakere soon after D'Rivera defected to the United States in 1981, touring with his own band and recording albums in several countries in Europe. Occasionally, the Castro government would allow Sandovál to appear in various international jazz festivals and with orchestras like the BBC Symphony and Leningrad Philharmonic. He also played European gigs with Dizzy Gillespie's United Nations Orchestra, a group of "international" young players Gillespie led just before his death. It was in July 1990, during a long European tour, that Sandovál defected at the American Embassy in Rome. Gillespie was instrumental in his defection, accompanying him to the embassy.

Sandovál signed a recording contract with GRP and settled in Miami. His first American album, appropriately titled *Flight to Freedom* (1991), demonstrated his versatility in several idioms. He later recorded fifteen albums, leaving GRP after 1996's *Swingin'*. Sandovál's work reflects his extraordinary talent as well as the political drama of his life—he is a true virtuoso who occasionally makes music with an overly commercial slickness. His recordings cover an eclectic range, from original jazz compositions to his remakes of Coltrane classics, to the Latin/salsa/pop excursions of 1995's *Arturo Sandovál and the Latin Train*, which featured a guest appearance by Celia Cruz. *Hothouse*, a collection of Afro-Cuban classics played in a jazz framework, followed in 1998, and a year later he returned with *Americana*, a syrupy anthology of U.S. pop classics from Al Green to Stevie Wonder.

After coming to the United States, Sandovál has dedicated much energy to recording the classics of North American jazz, music he was portrayed as being prohibited from playing by the Castro regime in the television movie *For the Love of Country*. In 2002 Sandovál released *My Passion for the Piano*, an album where he plays the piano instead of the trumpet. The typical Sandovál earmarks are here: several original compositions, the pop obscurity *Windmills of Your Mind*, and an Armando Manzanero bolero. The quality of the album is first-rate, although Sandovál had no intention of giving up his original instrument. While often overshadowed when it comes to publicity by his former Irakere mates Chucho Valdés and Paquito d'Rivera, Arturo Sandovál is recognized as a master trumpeter who plays both with incredible speed and deliberate grace. An unpretentious and serious player, Sandovál may be the best living session trumpeter in the world and is highly capable of playing on classical music recordings. And he really swings.

Two of the most talented graduates of Dizzy Gillespie's United Nations Orchestra were Puerto Rican saxophonist David Sánchez and Panamanian pianist Danilo Pérez. Sánchez is part of a young generation of Latinos struggling to make sense of transnationalism—the shifting back and forth of homelands and loyalties, fusing North and South. During his formative tutelage under Gillespie in the early 1990s, he was given a mandate by Dizzy to pursue the influences of various African traditions on music throughout Latin America. He turned that mandate into a mission to unite seemingly disparate countries from the Caribbean through Peru by focusing on their African roots.

Born in 1968 in Guaynabo, Puerto Rico, Sánchez left his native island to study music at Rutgers University in New Jersey in 1988 and shot to the forefront of young saxophonists on the New York scene in the early 1990s. While he is eminently capable of dazzling a crowd with sheer technical and emotional power, he seems obsessed with uncovering the buried legacies of the music itself. While his central project is the aforementioned uncovering of the influence of the African diaspora, he also pays tribute to influences from the free-wheeling John Coltrane to the great boleros of Latin America. Although the composition of Sánchez's band changed on each of his six albums, he has been collaborating consistently with Edsel Gómez, percussionist Pernell Saturnino, and saxophonist Miguel Zenón.

Obsesión (1998), a seductive collection of Latin ballad standards, is a distillation of Sánchez's efforts to compile the great Latin American Songbook. The intersection of sticks, strings, and standards makes *Obsesión* a statement album: Sánchez executes his rhythmic ideas in the context of a production by Branford Marsalis that, at times, recalled Gil Evans's lushness. But no matter how much of a flirtation Sánchez had with Stravinsky's chamber music and Schoenberg's *Transfigured Night*, some of his stated influences, his musical language crystallizes the basic elements of rhythm, drums, and love of country and family.

While Sánchez is a fan of bossa nova, the elegance of Jobim sometimes mutes the strong percussive energy of its root, samba. Sanchez's stripped-down version of Jobim's bossa nova *Omorro Nao Tem Vez* is infused with a dose of its street-drumming origins. It's almost all batucada—he duels with percussionist Pernell Saturnino, who flips between the surdo, repinique, and pandeiro

(Brazilian percussion instruments), creating a trancelike effect that seems like a missing link between *Black Orpheus* and Donna Summer's *Bad Girls*.

On 2000's *Melaza*, which translates into "molasses," Sánchez provides a strong catalogue of sweet moments, while remaining serious about his jazz ambitions. Here, Sánchez returns to his project of grafting traditional jazz influences onto an intricate core of unsung African rhythms from Puerto Rico and South America. His reinvestigation of the avant-garde possibilities of Puerto Rican bomba and plena beats make his project particularly exciting. On the symphonic *Canto a Loiza*, and even more clearly on *Sentinela*, Sánchez recruited two giants of new bomba, percussionist William Cepeda and Hector "Tito" Matos, to provide the rhythmic sorcery behind his quick, sharp Wayne Shorter-like riffing. These tunes provide a glimpse into the energy of Loiza, the town at the center of African culture in northeastern Puerto Rico, and nod to the influence of Rafael Cortijo, bomba titan of the early 1960s and one of Sánchez's spiritual heroes.

But Sánchez doesn't just want to lecture on the social anthropology of African diasporic rhythms—he wants to swing with the best of the bop and post-bop era. With his expressive phrasing, tunes like *Against Our Will* and the climactic *Canción de Canáveral* hint at what a new Miles or a new Coltrane might sound like. Pulsing through Sánchez's solos on *El Ogro* and *Centinela* there is even the lost-my-head loft feel of a young Ornette Coleman.

Sánchez released *Travesía* in 2001, continuing his collaboration with Saturnino and Zenón. The playing is even more innovative than on *Melaza*, perhaps because Sánchez himself was the producer. *Paz Para Vieques* combines a political protest with Puerto Rican folkloric tradition, this time in the song form of a seis chorreado; there is Brazilian ballad in *Pra Dizer Adeus* and an excellent reworking of Wayne Shorter's *Prince of Darkness*.

Sánchez's band makes the complex rhythms that survived more intact in the black Caribbean than in the American South look easy. In rehearsal, the band works out a Puerto Rican bomba or plena, or a Cuban changüí or guaguancó, by slapping on any object available, recalling the tradition of the box-playing rumberos. Sánchez's background playing for the salsa bands of Roberto Roena and Eddie Palmieri make him a throwback to old-school jazz players who had to play dances for a living—like Tito Puente, he seems to think, dance first, work out the rhythms later. As much as Sánchez mines the traditions of other countries, he is steadfastly loyal to that of his home island, Puerto Rico. He lionizes figures like composer Rafael Hernández by covering his classic *Lamento Borincano*, he covers classic bolero singers like Bobby Capó, and, as mentioned above, he has been at the forefront of an avant-garde bomba and plena revival.

Through Chucho Valdés's Havana Jazz Festival, Sánchez made a series of connections with Cuban musicians and took part in Roy Hargrove's Crisól band. In Cuba in 1996, Sánchez played with jazz-dance bands like Bamboleo and Klímax, straddling the territory between Afro-Cuban folklore and Earth, Wind, and Fire, as well as Isaac Delgado, one of Cuba's most important salsa singers. Most of this was done in live performance and not recorded.

Danilo Pérez, who was born in 1966, raised in the Dominican Republic and came to the United States to study in 1985, is a master of fusion and experimental playing within the context of Latin jazz. His Berklee School of Music conservatory approach mirrors many of his Cuban contemporaries and sets him a bit apart from the New York school of salsa-Latin jazz. His stint in the Dizzy Gillespie United Nations Orchestra anchored Pérez to a circle of young players that included Puerto Rican trumpeter Charlie Sepulveda, David Sánchez, and percussionist Pernell Saturnino. While his first few albums were more like those of his fellow Dominican Michel Camilo, Pérez helped contribute to a new chapter in Latin jazz with *Panamonk*, an album full of Thelonius Monk standards.

Pérez's 2000 recording *Motherland* showed him to be on a similar path as his friend David Sánchez. Like Sánchez, he has set
forth on a journey to collect and re-interpret the variety of African
rhythms found in Latin America outside Cuba. As Alejo Carpentier said in his book *La música en Cuba*, "There are great players in
Cuba, but there is a limit on the number of rhythms." On *Motherland*, Pérez used several traditional rhythms from the Panamanian
tamborito to the samba and baião of Brazil (see Chapter 6).

Cuban-born Gonzalo Rubalcaba is a master of jazz piano, ap-
proaching the process of making music from so many different directions that his work can be impossible to fully grasp in the first
listening. Born in 1963 in Havana and having studied classical piano
since age eight, Rubalcaba has no quarrel with what we know as the
popular Cuban sound, that familiar son swing that made Havana
famous. His trombonist-composer grandfather, Jacobo, was the
leader of the immensely popular Charanga Rubalcaba, and Gonzalo
appeared on five of salsa heartthrob Isaac Delgado's records. But
Rubalcaba is primarily known as an experimentalist, one who comes
down often on the side of free improvisation, almost to the point of
completely obscuring his Cuban roots—his 1997 duet with saxophonist Joe Lovano, *Flying Colors*, for example, is aimed at the serious jazz listener. His experimental wanderings are at times devoid of
swing; they are deconstructions of jazz traditions from New Orleans
to Havana. Rubalcaba seems determined to prove that Cuban music
itself is more than just a night out dancing.

On 1998's *Antiguo*, he is backed by fellow Cubans like Julio Bar-
reto on drums, Felipe Carrera on bass, and Reynaldo Melián on
trumpet, but this Cuban quartet functions more like a chamber
ensemble than a dance band. The playing is as brisk and precisely
angular as his previous efforts, but a special attention is paid to
Cuban spirituality. On tracks like *Circuito III*, *Circuito IV*, and *De-
sierto*, Rubalcaba leaps out of a melody at a frantic pace, favoring

one of several Roland synthesizers, much as Chick Corea did in the 1970s with *Return to Forever*. *Coral Negro* has a riveting ethereal quality augmented by the vocals of the classically trained Dominican singer Maridalia Hernández. But *Antiguo* hits its most swinging strides on *Elioko* and *Eshun Agwe*, driven by the trance-like rhythms of Yoruban spiritual dances, featuring appearances by Santería patriarch Lazaro Ros and the legendary Puerto Rican percussionist Giovanni Hidalgo.

On 2001's *Supernova*, an album that hinted at his explosive capabilities, Rubalcaba reveled in robust, authoritative exclamations of his jazz and classical influences. In the tradition of Afro-Cubana, he wielded the piano as a percussion instrument, but he's not as faithful to Afro-Cuban melodies as he was to a desire to break new avant-garde ground. On *El Cadete*, a classic danzón written by his grandfather, on which he incorporated *Stars and Stripes Forever* into the break, the effect is less ironic than it is cathartic—recalling the days before mambo, when it was typical for many American-influenced Cuban orchestras to incorporate a military march, or even Monk's *Round Midnight*—call it an early version of jazz sampling.

Drummer/percussionist Ignacio Berroa dispensed with the traditional clave rhythm on *Alma Mía*, a classic bolero written by Mexican songwriter María Grever, playing it as a jazz standard on brushes. Berroa is so deeply involved in the Afro-Cuban tradition that he flew through different versions of the son and rumba clave as if they were the key to his own existence. But his deepest desire is to be a jazzista, and with Rubalcaba he has found the perfect leader. Rubalcaba's version of *El Manisero* (The Peanut Vendor)—which also featured the Quintero brothers, who play timbales for salsa star Oscar D'Leon—is expertly recontextualized as a fusion between discordant improvisation, shifting time signatures, and trance-inducing tumbao riffs.

On *La Voz del Centro* (The In-Between Voice)—instead of playing on 2/4, Rubalcaba stresses the third beat. It's as if he's saying that instead of having to choose between someone's idea of an "American" voice and a "Cuban" one, he speaks with the one in between. As in much of Rubalcaba's work, he displays seemingly opposite kinds of virtuosity: the chaotic aggression of an Art Tatum, the moody colors Bill Evans might paint. But there's no contradiction in the playing. Rubalcaba's ability to embrace such polarities lets his spirit fly in a way no one could have quite imagined before.

When you're in the presence of Cuban jazz pianist Chucho Valdés, you can feel a certain sense of majesty. It's only fitting, because Valdés was born into Cuban music royalty. His father, Bebo Valdés, was the leader of the house band of the Hotel Tropicana, the most important orchestra in Havana during the 1950s. As if his lineage and regal bearing weren't enough, Valdés stands six feet four inches tall. After a long struggle to establish himself in the United States after the late 1970s U.S. recording of Irakere was forgotten and the Buena Vista Social Club revitalized traditional Cuban music at the expense of today's innovators, Valdés became the most dominant pianist in Latin jazz. Valdés, who still lived in Cuba, was able to make arrangements with American and European labels to distribute his work in the United States and released six albums as a soloist between 1997 and 2003, as well as *Yemayá*, which was released under the name Chucho Valdés and Irakere in 1999.

To call Valdés a master pianist is almost an understatement—he plays with incredibly skilled, lightning-quick hands and seems to have at his command the entire history of Cuban music. Valdés spent thirty years unearthing and re-interpreting roots. Irakere was famous for extravagant electronic experimentation, emphasizing electric lead and bass guitars on Cuban dance tracks, but Valdés's later work focused more on the simplicity of Cuban music's rustic origins. He continues a quest to foreground traditional instruments like the African batá drums.

Valdés is quick to acknowledge the influence of his father, Bebo, whom he calls a genius. Bebo did arrangements for classic Cuban singers like César Portillo de la Luz, Celia Cruz, and Sonora Matancera, and as a boy, Chucho rubbed elbows with everyone from Ernesto Lecuona to Arsenio Rodríguez.

Valdés's status and popularity have a lot to do with his position as head of the Havana Jazz Festival, a position he holds as the elder statesman of the new Cuban music of the 1970s, especially after his bandmates Paquito D'Rivera and Arturo Sandovál defected in the 1980s. Since the mid-1990s, David Sánchez and Roy Hargrove, who was inspired to create his Crisól project by his visits to Cuba, have been immersed in a new understanding of Afro-Cuban music facilitated by Valdés's festival. Chucho Valdés also continued to oversee, with the help of his son, Chuchito Valdés Jr., the current version of Irakere, which is more and more dedicated to resuscitation of the African roots of Cuban music. He also played an unforgettable duet, *La Comparsa*, with his father in Fernando Trueba's film *Calle 54*, and *Unforgettable Boleros*, his album of classics, was nominated for a Grammy in 2001.

Calle 54 and Beyond

Calle 54 (2001), a remarkable film by Spanish filmmaker Fernando Trueba, captured many of the greats of Latin jazz. Trueba got the idea for the film when he was shooting the Latin jazz jam finale for *Two Much*, a mid-1990s Antonio Banderas romantic comedy designed to break the director out of his native Spain. The performances in *Calle 54* are exhilarating. For the most part, Trueba let players like Paquito D'Rivera, Jerry González and the Fort Apache Band, Michel Camilo, Tito Puente, and Chucho Valdés speak only through their performances. Often they are seen bathed in primary colors in neutral studio settings, giving the feeling that they are timeless performers. The technique works best when Jerry

González seems to burst into red flames during a flugelhorn solo and Tito Puente's all-star configuration shimmers in spiritual white outfits. The film also has some of the last footage of Puente and Chico O'Farríll, who died before the release.

Latin jazz continues to proliferate in the big cities of the United States, like Los Angeles, San Francisco, and Miami, and in the major capitals of Europe. Acts like Bobby Sanabria's Ascensión (whose three albums, particularly 2000's *Afro Cuban Dream: Live and in Clave*, portend the genre's future) and the work of Conrad Herwig (his record, *The Latin Side of Coltrane*, was one of 1999's best releases in the genre) are extremely vital. Former Rubén Blades sideman Ralph Irizarry kept the scene in New York fresh. New York-based Brazilian pianist Elaine Elias, featured in *Calle 54*, released a strong, forward-looking album *Kissed by Nature* in 2002, and of course contemporary Cuban music is bursting with jazz talent like saxophonist Yosvany Terry and bassist Yunior Terry, brothers who are sidemen on releases by guitarist Juan Carlos Formell and percussionist Patato Valdez. A Latin jazz revival in New York was reported in 2002, and several small venues hosted new musicians from Cuba, such as percussionists Dafnis Prieto, Horacio "El Negro" Hernández, and Juan Carlos Formell, son of Los Van Van founder Luis Formell. They formed part of a scene that emphasized hybrid forms of jazz rather than traditional Afro-Cuban- or Brazilian-based Latin jazz.

One of Latin jazz's future bright lights is Omar Sosa, whose dissonant, idiosyncratic phrasing flows neatly into mannered renditions of Cuban danzón. Born in 1965 in Camaguey, he began studying music at age five at his hometown's conservatory. He left Cuba in 1995 for Ecuador, moved on to San Francisco's Bay Area soon after, and now lives in Barcelona, Spain. Sosa's playing is every bit as thrilling and engaging as the great pianists of the moment: Chucho Valdés, Michel Camilo, Gonzalo Rubalcaba, and Eddie Palmieri. His abstract moments are as challenging as his love for son, danzón, cha cha, and the blues—all are expressed with swing and exhilaration.

Sosa's 2002 album *Sentir* (Otá records) is a dazzling construction of fire, rhythm, improvisation, and vivid colors. It follows a
similar pattern to Sosa's eight other releases—it is part of a project
to combine the music of the African diaspora in countries as varied
as Cuba, Venezuela, the United States, and Morocco. While Sosa
is known for his ability to synthesize the rhythms and sensibilities
that hip-hop and Afro-Caribbean countries share, his incorporation of the Gnawa culture of Morocco is found only on *Sentir* and
his previous release, *Prietos*.

Recognizing the inevitability of his involvement with North
America, Sosa employs rapper Terence Nicholson (a.k.a Sub-Z) as a
kind of urban contemporary Greek chorus. When the energies swirl
together on a track like *Azul Yemayá*, the disparate energies appear
to merge, as if by magic, with Sosa's playing acting as the glue. A fol-
lower of the Afro-Cuban religion santería, Sosa takes the spiritual
grounding of an ancient earth religion and makes some of the most
contemporary Latin jazz available.

Re-imagining Brazil

The music of Brazil, from samba to bossa nova to the progressive Brazilian pop today, is as rich a story as any that exists in the Latin world. Like Afro-Cuban music, Brazilian music is an Afro-European fusion, but there are key differences. The samba beat, a shuffling, 2/4 rhythm, came about as a fusion between different African beats and does not conform to Afro-Cuban clave, although it is a two-bar pattern. The elaborate array of partner-dancing styles found in Afro-Cuban music is not as prevalent in Brazil. Finally, Brazilian music borrows more omnivorously from North American pop and jazz.

For various reasons primarily having to do with the difference between Portuguese and Spanish, Brazil is often left out of discussion of Latin music. But ironically, Brazilian music was one of the first Latin musics to cross over to a mass international audience with its own star, 1940s samba goddess Carmen Miranda. In fact, for a brief period, Miranda came to symbolize all of Latin music for an American public that didn't really get the diversity of Latin America. The next important moment for Brazilian music, which came in the waning years of the mambo era, the late 1950s, was the bossa nova of Antonio Carlos Jobim and João Gilberto. It was

an archetypal Latin pop sound that became misinterpreted in the
United States as "easy listening." When the 1960s arrived, a new
form of pop (Musica Popular Brasilera) and a countercultural rock
(tropicalismo) took over from bossa nova and became the soundtrack to social unrest fueled by a repressive military dictatorship.
In the 1970s, jazz fusion influenced the MPB stars, and a continuing cross-pollination between traditional styles and dynamic pop
made Brazil one of the largest music markets in the world, with a
dizzying array of musical genres.

The most important primogenitor of Brazilian music is samba,
which has evolved from earlier versions like choro (an instrumental, Dixieland jazz-ish genre) and frevo (a fast-paced, syncopated
marching music) to its contemporary derivation, pagode (a samba
with even more emphasis on percussion). Other major genres include bossa nova, tropicália and rock, baião (the lilting, balladic
form of the North, more characterized by use of accordions than
by percussion) and its offshoot forró, soul and funk, and music
with a more African bent, capoeira, axé, batucada and manguebeat, all highly percussion-oriented sounds from the northeastern region of Bahia. The expanding category of Música Popular
Brasilera, or Brazilian popular music, refers to any of these genres played in a more pop format.

Music evolved in Brazil in parallel fashion to the way it did in
the rest of Latin America, with the music of African tribes slowly
mixing with the European forms brought from Iberia. The original African form, lundú, was brought to Brazil by slaves from the
Bantu region of Central Africa. In the late nineteenth century, the
lundú began to mix with styles being brought to Brazilian cities
from Latin America and Europe, such as the polka, the habanera,
and the tango. This confluence begat what became known as the
maxixe, a sensuous hybrid of polka, lundú, and Cuban habanera,
and is often referred to as the first urban Brazilian dance. In the
early twentieth century, the maxixe evolved into the cornerstone
of twentieth century Brazilian music, the samba.

The Samba as Signifier

The Portuguese landed in Brazil in 1500 after a papal blessing, implemented through the 1494 Treaty of Tordesillas, granted them land in the eastern part of South America. By the middle of the sixteenth century, the Portuguese had set up a plantation-style economy, and like the Spanish, attempted to force the indigenous people (known as Guarani) into slavery. The indigenous people resisted, were championed by Jesuits, and began to die in massive numbers through diseases contracted from the Portuguese and other Europeans. For 300 years between 1550 and 1850, the slave trade brought hundreds of thousands of Africans to Brazil, and in northern areas like Bahia, they often outnumbered Portuguese settlers by three to one. In the early nineteenth century, when the rest of Latin America broke away from Spain, Portugal instituted a constitutional monarchy with an emperor from the royal family of Lisbon, who had escaped Napoleon's invasion. The Portuguese republic was not established until 1889.

Like the rest of Latin America, Brazil's society was structured in a class system that often corresponded to ranges of skin tone from black to white, with many mixed-race people forming an intermediate class. Similar forces were at work in the creation of Afro-Cuban music and Afro-Brazilian music, but in Brazil, the samba became a symbol of a society that was undergoing changes as a result of the world-wide economic depression of the late 1920s.

According to Hermano Vianna's *History of Samba*, samba became a national Brazilian music, central to that country's national identity. A series of scholarly works, most notably Gilberto Freyre's *Masters and Slaves*, which was published in the 1930s, made a case for celebrating the massive race-mixing that predominated in Brazil. In a moment when new political thinking was hungry to embrace specifically Brazilian nationalist characteristics, the philosophy of writers like Freyre, which celebrated race-mixing, coincided with the growing popularity of the samba parades held at carnaval. There continues to be a strong racism in Brazilian society, represented by the unequal distribution of wealth among the races, as well as police repression of dark-skinned youth, and it's possible to see this syncretism in national identity as a way of masking profound racism. But the rhetoric of embracing African-ness as a source of internal strength, even for Brazilians who were clearly "white," helped the purer African form of samba enter the mainstream of Brazilian music.

While there is some debate over which was the first recorded samba, it is widely considered to be *Pelo Telefone*, recorded by Banda de Odeon in 1917 in Rio de Janeiro. The advent of *Pelo Telefone* was an early manifestation of house-party music that was created in central Rio at the houses of influential members of an Afro-Brazilian community that had emigrated from the northern state of Bahia after slavery was ended in 1889 with the creation of the republic. These houses ultimately became known as samba schools, or ecolas do samba. Not unlike the cabildos of Havana, the samba schools, run like fraternities, protected African customs and nurtured musical training. In the late '20s, samba was repressed by the police, something ironic in view of the genre's rapid acceptance just a few years later. Schools like Portela, Imperio Serrano, and Mocidade Independente, which represented slightly different, but largely parallel, styles, grew strong roots in urban Rio. According to Hermano Vianna, samba's acceptance was fueled by the participation of upper- and middle-class residents of Rio (including Ary Barroso, a law student) in samba parties, as well as the advent of radio in the early '30s, a medium controlled by people in sympathy with the new nationalist project spurred by race-mixing celebrators like Freyre.

In the 1930s, samba evolved from its origins in house parties through composers who streamlined the sound, distinguishing it from maxixe and the proto-samba form marcha. Composer-singers like Ismael Silva and Armando Marcal helped to found the seminal samba school, Turma do Estácio. Orlando Silva, the first singer to have his own show on national radio, became one of the most popular singers in Brazil with songs like *A Jardineira*. Songwriters like Arturo Alves and singers like Moreira da Silva, who often improvised spoken-word "poetry" during improvisational breaks, held sway during this era as well.

The result of the middle- and upper-class mixing in the samba school era was the emergence in the 1930s of sambistas like Noel Rosa, Braguinha (Carlos Braga, credited with writing the original version of *Yes, We Have No Bananas*), and Ary Barroso. Barroso, who was born in 1903, is best remembered for *Aquarela do Brasil*, a legendary song of the era. But the most significant popularizer of samba from its early days was Dorival Caymmi, whose work spanned seven decades, beginning in the 1940s. Besides having a baritone that is often compared with Bing Crosby's, Caymmi is probably Brazil's most prolific popular music composer. Caymmi's early classic *Samba de Minha Terra* was part of the subgenre samba exatacao, sambas specifically designed to exalt the Brazilian ideal. But his main contribution may have been the songs he wrote for the Portuguese-born Rio transplant Carmen Miranda. He even taught her how to dance.

Born Maria do Carmo Miranda da Cunha in 1909 in Marco de Canavezes, Portugal, Miranda was moved to Rio de Janeiro as an infant and was raised a "carioca" (nickname for local residents). Not much of a student, Miranda became an overnight sensation when, as a shop girl, her singing talents were noticed, and she began singing in clubs. Seemingly overnight, Miranda emerged as one of the top attractions on the Rio club circuit, and upon signing with RCA in 1928 she became a massive star throughout Brazil. In 1930, she scored a major hit with *T'ai*, by Joubert de Carvalho. She then recorded a series of hit sambas written by Caymmi, whom she met at Rio de Janeiro's Radio Nacional radio station, and another samba giant, Ary Barrosso, among others. When Miranda began to perform Caymmi's sambas, such as *Roda Piao* and *O Que E Que a Baian Tem*, she was starring in major revues in Rio as well as some Brazilian films.

Backed by the Banda de Lua, an orchestral samba band overseen by Aloysio de Oliveira, Miranda's stage show, with its elaborate samba dancing and costuming, was the hottest thing in Rio
when Broadway producer Lee Shubert came to Brazil to scout talent in 1939. Miranda was immediately swept up as part of the
Good Neighbor Policy (a cultural exchange program designed by
the U.S. government to promote relations with Latin America) in
the 1940s. Thanks in part to Caymmi's sambas, Miranda's smiling
image became emblematic, in the United States, at least, of the entire Latin American milieu just before the mambo caught on. She
was a whirlwind success in New York, and soon one of the biggest
movie stars of her time as well. She was the highest-paid woman in
Hollywood in the late 1940s, fronting large-scale Busby Berkeley
musicals, and in a caricature of the carioca, modeling the famous
headpieces bursting with tropical fruit, a signifier of opulence during a time of war rationing.

The material she performed was a patchwork of samba, mambo,
and Cuban son that actually made more of a reference to Spanish-
speaking Latin America than to Brazil. Much of it was written by
the Tin Pan Alley songwriting team of Mack Gordon and Harry
Warren, the authors of *Chattanooga Choo-Choo*, although she managed to work in classic sambas by songwriters like Robert Ribeiro
and Silas de Oliveira, such as *O Passo Do Kanguru* and *Rebola a Bola*.

Miranda had attained a stardom that few Brazilians or Latin
Americans would ever hope to achieve, but it came at a cost.
When she returned to Brazil she found a public that was skeptical
of her Americanization. In response to this, she wrote a song
called *Disseram Que Voltei Americanisada* (They Say That I Returned Americanized), a samba in which she firmly reclaimed her
roots despite the path her career had taken. In the late '40s, a
period when the Axis threat in Latin America vanished and the
light musical comedies that cheered a war-trodden public gave
way to social issue films, Miranda was phased out of Hollywood.
In the final years of her life, Miranda suffered from severe depres-

sion. She returned briefly to Brazil in 1954, but soon returned to the United States to try to salvage what was left of her marketability. While taping an episode of *The Jimmy Durante Show* in August of 1955, Miranda suffered a heart attack at her Beverly Hills home. She died the following morning at age forty-six. Her body was flown back to Brazil where she was mourned across the country; a museum honoring her was constructed in Rio. Despite her love/hate relationship with her home country, she is revered as a figure of great historical importance.

Miranda's primary legacy may have been the fact that female samba singers Clara Nunes, Alcione, and Beth Carvalho were the most popular performers in the '50s. Songs like *Canto das Tres Racas* (Song of Three Races) and *Brasil Mestico, Santuario da Fe* (Mestizo Brazil, Sanctuary of Faith), written by Paulo César Pinheiro, celebrate the mixed-race Brazilian identity. The music's continually evolving percussion strategy, with faster tempos and different accents on particular drums and percussion instruments, brought samba the status that jazz had in North America. In fact, in terms of proficiency and refinement in the playing, samba was a much more widespread popular phenomenon than jazz.

Baião, the Music of the North

Brazil is an enormous country, with a total area larger than the United States. Although samba was the music of urban Brazil, and clearly the most important genre, there were regional styles that eventually had a strong influence on the development of music in the urban centers. One of those genres was baião, the music of the North.

Unlike the rest of Brazil, the provinces of the Brazilian north coast have a culture that is at least tangentially related to the Caribbean cultures of Spanish-speaking Latin America—their proximity to the Caribbean allowed for some cultural exchange,

and the concentration of Africans there mirrored similar populations in Cuba, Hispanola, and the West Indies. In fact, in the period between 1580 and 1640, when King Phillip II seized the
throne in Lisbon, the Spanish exercised considerable influence in
the region. The current music scenes in Salvador, and other
northern towns like Recife, which will be examined later, are some
of the most dynamic and fluid in Brazil today. The rhythm of the
region's original music, baião, however, holds a long-standing
place in Brazilian music history. It is perhaps the most important
music to emerge from the North.

The baião (Bahian), which features syncopated melodies, a gentle, pastoral rhythm, and lilting accordion, is relatively unknown
outside Brazil, surprising considering its considerable influence on
modern Brazilian music. The lyrics of the typical baião are compa-
rable to the Cuban trova—they are usually concerned with storytelling, and often describe the struggles of the people. In the
1930s, the original baião groups, fronted by vocalists, used pí-
fanos, small hand-carved bamboo flutes, a zabumba, a large bass
drum, and other forms of percussion. The rhythmic pattern of
baião is set by the zabumba drum, which has skin on both sides,
reminiscent of the tambora drum used for merengue. One side is
used for bass tones and the other for a higher pitch, usually playing a syncopated rhythm. The 2/4 rhythm is based on ballroom
dancing of European origin, as well as an African circle dance
done in the interior, arid areas of the northeast.

Because of the region's proximity to the Caribbean, the baião
may be related to the French-African variation of the contradanza
that in Cuba eventually evolved into the danzón. The instruments
used in this form vary from those used in the Caribbean, probably
influenced by Congolese folk craft as opposed to the Yoruban instrumentation that dominated Cuba. The rural baião was taken to
the urban masses in the late 1930s and early 1940s by a charismatic
accordionist named Luis Gonzaga. His landmark tune, *Baião*,
written in 1946 with Humberto Teixera, a lawyer, formalized the

varied tendencies of the genre to create a popular music form with an easy dance beat.

Gonzaga was followed in the '50s by singer/songwriter Jackson do Pandeiro, who incorporated more coastal rhythms, especially the coco, another African circle dance with long roots in Brazilian history. By using the coco, Pandeiro was essential in the development of forró, a grittier, more urban version of baião, and a form that continues to rivet Brazilian listeners through performers like Chiquinho do Acordeon and Jacob do Bandolim. But, in the wake of the invasion of North American musical styles, especially jazz, baião was relatively neglected in the 1950s. Gonzaga's seminal work was revived by the tropicália movement using rock instrumentation in the 1970s, highlighted by Caetano Veloso's recording of *Asa Branca* in 1971.

Baião also had a modernizing, hybridizing influence on the development of Brazilian popular music in the North. Many of the descendants of baião, like embolada (a more lyrically complex version of coco), desafio (an embolada for dueling poets, recalling Cuban contraversias), axé (samba mixed with Caribbean beats like reggae, calypso, and merengue), even the 1990s hybrid creation lambada, and the popular recordings of Elba Ramalho, one of the foremost pop singers of the region in the 1980s, are strongly influenced by Gonzaga's trailblazing work.

Bossa Nova

Bossa nova was the first truly pan-hemispheric music of the Americas. Its first major manifestation was the music written by Antonio Carlos Jobim and Vinícius de Moraes for a stage play called *Black Orpheus* in 1956. Bossa nova was a slower, cooler samba that flowed lazily like the West Coast groove of Chet Baker and Gerry Mulligan, which directly influenced it. Although Jobim, who wrote one of the most famous songs of the twentieth century, *The Girl from*

Ipanema, was at bossa nova's compositional center, it was the sleekly cerebral tenor João Gilberto who was credited with inventing bossa's guitar style. He made Jobim compositions like *Corcovado* and *Desafinado* into pan-American pop classics and hits around the world.

Bossa nova is sometimes misinterpreted as lite music because it seemed to mute the strong Bahian drumming tradition that created the samba, stripping it down to its bare essentials, and retaining its syncopation. The haunting chords of bossa nova are best heard on guitar. The harmonic variation employed by Gilberto in *Desafinado* (which translates into "out of key") was one of bossa nova's revolutionary stratagems. While it sounded out of key, Gilberto was using a melodic shift that was a bit of a shock to listeners accustomed to a standard operatic style of singing. The song speaks about an imperfect guy in love with the perfect girl, with Gilberto demonstrating that his vocal "imperfection" was extremely seductive.

Jobim's music merged the experimentalism of composers like Ravel and Debussy with nationalist Brazilian composer Heitor Villa Lobos, who combined European classical forms with folkloric music and rhythms, emphasizing accelerated and highly chromatic melodic lines. Jobim's obsession with these harmonics, whether the mood paintings of Debussy, the mutated gypsy progressions of Ravel, or the flatted fifth notes of bebop, shaped his compositional creativity.

Born in 1927 in Rio de Janeiro, Antonio Carlos Jobim (often affectionately referred to as "Tom," his nickname) originally wanted to become an architect. In his early twenties, he began to play piano in nightclubs. His collaboration in 1956 with poet Vinícius de Moraes on the play *Orfeo do Carnaval*, a Brazilian retake on the Orpheus myth, which two years later was made into the French film *Black Orpheus*, established him as a composer who knew how to take artful lyrics (he would later write most of his songs) and put them into a moody, romantic context.

Guitarist João Gilberto was born in 1931 in Juazeiro, Bahia, and began playing guitar at age fourteen. At eighteen, he moved to

Bahia's largest city, Salvador, and performed on live radio shows with a band called Garotos da Lua. Upon reaching Rio a couple of years later, Gilberto entered into an unproductive period said by many to have been caused by excessive marijuana consumption, going ten years without producing an album. He eventually moved to the smaller town of Porto Alegre, where he perfected his unique vocal style and guitar playing. By 1959, when he recorded his first album, *Chega de Saudade* (No More Blues), a classic collection of bossa nova tunes mostly written by Jobim, his nasal singing style had become the voice of a new generation.

João Gilberto's staccato playing style, suggesting a kind of edgy fire behind the music's calming melodies, was singlehandedly responsible for the way bossa nova was played on the guitar. In the late '50s, Jobim became his most crucial collaborator, composing and accompanying him on the piano. Gilberto's personal demons—he suffered from constant bouts of depression—may have helped him express bossa nova's feeling of saudade. An untranslatable Portuguese word roughly meaning melancholic nostalgia, or a longing for homeland, saudade is key in the bossa nova aesthetic. The sadness of saudade has obvious roots in the travails of the Portuguese settlers wandering in the vast, semi-arid expanse of Brazil's interior, the plight of a displaced African slave, and the more recent experience of European immigrants in a land relatively isolated from the rest of the world. Perhaps its definitive expression is *A Felicidade*, the signature tune of the movie *Black Orpheus*. "Sadness has no end," says the song's narrator. "Happiness does."

But bossa nova also expressed the dare-to-be-different aspect of the Brazilian psyche. Ahead of the rest of Latin America, Brazil posited itself as another country in the Americas with a strong enough history and cultural development to become a cultural peer of the United States. Despite the irony buried inside it, bossa nova is the creation of men and women who wore their hearts on their sleeves. João Gilberto, the figurehead of the movement, wrote home from New York after hearing the Fifth Dimension's

1967 hit *Up, Up and Away* that it was one of the most beautiful songs he'd ever heard. The mystery of bossa nova is how it manages to be cool when the vast majority of its lyrics are so sentimental. You can't get much mushier than Jobim's lyrics to *Corcovado*: "I, who was lost and lonely/Believing life was only/A bitter, tragic joke,/Have found with you/The meaning of existence/O my love." Yet the song is a masterpiece.

With its accessible melodies, seductive harmonics, and air of tropical elegance, bossa nova traveled well outside of Brazil. In North America it became a much-welcomed alternative to the over-intellectualization of post-bebop jazz; Thelonius Monk was quoted as saying that bossa nova "gave the New York jazz intellectuals what [they were] missing—rhythm, swing, and Latin warmth." Through North American musicians who played bossa novas, like flutist Herbie Mann and horn players Cannonball Adderley, Horace Silver, and Dizzy Gillespie, bossa nova provided an opening to a jazz listener to hear improvised music without threatening them with lack of melody and classic song structure. It was as if bossa nova were saying, you can stop taking notes now and just groove.

In 1963, a collaboration between Jobim and João Gilberto with saxophonist Stan Getz and guitarist Charlie Byrd produced one of the great jazz albums of all time, *Getz/Gilberto*. Gilberto's wife, Astrud, made a deep impression on a worldwide commercial scale with her classic, whispery version of *The Girl from Ipanema* on *Getz/Gilberto*. The West Coast tendencies that Getz had appropriated from Gerry Mulligan had found vocalists for that peculiar strand of jazz, equivalent to Ella Fitzgerald and Nat King Cole. Bossa nova was more broadly popularized outside of Brazil by Sergio Mendes and Brasil 66, a kind of Brazilian jazz group with a chorus that sang soaring harmonies not unlike the Fifth Dimension. In the late 1960s, bossa nova's popularity began to wane. But when vocalist Elis Regina and Jobim recorded *Águas de Março*, included in *Elis and Tom* (1974) it seemed as if bossa nova were briefly returning to rule the world of melody and harmony. For several years the Gilbertos made recordings and continued to play in concert, but in 1994 Jobim died suddenly in New York of heart failure, and bossa nova never really regained its prominence. João Gilberto went through bouts of reclusiveness until the late 1990s,when he returned to record and perform, making a journey to New York in 2001. His 2000 release, *João Voz E Violão*, was a well-received collection of Brazilian classics produced by Caetano Veloso, whose *Coração Vagabundo* appears here.

In recent years, proponents of bossa nova in its pure form or slightly updated fashion include singers like Joyce, who has recorded twenty-one albums; Vinicius Cantuaria, who is part of New York's growing Brazilian scene; and Celso Fonseca, whose 2003 album *Natural* (Six Degrees), takes a minimalist approach to revitalizing the genre and hints at Gilberto and/or Veloso as very few have done.

Following the peak years of bossa nova in the mid to late 1960s, a new Brazilian music began to take form, one that was partially shaped by the imposition of military dictatorship in 1964. A wide variety of performers from early rock performers on singer Roberto Carlos's television show to singers like Djavan, Elis Regina, Chico Buarque, Milton Nascimento, Gal Costa, and the revolutionary tropicalistas, Caetano Veloso, Gilberto Gil, came under a category called Musica Popular Brasilera (MPB). Popular is here loosely defined as not very experimental or ethnic, much like the North American idea of popular music. MPB is one of the largest-selling genres in the Americas, largely because Brazil, the most populous country in South America, more effectively creates larger numbers by avoiding regionalization—music from all areas of the country is promoted as "Brazilian." The rest of Latin America's music can be fragmented into regional categories that don't transcend national differences, with the exception of Afro-Cuban, tropical and pop. MPB succeeded the bossa nova and samba eras, but despite its essential popularity it is one of the most innovative and eclectic popular music in the world.

A recent biography of singer Nara Leão, often cited as one of bossa nova's key vocalists post-Astrud Gilberto, claims that Leão's break from bossa nova on her first album (*Nara*, 1964), was MPB's moment of creation. But a phenomenon of televised music festivals that began in 1965 went a long way to establishing the stars of the genre. In a raucous atmosphere of booing and cheering, young singers and songwriters competed against each other in a proto-*American Idol* format. Nationalism and authenticity were valued over looks and commercialism, and protesting injustice was the order of the day. The prize-winning song at the first festival, held in Guarujá, a beach town outside of São Paulo, was *Arrastão*, as interpreted by a young singer named Elis Regina. The song, written by Vinicius de Moraes and Edu Lobo, established Regina as a star at the age of twenty and also made Lobo one of the most significant composers of the era—he combined aspects of traditional folk music with the harmonic and melodic innovations of bossa nova.

Chico Buarque

Chico Buarque's singing style was at best warmly seductive and at worst overly sentimental, but as a provocateur and heroic figure, he was one of the first stars of MPB in the 1960s and 1970s. He was seen by many as a defender of the nationalist folkloric values against Roberto Carlos's teen rock and the transgressive tropicalistas. Buarque was born in Rio de Janeiro in 1944, and his early years were strongly influenced by his historian father, who wrote about the emerging notion of Brazilian nationalism in a way similar to Gilberto Freyre. At twenty-one Buarque recorded *Pedro Pe-*

dreiro, a bossa nova, his signature song. A precursor to and perhaps direct influence on Rubén Blades's *Pablo Pueblo*, the song is the story of an average laborer and a work of social realism resonant with the aesthetic developed by director Glauber Rocha's Cinema Novo in the 1960s.

In 1968, already massively famous at the age of twenty-four, Buarque wrote and scored a relentlessly dismal work of existential theater called *Roda Viva* (Confusion). The play was a strong critique of obsessive fan worship—in the end, the star protagonist is torn limb from limb and his "flesh" is consumed by fans, with audience members invited to eat chicken meat that represents his flesh. Brazil's conservative military dictatorship was offended by the play, and there were several incidents where the military police disrupted it and arrested the cast. All this made Buarque an instant persona non grata.

Although Buarque's music was considerably more conventional than that of the tropicália movement that he found himself at odds with, he was forced into exile by the Brazilian government. When he returned in 1970, Buarque made *Construcão*, breaking from the bossa nova style that made his early career. Government repression of his lyrics became more intense. When tropicalistas Caetano Veloso and Gilberto Gil returned from their own exile, they reached an accord of sorts with Buarque, and he recorded one of his most penetrating records, *Caetano e Chico Juntos E Ao Vivo* with Veloso in 1972.

Buarque's post–exile career was marked by attempts to capture his original power. Highlights were his *Calice* duet with Milton Nascimento on a 1978 self-titled album, and more pairings with Caetano and his sister Maria Bethania. His 2000 album, *O Sambista*, was something of a comeback, including a remake of *Samba de Orly*, from *Construcão*, but it didn't resonate outside of Brazil. Still considered something of a national hero, because of his immense popularity and political defiance, Buarque represents the glory of MPB's beginnings.

Tropicália

The musical and cultural movement that at the same time opposed and synthesized the nationalist and rock strains of the MPB festival era, tropicália seems to stay modern even today, thirty-five years after it began. The tropicalistas were a radical reworking of the teen rock format of pop singer Roberto Carlos's mid-1960s *Jovem Guarda* television show, which, like Puerto Rico's nueva ola portoricenis (see Chapter 5), was showcasing Brazilian lite rock (sometimes called "ye-ye-ye," as in, she loves you, yeah yeah yeah). Discordant, iconoclastic, and rebelling for rebellion's sake, the early tropicalista recordings took the youthful energy of Jovem Guarda and updated the adult seriousness of bossa nova. Led by singer-composers Caetano Veloso and Gilberto Gil, tropicália, which distinguished the hybrid Brazilian point of view from the European idea of the avant-garde, was the ultimate expression of Brazil's version of the countercultural '60s.

With distortion-laden, psychedelic electric guitar blasts and tinny keyboard runs, the tropicalistas espoused the *Cannibalist Manifesto*, a document written in 1928 by Brazilian anthropologist, poet, and playwright Oswaldo de Andrade, which advanced a model for critically "devouring" cultural inflows from abroad. De Andrade thought the best way for Brazilians to make art was to swallow up outside (mostly European, some American) influences and spit them back out in a new kind of stew. The music tropicália produced following this philosophy seemed to predict every postmodern cliché you've heard about hip-hop, sampling, and the continual recycling of twentieth century pop culture. Singers like Veloso, Gil, Gal Costa, Jorge Ben, Maria Bethania, and Tom Zé dared to question the authority of the military dictatorship that ascended to power in 1964. Many of this group, most famously Veloso and Gil, were forced into exile in Europe for insisting, in the words of Veloso's 1968 song *E Proibido Proibir*, that to forbid is forbidden.

Caetano Veloso

Born in 1942 in Santo Amaro, Bahia, Veloso absorbed the region's musical heritage, which was more influenced by Caribbean, African, and North American pop music than the rest of the country. In his memoir, *Tropical Truth*, Veloso also pointed out a strong influence from French New Wave cinema. But it was the bossa nova sound of his predecessor and fellow Bahian, João Gilberto, that inspired him to become a pop singer. As his younger sister Maria Bethania became an overnight star singer in 1965, the twenty-three-year-old Veloso won a lyric writing contest with his song *Um Dia* and was signed to a recording contract with Phillips. Having moved from Salvador to Rio, he was introduced to Dori Caymmi, who wrote guitar arrangements for him, and Gal Costa, who sang backup vocals. He immediately became involved in resolving genre contradictions between pop and rock, traditional samba and bossa nova, modern and folkloric Brazilian music. Joined by Gilberto Gil, who also arrived from Bahia, Veloso plotted the tropicalista project as one that would use the commercial appeal of rock to transmit what they felt were revolutionary ideas.

One of the most gifted Brazilian musicians, Veloso is that rare combination, a singer of incredible vocal talent—his silky smooth tenor leaps operatically into high registers with shocking ease— and a masterful poet and composer. He is also perhaps the most striking embodiment of the postmodern turn Latin American has taken in the last half of the century. Growing up in the late 1950s and early 1960s, Veloso and his tropicalista contemporaries developed an ironic take on rock and '60s counterculture from the perspective of underdeveloped, wildly rhythmic, and mystical Brazil. It was a double consciousness parallel to the one African-Americans used to create jazz and later, hip-hop.

The preliminary phase from which tropicália was born was crystallized in a show Veloso was commissioned to put together in 1965, while still in Salvador, called "Nova Bossa Velha, Velha Bossa

Nova" (New Old Bossa, Old New Bossa), in which Veloso, Gil, Gal Costa, Maria Bethania, and Tom Zé performed. As the title implied, the group was struggling to move beyond bossa nova while trying to pay homage to it at the same time. The contradictory goal of preserving tradition while shattering it was the essence of tropicália. When the tropicalistas played their first concerts, their modernist affronts to Brazil's traditionalism were parallel to the challenge Bob Dylan issued when he played the Newport Folk Festival with an electric guitar.

When it hit in 1967, tropicália caused scandal. At one of the group's first concerts, which Veloso and Gil staged to promote their extravagant rebelliousness, the audience expressed its unambiguous distaste for Veloso's tropicália anthem, *Alegria, Alegria*, which was unlike anything they had ever heard. However *Domingo Na Parque*, which loped along to an Afro-Brazilian capoeira beat, met with enthusiasm from nationalist fans obsessed with Brazilian authenticity. *Alegria, Alegria*, wrote Veloso in *Tropical Truth*, "says a great deal about the intentions and possibilities of the tropicalista movement. In striking and intentional contrast to the manner of bossa nova—a formal structure in which altered chords move with natural fluency—here the perfect major chords are oddly juxtaposed. This derived largely from the way we heard the Beatles."

The first collection of these songs appeared in 1968's *Tropicália ou Panis et Circensis*, the title making an obvious reference to the bread and circuses used by the Roman empire to distract citizens from its corruption. The album featured songs by Veloso, Gil, Gal Costa, Os Mutantes, and Nara Leão. Many singers of the time, such as Chico Buarque, were already reacting against the military dictatorship, so tropicália's scathing, confrontational lyrics were not necessarily new. The true scandal, as Veloso once told me, was the electric guitars, clothes, hair, and the wild mixture of styles that characterized tropicalismo. Nevertheless, when the tropicalistas dared to question authority, they met with secret government repression.

The military dictatorship that ran Brazil in the late 1960s and early 1970s punished artists who were critical of the regime. Veloso and Gil were favorite targets—both spent two months in prison for "anti-government activity" and another four months under house arrest. The government "invited" them to leave the country, and since the two had no money to cover their expenses, they staged a defiant 1968 concert. In exile in London Gil and Veloso each recorded two almost-forgotten albums—Veloso's, another self-titled one released in 1971, was all in English save for a cover of Luis Gonzaga's *Asa Branca*. After their return to Brazil in 1972, prompted by the presence of a less hardline military ruler, their careers flagged. Veloso's reached a commercial low point in 1978, when he released *Muito*. Among this album's quirky collection of sparse, moody songs was *Terra*, which David Byrne would include in his first influential compilation of Brazilian music, *Beleza Tropical*.

Veloso had managed to keep together the same band, Da Otra Banda da Terra, during this period and began to build enough momentum in his career that he eventually made his way to New York, debuting at the Public Theater in 1983. Among those attending the show were Bob Hervitz, CEO of Nonesuch Records, and Arto Lindsay, a Downtown musician who grew up in Brazil, was influenced by the tropicalistas, and whose main claim to fame at the time was being a seminal member of the radical jazz-punk No Wave movement. They became fascinated with Veloso, and Hervitz signed him to a record deal. A live-in-the-studio, self-titled album was recorded in 1986 with Hervitz producing. It was followed by an experimental album, *Estrangeiro*, released in 1989 with Lindsay and his partner Peter Scherer, with whom he had formed the avant-rock duo Ambitious Lovers in 1984.

The cover of *Estrangeiro* is a painting of a stage set for a play by Oswaldo de Andrade. Veloso's project on *Estrangeiro* is to talk about the image that foreigners have of Brazil and how these perspectives can be more important to Brazilians than they are to the outsiders themselves. In the title track, *O Estrangeiro*, Veloso acknowledged

his panoply of outside influences as well as a playful aesthetic of
self-contradiction. Amidst a cacophony of scratching guitars, unlikely Bahian beats, and the scratchy one-stringed berimbau, he re-
veals a catalogue of his philosophical development. The critical
acclaim *Estrangeiro* earned allowed Veloso to stage almost yearly
appearances in the United States, launching a second career as a
solo artist.

After *Estrangeiro*, Veloso released three more high-concept albums for Nonesuch, as well as various collaborations (one with
Gil), movie soundtracks (most famously, *Orfeu*, a contemporary remake of *Black Orpheus*), and some homages (to the Latin American
bolero, *Fina Estampa*, and filmmaker Federico Fellini, *O Maggio a
Federico e Giullietta*). One of these, *Circulado* (1991) ambitiously
meditated on the circular nature of existence. With its weirdly Italian cadence, Latin grounding, and Slavic aftertaste, Veloso's Brazilian Portuguese gently insinuates itself into the neo-bossa novas,
deconstructed sambas, or Downtown funkoramas he frames his
songs with. An example is *Santa Clara, Padroeira de Televisao* (Pa-
tron Saint of Television), with its rippling Portuguese guitar paced
by percussive maculele sticks (similar to Afro-Cuban clave sticks),
praying that "Video be a pool where Narcissus/Shall be a god who
will also know how to resurrect." Many of Veloso's lyrics are as-
tounding feats of pure poetry. Simple, beautiful songs like *Itapua*—
garnished by a string quartet and set on a beach in Bahia, the center
of black Brazil—resonate as strongly as the disc's more complex
ones, like *Fora da Ordem*, which asserts that something is wrong
with President George Bush's New World Order.

1994's *Fina Estampa* is one of the finest albums of traditional
Spanish pop songs ever recorded, albeit by someone whose native
language was Portuguese. Veloso's choices of Rafael Hernández's
Lamento Borincano, and Agustín Lara's *María Bonita*, often associated with Julio Iglesias, were modernized, stripped down, and embellished by arranger/cellist Jacques Morelenbaum's muted
accompaniment. His next three albums, *Livro* (1998), *O Maggio a*

Federico e Giulietta (1999), and *Noites da Norte* (2001) continued to expand his work with Morelenbaum, covering various topics from the films of Fellini to the legacy of slavery in Brazil.

Gilberto Gil

In terms of the power and melodic force of his music, singer/song-writer/guitarist/bandleader Gilberto Gil could be compared with both Stevie Wonder and Bob Marley, but neither comparison conveys his impact. Whereas Veloso seems to lock himself into a room and return with hard-fought abstract paintings, Gil appears to roll out of bed into greatness—when they click, his songs become instant anthems. As a singer, his commanding voice is unflappable, malleable, and effortless.

Born in 1942 and raised in Salvador, Bahia, Gil played the accordion as a child, going on to study in an accordion academy at age eighteen, but as he grew into early adulthood he was composing songs. Like Veloso, he was greatly influenced by João Gilberto, whom he first heard on the radio in the late 1950s, so he learned to play the guitar. In 1965, after composing some television jingles, he got his first break when Elis Regina recorded his song *Louvacao*.

For many years Gilberto Gil seemed to play Caetano Veloso's alter ego. From their youth in Bahia through the heady days of the Tropicália movement in Rio, through their imprisonment, exile, and return to Brazil, their careers were inextricably linked. His first album, 1967's bossa-nova influenced *Louvacao*, contained elements of forró. It was followed by two eponymously titled albums. One, a collaboration with tropicalista house band Os Mutantes, contained *Domingo Na Parque* and made his introduction to the Brazilian music world strongly psychedelic. The second of the two, released in 1969, included his signature song *Cerebro Electronico* (Electronic Brain). His English album, *Gilberto Gil*

1971, included a version of Steve Winwood's *Can't Find My Way Home*. When Gil returned to Brazil, he resurrected the work of Jackson do Pandeiro, covering his classic *Chiclete com Banana*. Perhaps the strongest work of his pre-1980s period was *Refazenda* (1975), in which he revitalized forró, bringing it into the post samba-funk era with a heavy electric/fusion-influenced sound. Although there was much political content in his songs' lyrics, his music itself was often less experimental than Veloso's, anchored by easy funk dance grooves.

In the late '70s, Gil became something of a jazz fusion artist with albums like *Nightingale* and *Realce*. The Portuguese version of Marley's *No Woman, No Cry* on *Realce* began Gil's love affair with reggae music. In the early '80s, after the end of the Brazilian dictatorship that exiled him, Gil became a local councilman in Salvador. He also spent many years as an environmental activist. There were moments of brilliance in Gil's work over the next several years, such as *Andar Com Fe* from *Um Banda Um*, *Quilombo*, from that film's soundtrack, which celebrated the moment in Brazilian history when escaped slaves founded their own country within Brazil. Toward the end of the 1980s, Gil, inspired by a search for African diasporic musics, began to incorporate more reggae, reprising his cover of *No Woman, No Cry* on 1989's *A Gente Precisa Ver o Luar.*

On Gil's collaboration with Caetano Veloso in 1993's *Caetano e Gil: Tropicália 2*, the greatness of the early tropicália days is resurrected and enhanced by these two artists's maturity. Sharing the vocals with Caetano on *Tradicão*, Gil leaves his imprint as a chronicler of everyday lives on an album largely dominated by Veloso's big-picture poetry. He delivers songwriter Arnaldo Artunes's *As Coisas* with downtown industrial panache, and revives the baião on *Baião Temporal.*

Quanta, released in 1998, renewed interest in Gil particularly outside of Brazil, reestablishing his songwriting and emphasizing the link to Marley. In 1998's *Sol de Oslo* and 2000's *Eu, Tu, Eles* (the

Me, You, and Them soundtrack), Gil abandoned disco-pop and reinserted folkloric influences, particularly the accordion. *Eu, Tu, Eles* in particular is a paean to Luis Gonzaga and the tradition of forró. The presence of venerated accordionist Dominguinhos recalls the ebullience of *Refazenda*. Throughout, Gil's generous warmth and reinvigorated songwriting indicate that he finally found his way. In 2001, he was nominated for a Grammy for the soundtrack to *Me, You, and Them*. Later releases include *Gil and Milton* (2001), a duet album with Milton Nascimento; *Kaya N'Gan Daya* (2002), a tribute to Bob Marley; and *Z: 300 Anos de Zumbi* (2002), an experimental homage to rebel slave hero Zumbi.

After the modest success of the Gil and Milton duet and his Bob Marley tribute *Kaya N' Daya*, Gil embarked on a dramatically new phase of his life when he was named minister of culture in the government of leftist president Luis Inacio Lula da Silva in 2003, temporarily putting his music career on hold. More than thirty years after being exiled, he was finally an insider.

Os Mutantes

Os Mutantes was tropicália's most psychedelic and irreverent configuration. Formed in 1965 in industrial São Paulo, the group was the core of what Caetano Veloso called the "Paulista" contingent of the movement. They took their name, which means mutants, because they felt they were outsiders in Brazilian society. Singer Rita Lee was descended from a line of immigrants who came down from the United States South after the Civil War, and brothers Sérgio and Arnaldo Baptista divided guitars, keyboards, bass, and drum between them. Os Mutantes was the radical wing of tropicália—its original project was to tear down the musical conventions of Brazil, with absolutely no mercy for that country's traditions.

It was Os Mutantes's audacity that encouraged occasional collaborators Caetano Veloso and Gilberto Gil to face an audience

of leftist college students at a 1968 cultural festival and play electric guitars. The group's albums are noisy and decadent, trippy
and introspective. They were strange innovators—in one live gig,
they used an aerosol can of a popular brand of bug spray as a
high-hat for their drum set. When Sérgio distorted his vocals
through a rubber hose connected to a wired hot-chocolate can,
they called it the Voice Box.

Os Mutantes wasn't concerned with either Gil's africanidade
(celebration of things African) or Chico Buarque's quest to protect
nationalist ideals. While they were never formally banished by the
Brazilian government, the three went into a self-imposed exile in
Britain and France in the early 1970s. Their rejection of nationalist concerns and fetishization of discarded consumer items may
have made them poster children for Latin American postmod-
ernism, but their musical influence can be heard in contemporary
musicians like Stereolab and Beck. They were also remembered
for Rita Lee's pop-bossa versions of Caetano Veloso's *Baby* and
their own Electric Prunes-ish classic *Ando Meio Desligado*. Still
their relentless parodying of Latin traditional styles of great substance, as in *Cantor de Mambo*, an Afro-Cuban lark, and *Adeus
Maria Fuio*, a lampooning of baião, seems pointless and relegates
them to secondary status behind their contemporaries and occasional collaborators Veloso, Gil, and Jorge Ben.

Rita Lee left the band in 1972 and carried on a solo career that
continued her status as Brazilian rock queen, producing fourteen
albums, including 2002's *Bossa n' Beatles*, an album of Beatles covers (some in Portuguese, some in English). While the band
moved more toward an English progressive-rock sound, Os Mutantes's most sustained influence on Brazilian music probably
came through Liminha, who played bass with them in the middle
of their run and went on to become Gilberto Gil's producer and
collaborator from the mid-1980s on. In 1993, the band was discovered by U.S. rock fans when Kurt Cobain requested they re-

unite for a concert, an offer they declined. When David Byrne's Luaka Bop label released a compilation of their 1968–1972 work, *Everything Is Possible: The Best of Os Mutantes*, in 1999, the band was recognized by the North American press as a cornerstone of psychedelia on a par with the Beach Boys's *Pet Sounds*.

The Women of MPB

Three of the most important female singers in Brazil since the '60s—Elis Regina, Gal Costa, and Maria Bethania—had careers that spanned developments in the bossa nova, tropicália, and MPB eras. Regina, who was born in 1945 in Porto Alegre, was known for a tempestuous personality, a husky voice, and brusque stage presence. Her fiery style has drawn comparisons to Janis Joplin, but her voice, though possessing a bit of a rough edge, is much more nuanced. She spent the 1960s and 1970s performing songs by Brazil's best songwriters, including Edu Lobo, Milton Nascimento, Caetano Veloso, and Chico Buarque. During the period of political tumult of the military dictatorship, she drew a lot of criticism from nationalist groups for singing the national anthem at a ceremony celebrating Brazil's independence, but it was only revealed years later that she did so under the threat of imprisonment.

Few moments in Brazilian music history have had the heart-stopping impact of Regina singing *Aguas de Março* (Waters of March) with Antonio Carlos Jobim on their 1974 album, *Elis and Tom*. With its jazz-influenced arrangements, it sounds like chamber music with voice. A cascade of mournful cellos and violins surround her starkly beautiful performances of *Modinha* and *Corcovado*. On *Transversal do Tempo* (1978) and *Elis, Essa Mulher* (1979) she turned in haunting, mature performances that seemed to capture the ecstasy and melancholy of the Brazilian sentiment. But the highs and lows she projected as a singer caught up with her. Rumored to have entered into a cocaine dependency in the late 1970s, she died tragically of cocaine and alcohol intoxication in 1982.

Gal Costa and Maria Bethania had somewhat intertwining careers—they were two of the earlier stars of MPB and the festival era and were closely involved with Caetano Veloso and the tropicalistas. Costa and Bethania have left a recorded legacy spanning thirty-five years. From Costa's appearance on Bethania's first album in 1965, singing Caetano Veloso's *Sol Negro*, to their collaboration on one of MPB's most stunningly exhilarating songs, *Sonho Meu* (My Dream), in 1978, the two have been inextricably linked.

Costa's version of the tropicália anthem *Baby* (with English and Portuguese lyrics) is the most memorable. With a powerful, full-bodied soprano, Costa has recorded the work of all the great Brazilian songwriters, including Lobo, Veloso, Gil, Dorival Caymmi, and Jorge Ben. Her career got even bigger in the '70s and '80s, particularly through the success of 1984's *Aquarela do Brasil*, a tribute album to sambista Ary Barroso. She toured over the last decade performing a kind of revue that featured a collection of greatest hits of bossa nova, tropicália, and MPB.

Bethania, who began her career before her brother Caetano Veloso and was in some ways instrumental to launching his career, recorded close to forty albums after she began to supplant Nara Leão, an extremely popular early 1960s bossa nova singer, as the queen of the Rio scene. Like Costa, Bethania recorded most of Brazil's top songwriters' material, and she reached back into the samba era as well. She also recorded two classic duet albums with Chico Buarque (1975) and her brother, Veloso, in 1978. Her strongest later success was 1997's *Ambar* and a follow-up live album reprising the songs on *Ambar, Imitacão da Vida*, which was released a year later. A penetrating collection of songs from newer composers like Carlinhos Brown and old sambas from Ary Barroso, the album presents a more introspective style than Costa's, preferring minimal acoustic instrumentation.

Jorge Ben

Singer/songwriter/guitarist Jorge Ben was a contemporary of the tropicalistas, but his individualism set him apart from them. Like most of the Brazilian musicians of his day, Ben was inspired by João Gilberto, but rather than try to duplicate Gilberto's lyrical picking, he reinterpreted bossa nova from the perspective of a bass guitar. An eclectic performer refusing to commit himself to a particular genre, Ben was one of the forerunners of folk tendencies of Brazilian pop, and he slipped easily among samba, rock, bossa nova, and reggae.

Jorge Duílio Ben Zabella Lima de Menezes was born in 1940 in the Rio de Janeiro slum of Madureira. As a youth in the mid to late-'50s. Ben, like others of his class and African heritage, was drawn to the Mangueira and Salguiero samba schools. Ben, who changed his name to Jorge Ben Jor in the 1990s, allegedly because American guitarist George Benson once received payment for a Jorge Ben European tour, makes a strongly American-influenced funk music. Like the music of his heirs, the twenty-first century rappers of the contemporary style manguebeat (see below) as well as the Rio hip-hop world, Ben's music has the bluesy, funky edge that you hear in African-American music from Robert Johnson to Sly Stone.

Ben began his career playing in bars in the Rio district that produced bossa nova, but he strongly identified with the samba schools of the carnaval parades. He is credited with being among the first to play a samba on an electric guitar and he predated the tropicalista movement that he peripherally participated in. His political inclinations were not as pronounced, so he managed to escape the overt oppression that came down on them—symbolically, his song *Mas Que Nada* became a big hit for the conventional poppers Sergio Mendes and Brasil '66. *Mas Que Nada* and *Balanca Pema*, later revived by 1990s MPB diva Marisa Monte, were culled from 1969's *Samba Esquema Novo*, which straddled bossa nova and samba.

But like the tropicalistas recordings, Ben's 1970s albums, especially *A Tabua de Esmeralda* (1974) and 1976's *Africa Brasil*, became classics of Brazilian pop music. The former features *Zumbi*, a ballad honoring the slave liberator/hero of the nineteenth century, and *Os Alquimistas Estao Chegando*, a samba anthem that posits Africanidade as a mystical liberating force. *África Brasil* contains *Umbabaraumba*, a driving bass-driven funk tune later given a new life in David Byrne's *Beleza Tropical* compilation, and *Taj Mahal*, a song whose basic melodic line was borrowed by Rod Stewart on *Do Ya Think I'm Sexy*. Ben's soul-funk sound was ahead of its time, but it was at times undermined by the demise of tropicália and the general indifference outside of Brazil.

Although probably best known for the pop accessibility of *Mas Que Nada*, a frenetic, melodic pop samba with lush choral harmonies, Ben's two defining songs are *Caramba . . . Galileu de Galilea*, from 1972's *Ben* and *Umbabaraumba*, from *África Brasil*. In *Caramba*, he spouts a kind of popular liberation theology not unlike Tupac's gangsta rap in sentiment: "If a hustler knew how to be honest/he'd be honest for hustling's sake." In other words, survival is the only truth. *Umbababaraumba*, a rollicking tribute to a Brazilian soccer star, has been covered several times—musicians are in love with its driving rhythm, cutting guitar adornments, and Ben's "the party starts here" urgency.

Ben kept a low profile after the 1990s, playing occasional shows, but producing relatively few recordings. In 1997, he released *Musicas Para Tocar Em Elevador*. Unlike its title, which suggests elevator music, the album collects a number of contemporary Brazilian pop musicians (Carlinhos Brown, Funk n' Lata, Paralamas do Succeso) to reinterpret some of his classics with the freedom that many of today's rock tribute albums use. In 2002, Ben released two live albums that were the result of an unplugged session he did for MTV Latin America. Hits like *Balanca Pema*, *Mas Que Nada*, and *Taj Mahal* are revisited in a high-quality live recording.

Tom Zé

Art-samba pioneer Tom Zé was a charter tropicalista in the 1960s and 1970s and in some ways helped to spur the entire movement. But while his contemporaries went on to stellar careers, he remained fairly obscure until David Byrne essentially resurrected him in the late 1980s. Zé was born in 1936 and like Veloso and Gil, spent his childhood in Bahia. In 1964 and '65, he performed in musical revues that were staged by Veloso, with Gil, Gal Costa, and Maria Bethania. Zé's song, *Parque Industrial*, which reflected his lifelong theme of alienation from the modern world, was included in the manifesto album *Tropicalia: Ou Panis Et Circenses*, released in 1967. Zé went on to record eight albums during the 1960s and 1970s, starting with *Tom Zé*, in 1968. He had the same run-ins with the censors that his peers did, and took the extraordinary extra step of performing the transcript of his censorship court orders in the middle of his live sets.

Not much of Zé's early music survives, and evidently its experimentalism irked listeners accustomed to Brazil's mellifluous music. He once constructed an instrument that was a cabinet with blenders, vacuum cleaners, floor polishers, and other appliances and played with a "keyboard" made of doorbells. Zé played the odd university tour, took part in the Brazilian staging of *The Rocky Horror Picture Show*, and even went back to his hometown to work in his brother's gas station.

David Byrne's *Brazil Classics* compilations were influential in the revival of interest in Brazilian music in the '80s. When Byrne first heard Tom Zé's music in 1986, he was shocked. Combining Dadaesque ruminations, poetic balladry, eccentric minimalism, gritty guitar rock, and Brazilian pop, Zé was a cult figure waiting to be discovered. With Byrne's help, he began making some of the most relevant music of his career. The eccentric but playful Zé, sometimes known as the Captain Beefhart of Brazil, is fond of mythologizing his rural Brazilian upbringing. By his account, he grew up surrounded by dazzlingly musical but illiterate people. His songs play on the irony of their essentially medieval nature clashing with the sudden modernity that globalization brings. Zé's response to this is paradox. On *To*, from the first Byrne-sponsored release *Brazil Classics 4, Massive Hits (O Melhor de Tom Zé)*, he sings, "I'm confusing you to make things clear. I'm illuminating so I can blind. I'm going blind so I can lead."

To Zé, the settlers of the inner expanse of northeast Brazil, the birthplace of the baião, developed a kind of Europeanized form of the African oral tradition—instead of recording culture and discussing it in academies, his people lived culture, recited culture, danced culture. While it may be unfortunate that he calls this "illiteracy," it still leads to an interesting truth about Brazil and Latin America.

The instrumental *Toc*, from *Brazil Classics 4*, is playfully discordant, with irregular clock beats epitomizing Zé's abrasive experimentalism. The opening and closing tracks, *Ma* and *Nave Maria* use Brazilian ukuleles, called cavaquinhos, in eerie, nontraditional ways. His eccentricity extends even to his deconstruction of Antonio Jobim and Vinicíus de Moraes's *A Felicidade*. The odd time signatures and bizarre chord changes are one of the hallmarks of tropicália.

Zé's second Byrne-sponsored album, *Com Defeito de Fabricacão* (With Fabrication Defects), issued in 1998, is more lucid and melodic, less intent on proving his experimentalism. But his happy sarcasm grows even more profound, as he continues to hold that the "defects" of working-class Brazilians are their enduring humanity in the face of globalization. In 2001, he released *Jogos de Armar* on the Brazil-based Trama label, in which he employs the homemade instrument the businorio, essentially a car horn. He covers *Asa Branca* and continues down the same idiosyncratic path, while still broadening his influences and paying attention to vocal harmonies and lilting melodies.

Milton Nascimento and Minas Gerais Pop

Born in 1942 in Rio de Janeiro and raised in a rural town in the southern state of Minas Gerais, singer/songwriter Milton Nascimento was a contemporary of the tropicalistas, but he was not a part of that movement. His voice, which reached high registers without betraying too much of a falsetto, caused him to be noticed by U.S.- and Europe-based jazz fusion pioneer Eumir Deodato in 1967. That meeting eventually led Nascimento to collaborate with saxophonist Wayne Shorter on the most successful jazz-Brazilian fusion record ever, 1974's *Native Dancer.*

In his music, Nascimento reflected the pastoral, rural area where he grew up, the adopted black son of a white family. He was profoundly affected by bossa nova when he first heard it in the late 1950s, and when he moved to Belo Horizonte, the region's capital, he evolved from a pop-rock singer to embrace the complex chord changes and harmonies of jazz. There he also became part of an informal group of musicians called Club da Esquina (Corner Club), which included artists like composers Lo Borges and Guedes, guitarist/composer Toninho Horta, and percussionists Nana Vasconcelos and Robertinho Silva. This collaboration was celebrated on two discs, *Club da Esquina* and *Club da Esquina 2*, released in 1972 and 1978, respectively. These albums, as well as the Wayne Shorter experiment and *Courage*, an album Nascimento recorded with Herbie Hancock, Airto Moreira, and Deodato in 1968, had a profound effect on the fusion music community in the United States.

Nascimento recorded eleven albums in the 1980s, all of them wildly different, establishing him as an eclectic, unpredictable artist. Everything was fair game for Nascimento, from a mass based on the traditions of escaped slaves (*Missa dos Quilombos*, 1982) to records featuring collaborations with a folkloric group called Uakti, Caetano Veloso, and Elis Regina (*Anima*, 1982), and *Yaurete* (1987), which included Paul Simon and Herbie Hancock.

The one consistent theme in his music during this period was his commentary on life in post-dictatorship Brazil and on the possibilities of this newfound freedom.

Over the 1990s Nascimento continued producing strong albums, particularly 1990's *Txai*. He retained a commitment to the simple pairing of the singer and the acoustic guitar, and the lightness and poignant melancholy of his voice have inspired the singing of Virginia Rodrigues, from Salvador, and Cesaria Evoria, from the Portuguese-speaking Cape Verde islands.

Contemporary MPB

While Música Popular Brasileira has its roots in performers like Chico Buarque, Elis Regina, and Gal Costa, it became the central genre for Brazilian pop after the tropicália and bossa nova eras died out in the late 1970s. MPB, the pop standard for the sixth-largest music market in the world, reinvestigates and reinvigorates Brazilian pop and an array of regional ethnic music with American styles from folk-rock to funk to acid jazz to hip-hop. For artists like Zélia Duncan—whose throaty voice can sound like Bonnie Raitt's to North Americans—MPB is a chance to incorporate American influences without losing their traditional grounding. Finding a place for everything from the extravagant samba-pop of Daniela Mercury, whose every show seems like a carnaval, to the understated Bahian grace of Margareth Menezes, to the Funkadelic-*batucada* fusion of Carlinhos Brown, MPB serves a function a little like North American R&B. The artists have, as always, a samba in their hearts, but they've been listening to the cooler textures of North American and European music and don't need to live up to the pressure of following the "old guard" tropicalistas like Caetano Veloso, Gilberto Gil, and Gal Costa.

Marisa Monte

Born in 1967 in Rio de Janeiro, Marisa Monte was the daughter of Carlos Monte, who sat on the board of directors of the Portela samba school. She took up drumming at an early age and studied music theory, ultimately leaving for Italy at eighteen to study opera for a little over a year. She returned to Brazil and became a kind of soul-jazz chanteuse under the guidance of Brazilian soul pioneer Nelson Motta. When her first live album was released in 1989, she almost immediately became MPB's new star.

Though she has a dizzying swirl of long curly black locks, wears elaborate stage costumes, and embodies an Ibero-Brazilian sensuality, it seems limiting to dub Monte a diva. She may tread into a chic erotic space when she sings love songs written by men about women without changing the gender in the lyrics, but Brazilian singers do this all the time. A Monte show is like a dreamlike revue of an utterly modern Carmen Miranda, one with friends like Lou Reed, Philip Glass, and Arto Lindsay. Monte's four albums, *Mais* (1991) *Rose and Charcoal* (1994), *A Great Noise* (1997), and *Memories, Chronicles, and Declarations of Love* (2000), have been released in the United States as well as Brazil. Made under Lindsay's supervision, they have established her as the queen of an art-samba, neo-bossa aesthetic that bridges Downtown with Rio. While 1991's *Mais* elegantly defined Monte's niche, *Rose and Charcoal* strengthens her resolve, re-emphasizing her roots. Definitive Downtown sessionists like Marc Ribot, John Zorn, and Ryuichi Sakamoto are replaced by Gilberto Gil and the funky *baião*, Carlinhos Brown, a Jorge Ben-like Africanist and long-time collaborator with the pop stylist Sergio Mendes. The effect is a new sense of cool hinted at, but hardly ever attained by, jazz-infused hip-hop.

Monte's strategy in *Rose and Charcoal*—the title refers the multiracial character of Brazil's people and culture—is to mix several traditional and modern tendencies. Lindsay's incredibly crisp, spare

production enables her to crystallize varied tendencies into a definitive style. Collaborating with Nando Reis and Arnaldo Antunes,
from São Paulo's leading avant-rock band Titas, Monte sings their
lyrics, sometimes derived from the concrete poetry that inspired the
tropicalistas, over an airy, elongated samba. In *O Céu* (The Sky), on
the wings of Gil's plucky acoustic and Bernie Worrell's Hammond
organ, she fancifully intones, "The sky parachutes and high
heels/Nobody can catch the sky," while *Bem Leve* ends abruptly
with "A wooden word falls to the ground/A coffin/Just like that."

Her *Rose and Charcoal* cover of the Velvets' *Pale Blue Eyes* is a
haunting tease, making it a kind of a gypsy lament. But even as she
can mix Lou Reed with Philip Glass, who arranges strings on *Ao
Meu Redor* (All Around Me), and Laurie Anderson, who does a
guest vocal on *Enquanto Isso* (Whenever), her nods to North
America are merely window dressing. Monte is more a postmodern Gal Costa than a female Sergio Mendes.

Looking to the northeast corner of Brazil for deeper African
roots, Monte bonded with Mendes alumnus Carlinhos Brown,
purveyor of a loping, rustic-percussive baião beat, on *Rose and
Charcoal*. *Segue O Seco*, powered by Brown's drumming muscle and
background vocal, egged on by the squeaky one-stringed berimbau, is the record's roots triumph, a prayer for rain on a drought-
stricken land that becomes a celebration. A similar epiphany is
accomplished in *Maria de Verdade*, written by Brown, but the album's purest moment of ecstasy occurs in Monte's duet with Gil,
Danca da Solidao, a 1972 Paulinho da Viola bossa nova.

Brown also figured strongly in 1997's *A Great Noise*, writing four
songs, playing organ and guitar, and contributing backup vocals. The
spirit of tropicália is revived through covers of Gilberto Gil's *Cerebro
Electronico* and a live version of *Panis et Circenses*, the latter featuring
chiming guitars and glittery choruses. But the core of the album are
Brown compositions like *Maracá*, a bass-heavy, funk-driven vehicle
for Monte's airy ecstasy. *Memories, Chronicles, and Declarations of Love*
featured the nostalgic lilt of the ukulele-like cavaquinho that embel-

lished Paulino da Viola's *Para Ver as Meninas*, and Monte's riveting, nuanced delivery created a kind of *My Funny Valentine* catharsis on *Gotas de Luar*. Monte's 2003 release was *Tribalistas*, a collaboration with Brown and songwriter Arnaldo Antunes. Simple, effective pop done with spare acoustic instrumentation (with some ambient electronic backing), the songs here are state-of-the-art MPB, hinting at surrealist poetry, Tom Zé's deconstructed samba, and the tropicalista movement. The title track is a manifesto of sorts, announcing "Tribalistas" as an "anti-movement" that "doesn't have to be anything."

Carlinhos Brown

The Babyface of MPB is singer/songwriter Carlinhos Brown, whose ultra-modern update of Bahian rhythms and Gilberto Gil-like songcraft is brilliantly displayed on his second album, 1997's *Alfagamabetizado*. Brown brings the charismatic momentum of Bahian axé and batucada, musics derived directly from Afro-Brazilian drumming, to create a sound for new-jack funkateers of North and South America. Born Antonio Carlos Santos Freitas in Salvador, Bahia in 1963, Brown renamed himself after the hardest working man in show biz, and has lived up to that sobriquet. He's collaborated with everyone from bossa legend João Gilberto to Veloso, Costa, Monte, Gil, Daniela Mercury, reggae-ska group Paralamas, and even thrash metal homies Sepultura. He also wrote five of the twelve songs on Sergio Mendes's 1993 Grammy-winning *Brasilero*.

In the carefree spirit of a street drummer, Brown writes songs about simple emotions with joyful, catchy choruses, and belts them out in styles reminiscent of Fela, Gilberto Gil, and R&B crooner Maxwell. But for every carnavalesque neo-samba like *Alfagamabetizado*'s *A Namorada* (In Love), with its Prince-like funk structure and celebratory singalong chorus, there's a screechy guitar, or a snarling Chico Science-like harangue. Brown trades on his urban griot status as the harder-edged rapper Science would, but in *Tour* turns the hard-knocks tribulations of proletarian *descamisados* (shirtless ones) into a poppy, jubilant chorus of resistance.

Alfagamabetizado announces itself as a language experiment, peppering several songs with English lyrics, some French, and a playful private dialect, hinting at the hybrid Tower of Babel we're becoming. "I'm all right! All right!" bellows Brown in English. His poetic gymnastics most often appear in his sometimes effortlessly flowing, sometimes jagged ballads, as in *Argila*'s moody refrain, "E zuzue/e zum zum zum."

Alfagamabetizado's, and Brown's, most crucial innovation is the juxtaposition of new tribal energy with a minimalist studio cool. In *Cumplicado de Amario*, Brown layers the flat and spooky sounds of two different Bahian drumbeats with cutting, percussive guitars and a full jazz brass section.

Brown's subsequent effort, *Omelette Man* (1999), displayed increasing eclecticism. As if inventing a funkier Sergio Mendes sound, the title track bubbles along to several climaxes. *Vitamina Ser* is a hard-driving reggae tune. *Soul by Soul* is a Beatles-esque rock ballad, and there are stripped-down sambas punctuated by celebratory horn charts and of course, strong batucada rhythms. The 2001 release *Bahia do Mundo* is fully realized Brown—surdo drums and wah-wah guitars grapple for dominance, and *Carvalo da Simpatia* captures his ability to bask in melody and emotion.

Manguebeat

Many U.S. Brazilophiles first heard of Recife, the capital city of the northeastern province of Pernambuco, through the efforts of the late Chico Science, a visionary rapper who was at the root of the fusionist scene known as manguebeat in the mid to late 1990s. Chico Science and Nação Zumbi, a group of drummers who updated traditional northeastern genres with rap, funk, reggae, and rock, captured the angst of urban working-class Brazilians. Their two albums, *Da Lama*

Ao Caos (1996) and *Afrociberdelia* (1997), were defining moments in the creation of a new Brazilian music sensibility. Manguebeat, like so much in Latin American music, is a postmodern mixture of several northeastern styles, such as forró, coco, and maracatú, which were pioneered in the '50s by baião stars Luis Gonzaga and Jackson do Pandeiro. Manguebeat experimenters like DJ Dolores Mestre Ambrosio, Sheik Tosado, and the electronica-influenced Otto, captured effectively on *Baiáo de Viramundo: Tributo a Luiz Gonzága* (2000), paint a picture of yet another Brazilian music renaissance.

Otto, who was a percussionist for Chico Science, is a primary muse of manguebeat. His landmark album, *Samba Pra Burro* (1999), was a DJ-culture influenced rhythmic and melodic odyssey of manguebeat, so influential that it was quickly deconstructed by several Brazilian underground DJs, including Apollo 9, DJ Dolores, and Andre Abujamra. Recife's location on the edge of the northeastern desert known as the sertao has in the past made it an undesired stop for touring Brazilian musicians, but due largely to the movement led by Nação Zumbi, it is becoming a trendy destination. Chico Science died tragically in an automobile accident in 1997, but Nação Zumbi continued to perform, with percussionist Jorge Dupeixe on vocals. Drawing heavily on batucada, axé, and capoeira traditions, the current version of Nação Zumbi mixes African drumming with a punkish, speed-metal sensibility, releasing *Radio Samba* in 2000.

New York, Brazil

The American boy who grew up in Brazil, then came to New York to help invent Downtown, Arto Lindsay had a major hand in mainstreaming tropicália. Originally part of New York's No Wave punk movement, which featured largely atonal, abstract noise-rock, Lindsay returned to his Brazilian roots in the mid-1980s, spurred especially by Caetano Veloso's first area show at the Public Theater. He quickly made an alliance with Veloso and parlayed this alliance into producing him as well as Marisa Monte. In the late '90s he issued a trilogy of solo mood albums, *Corpo Sutil/Subtle Body*, *Mundo Civilizado*, and *Noon Chill*, that featured many songs written in Portuguese, affecting a style reminiscent of Veloso's and Tom Zé's. Lindsay has also worked with bossa nova revivalist Vinicius Cantuaria, whose solemn, spare recitations fit right into the Lindsay/Byrne Downtown nexus.

Another Brazilian artist who has benefited from the Downtown Brazilian alliance is Bebel Gilberto, daughter of bossa nova founder João Gilberto, born in 1966. Bebel kicked around the New York Brazilian music scene for a decade, playing with local sessionists Romero Lubambo and Claudio Roditi, trying to survive on the interest in Brazilian bossa jazz, which had been nurtured in the 1970s by Airto Moreira and Flora Purim. Gilberto did a version of MPB, her stage shows combining a bit of Daniela Mercury-style samba-pop and Gal Costa-ish cabaret Brazilian.

In 2000 Gilberto capitalized on New York's growing fixation with cocktail lounge ambient music, an offshoot of the dance club scene that focused on drum and bass remixes with Brazilian sources. Collaborating with club music maestros like Suba and Thievery Corporation, Gilberto thrust herself into the leading edge of the emerging Brazilian electronica movement. On her immensely popular *Tanto Tempo* (2000), Gilberto breathes new life into classics by Brazilian songwriter Baden Powell (*Samba da Bancao*) and Chico Buarque (*Samba o Amor*), as well as the English-language bossa-pop classic *So Nice*, written by Norman Gimbel, who had collaborated with Antonio Carlos Jobim on English lyrics to classics like *Girl from Ipanema*.

The effect of Gilberto's vocal is similar to that achieved by most of the MPB giants, although in the spirit of bossa nova, she sets a mood that doesn't overwhelm the backing music, steering clear of dominating it. This new direction for Brazilian music is a natural one, for several reasons: the samba drum pattern is easily replicated by rapid-fire sequencers and samplers; bossa nova introduced a cosmopolitan cool to Brazilian music long ago; it fits in with the new hunger for the modernization of world music, pioneered by Fela and Peter Gabriel in the '70s and rapidly gaining momentum in the early twenty-first century.

Since the turn of the century, Brazilian music has continued to evolve rapidly, with new artists like Zuco 103, based in the Netherlands, exploring electronica, and Otto's *Condom Black* (2001) further pushing the boundaries of manguebeat. A pairing of bossa nova pioneer guitarist Roberto Menescal with his son Mario produced two bossa/electronica albums under the name Bossa Cuca Nova. The second, *Brasilidade*, was nominated for a Grammy in 2001, reinterpreting classics like *Agua de Beber*, and *Girl from Ipanema*. Celso Fonseca's 2003 album *Natural* features this Gilberto Gil collaborator's subtle vocal work layered over spare, mostly acoustic instrumentation. Somehow lurking behind almost all of these cutting-edge efforts is the steady, sure beat of samba. While the different paths of Brazilian melody, harmony, and rhythms have diverged and converged so often since *Pelo Telefone*, there is such a strong integrity to what samba has wrought that it never seems to get erased by the wild experimentalism that accompanies Brazil's headlong dive into the global technological future.

•8•

Other Latin Beats from Mexico, Colombia, and the Dominican Republic

Besides Cuban, Brazilian, and to a lesser degree, Argentinian and Puerto Rican music, and North American jazz, rock, and R&B, the musical styles of three other countries—the Dominican Republic, Colombia, and Mexico—have left their mark on Latin music. Like Brazil, each of these countries has several genres associated with different regions. The music of the Dominican Republic, particularly the merengue, and Colombia, particularly the cumbia, has transcended national boundaries to become "mainstream" Latin music. Right now there may be more commercially successful merengue bands in Puerto Rico than in the Dominican Republic, and there are so many Mexican groups playing variations of the cumbia that many Latinos have forgotten its Colombian origin, although it is still Colombia's national music. While the folk styles of Mexico—the corrido, ranchera, and Texan conjunto music—remain regional phenomena that have not broken across the Mexican border to the rest of Latin America, they have strongly influenced North American music, particularly Texas and California rock, and are popular across the entire Southwest border region.

This chapter will discuss the origin of merengue and cumbia, their spread within and outside the Dominican Republic and Colombia, some of the other genres of those countries (including the development of salsa in Colombia), and survey the influential styles of Mexican regional music. Artists from other countries who play merengue and cumbia will be included within the discussion of particular styles.

The Dominican Republic: Merengue, Perico Ripiao, and Bachata

Merengue, like many of the Afro-Caribbean dance rhythms such as the Cuban danzón and the Puerto Rican danza, came about by fusing the European contredanse with African drumming traditions. It features the central use of the five-beat cinquillo rhythm, the one that became the basis for the Cuban habanera and Argentine tango and is found in Brazilian samba. Its structure is similar to the Cuban son in the way that it introduces a theme and proceeds to an improvisatory section, and call and response is featured. But somehow its sound is more visceral, dancing to it centers more on hip movements than complicated steps, and the drum that drives it, the tambora, drives the music in a less subtle, primordial way. The dance was once thought so licentious that it was banned in Puerto Rico in 1849.

Because of the Dominican Republic's European-identified elite, island scholars refused to recognize merengue's African origins until the 1970s. Actually, Dominican merengue originated in the slower Haitian mereng and traveled across the border to the Dominican Republic in the mid–nineteenth century, shortly after that country's war of independence in 1844. Merengue's fusion between African and European musics was a social process much like Cuba's. The drum-oriented African chica and calenda were grafted onto the ballroom-friendly contredanse, using the cinquillo rhythm. But instead of the line-dancing style of the contredanse, couples danced free-style in what many authorities considered a lascivious manner.

Although rural, folk styles of the merengue eventually evolved, the original merengue ensembles performed the music in a ball-room for the Dominican elite. The lineup featured some or all of these instruments: flutes, violins, guitars, mandolins, cuatros, and on percussion, the timbál, the güiro, and the characteristic merengue drums, the tambora (a double-headed drum played sideways) and the pandereta (a handheld tambourine-like instrument). Some ballrooms in the countryside banned merengue, but the music thrived in less formal settings. It was often used during the patron-saint festivals, yearly gatherings that symbolized the union of African culture and Catholicism in a way similar to Cuban Santería and Brazilian candomblé.

Because of distrust of the island elites' collaboration as significant trading partners with Germany during World War I, the United States occupied the Dominican Republic from 1916 to 1924. The region to the north and west of the capital city of Santo Domingo, called Cibao, waged a propaganda war against the occupation. As part of that campaign, the landed gentry from plantations and other old money families used the folkloric music of the peasantry, a stripped-down form of merengue, played with groups of accordion, tambora, güiro, and saxophone, that would become known as merengue típico cibaeño, or merengue from Cibao. This folk-influenced merengue had a shuffling four-beat rhythm that was easy for dancers, and it became the dance salon merengue that attracted all levels of society. The Cibaon merengue downplayed the music's African influence, a denial that may seem absurd in a country where the population is close to 80 percent mixed-race, but that can be partially explained by the fear of association with Haiti. Through this political and social context, it was the Cibaon form of merengue that first became a nationalist music. Accordionists Francisco "Nico" Lora and Antonio "Toño" Abreu were the most prominent bandleaders of this period.

Cibaoan merengue ultimately set the stage for the next era of merengue, which firmly established the genre as *the* Dominican nationalist music. This modern era merengue was ushered in by the coming to power of Rafael Trujillo, one of Latin America's longest-lasting strongmen—he ruled from 1930–1961. Trujillo, a military man of working-class origins, wanted to solidify the Dominican Republic's national identity in his own image. Remodeling merengue as a polite ballroom dance was a way he saw of distinguishing Dominican music from the music of Cuba and Puerto Rico.

The Luís Alberti orchestra, which Trujillo favored because it harnessed Cibaon merengue's rustic qualities in a sophisticated, jazz-influenced presentation, was brought to Santo Domingo and renamed Orquesta Presidente Trujillo. Alberti's style was modeled on North American big-band jazz, with the additional input of local instruments such as the tambora, the güiro, and the piano accordion. Other early stars of Trujillo-era merengue included Super Orchesta San José, led by Papo Molina, Los Hermanos Vásquez, and El Trio Reynoso.

The mid-1930s also saw the development of an important merengue variation, the perico ripiao, which stressed accordion solos. The origin of this name, literally meaning "ripped parrot," has been interpreted in two ways. One, it was the name of a brothel, and the ripped parrot was a euphemism for a serviced penis. Or two, the name referred to the humble musicians who played the music—they could only afford meager meat like that from an eviscerated parrot. Perico ripiao has come to signify the more rustic forms of merengue performed today as an alternative merengue genre.

The assassination of Trujillo in 1960 ended his reign of terror and intimidation, and a great wave of euphoria swept the Dominican Republic. With the new democratic government, the form of merengue didn't change, but its lyrics spoke unabashedly of this happiness. One of the first stars to emerge in the atmosphere of

the 1960s was Johnny Ventura, who began in Luís Pérez's orchestra, but eventually formed his own band, Johnny Ventura y su
Combo-Show, in 1964. While the word *combo* reflected the influence of Puerto Rican Rafael Cortijo's compact combo format, the
show part indicated another influence entirely. Known to dress as
flamboyantly as Elvis Presley and to stress the dancing performance of his sidemen, Ventura presented a merengue that was to an
extent influenced by North American rock and roll. Many of his
early hits, such as *Ah Yo No Se Yo* and *Un Poquito Para Atras*, are
captured on a 1987 compilation, *Johnny Ventura y Su Combo*, on
Kubaney Records.

While Ventura ultimately went on to incorporate disco influences in the late 1970s, his reign as merengue king was usurped by
the dominant merenguero of the '70s and '80s, Wilfrido Vargas.
Vargas was a master hybridizer, turning merengue into the international music that it is today. He brought the tempo of the
merengue to breakneck speeds and went much further than Ventura in incorporating outside musical influences, drawing from
Haitian konpa (similar to Puerto Rican bomba) music, Colombian
cumbia, and, eventually, American hip-hop. Vargas also initiated a
trend of covering hit Latin American ballads in an attempt to open
up merengue to a wider international audience. His first release, in
1974, was under Wilfrido Vargas y sus Beduinos, the name of his
long-time band. He went on to record seventeen albums on the
Karen label. A key collaborator was pianist and composer Sonny
Ovalle, who helped develop the band's signature sound. *El Bar-
barazoí*, released on 1978's *Punto y Aparte*, was key in the international popularization of merengue, and Vargas went on to record
several hit albums with vocalist Sandy Reyes. In 1989 he received a
Grammy nomination for *Animation*, and his 2002 hit album, *El
Jardinero*, incorporated rap music.

As Paul Austerlitz related in his book *Merengue: Dominican Music and Dominican Identity*, a major transformation in merengue
style took place in the 1980s. The mangue beat, also known as the

maco beat, originally pioneered in the '60s by Cheché Abreu, began to have a major influence on mainstream merengue in the early '80s. The rolling four-beat rhythm of the Cibao-oriented style of merengue was replaced by the two-beat rhythm of the more primal African maco beat, one of the many subsidiary rhythms found in the Dominican Republic and other Caribbean islands. With the maco beat, which was parallel to the marching disco beat, merengue was even easier to dance to, which led to an explosion of interest in merengue outside of the Dominican Republic. Merengue became a staple of dance floors from Santo Domingo to Miami to New York, and the genre began to sell as much as salsa, and sometimes outsell it. The stars of this new maco movement were Pochi y su Coco Band, Jossie Esteban y la Patrulla 15, and Los Hermanos Rosario, bands that began touring in the United States in the mid-1980s.

The '80s also saw the emergence of Juan Luís Guerra, who deviated from the maco trend and incorporated troubadour elements and high-quality production in his records, which prompted a generation of salsa loyalists to embrace the merengue beat. Born in Santo Domingo in 1957, and influenced by boleros, the nueva canción movement, and the Beatles, he left the country in 1980 to study at the Berkelee School of Music in Boston. Guerra turned away from the speeded-up, mass-market versions of merengue music and celebrated its more folkloric roots, particularly bachata. A kind of rural troubadour singer-songwriter form, bachata is played with traditional guitars or a requinto similar to the one used in trío music.

At once traditional and celebratory of Africanness (his song, *Guavaberry*, from 1987's *Mientras Mas lo Pienso*, celebrated English-speaking Africans in an obscure corner of the Dominican Republic), he is also an exponent of Western rigor. His band, formed in 1984, was called Juan Luis Guerra y 440, the 440 representing his backup group of vocalists, their moniker referring to the number derived from the standard pitch of the A note: 440 cycles per second. His backup singers helped Guerra fuse the harmonic perfection of Manhattan Transfer with world music influences from Africa and Brazil and native styles like merengue and the slower, folkier bachata variant. His compelling, poetic lyrics and his obvious concern for continuing bachata's social protest tradition have made him one of Caribbean music's most cherished musical figures. In 1990, Grupo 440 got its first break when Guerra's 1988 composition, *Ojalá Que Llueva Café* (I Hope It Rains Coffee), a plea for better economic conditions for the island's poor, became widely known as the backing track for a TV commercial about a local brand of coffee. The album of the same title kicked off an international tour during which crowds would open and spin umbrellas when the song was played. Guerra and 440's next release, *Bachata Rosa* (which came out later in 1990), won the first Grammy for any merengue-oriented group.

With *Bachata Rosa*, Guerra established himself as a purveyor of intelligent, sexy dance music with excellent musical arrangements and attention to perfect-pitch harmonies. The album is well-paced, moving from the mid-tempo bachata form to more frenetic merengue numbers. What gives Guerra broad appeal as a recording artist is the way his bachatas feature Cuban-style bolero trumpet figures, and his merengues evolve into the supple rhythms of the Cuban son. Upbeat, danceable songs like *Rosália* and the monster hit *La Bilrrubina* are Guerra at his most infectious, while slower boleros like *Como Abeja al Panál* and *A Pedir Su Mano* can inhabit your body like a romantic fever. Throughout, Guerra maintains a poetic quality in his lyrics, as in the title track, which is a décima, its first four lines taken from Neruda's *Book of Questions*. But perhaps Guerra's strongest suit is in his journalistic tone, as in *Carta de Amor*, where he pleads with an estranged lover: "As you can see I think only of you/I'm not interested in Perestroika/nor basketball/nor Larry Bird." Guerra's back-up vocalists are in top form here, and Cuban jazz pianist Gonzalo Rubalcaba makes an appearance.

In the tradition of the nueva canción movement of Silvio Rodríguez, Victor Jara, and Pablo Milanés, Guerra continued his socially conscious lyrics and musical innovation on albums like *Fogaraté* (1994) and *Ni Es lo Mismo Ni Es Igual* (1998). Their songs worked metaphoric themes about immigration, the onset of high technology, and the preservation of the island's cultural past and its environment. Guerra, a somewhat reclusive figure, could take up to four years to release an album. After *Ni Es lo Mismo*, he released *Colección Romantica* (2000), a greatest-hits compilation of love songs.

Guerra's merengue-bachata style reflects bachata's influence from the 1960s days of the Chilean nueva canción movement. The lyrics of bachata often express the social protest that coincided with the Joaquín Balaguer presidency, which despite its democratic pretensions was often referred to as the second Trujillo regime. Bachata is one of the most clearly rustic-sounding musical styles in Latin America, and it is associated with the poverty of the countryside. With its quirky, repetitive, rolling guitar-picking style, bachata is a countrified bolero, with lengthy verses that poetically express dismay with socio-political conditions, as well as laments of love. A singer-songwriter like Raulín Rodríguez, for example, can wallow in the disappointment of a lost love, in a song like *Anoche* (Last Night), and Blas Duran can indirectly criticize Balaguer with his song *Ojo Pela'o* (Eyes Peeled). Many bachata singers of the '70s and '80s took the lead of openly political merengue singer Cuco Valoy, who once portrayed himself (albeit somewhat humorously) as the victim of police brutality on the cover of his album *No Me Empuje* (Don't Push Me).

Many of bachata's bigger stars, such as Alex Bueno, Antony Santos, Elvis Martínez, Francis Deo, Joe Veras, and Luis Vargas, known as "The Supreme King of Bitterness," toil in relative obscurity. (Vargas's 1997 album *Volvió el Dolor* is considered one of the best of the genre.) Juan Manuel is one of the few recent bachateros to cultivate a less anonymous image. On 1998's *Corazón de Bachata*, Manuel manages to glamorize the hokey twanging guitars of bachata with charismatic, Cuban son-influenced music, at times evoking North American blues greats like Robert Johnson. On *Para qué Me Mate un Hombre que me Mate una Mujer* (literally, "Why does a man kill me when it's a woman who does"), Manuel, as a hard-drinking ne'er-do-well, proposes that the House of the Rising Sun is in Santo Domingo. *Asesina de Amor* continued Manuel's pursuit of violent emotion (the song is about an unfaithful woman who is a "murderer" of love) in the context of a happy crescendo of guitars that are reminiscent of African guitarist King Sunny Adé and Hawaiian slack-key style.

Compilations like the Bachata Hits series on J&N/Sony, can offer a quick education to a bachata neophyte. The 2003 edition contained some of the previous year's top hits by Monchy & Alexandra, Alex Bueno, Raulín Rodríguez, and Vanessa. The album also featured a merengue version of Mexican singer Juan Gabriel's *Tus Ojos Mexicanos Lindos*, probably in an effort to cement that community's interest in bachata. Bueno's 2002 release, *Pídeme* (J&N/Sony), was one of the year's strongest releases in the genre. Bueno has one of the better voices in bachata, he possesses a charisma not unlike Victor Manuelle's, and the studio musicians are superior. Andy Andy's *Aquí Conmigo* (Sony Discos) is an even more ambitious pop-bachata experiment, with three boleros from Mexican singer Marco Antonio Solís and one by Ricardo Montaner. But for something with a little more of an air of authenticity (without sacrificing modern recording techniques), Zacarías Ferreira's *Adios* (2001) and *Novia Mía* (2002) are state-of-the-art. Ferreira, for the most part, writes his own songs and comes closest to being a true poet.

The Merengue Diaspora: From the Dominican Republic to Puerto Rico and New York

In the 1990s, merengue occupied a central position in the tropical music world. After some initial resistance—dancers found merengue too simplistic—New York audiences finally accepted the genre, and double bills featuring both salsa and merengue acts became common. Merengue also helped smooth the interaction between house music and the kind of music alternately called freestyle and Latin hip-hop, club music popular among young urban Latinos from several countries of origin. Freestyle/Latin hip-hop was made by club singers like Brenda K. Starr, Lisa Lisa, and Safire (as well as, eventually, La India), whose recorded output fit well into a format that mixed salsa with the disco-influenced merengue.

Several flashy stars emerged in the 1990s, including Jossie Esteban y La Patrulla 15, a workmanlike, intense group whose songs seem to run together. Polished and steady and enormously popular, they are El Gran Combo of merengue. Standout albums include 1986's *Noche de Copas*, 1990's *El Cantinero*, and 1997's *La Colota*—all adhering to a relentless rhythmic intensity. Sergio Vargas's soap-opera-star looks, elaborate costumes, and smooth interpretations of ballads, and his forays into world and African music, have made him an enduring force in merengue. Vargas released twenty-seven albums between 1988 and 2001, with highlights including his self-titled Sony Discos debut in 1992, 1994's *Brillantes*, and 1999's *A Tiempo* (RCA).

Bonny Cepeda, who released fifteen albums between 1985 and 2003, and received the first Grammy nomination for a merengue album, is one of merengue's more eccentric acts. He would often dress his band in French colonial costumes and stage elaborate dance routines. Cepeda's music is tight and challenging, shifting tempos to challenge dancers and poke fun at the frenetic charm of merengue. Cepeda's finest work was on 1992's *A Nivel Internacional*, which includes the Spanglish playfulness of *Baby, Say Yes*; *La Isla del Encanto*, a travelogue tribute to Puerto Rico; and the renegade frenzy of *La Chica de los Ojos Café*.

Las Chicas del Can, featuring four attractive women on high-pitched lead vocals, at first appeared to be a novelty act—in their videos they are all pictured playing horns and drums in tight dresses and high heels. Created and overseen by Wilfrido Vargas, the women are a formidable live band and terrific instrumentalists. Their cover of *Juana La Cubana* (written by Mexican cumbia orchestra leader Fito Olivares), which appears on 1990's *Caribe*, was one of '90s merengue's most exhilarating moments. Original members like Belkis Concepción began splitting off from the band in the mid-'90s, although Las Chicas continued to release albums with different members.

Quezada is one of merengue's most talented vocalists—and one of its few female lead singers. With her charismatic presence and emotive powers, she does for merengue what Mexican singer Rocio Durcál did for rancheras. Quezada is the one-time leader of Milly y los Vecinos, one of the first merengue bands to base themselves successfully in New York, which it did beginning in the late 1980s. On her 1999 album *Vive*, Quezada, who does not write her own songs, showcased her wide range and easy-flowing improvisational skills with a collection of pop merengue tunes in the tradition of Juan Luís Guerra. She established her breathy, sensual approach on the opening track, *Para Olvidarte*, which, like *Si Piensas en Mi*, evolves into rousing mid-tempo merengue from a balladic beginning. A duet with Puerto Rican megastar Elvis Crespo, *Para Darte Mi Vida*, is as winning as it is curious—Crespo is more of a straight singer here rather than the rhythmic, percussive improviser he is on his own songs. Quezada's 2002 album, *Pienso Así*, mixes in some ballads and salsa-like tunes, with *Tanto Que Dije* written by salsero Gilberto Santa Rosa.

Puerto Rican Merengue

In the 1990s, after a long and sometimes rancorous process, merengue finally conquered Puerto Rico. Outlawed in the nineteenth century as lewd, merengue later clashed with salsa in a club and music-promoter battle that resonated with the coexistence of newer Dominican immigrants in Puerto Rican-dominated New York. In Spanish Harlem and the rest of New York, Dominican entrepreneurs slowly bought up the majority of the Puerto Rican bodegas, and on the dance floor and radio stations, they finally attained something of an equal footing with salsa.

While New York Puerto Ricans gave in by dancing, their ancestral island began to develop its own merengue stars, some of whom became bigger than those from the Dominican Republic. Many of the top-grossing merengue acts in total Latin music sales in the United States and Latin America now are Puerto Rican. Two of Puerto Rico's biggest solo merengue stars tried to go down the rock-pop route, a path followed only by singers with considerable commercial success.

Olga Tañón

Born in 1967 and raised in Cataño, Puerto Rico, Olga Tañón not only successfully popularized merengue on a salsa-dominated island, she also established herself as one of the genre's few female stars. Originally wanting to be a dancer, she sang for the church choir and fostered dreams of a singing career. Tañón got her first break as a professional singer in the late 1980s with Las Nenas de Ringo y Jossie, an all-female merengue group. Soon afterward she received an offer to be part of another all-female group, Chantelle. The unbridled success of Chantelle afforded her the opportunity to sign as a solo artist with WEA Latina. With a battery of professional songwriters providing the lyrics and music, in 1992 her first album, *Sola*, went platinum in the United States and Puerto Rico. Her next album, 1993's *Mujer de Fuego*, in which she also debuted as a producer, and 1994's *Siente el Amor* both outsold her previous effort.

Although her chosen format is merengue, Tañón's aggressive contralto carries echoes of the Andalusian gypsy style, unleashing a passionate inner howl and letting it loose over a barrage of rhythm. Her unapologetically sexy delivery on songs like *Vendrás Llorando* and *Muchacho Malo* made her a tropical music phenomenon. With her next album, *Nuevos Senderos*, produced by renowned regional Mexican singer and composer Marco Antonio Solís, she began to expand her style to include ballads. *Llévame Contigo*, Tañón-produced and released in 1997, returned to merengue; the album was nominated for a Grammy for best tropical performance. 1998's *Te Acordarás de Mi*, produced by Rudy Pérez, continued her experimentation with variations on merengue and her occasional foray into salsa and included a duet with pop singer Cristian Castro.

Yo Por Ti, released in 2001, continued in this vein, combining arrangements reminiscent of Juan Luís Guerra's with the emotional delivery of a pop queen. There was even room for salsa, on *Pegadito*, and a Santana-ish, guitar-tinged son, *Me Gusta*. *Sobrevivir*, in 2002, produced a huge single, *Así es la Vida*, which is more like the Miami-style international Latino dance pop that fuses merengue with disco-style rhythms.

Elvis Crespo

Elvis Crespo is more than just another Puerto Rican jumping on the merengue bandwagon. With his neo-mod long, straight black hair, Andalusian eyes, and spacy demeanor, he is the perfect pin-up idol for his hordes of female fans. But his oddly seductive tenor, tinged with a flamenco-style lament, is a key to his popularity.

Born in New York in 1971, Crespo was raised in Puerto Rico—he auditioned for the kid group Menudo at age fourteen. His first gig was with a salsa-merengue orchestra headed by Willie Berríos, but he also sang with Toño Rosario, a merengue singer who moved to Puerto Rico from the Dominican Republic in 1991. Crespo was originally a vocalist for the seminal Grupo Manía, and his tenure with that group lasted from 1994–1996, peaking with the release *Está de Moda*. Crespo released his first solo album, *Suavemente*, in 1998. His massive hit single by the same name had the staying power of a classic salsa or pop hit. Propelled by his hyperkinetic rhythm section and the controlled hysteria of his backing horns, Crespo draws the focus back to the singer while not entirely distracting the listener from merengue's insistent dance beat. An unspectacular subsequent album of dance remixes that featured English-language vocals in certain choruses and a duet with Argentine vocalist Giselle D'Cole (*Come Baby Come*) were less satisfying, and Crespo appeared to miss his chance to be part of the Latin pop explosion. *Urbano* in 2002 was a return to form, featuring a cover of Spanish vocalist Lorca's *Bésame en la Boca*, strong original compositions like *Ojos Negros*, an unplugged version of *Como Fingir*, and a duet with Sergio Vargas.

Despite losing one of its most dynamic performers when Crespo left, Grupo Manía continued to be one of Puerto Rico's most dynamic purveyors of the tropical two-step, merengue. Formed in the early 1990s by brothers Henry and Omar Serrano, Grupo Manía struck gold by combining a youthful appeal and giving merengue a Puerto Rican feel. Using the format of one lead singer and a trio of chanting back-up singers, Grupo Manía has all four members take turns as the lead vocalist. The strongest of the four is probably Alfred Cotto, but the other three members, the Serrano brothers and Reynaldo Santiago, all have their moments. The rhythmic interplay between Grupo Manía's typical contemporary merengue instrumental lineup of horns, piano, and percussion is satisfyingly intense. Songs like *Como Baila* and *Pa'l Bailador* go through a number of time-signature shifts that make dance parties rock. Manía isn't stuck in a merengue groove, however. They stray earnestly into 1980s-style R&B in *Tú y Yo*, scratchy reggae dance-hall minimalism in *Ragga Manía*, and a syncopated salsa workout in *Lloro Por Tí*. Grupo Manía's later releases, 2001's *Grupo Mania 2050* and 2002's *Latino*, gravitate toward the hybrid genres of meren-house and reggaetón, currently hugely popular with Puerto Rican youth on the island and the United States. Toasting and rapping over a Jamaican dance-hall beat, and incorporating the synthesized keyboard figures of house music, Grupo Manía kept up its youth appeal while often going back to its basic merengue sound.

Merengue, like Afro-Cuban music in the 1940s and 1950s, evolved a bit when exposed to the urban sensibilities of New York. Fulanito, a diminutive of *Fulano de tal*, a street term meaning so-and-so, is an eccentric posse of transnational caribeños with island roots—five singer/rappers in derbies and suits, the elder musician, El Maestro, with an accordion painted like the Dominican flag, and a timbál player with a T-shirt that says www.fulanito.com. Belting out flag-waving odes to the beaches and mountains of the Dominican, and sarcastic laments about the women who cheat on them, the charismatic Dose and his Dominican and Puerto Rican bandmates from Upper Manhattan and New Jersey are an older school hip-hop crew, with roots in the mid-1980s, masquerading as a merengue band. Formed in the mid-1990s, they may introduce a tune like *Baile del Cepillo* with bilingual hip-hop patter, but El Maestro always brings the music back home with his accordion and the tambora drum.

Fulanito reminds us of the transnational nature of tropical music—the group not only draws from Dominican experience, even though its members live in New York, but they see the multinational appeal of rustic forms of merengue. Reviving perico ripiao, they demonstrate how it can sound like Colombian vallenato played at 78 r.p.m. at a Port Au Prince carnaval. Dose and bandmate Winston Rosa together released Latin house records like *2 in a Room* and *740 Boyz*, producing dance-floor hits such as *Wiggle It* and *El Trago*, a Spanglish house stomp. Despite being an "underground" band, Fulanito maintains an impressive degree of popularity, playing shows throughout the Caribbean as well as in New York, and posting moderate sales figures. The group's 2001 album, *Americanizao*, showed a continued streamlining and perfection of its concept, increasing the use of Spanglish in the lyrics, and deepening the perico ripiao backing sound.

The Rhythms of Colombia:
Cumbia, Vallenato, and Beyond

With its coastal regions straddling the Pacific and the Caribbean, as well as diverse regions in the interior, all creating different forms of music, Colombia is one of the most dynamic musical environments in Latin America. Colombia's music evolved under different conditions from those of the island nations of the Caribbean. Colombia is much larger and had an indigenous population that was far more populous and somewhat more advanced than their Caribbean counterparts, who were quickly wiped out by disease spread through Spanish conquerors. And unlike Mexico, Colombia's African populations were not largely confined to one coastal area. They established numerous escaped slave communities and moved in considerable numbers to cities in the interior. So conditions in Colombia nourished a tri-cultural hybridism in music unlike that found in most Latin American countries.

Four regions of Colombia have produced distinct musical styles. The Atlantic Coast achieved an extraordinary mixture of influences among its Spanish, indigenous, and African inhabitants, producing rhythmic genres like porro, gaita, mapalé, bullerengue, paseo, and the most important style, cumbia, and its offshoot vallenato. The rhythms of the Pacific Coast, currulao, jota, juga, aguabaja, and potacore, preserved African culture and escaped-slave culture intact, with some indigenous influence. The Andean region produced bambuco, torbellino, guabina, pasillo, bunde, and danza, musics which combined Spanish and indigenous influences from the Chibcha tribes. The musical styles of the plains, or Llanero region, joropo, galleron, pasaje, corrido, and seis, have a strong flamenco feel, but with traces of indigenous influence.

These different influences manifest themselves in various ways, but in general the use of guitar and song structure is rooted in Spain, the large gaita flutes and some percussion and rhythmic influences are indigenous, and the percussion structures, dance, and some choral techniques come from Africa. Both the indigenous and African influence also contain within them a magic or religious significance, as their original purpose was to communicate with deities.

Cumbia: Colombia's National Pastime

The cumbia became popular in Colombia around the 1820s, during its struggle for independence, when it became a song and dance of national resistance, evolving from its history as an entertainment for African and indigenous laborers and slaves. Its essential elements, the tambor drums and enormous gaita flutes, combine to give the music a rolling, infectious 2/4 beat that seems like a fusion between merengue and reggae, with a similar backbeat that sends it surging forward. The cumbia dance is based on hip-rocking that is much more subtle than merengue's.

The cumbia was different from Afro-Cuban music because the African element, like Brazil's samba, derived primarily from the Congo-based cultures rather than the Yoruban-based cultures. In addition, the cumbia is different from salsa, merengue, and Afro-Caribbean music because it contains not only African but indigenous influences—although the gaita flute had an African analog and the cumbia dance itself is thought to be a mating dance between an African male and an indigenous woman. John Storm Roberts suggested that while indigenous Colombian tribes did manufacture gaitas early on, the "instrument and name alike are found in both Spain and West Africa, and they are much the same as reed instruments found almost everywhere in the Islamic world." The cumbia tempo stresses the upbeat, allowing the cumbia to "float" and giving it a kind of perpetual optimistic lilt.

Perhaps because of its complexity and variety, the music of Colombia has remained relatively obscure outside the country, even though it shares the same Caribbean cultural nexus in cities such as Havana, San Juan, Santo Domingo, and Caracas. Despite the evolution of cumbia in a fashion parallel to the Cuban son and the Argentine tango, for instance, outsiders have had difficulty in interpreting the subtly complex cross-rhythms exchanged among the rhythm section members. With its unique syncretism between African and indigenous elements, the cumbia did not lend itself to dance halls outside Colombia.

Eventually, in the early 1920s in the port city of Barranquilla, Colombian dance bands began to play cumbia, adding horns, bass, and other instruments to the traditional lineup of three African drums, the llamador, allegro, and the tambora, and two gaitas. When Colombian bandleaders tried to bring the cumbia to be recorded in New York in the 1930s, they could not afford to bring their orchestras. Instead, they had to record with orchestras such as the one led by Puerto Rican legend Rafael Hernández, which interpreted the cumbia as a contradanza, giving it a more ballroom salon feel.

Cumbia tended to get submerged in its interactions with musical styles from other parts of Latin America. In New York, where the main influences were either the African-American jazz tradition or Afro-Cuban mambo, the cumbia became a son variation, and in Texas and Mexico, where a major influence was the German folk tradition, the cumbia became a kind of polka. When the 1950s revolution in dance music brought the mambo, the cha-cha, and rock and roll to Colombia, its orchestras incorporated Afro-Cuban drums but not Colombian tambores (large drums similar to the ones used in the Dominican Republic). In 1955, with the song *Cosita Linda*, Barranquilla-based bandleader Pacho Galán invented the merencumbe, a fusion between merengue and the cumbia, and over the next forty years Colombian musicians like Lucho Bermúdez became very adept imitators of the salsa mainstream sound.

The basis for the development of modern Colombian cumbia was Discos Fuentes, a record company founded in 1934 by a sound engineer named Antonio Fuentes. Discos Fuentes was the home of most of cumbia's biggest recording stars, such as Rodolfo y su Tipica R.A. 7, Gabriel Romero, Adolfo Echeverría, Pastor López, and La Sonora Dinamita. Accordion players like Lisandro Meza were perhaps the genre's only important instrumentalists, but by the 1950s the trumpet became the genre's most important jamming instrument and the accordion became more characteristic of vallenato (see Carlos Vives below). An excellent introduction to Colombian cumbia is a two-disc compilation, *Cumbia Cumbia* volumes 1 and 2, issued by World Circuit Records in 1989 and 1993, respectively. The compilation features classics like Gabriel Romero's *La Piragua*, Los Inmortales's *La Pollera Colorá*, and Rodolfo y su Típica RA 7's *La Cologiala*.

The evolution of Colombian music over the last fifty years has been tied to its urban, coastal areas such as the port city of Barranquilla, located at the mouth of the Rio Magdalena. Barranquilla is a modernist city with a shabby downtown surrounded by miles of suburban-ish housing and some art deco structures reminiscent of Miami's South Beach. It sits at the center of a region including three other cities that had a great influence on Colombia's musical tradition: Cartagena (site of cultural exchange with the rest of the Spanish-speaking Caribbean); Mompós (river-based city of the interior where African and folk traditions developed); and Santa Marta (a place with strong indigenous presence). During the rapid industrialization of twentieth century Colombia, and in the years following World War II, Barranquilla experienced an influx of European immigrants, particularly Italians and Jews, who helped develop the postwar consumer economy. They brought European fashion, theater, classical music, rock and roll, and modern aviation to the country. During the 1950s and 1960s, Barranquilla was the music capital of the country, thanks to two factors: the tienda phenomenon and the yearly carnival.

The tiendas of Barranquilla are small convenience stores with wooden benches in front, where people linger to drink their beer, listen to radios, and show off the latest dance steps. To really make it in Colombia, an artist had to reach the people who hung out at the tiendas, so they had to make a danceable, catchy music that would be played on the radio stations.

The yearly carnivals were places to hear obscure local rhythms from surrounding areas like Santa Marta, Malambe, and Soledad. They continue to be an opportunity for Barranquilla not only to demonstrate its urbane social atmosphere, but to celebrate its contributions to the international music scene, through competitions between invited international bands and local groups. In 2000, famed Colombian salsa singer Joe Arroyo presented the honor of Queen of the Carnaval to Colombian pop singer Shakira.

Colombian Salsa

In many ways Colombians are more ardent and knowledgeable salsa fans than most of the rest of Latin America. Like the Japanese, who buy up every known African-American blues and jazz recording, Colombians, particularly in the Cauca Valley region, which includes the cities of Medellín and Cali, know the Fania era like the back of their hands. Although variations of the Cuban son were played in Colombia much earlier, the country seemed to go crazy for salsa in the 1960s. After New York salseros Richie Ray and Bobby Cruz were feted in Barranquilla in 1968, a new movement for Colombian salsa began. Visits from New York salseros like Willie Colón and Rubén Blades during the 1970s Fania era created a large and enthusiastic following among Colombians.

Beginning in the '60s, Discos Fuentes hired an in-house producer named Julio Ernesto Estrada Rincón, otherwise known as "Fruko." Estrada was originally with a group named Los Corraleros (which included accordionist Lisandro Meza), who provided a conjunto or típico-style alternative to the orchestras led by Lucho Bermúdez. Eventually Estrada led an orchestra that covered Cuban son and mambo bands, but when he played New York in the early '70s, he began to pick up on the Fania-era innovations. When he came back to Colombia he began recording with a new band, Fruko y los Tesos. This band, as well as the Latin Brothers and La Sonora Dinamita, were all nurtured by Fruko, in effect creating a salsa scene in Colombia.

Helping Colombia secure its reputation for producing some of the most authentic salsa in the world was Álvaro José "Joe" Arroyo, one of salsa's most dynamic tenors. Born in 1955 in Cartagena, he began singing at age eight and did time in church choirs and houses of ill repute. Arroyo began his formal career in the mid-1970s as a seventeen-year-old singer for a band lead by Fruko Estrada. Arroyo left Fruko y sus Tesos in the late '70s and formed his own band, La Verdad, in 1981. Health problems affected his ability to create music for about a year, but he returned to participate in the Barranquilla carnival of 1984, in place of Venezuelan salsero Oscar D'León. After he won the Colombian salsa capital Cali's "Congo de Oro" prize six times, a new award, the "Super-Congo," was created for him.

With his high-pitched vocal style reminiscent of the Cuban legend Beny Moré, Arroyo has been one of Colombia's greatest salsa singers. His expansion of the range of salsa rhythms by incorporating the incredible variety of influences that permeate his hometown also made Arroyo one of the most significant innovators in the genre. Exploring native Colombian rhythms such as the cumbia, vallenato, and porro, and West Indian influences like compas and soca, Arroyo devised his own hybrid rhythmic styles—the cumbión and the self-referential Joesón.

Many of Arroyo's songs carry a social and political commentary, most famously his big hit *Rebelión* (1988), which directly addressed the legacy of slavery along the South American coastline. ("An African marriage/slaves of the Spaniard/He treated them very badly/And he beat his black woman," says one verse, to which the chorus responds, "Don't beat the black woman!") Enormously popular in Colombia, he recorded about ten albums for Colombia's Sonotone Latin and Discos Fuentes labels as well as several in the '90s for Sony International. Most of his music is available in the United States through original issues or was re-released in compilation form. Arroyo continued to experiment with different rhythms, particularly from the English- and French-speaking

Caribbean and Africa, using both electronic and traditional arrangements in his inventive combinations of rhythmic styles. Albums like *Cruzando el Milenio* (1999) make extended reference to African-derived spiritual religions.

With ambitious arrangements that recall Fania-era Willie Colón and lyrics that confront Colombia's history of slave rebellions, *Rebelión*, available on various greatest hits compilations like *32 Cañonazos* (Discos Fuentes, 2002), combined Arroyo's vocal authority with his well-drilled band's irresistible energy. *Fuego en Mi Mente* (1990) is one of Arroyo's best. Kicking off with the minor-scale flourishes that Eddie Palmieri might use, *Por ti no Moriré* is another triumph of Arroyo's storytelling savvy and the salsa wall-of-sound erected by his aggressive horn section. *Te Quiero Mas*, played in Arroyo's own Joesón (Joe-style son) arrangement, is a soca (soul-calypso)-flavored son, featuring the chugging horns associated with merengue and Afro-pop-like minimalist electric keyboard, over a loping soul-calypso rhythm. Merengue gets another nod on *Echao Pa'lante*, although he prefers to describe that song as a Joesón. Arroyo's fond attention to Colombia's homegrown rhythms, like the smooth porro of *Vuelve* and the rollicking cumbia of *Suave Bruta*, are a big part of what makes him a national treasure. But he can swing with the best of salsa's hitmakers, as he does on *Fuego en mi Mente*, which alludes to both the 1950s mambo era and the 1970s Fania era.

Arroyo's recent albums, *En Sol Mayor* (2000) and *A Duo: Los Reyes del Trópico* (2001) did nothing to diminish his enduring popularity, but broke little new ground. The latter, a duet with pop balladeer Juan Carlos Coronel, was a significant departure for Arroyo, whose tenor is crisp enough to switch to the bolero genre with ease.

One of Colombia's great salsa groups, Grupo Niche was formed by arranger/vocalist Jairo Varela in 1980 with the release of *Al Pa-*

sito. Despite several lineup changes, Niche remained a favorite among salsa fans who prefer what is known as salsa dura, or hard salsa, to salsa romantica. Songs like *Mi Negra y su Calentura* and *Listo Medellín* play like the great Johnny Pacheco-Willie Colón collaborations of the 1970s. With a particularly strong horn section and an impeccable legacy of conga players, Niche leads the Colombian pack, which also includes acts like Sonora Carrusell; an old-school salsa brava band, Grupo Gale; a nine-piece orchestra with three lead singers, á la El Gran Combo, featuring ex-members of Niche and Sonora Carrusell; and newcomers like Los Titanes, who feature heavy trombone parts and electric guitar.

Carlos Vives and Vallenato

As in much of the rest of Latin America, the Colombian coast housed a legacy of romances, trovas, and décimas, an oral tradition with direct lineage to Spain. According to Peter Wade's *Music, Race, and Nation: Música Tropical in Colombia*, the genre of vallenato continues this tradition. Gabriel García Márquez once described his most famous novel, *One Hundred Years of Solitude*, as a 350-page vallenato. While Wade noted that there are disputes as to whether the music began in the late nineteenth century, or was primarily a product of the radio commercialization of music in the 1940s, vallenato is a kind of remote, romantic cowboy music preferred by mestizo ranchers and campesinos that provided a running commentary of the lives of a people cut off from the urban elites.

According to Wade, vallenato had a "mythical" origin in the area of Valle de Upar, in northeast Colombia, an agriculture-rich valley region that begins on the northern Caribbean coast and follows the César River into the interior. As the seeds of the music that would become vallenato spread from the Atlantic Coast's Santa Marta mountain chain, it added the gaitas made of bamboo that indigenous people played and African drums made of hollow wood with goat skins secured by wooden rings and strings. While there is evidence that the accordion was introduced into the coastal regions of Colombia in the nineteenth century, Wade cited several Colombian ethnomusicologists who believe that the modern type of accordion associated with the genre only appeared in the Valledupar in the late 1930s. With its simple lyrics about the trials and tribulations of everyday people echoing the décima tradition, vallenato has been known as the music of the poor, but Wade presented evidence that it was appropriated by local elites in a way similar to Brazilian samba. A classic vallenato, *Los Caminos de la Vida*, begins with this verse:

•••••

Los caminos de la vida	*The paths of life*
no son como yo pensaba	*Are not what I thought they'd be*
como me los imaginaba	*As I imagined them*
no son como yo quería	*They aren't as I would have liked*
los caminos de la vida	*The paths of life*
son muy difíciles de andarlos	*Are very difficult to travel*
difícil de caminarlos	*Difficult to travel*
y no encuentro la salida	*And I can't find an escape*

•••••

Originally called música provinciana, vallenato has been used as a collective term for a wide range of styles. The contemporary vallenato, like cumbia, features both African and indigenous elements—the indigenous guacharaca, something like a Cuban güiro, and the African caja vallenata. The accordion, which typifies its sound, is augmented by the Spanish/indigenous gaita flutes and the clarinet. Its different permutations include native Colombian rhythms with varying meters called paseo, son, merengue (not related to Dominican merengue), and puya. When the paseo rhythm is performed, there is more emphasis on harmony. Merengue is played in a two-beat pattern; both the son and the puya are more rhythmically complex, played at 6/8 rhythms, and resembling something similar to the Cuban guaracha.

The use of the accordion distinguished vallenato from the cumbia. The musicians of Valle de Upar adapted the accordion to interpret the different rhythmic styles of vallenato. It became a recorded music that was heard in the rest of Colombia in the 1950s and 1960s, when it was pioneered by songwriters like Rafael Escalón and accordionist Alejandro Durán. A more modern vallenato school, incorporating Afro-Cuban drums, emerged in the 1960s, headed by prolific songwriter Gustavo Gutiérrez Cabello. Currently the stars of traditional vallenato are Los Hermanos Zuleta, Jorge Oñate, and Diomedes Díaz.

The vallenato had always had loyal following in the countryside and in some northern cities, but in the early 1990s an unlikely charismatic figure created a small explosion in the music's popularity. In 1994, a one-time soap opera star, Carlos Vives, assembled an impressive group of older-line folkloric players, and some of the best young musicians from the coast, in the capital city of Bogotá. They included singer/songwriter Ivan Benavides, guitarist José "Teto" Ocampo, and flutist Mayte Montero.

Meticulously reproducing a variety of vallenato styles on albums like *Clásicos de la Provincia* (1994) and *Tierra del Olvido* (1995), the band transformed a rustic music into the highest quality tropical world-beat bliss, incorporating típico (traditional) instruments like the caja vallenata and the güiro-like guacharaca, as well as a full set of tropical percussion instruments and the oversized gaita flute played by the petite Mayte Montero. With 1999's *El Amor de mi Tierra* and 2001's *Déjame Entrar,* Vives cemented a relationship with the Emilio Estefan Miami-based production machine without compromising the quality of his music. In fact, the collaboration of Vives and Colombia-born producer/songwriter Kike Santander was a major force in the ability of the Miami sound to establish itself as an international Latin pop force.

Contemporary Colombian musicians have become quite influential on the Latin pop scene, from Vives's streamlining of the vallenato to Santander's pervasive presence as a producer in Miami. Rock and pop-rock acts like Shakira, Aterciopelados, Juanes, and Cábas (see Chapter 10) have gone a long way in dissipating the barriers between Latin alternative and mainstream pop. But the traditional music of Colombia continues to be celebrated as well, particularly by the singer Totó La Momposina. Born in the mid-1940s in a small village outside the town of Mompos, she was trained by a famed local singer, or cantadora, named Ramona Ruiz. In her twenties, she began traveling up and down the Atlantic coast, stopping in small towns, some called palenques, or escaped slave communities that preserved various traditions intact. By the mid-'80s she started recording, and she became a sought-after performer, once appearing at a ceremony honoring Gabriel García Márquez's receiving of the Nobel Prize in Literature.

Totó became a kind of ethnomusicologist/performer, continuing to sing the various genres of the Atlantic Coast and studying dance at the Sorbonne in Paris. After performing at Peter Gabriel's WOMAD festival in the early '90s, she secured a recording contract with his label, Real World records, and exposure to an international audience. Her debut album, 1983's *Cantadora*, was re-released in 1998 on the MTM label. Totó takes the listener on a tour of the festive porro (*Aguacero de Mayo*), the Puerto Rican plena-like chandé (*El Tigre*), the shuffling bullerengue (*El Piano de Dolores*), and a fandango (*Le La Le La*) that, despite being from a palenque, demonstrates an Andalusian/Arabic influence in the vocals.

The growing popularity of traditional Colombian music in cities like New York—exemplified by grassroots acts like Cumbiamba (which takes its name from a cumbia party), the singer Lucía Pulido (who collaborates with Downtown jazz musicians), and rock-pop singers like Cábas and Vives veteran Ivan Benavides—suggests that Colombian music continues to strive for modernity while remaining thoroughly authentic. It's a form of self-preservation that is growing, evidenced by the revival of interest in the Puerto Rican bomba and plena by groups like Plena Libre, Yerba Buena, and William Cepeda's orchestra and the resuscitation of various Venezuelan coastal rhythms by the singer Irene Farrera, based in Eugene, Oregon.

Mexico: Corrido, Tejano, Norteño

Mexican music follows a parallel path to that of the rest of Latin America in that it arises essentially from the mixing of indigenous, Iberian, and African cultures. The Spanish influence is evident through the use of stringed instruments and the survival of the décima tradition in the verses, and the African influence appears in rhythms that resemble Afro-Caribbean ones, as well as the presence of the marimba, a kind of xylophone which is sometimes misinterpreted as being of indigenous origin. The indigenous influence appears more muted than in, say, Colombian music, although small bands and orchestras include indigenous flutes.

Dating to the early colonization of Mexico in the seventeenth century, which included a sizable number of African slaves, the Mexican son began to appear in various forms that corresponded to different regions. There were son calentanos, son Rio Verde, son Costa Chica, son isthmeño, and the most important, son jalisco, son huasteco, and son veracruzano. As discussed in Chapter 5, these sones had rhythmic variations, used local versions of guitars and harps, and expressed the concerns of each region in their verse. The African participation in the sones is clearest in the son veracruzano, and Veracruz is the last region where

Africans remained in large numbers after the Mexican experiment with slavery dissipated in the nineteenth century.

The tradition of norteño, Tejano, and corrido music along the border between Mexico and the United States in the nineteenth century was another crucible for the development of Mexican music. Many musicologists insist that the Mexican corrido is a product of the confrontation between the United States and Mexico following the Mexican War of the 1840s. But there is undoubtedly a link to the Spanish romance, which was brought to Mexico during the beginning of the conquest in the sixteenth and seventeenth centuries. The corrido's octosyllabic verses and storytelling capabilities are clearly linked to the earlier Spanish romances, and its epic lyricism again refers to characteristics of the Spanish troubadour. Regardless of its origin, the corrido became particularly popular along the border of Mexico and the American Southwest in the late 1800s.

A third stream of Mexican music resulted from the evolution of the mariachi and ranchera in the state of Jalisco (see Chapter 5). But by the 1950s the whole country seemed to be dancing to the mambo and crooning the bolero. It says a lot about Afro-Caribbean rhythms' dominance of Latin America that at different points danzón, the bolero, and the mambo, genres native to Cuba, were national music genres of Mexico. Due to Mexico's unique position of proximity to the media and recording industry of North America and the success of its economy in developing a strong recording and film industry, it became a staging ground for many Latin American genres in a way similar to how Chicago and New York platformed jazz, which began in New Orleans.

Mexican music's dominance in the North American consumer market is a function of that community's buying power—Mexican-Americans account for 66.9 percent of the total Latino population in the United States. Stalwarts like Los Tigres del Norte and Los Angeles Azules hover around the top of the Billboard Latin Charts, but Mexican/Tejano music, which incorporates subgenres like

Tejano, norteño, banda, ranchera, conjunto, and others, doesn't seem to transcend the Mexican and Mexican-American communities to capture substantial attention of the rest of the Latinos, Latin Americans, and non-Latinos in the United States.

Tejano and Mexican Regional Music: Straddling the Border

The constellation of styles that characterized Mexican music mutated into something new in the years after the North American takeover of large parts of Mexico as a result of the U.S.-Mexican war of the 1840s. The genres norteño and Tejano encompass styles ranging from ranchera, polka, the story-telling corrido, and American styles like blues, pop, and country music. Tejano evolved from a big band style to its modern incarnation just as rock and roll was becoming popular in the United States. In the mid–1950s, bandleader Isidro López ushered in this change when he began to use the accordion up front and give Tejano more of a funky sound. These innovations brought about the institutionalization of the Mexican conjunto, which like the Cuban conjunto was a standard group style featuring an evolving set of instrumentation. Since the 1960s Tejano has been incorporating influences from R&B, rock, disco, and hip-hop. Analogous to Tejano conjuntos were norteño's "gruperos," groups that are today exemplified by Los Bukis and Los Temerarios. Almost coincidentally, norteño evolved in northern Mexican states like Sonora and Sinaloa, combining Colombian cumbia and corrido with other regional Mexican and U.S. pop influences.

Modern norteño stars like Los Tigres del Norte and Grupo Límite often share popularity with fans of Tejano music made by Intocable, Michael Salgado, Joel Nava, and Jay Pérez. Norteño/Tejano music isn't heard very much outside of northern Mexico, the American Southwest, or the large Mexican communities in California, Illinois, and New York, although I once had a cab driver in

Colombia who loved Tigres del Norte. The genre did have one breakthrough artist in the early 1990s, Texan singer Selena. She almost made the music an international Latino music, something that would have changed Latin music history forever.

Selena

Born in Corpus Christi, Texas, in 1971, Selena Quintanilla-Pérez, during her brief life, became one of the most celebrated figures in the history of Tejano music. In 1989, Selena and her siblings formed a Tejano group at the urgings of their father, Abraham Quintanilla, a frustrated Mexican-American rock and roller. The band cut its chops playing at local restaurants, clubs, and outdoor festivals, sticking to the Spanish-language ethnic style even though they themselves were predominantly English-speaking. After winning female vocalist of the year and performer of the year at the 1987 Tejano Music Awards, Selena was signed to EMI records and released her first album in 1989. Her brother Abraham Quintanilla Jr. wrote most of the material for the band, which also covered singers like Juan Gabriel. In her early twenties, Selena recorded two albums, *Entre a Mi Mundo* (1992) and *Amor Prohibido* (1994), which went gold, while a third, *Live* (1993) reached platinum status.

Selena had grown up listening to American pop (she had a great affinity for Donna Summer and Diana Ross), and she wasn't content to merely reproduce the cumbia sound of contemporaries like La Mafia. She began to inflect her work with a different accent, as shown in songs like *Techno Cumbia* and her re-working of the Pretenders' *Back in the Chain Gang* (Fotos y Recuerdos), on *Amor Prohibido*. She worked on her Spanish to communicate better with her Spanish-speaking fans and was beginning to master the language in press conferences in Mexico just before her death. On March 31, 1995, two weeks before her twenty-fourth birthday, she was gunned down by Yolanda Saldívar, the president of her fan club. Already established as the undisputed queen of norteño music, Selena had been putting together what would have been her breakthrough. Released in the summer following her death, *Dreaming of You* was an eclectic work featuring R&B, disco, flamenco, and a collaboration with David Byrne. In 1996, *Selena*, a film based on her life, directed by Gregory Nava, was released, starring Jennifer Lopez—who would ironically later accomplish Selena's crossover dream.

Much of Selena's last Spanish-language album, *Amor Prohibido*, is recorded in the minimalist Tejano style typical of the early '90s, but there are hints of a subtle evolution in her music. The title track is a classic mass-market hit that inhabits the memory, easily floating in the summer air from radios on the street. It is catchy, but it is also a parable about love and social class that reflects the strains of immigration on the barrio while resonating with Romeo and Juliet. While there is a tradition in Latin pop as well as in 1950s and 1960s R&B to take mainstream hits and refashion them for minority communities, *Fotos y Recuerdos* has so much personality that it's almost an improvement on the Pretenders' AOR hit *Back in the Chain Gang*. Selena's delivery makes tunes like *Bidi Bidi Bom Bom* and *Techno Cumbia*, which would be catchy but forgettable throwaways in the hands of the average performer, stick in your gut. Further expanding her range, Selena becomes a raunchy rocker on *Ya No*, a song that also features a preview of the sound her boyfriend Chris Perez would use in the late 1990s to garner a Grammy for best Latin alternative performance. The only thing about *Amor Prohibido* that disappoints is the knowledge that it was only leading up to Selena's best work, which she never got to do.

After her death, Selena's surviving brother, A. B. Quintanilla III, pioneered a Tejano/pop/hip-hop fusion, trading on a timely bilingual border-culture attitude. With *Shhh* (2001), recorded with his band A. B. Quintanilla y Los Kumbia Kings, and *4*, a bestseller in 2003, he took even further what Selena had been working toward in her last two recorded efforts. Lurching back and forth between the roughneck, rap-flavored title track and the teen pop balladry of *Me Enamoré*, A. B. and the Kumbia Kings project a hard-on-the-outside, soft-on-the-inside attitude. More akin to merengue-hip-hop bands like Fulanito, discussed earlier in this chapter, than to their Tejano counterparts, the Kumbia Kings might someday break through to a nationwide urban audience. On 2003's *4*, the band grows even more eclectic, with a hit single, *No Tengo Dinero* featuring alternative band El Gran Silencio and pop vocalist Juan Gabriel.

Tex-Mex, Corridos, Narco-corridos, and Banda

In the American Southwest, the legends of banditry became an important root of the hybrid Mexican border culture of the early nineteenth century. Since Mexican-Americans were denied the right to acquire property and establish political power, banditry was at once a legitimate form of social protest and a symbol of the spirit of an oppressed people. Men like Gregorio Cortez, who killed a lawman in the early 1900s, and Joaquín Murieta, a Californio (a Mexican living in California when it was taken over by the United States), were lionized in the corridos, or popular songs, of the early twentieth century. The Texas-Mexican corridos survive in Texas Tejano and the norteño format of northern Mexico, generally carrying some kind of antiestablishment message that aggrandizes the working class and its concerns.

"Narcocorridos" are a contemporary form of corridos, songs about the drug smuggling and dangerous border crossings that helped shape Latino life in California and the Southwest from the 1980s to the present. They typically combine gritty, gangsta tales with festive rhythms and yearning harmonies that would sound more at home at a mariachi-splashed wedding. Fonovisa is the home for the stars of corrido such as Tigres del Norte, Grupo Exterminador, and Luis y Julián. In a compilation released in 2001, *Corridos y Narcocorridos*, the label issued some of the most important songs of the genre.

Starting off the Fonovisa compilation is Los Tigres's *Contrabanda y Traición*, recorded in 1972 and probably the first narcocorrido. Led by founding members Jorge, Raúl, and Herman Hernández, who are brothers, Los Tigres has been together for over thirty-three years, has sold over 32 million units, and has been nominated for twelve Grammy awards, seven of those in consecutive years. With its jauntily rhythmic guitars and lilting accordions leading the way, *Contrabanda y Traición* starts its tale with a car crossing the border, its tires filled with marijuana, and ends in double-cross and a murder. Not all of Los Tigres's output is about illegal activity, however; in 1988's *La Jaula de Oro*, the narrator describes an immigrant who has worked hard for ten years and built a stable life, only to face the disappointment that his children refuse to learn Spanish and deny their Mexican identity. Los Tigres has been particularly successful with albums like *Unidos por Siempre* (1996), *Así Como Tu* (1997), and *Herencia de Familia* (1999).

In 2003, Los Tigres enjoyed an unusual benefit of marketing synchronicity when its album *La Reina del Sur* was released at the same time that a novel by the same name, written by a Spanish novelist, Arturo Pérez-Neverte, was topping the best seller lists. The first page of Pérez-Neverte's novel has La Reina, a female narco-trafficker, contemplating her death while listening to Los Tigres's famous song *Contrabanda y Traición*, and Los Tigres's album opens with a song in tribute to La Reina.

Lupillo Rivera is one of the hottest-selling artists in the contemporary Latin music scene. Born and raised in Long Beach, California, Rivera broke through in 1992 with the catchy, tuba-driven *Sustancias*

Prohibidas (Prohibited Substances), in which the song's narrator boasted that the government can't catch him selling drugs because he has bribed everyone in the judicial system. Later Rivera preferred to sing drinking songs—included on *Sufriendo a Solas* (2001) are *Siempre Siempre Borracho* (Always, Always Drunk) and *Nací Borracho* (I Was Born Drunk). On *Despreciado* (Unappreciated) he sings *Copa Tras Copa* (Drink After Drink). Backed by a fluttering flourish of brass instruments, Rivera's slurring vocal style sounds as if it's coming from the back table of a busy cantina. On his 2002 album, *Amorcito Corazón*, Rivera strays further to the mainstream, including a Juan Gabriel cover, *Se Me Olvidó Otra Vez*.

Rivera is the son of Pedro Rivera, the producer of the singer many say is the pivotal figure in the new popularity of corridos, Chalino Sánchez. You'll sometimes see Sánchez's image on silk-screen posters at concerts given by the Tijuana-based techno band Nortec. Born in 1961 in Sinaloa, Mexico, Sánchez was forced to move to Los Angeles at age fifteen, after shooting to death his sister's rapist at a local party. In Southern California, he suffered through low-paying jobs. Ultimately his brother was murdered in Tijuana, further fueling a tragic life that would be turned into narco-corrido verse.

With a no-frills approach that contrasted with Los Tigres's established performance style, Sánchez's songs told a story in the plain language of the working class, backed by twangy guitars and the oompah beat of a German polka. One of his classics, *El Crimen de Culiacán*, tells of the gory end of two men who had murdered another over a woman. But the corrido-like twists of his own life continued to their own violent end. In 1992, when he was beginning to attain a measure of fame in California, he got into a gunfight during a club appearance. Five months later, apparently the victim of a contract murder, he was found dead in an irrigation canal near a highway leading north from Los Angeles.

As if to demonstrate the appeal of narcocorrido to a younger generation, Los Tigres was the subject of a 2002 album called *El*

Más Grande Homenaje a Tigres del Norte (Fonovisa), on which a new generation of Mexican rockers pays homage to these norteño heroes. Maldita Vecindad offers an upbeat ska remake of *El Circo*, La Barranca offers spacy guitar noodling in a cover of *La Banda del Carro Rojo*, and Ely Guerra coos over a grungy, tuba-sampled version of *La Tumba Falsa*. Rap-rockers Molotov and the techno-dance band Titan are in the house, and Latin alternative stars Café Tacuba pitch in a dizzyingly original *Futurismo y Tradición*.

The Brave New Wave of Banda

Probably the most popular and scintillating of current Mexican-origin popular music is banda, a style that, like Tejano, incorporates various other Mexican genres. Primarily a dance music, banda is played by big brass-heavy bands that come from the northern state of Sinaloa. Thought to have an origin in military bands, banda's most salient characteristics are the peppery use of tubas in a percussive fashion and the extensive embellishment from trombones, trumpets, and sometimes clarinets. These bands often have over twelve members and dabble in cumbia, corrido, bolero, and the son huapango. The most famous banda group is probably Banda el Recodo.

Formed in 1951, La Banda el Recodo was originally led by self-taught clarinet player Don Cruz Lizarraga. After moving to Mazatlán, Sinoloa, he signed with RCA Victor. Although he recorded his first two tunes, *Mi Adoración* and *El Callejero* with a quintet, he soon formed Banda El Recodo with its classic lineup of two clarinets, two trumpets, two trombones, bass drum, and snare drum. Lizarraga continued to front the band until he died in 1995. The group continued to tour in Mexico and the United States, led by his clarinetist sons, Germán and Alfonso. The band's most successful records were 1997's *De Parranda con la Banda* and 2002's *No Me Se Rajar*, both of which dabble in ranchera and mariachi flavors (the group recorded a tribute to Juan Gabriel in 1997), as well as the souped-up tambora beat that is the essence of the banda sound.

A popular dance associated with banda called the quebraditas took Mexican Los Angeles by storm in the 1990s. The dance features outlandish, unorthodox partner-swinging that seems to have been influenced by the Brazilian lambada. The most resonant of the banda classic hits are *Provócame* by Banda Vallarta Show and *Al Gato y al Ratón* by Banda Machos. Banda Machos's CD *Machos Tambien Lloran* (Machos Cry Too), released in 1993, is noted for its revival of ranchera-boleros by Javier Solís. Banda groups can easily be recognized by the use of banda as a prefix, including Banda El Limón and Banda Maguey.

Banda remains one of the most popular genres in Mexican regional music, especially in the Los Angeles area. The banda dancing scene is as competitive and intense as the salsa dancing scene in New York, and its followers go to great lengths to costume themselves in the ten-gallon hats, tight jeans, and boots that capture the Sinaloan cowboy lifestyle. Banda's popularity with the narco chic that prevails in northern Mexico and is mirrored in Southern California continues to fuel the music and its scene.

Since the first Latin Grammy presentation in 2000, when the Mexican-owned label Fonovisa called for a boycott because of the lack of Mexican performers in the presentation show, there has been some controversy over the representation of Mexican music or how Mexican music fits into the image of Latin music in general. The boycott challenged the perception that for music to be considered mainstream Latin it must either be "tropical," that is, some variation of salsa or merengue, or "pop" as defined by Miami-based hitmakers like Emilio Estefan.

While Mexican music sales account for just over half of the total dollar value of all Latin music shipments in the United States, it has yet to break into the mainstream Latin Album of the Year or Record of the Year categories at the Latin Grammys. While this may reflect bias among the record executives, producers, and tastemakers in Latin music, the case can be made that Mexican music has not transcended its national boundaries to become an international Latin music. Still, the increasing Mexican immigration to non-traditional areas, such as the Southern states of Alabama, Okalahoma, and the Carolinas, as well as New York City, will continue to spread the music's popularity. There is no telling what future musical hybrids this continued spreading of the Mexican population will yield—another Selena is probably on the horizon who may yet make Mexican regional music a crossover cultural force.

9

The Hidden History of Latinos and Latin Influence in Rock and Hip-hop

Rock covers music from the soul, R&B end of the spectrum to the guitar-based riff-rock that evolved from hard rock to metal to punk and alternative, often played with a kind of raw, some might say sexual, energy. But while it is often a given that rock is a purely North American creation, at almost every turn in the history and development of rock and roll there has been a Latino influence. It could be something as intrinsic to the music as the beat, or merely a matter of consumer preferences, as was the case when Chicano loyalties helped shape the rock market in California in the 1950s or 1960s. Long before there was such a thing as Latin rock, there were Latino musicians in various rock groups. Many people today have only a vague idea of the Latin influence on rock, and no idea of rock's Latin roots, so it's fair to speak of this as the hidden history of Latinos in rock.

The influence of Latin music on rock can be traced to several sources, primarily from Africa, some from the Islamic world, and some from the New World-formed Afro-Caribbean and Mexican traditions. Rock music is often assumed to be a synthesis of

African-American blues and country blues, as well as European-American country and folk traditions. As John Storm Roberts stated in *Black Music of Two Worlds*, "There does not seem to be the same African quality in blues forms as there clearly is in much Caribbean music." For Roberts, the blues has a harmonic structure based on European theory, and the call and response that typifies African music is transformed from a dialogue between rhythmic instruments into an interaction between the singer and the guitar. Importantly, a direct Afro-Caribbean influence on rock stems from the way boogie-woogie piano-playing, a kind of stride technique, was the basis of blues piano. The rhythmic strumming of the guitar that is a characteristic of rock music seems to reflect the Islamic influence on African playing, as well as the obvious Moroccan component of the techniques of Spanish guitar.

While these are basic elements that were transferred through African traditions to African-Americans, who created the blues, crucial elements of Latin music, particularly Afro-Cuban bass and percussion patterns, as well as Afro-Brazilian drumming techniques and the harmonies of Brazilian bossa nova, were directly incorporated into rock music. Finally, the Mexican influences on country-western music, the structure of the Tex-Mex conjunto, and the formation of Mexican-Americans as a mass audience for rock and roll all had a considerable impact on the genre in the 1950s and 1960s, a period crucial to its development to a hegemonic mass-market music.

The Latin Roots of Rock and Roll

The origins of rock and roll are variously located in mid–twentieth century American popular music like blues, jazz, jump blues, and rhythm and blues. Coming into being in the late nineteenth century as a coping mechanism for the difficult lives of post-slavery African-Americans, the blues is a unique and original form of popular music. Several elements of the blues distinguish it from Latin or Afro-Cuban music: its twelve-bar structure, its use of repeating lyrical lines, and the phenomenon of the "blue" note, with a minor-scale affectation that is not present in traditional Afro-Cuban music. Still, Yoruban mythology is present in the early blues, at least in Robert Johnson's signature song, *Crossroads*, which is a thinly veiled reference to Eleggua, the orisha in charge of the crossroads.

But at almost every step of the blues' development from its early incarnation to rock and roll, this music inherits a significant Latin or Afro-Caribbean influence. The merger of blues with ragtime and jazz, pioneered by New Orleans pianist W. C. Handy, was accomplished in part through his use of the habanera rhythm, which had been present in ragtime compositions since the work of Scott Joplin. The boogie-woogie or barrelhouse style of piano developed in the South in the 1920s is basically a mirror of the stride piano-playing of New Orleans, in which cross rhythms are prevalent and bass patterns parallel to Afro-Cuban tumbaos are played on the left hand, while the right hand improvises. The jump blues pioneered by Big Joe Turner and Louis Jordan had strong New Orleans R&B and boogie-woogie foundations, and the swing influence on jump blues contained the contributions of Latin musicians like Mario Bauzá and Tito Puente.

Most of the direct antecedents of rock and roll were in some way affected by the evolution of Latin music in the United States. Rhythm and blues giant Fats Domino's sound was New Orleans-oriented, and rockabilly, a major thread in the music of Elvis Presley, contained a lingering vestige of the habanera rhythm. The Bo Diddley beat, although most likely derived from vestigial African musical traditions of the American South, is basically a son clave, and Buddy Holly also employed this beat on *Not Fade Away*.

It can even be argued that the dynamic that created rock and roll is typical of the dynamic that created Afro-Cuban music, in which a European influence mixes with the minor-key and rhythmic tendencies in the African traditions to create a new kind of music. In fact, through their connection to New Orleans stride piano and the parallel between the strong accent on the backbeat—the second and fourth beats of African American blues—and Afro-Cuban syncopation, rock and roll and Afro-Cuban music are distant cousins.

In Latin America, hybrids between African and European music were percolating as early as the seventeenth century, particularly in Cuba. But in North America, the influence of African-Americans on popular music wasn't strongly felt until the beginnings of jazz in the late nineteenth century. (Stephen Foster's popular songs, with their evocation of minstrelsy and slavery-derived work song, and gospel-influenced bluegrass songs such as those heard on the Grammy-winning soundtrack to *O Brother Where Art Thou* adapt African influences, mainly in terms of melody and harmony rather than rhythm, so these crosscultural fusions are less dramatic in comparison to Afro-Cuban music.) In this period the two strongest influences on popular music in the United States were jazz and blues.

Afro-Caribbean rhythms and the blues were as crucial to the development of jazz as they were to rhythm and blues and rock and roll. Music historians theorize that Afro-Caribbean rhythmic patterns and phrasing were rapidly absorbed into American popular music after they fanned out from New Orleans into surrounding Southern states. As the late music critic Robert Palmer pointed out in a *Spin* magazine article that appeared in 1989, Afro-Cuban influences were a deciding factor in every major transition American music underwent after World War II—from swing to modern jazz; from R&B to rock and roll, from R&B to funk; from the musical convention of verse and chorus to open-ended one-chord vamps. When, through mambo, bebop and Cubop, the syncopation of Cuban music augmented the even flow of swing, this new feel marked a change in the American musical mindset.

Robert Palmer cited observations Mario Bauzá made about the influence he and Machito's Afro-Cubans had on American music when their techniques were picked up by Dizzy Gillespie.

"We made changes starting from the bottom—the bass, the drums," Bauzá said in an interview with Palmer. "Before they started to listen to [the Dizzy Gillespie Orchestra] in the 1940s, all the American [jazz] bass players played nothing but dum-dum-dum, 1–2–3–4, 'walking' bass. Then they heard the Cuban tumbaos Cachao was playing and they started to go da-da-*dat*—stop and rest—da-*dat!* And the American [jazz] drummers the same. They were playing this even swish-swish-swish-swish on the ride cymbal, you know? Then they hear us and the snare and tom-tom start talking back and forth, like Cuban congas and bongos. When the electric bass guitar comes in around 1957, the style people develop for that instrument, the pattern, the whole feel, it's Cuban."

The dramatic shift in the rhythmic base of jazz bands that Bauzá is essentially describing—from square 4/4 time to the layered syncopation that is the basis of Cuban music—would eventually find its way into rhythm and blues and rock. And while there were already African call-and-response influences in jazz through its blues origins, the Afro-Cuban influence was opening up African-American music, essentially becoming the "rhythm" behind rhythm and blues. This combination of Cuban music with American pop, an already evolved Afro-European mixture of styles, created even newer hybrids.

Pioneered by guitarist B. B. King, Otis Rush, and New Orleans mainstay pianist Professor Longhair, the "son-blues" style, as Palmer referred to it, is identified as a direct antecedent to the Latin-style bass feel in Little Richard and even James Brown recordings—bass players for both admitted to being influenced by mambo recordings. By son-blues, Palmer is alluding to the way a triplet son bass pattern, basically a habanera that goes back to the days of Septeto Habanero, was fused with blues to form a new sound, which can be found in New Orleans pianist Professor

Longhair's *Hey Little Girl*. When the bass line was transposed to the saxophone by bandleader and songwriter Dave Bartholomew in his late 1940s recording *Country Boy*, it formed the basis of a jump blues style that was called "the Big Beat." The major beneficiaries of Bartholomew's Big Beat were Fats Domino and Little Richard, believed by many to be the original stars of rock and roll.

The triplet bass patterns that are salient features of Fats Domino's *Blue Monday*, Lloyd Price's *Lawdy Miss Clawdy*, Bill Haley's 1954 version of *Shake, Rattle, and Roll*, and Little Richard's *Slippin' and Slidin'*, Palmer wrote, are essentially the same patterns found on Cuban son records of the 1930s and 1940s. Palmer pointed out that *For Your Love*, a song written by the Yardbirds' Graham Gouldman, then covered by the Jon Mayall Bluesbreakers, featured a prominent clave rhythm and drum accents derived from Cuban conga and bongó patterns.

Musicologist Roy Brewer, in an essay published in 1999 in the journal *American Music*, highlighted the use of the habanera rhythm pattern in rockabillly. Brewer defined rockabilly as "the hybrid of blues and country that became rock & roll" or "the earliest style of white rock-and-roll, which blended blues with country music." He assumed that many rockabilly musicians were not aware of the habanera's Afro-Cuban heritage or even its proper definition, but rather associated it with exotic and erotic striptease acts, a source for their learning of the beat, along with the general influence of New Orleans dance bands up to boogie-woogie and jump blues. In rockabilly, as well as boogie-woogie and jump blues, the habanera was played often in triplets by the pianist's left hand or played on the string bass and saxophone.

Brewer pointed out that Elvis Presley began to employ a syncopated habanera rhythm as the central, continuous beat pattern in his Nashville RCA session recording of *Hound Dog* in 1956. The song, which began as a novelty tune but ultimately became one of Presley's most requested tunes in live shows, was performed to death by his band, prodding them to find new ways to play it. Brewer observed that during Presley's performance on the Milton Berle show in June 1956, his guitarist, Scotty Moore, bassist Bill Black, and drummer, D. J. Fontana, played a habanera figure at a slower, provocative tempo that encouraged Presley to exaggerate his hip gyrations, outraging much of the older viewing public. "Perhaps because of the controversial television appearance," claimed Brewer, "Presley's producers did not exploit the habanera pattern with his subsequent releases regardless of the overwhelming success of *Hound Dog*."

In later recordings, the habanera began to be phased out of Presley's recordings. His follow-up hit to *Hound Dog* was *Jailhouse Rock*, which was "driven by straight eighth-note subdivisions rather than boogie-woogie or Latin rhythms." As Brewer noted, "The habanera was played by Scotty Moore (with lowered string pitch) for the introduction of *Don't Be Cruel*, but the rhythmic drive for the remainder of the recording shifts to a shuffle beat dominated by the piano and backup vocalists." By the end of the 1950s, other rhythms had replaced the habanera traces completely, and Moore and Black were phased out of Presley's influential band. As rock emerged from the end of rockabilly's heyday, its musicians preferred a more conventional rhythmic structure, which was finally codified by the straight-ahead rhythms of Chubby Checker's *The Twist* in 1960.

But despite this seeming move away from syncopation, the Latin influence on rock music persisted. One of the most important milieus where it was kept alive was in many of the songs written by the songwriters of New York's Brill Building. Among the best of the Tin Pan Alley-influenced Brill Building writers, who were at their peak in the early '60s, were Gerry Goffin, Carole King, Barry Mann, Cynthia Weil, Jerry Leiber, Mike Stoller, Jeff Barry, Ellie Greenwich, Doc Pomus, and Mort Shuman. These writers penned tunes for acts like girl groups the Shangri-Las, Ronnettes, and

Dixie Cups, Connie Francis, Neil Sedaka, the Drifters, and the Righteous Brothers. As critic Ken Emerson noted in the *New York Times*, "The Brill Building songwriters enriched rock 'n' roll, originally the miscegenated music of black and white Protestant men, with a Jewish sensibility, a Latin beat and a stronger voice for women." The Brill Building was just blocks away from the Palladium, the capital of the Latin music universe in the 1950s.

According to Emerson, the Brazilian baião was the basis of the songs Jerry Leiber and Mike Stoller produced for the Drifters and Ben E. King, such as *Under the Boardwalk* and *Stand by Me*. Songs by the Isley Brothers (the piano vamp in *Twist and Shout*) and the Dixie Cups (the hand-clapping and incidental percussion of *Iko Iko*) were clearly influenced by Latin rhythms. Carole King, a Brill Building songwriter who later became a star in her own right, had evident Latin influences on *Will You Still Love Me Tomorrow?*, recorded by the Shirelles and co-written by her husband, Greg Griffin. Even the Beatles were influenced by the Brill Building songwriters and arrangers, having covered *Twist and Shout* and using Latin rhythms in *And I Love Her*. The current age of rock and pop music would be hard to imagine without them.

In the mid-1960s, rock's African roots would reassert themselves with funk, an outgrowth of the intersection between jazz, R&B, and rock. Perhaps originating with Mongo Santamaría's Afro-Caribbean jazz classics, *Watermelon Man* and *Afro-Blue*, funk became important in rock primarily because it adapted Latin techniques like syncopated polyrhythms to the bass guitar and encouraged open time signatures and extended improvisation. The word funk suggests an earthiness and rustic authenticity that evoke an Afrocentric approach to R&B, jazz, and rock. The main stars of funk music, James Brown, Sly Stone, and George Clinton's Parliament-Funkadelic, all adhered to these essential elements of funk. These are the same elements that were passed from funk onto what many consider its bastard child, disco.

The Latin Presence in Rock and Roll

While it is evident that there was a widespread absorption of Latin music elements into rock and roll, Latinos who lived in the United States also participated directly in the genre. The influence of Latinos on rock and roll began virtually at the same time the music itself was coming into being, as early as the 1940s. On the West Coast, Mexican American groups, notably Don Totsi's Pachuco Boogie Boys and Lalo Guerrero y Sus Cinco Lobos, were actively engaging in fusions of mambo and boogie-woogie in songs like *Pachuco Boogie* and *Muy Sabroso Blues*. In the early 1950s, New York Puerto Ricans were sharing the same street-corners with African-Americans and other ethnic groups who were helping to create doo-wop music—for example, Frankie Lymon and the Teenagers included two Puerto Rican members, Joe Negroni and Herman Santiago.

West Coast Chicanos were embracing African-American doo-wop performers like Johnny Ace and the Drifters and forming groups of their own that mixed R&B, doo-wop, and rock and roll, most notably doo-wop singer Little Julian Herrera. The cultural fusion that was going on with Mexican-Americans in California and the Southwest would lead to the longest-running rock scene dominated by Latinos in the United States, producing several Chicano bands and strongly influencing the development of California garage rock in the 1960s and punk rock in Los Angeles in the late 1970s.

The Chicano appreciation of doo-wop and rhythm and blues is one of the factors in the creation of the rock and roll audience in California in the 1950s. David Reyes' and Tom Waldman's book *Land of a Thousand Dances* told the story of racially mixed groups in Southern California that were sometimes fronted by Chicano members. According to Reyes and Waldman, African-American doo-wop groups like the Penguins, the Five Satins, and the Brothers of Soul drew heavily on Chicano audience support, and individual singers like Tony Clarke and Brenton Wood actively recruited a Mexican-American following. The Penguins' *Hey Señorita* and Chuck Higgins's *Pachuko Hop*, both recorded by African-American acts, were songs that made reference to Chicano culture and language.

The obvious starting point of West Coast Latin rock history is the 1957 hit single *La Bamba*, which catapulted Richard Valenzuela, also known as Ritchie Valens, to success. Valens was a relatively Americanized rocker who was mostly interested in mainstream rock, doo-wop and country-western until he found his Mexican self on a trip to Tijuana. Unearthing *La Bamba*'s origins in Mexican folkloric tradition, Valens brought the basic element of Latin music, the Afro-Cuban tumbao, into American pop music while singing in Spanish. *La Bamba* is based on the Mexican son jarrocho, which originated in Veracruz, one of the few areas in Mexico to have a significant African and Afro-Cuban influence. *La Bamba* has the same vamp you can hear in *Twist and Shout*.

Valens was the first American-born Latino singer to record a mainstream rock hit in Spanish, and he reflected the polyglot tastes of Mexican-Americans in California in the 1950s. A Valens song like *C'Mon, Let's Go* was the kind of habanera-laced rockabilly still popular at the time; his covers of Leiber and Stoller's *Framed* (originally recorded by the Coasters) and *Bluebirds Over the Mountain* (by country-western singer Ersel Hickey) reflected a wide range of musical influence. Tom Keane, who owned the label Valens recorded for, felt that Valens was the only artist of his time who would include these seemingly opposite genres within a single record album. *La Bamba* would not have been the massive hit it was if Valens's fans were not listening to him in the first place because of his earlier doo-wop-style hits like *Donna*. Valens died in a plane crash in 1959 after playing a show with two of the biggest rock stars of the time, Buddy Holly and the Big Bopper, who were also killed in the accident. After Valens's death Keane's Del-Fi records became one of the primary labels for the development of surf music—the label entrepreneur also fostered the career of El Paso, Texas, native Bobby Fuller, whose *I Fought the Law* incorporated a bit of an habanera rhythm as well as Tex-Mex and country-western influences.

Mexican-Americans had a subtle effect on the development of rock music. The corrido tradition of Texas undoubtedly bled through into the storytelling nature of country western and folk artists—Woody Guthrie wrote his *Dust Bowl Ballads* while traveling through Texas and the Southwest in the late 1930s. Texas conjunto bands began substituting the Farfisa organ for the previously de rigueur accordion in the late '50s. Among the significant Top 40 hits produced by Chicano R&B groups in the late '50s and early '60s, the most notable was Cannibal and the Headhunters' version of *Land of a Thousand Dances*, a tune written by Fats Domino and Chris Kenner and made famous by R&B heavyweight Wilson Pickett.

Cannibal and the Headhunters were from East Los Angeles, the undisputed crucible of California Chicano and Mexican rock culture. Made up of working-class singers Robert "Rabbit" Jaramillo, Richard "Scar" Lopez, "Yo Yo" Jaramillo and Frankie "Cannibal" Garcia, the Headhunters modeled themselves after R&B groups like the Miracles, the Motown prototype of the early 1960s. Their enormous popularity led to a tour with a Motown revue, appearances on popular TV shows like *Hullabaloo* and *Shindig*, and, in 1965, a spot opening for the Beatles on their most famous American tour, which began at Shea Stadium in New York City and ended at the Hollywood Bowl. This turned out to be a high point of their career, however, and they were relegated to the oldies circuit in the late 1970s.

California Chicano rockers Chan Romero and Chris Montez also played a role in the early years of rock and roll—their songs *Hippy Hippy Shake* and *Let's Dance* were recorded and covered by key figures in rock history. Romero, who was from Billings, Montana, and moved to Los Angeles as a child, was thrust into the limelight in the wake of Ritchie Valens's death because promoters saw him as a replacement for Valens. Valens's manager, Bob Keane, signed Romero to a recording contract, and he wound up recording in the same studio, with the same musicians and on the same label as his idol. Romero did a major national tour with Jerry Lee Lewis in 1960 and his song *Hippy Hippy Shake* was recorded by the Beatles during their Hamburg, Germany, period in 1962.

Chris Montez's hit single *Let's Dance* went to fourth place on the national pop charts in 1962, enjoying a similar level of success to early 1960s pre-discothèque pop like *Land of a Thousand Dances* and *The Twist*. Born in 1943 in Los Angeles, he was a contemporary at Hawthorne High School with the Beach Boys' Brian Wilson. Montez toured with major R&B acts Sam Cooke, the Drifters, Smokey Robinson, and Screamin' Jay Hawkins in 1961, and in 1963, he toured England with the still relatively unknown Beatles. The Ramones' 1976 cover of *Let's Dance* was one of the single most influential punk rock songs ever recorded, largely because it accomplished punk's mission to recapture rock's roots.

Another Southern California Chicano band was Thee Midniters, a rock and soul band from East Los Angeles that also succeeded with a cover of *Land of a Thousand Dances*. Anchored by guitarist George Dominguez and the charismatic vocals of Little Willie G., Thee Midniters had a raucous sound that was somewhere between the Rascals and the Beach Boys, doo-wop and garage rock. The band was influenced by everything from jump blues, jazz, and rock to classical Spanish guitar and Mexican boleros. *Whittier Boulevard*, an anthem for a famous cruising strip in East L.A., has all the earmarks of the period: wailing guitars that evoke everyone from the Yardbirds to the Velvet Underground and today's indie rock music; a psychedelic Vox organ; and a horn section straight out of Wilson Pickett-style R&B. After a few albums and an interesting detour into social consciousness with the single *Chicano Power*, the group split in the early 1970s, though its legacy (part community feel, part rock and roll) is felt in the work of Los Lobos.

Thee Midnighters and other Chicano bands like the Blendells, the Premiers, Tierra, and El Chicano all had relatively minor impact, solidifying the audience for rock music in Southern California at a time when regional music scenes had intense followings. The same audience would soon support surf music (some surf-oriented bands, like the Champs, featured Latin members), but there weren't many formal musical connections besides the Latin elements in rockabilly, which, along with the British invasion, was the key precursor to the full-blown 1960s rock sound.

Louie Louie, a song that is often cited as containing the essence of rock's primal energy, was another key moment in the genre's history because of the song's Latin influences. The most famous version of the song was done by a Seattle group called the Kingsmen in 1963, but the original is credited to Richard Berry, an African-American graduate of Jefferson High School in South Central L.A. in the early '50s. Berry was a doo-wop/R&B singer— he was the uncredited lead singer on Leiber and Stoller's *Riot in Cell Block #9*, recorded by the Robins, a group that later became the Coasters. He has said in published interviews that when he was in the process of writing *Louie Louie* in 1956, he based it on the chord progression from the Cuban-born René Touzét's *Loco Cha Cha*. In fact, his original plan for recording the song included using timbales and congas, but the producer turned him down.

The ethnic mix of Berry's rock band, the Soul Searchers— blacks, Latinos, and Filipinos—wasn't all that unusual in southern California. The late avant-garde rocker Frank Zappa, whose 1968 recording *Cruising With Ruben and the Jets* is a tribute to Southern California's doo-wop scene, began his career in several such bands. One was the Soul Giants, which featured Mexican-American bassist Roy Estrada and Native American guitarist Jimmy Carl Black, who both appeared on *Cruising*. Zappa was also rumored to have stolen money from his father to buy a ticket to a Ritchie Valens show in El Monte Legion Stadium. Posted in the liner notes of Zappa's first album, *Freak Out*, which appeared in 1964 and is widely acknowledged as the first avant-garde rock record, is the slogan: "The present-day Pachuco refuses to die."

The legacy laid down by Ritchie Valens and the Chicano rockers of the early 1960s was at the root of an entire branch of American rock history, one that many consider to be the most authentic "American," do-it-yourself style. Afro-Cuban music had been absorbed into rock through rockabilly, rhythm and blues, and funk, largely without the participation of actual Latin musicians. But genres popularized in the early to mid-'60s, such as frat rock, party rock, and garage rock, and possibly surf music, all sounds that immediately preceded or developed in tandem with the Beatles and the British invasion, were at least partly grounded in the hybrid Mexican-American culture that had already absorbed Afro-Cuban music through Mexico's mambo period in the 1950s.

A classic early example of Mexican-American influence came in the form of the Champs's *Tequila*, which rose to national prominence in 1958. The band included saxophonist Chuck Rio (born Daniel Flores), a Texas-born musician whose characteristic Tex-Mex or Tejano signature, essentially playing an Afro-Cuban tumbao, was essential to the song. *Tequila*'s association with comedian Pee Wee Herman in the 1980s made it synonymous with frat rock, a lowest-common-denominator rock genre associated with partying college fraternities, eliding the Latin essence that was more appreciated in the 1960s, when rock music had a broader audience. The association of Latin or tropical music with frat rock probably follows from the popularity of places like Tijuana and Cancun, Mexico, as spring and winter break sites for college fraternities.

Since songs like Valens's *La Bamba* and *C'Mon Let's Go*, covered by the Ramones, and Chris Montez's *Let's Dance* and Chan Romero's *Hippy Hippy Shake* are at the backbone of what roots rock purists consider essential, what came to be known as garage rock would have been inconceivable without Mexican-American influence. Just scanning the participants in the anthology *Nuggets*, considered the bible of American garage rock, you'll find the following: The Chocolate Watch Band, which contributed *Let's Talk About Girls*, had two Latino members, Dave Aguilar and Bill Flores; the Five Americans, who had a top five hit with *Western Union*, had two Mexican Americans, Mike Rabon and John Durrill, at the core of its songwriting; and the Syndicate of Sound, which did *Little Girl*, had a Latino bass player, Bob Gonzalez.

The pantheon of garage rock is dotted with Mexican and Latino participation. The Thirteenth Floor Elevators' *You're Gonna Miss Me* was propelled by a clave beat and featured a Mexican-American bassist, Dan Galindo. In 1966, Los Bravos, a Spain-based group, had an almost freakish overnight success with the seminal *Black Is Black*. Overwrought pop/R&B style vocals, tinny organ, and crashing guitars anchored Los Bravos, who were often mistaken for a British invasion band because they were based in Europe. Another band that became a favorite of garage aficionados was Los Mockers, who hailed from Montevideo, Uruguay, and performed what seemed like direct parodies of the Beatles and the Rolling Stones. Its 1966 self-titled debut was re-released in 1994 by Get Hip, a label based in the United States.

Garage rock can't be understood apart from its simple origins, in garages, with whatever instruments are at hand. While Mexican-Americans didn't have a monopoly on economic disadvantage, their relative inability to purchase expensive instruments put them on common ground with working-class America. Mexican-American music traditionally is characterized by a flexibility to use whatever instruments are available, anyway. In the years after World War II, the corrido conjuntos in Texas and northern Mexico began to augment the basic instrument of the corrido, the accordion, with the organ. The conjuntos were expanding at the time, incorporating additional electric and brass instruments, trying to seem modern and escape the poor-people's stigma of the accordion that began to creep into Tejano attitudes in the '50s and '60s.

The widespread use of the organ in Mexican-American music in turn may well have led to its use in garage rock. Mexican-American conjuntos used Farfisa organs that had a tinny, cheesy sound, one that ultimately became identified with garage rock and today has been elevated to exalted status among rockers.

Two of the earliest overlaps between Texas conjunto music, the British invasion, and garage rock involved Doug Sahm, an Anglo based in San Antonio who fronted a band that included legendary Tejano accordionist Flaco Jimenez, and ? and the Mysterians, a Detroit-area band who recorded the first garage rock classic. Sahm's group, called the Sir Douglas Quintet, released a song in 1965 called *She's About a Mover*, with a characteristic cheesy-sounding organ riff supplied by Augie Myers. The fanciful name Sahm chose for his group led many to believe they were a British invasion group.

A year later, ? and the Mysterians' *96 Tears*, with its strident, out-front organ commanding the melody, became an instant classic. The Mysterians, who took their name from an obscure science-fiction movie, were Mexican-Americans, the children of migrant agricultural laborers who had moved to Michigan from Texas and northern Mexico. They recorded *96 Tears* for a local Spanish-language music label, Pa-Go-Go, but it ultimately received national distribution because of its enormous local popularity and driving, contagious beat. The band's lead singer, ?, (a.k.a. Rudy Martinez) was still active in 2003 and a major eccentric, often performing in masks and sunglasses. The group consisted of Frank Rodriguez Jr. on keyboards, Larry Borjas on guitar, drummer Robert Martinez, and lead guitarist Bobby Balderrama. *96 Tears* uses the organ as a percussive instrument, the way Afro-Cuban music does, building to an other-worldly, moody apotheosis, especially when combined with Martinez's eerie vocals. The Mysterians' music seemed to announce that as Mexican-Americans, they felt like aliens.

Another proponent of the Farfisa sound was Sam the Sham and the Pharaohs, who straddled the border between garage rock and

Tex-Mex. Led by singer Domingo Samudio, the band was best known for its 1965 smash *Wooly Bully*, which helped introduce Tex-Mex rhythms to mainstream rock and roll. Samudio described his performing style as half-Spanish and half-Anglo—much of the rest of his band included Anglo-Americans. Introduced by Sam counting "uno, dos, tres, cuatro," *Wooly Bully* was another electric-organ-dominated song whose Latin rhythm, transferred to the keyboards, created a boogie-woogie sound that was irresistible dance music. After breaking up the band in 1967, Domingo Samu-dio ultimately changed his name to Sam Samudio and had a more modest success with the arch *Li'l Red Riding Hood*. He later collab-orated with Duane Allman of the Allman Brothers on a failed solo project and wrote music for the Jack Nicholson film *The Border* before becoming a street preacher in Dallas. In the late 1990s, Samudio returned to the stage for revival tours with surviving members of the Pharoahs.

The San Antonio Sound straddled both rock and roll and more traditional music, spearheaded by the Sir Douglas Quintet and Sam the Sham and the Pharaohs. The style was revived in the '80s by Joe "King" Carrasco who had his fifteen minutes of fame playing along-side CBGBs punk acts like the Ramones and Television. The Sahm brand of Tex-Mex also embraced Mexican-American players like singer-guitarist Freddy Fender and Flaco Jimenez, who in the late 1990s recorded nostalgia albums with Mexican-American rockers Los Lobos (see below) under the name of Los Super Seven.

Flor Power

As rock reached its psychedelic phase in the mid to late 1960s, it seemed to tune out the Latin influence—if expressed, it was sub-dued. Pseudo-bugaloo hits like Jimmy Castor's Afro-Caribbean-inflected *Hey Leroy, Your Mama's Callin You* in 1967 and the Blues

Magoos' vibe-heavy cover of Tito Puente's *Never Goin' Back to Georgia* in 1969, were very successful. (The entire Blues Magoos' album *Never Goin' Back to Georgia* was a departure from the band's Farfisa organ-driven psychedelic sound, typified by 1967's *We Ain't Got Nothin' Yet*. It had a strong Afro-Latin feel and lists a "conductor" named "Tito" in the credits.

From the flamenco overtones of Love's *Back Again* (which was covered by the late Selena's husband, Chris Perez, in a 1999 album), to the Doors' *Break on Through to the Other Side*, a weird overlapping of bossa nova and Afro-Cuban rhythm, the musicians of America's late 1960s counterculture appropriated Latin elements for superficial or synthetic effects. The lavish, frenetic organ introduction (a vestige of the garage-rock Farfisa sound) to *Light My Fire* set up what resembled an Afro-Cuban tumbao. The bolero-inflected blues version by the blind Puerto Rican singer, Jose Feliciano, explored the song's buried Latin roots. (In 1968, at the World Series in Detroit, Feliciano was the first musician, well before Jimi Hendrix, to perform a controversial, rock-inflected version of *The Star-Spangled Banner*.)

One important branch of 1960s pop that wound up strongly influencing both psychedelia and folk-rock was the folk movement of Greenwich Village cafes in the early 1960s. The scene that produced singers like Bob Dylan was profoundly influenced by a married couple, Richard and Mimi Fariña, both of whom had partial Hispanic roots. Richard was the son of a Cuban immigrant and an Irish woman, and Mimi, who was the sister of singer and one-time Dylan romantic partner Joan Baez, had Mexican and Scottish parents. While there may not be strongly apparent Latin influences in their music, their compositional style, which they developed together in 1964, was polyrhythmic and featured improvisation between guitar and dulcimer, characteristics that allude to the Hispano-Arabic roots of Latino culture. A 1971 Rolling Stone article quoted Rolling Stones member Brian Jones as saying that his use of the dulcimer in the hit single *Lady Jane* was inspired by Fariña.

The California hippie counterculture was nostalgic for Native America but rarely connected with the 1960s Chicano movement's recognition of indigenous roots. It was, however, unflaggingly loyal to Jerry Garcia's Grateful Dead. Born in 1942 in San Francisco, Garcia was only half Spanish, but his band's symbolism reflected California's Mexican roots (Day of the Dead is one of the most spiritually important days on the Mexican calendar). Judging from the group's self-titled 1967 debut, the Grateful Dead's sound had its roots in the psychedelia/garage rock that flourished in the West and Southwest—many of the album's songs feature the frenetic tinny organ sound of that milieu. While most of the Dead's oeuvre, from its early psychedelic improvisation to the 1970s turn to electrified country and bluegrass, was based on North American styles, several of the group's most popular songs (particularly concert favorites) had strong Latin influences. The cover of Buddy Holly's *Not Fade Away* clearly elicited its Bo Diddley/clave beat, and tunes like *Good Lovin'*, *Uncle John's Band*, and *Sugar Magnolia* built on Afro-Cuban rhythms.

Santana became a quintessential 1960s San Francisco psychedelic rock group because of lead guitarist Carlos's understanding of the blues and psychedelic potential of the electric guitar. But Santana went further because of Carlos's friendship with Oakland-based Afro-Cuban music devotees like Pete Escovedo, father of pop artist and former Prince protégé Sheila E., and Chepito Areas, who successfully incorporated Afro-Cuban rhythms into his music. Santana was born in 1947 in the small town of Autlán de Navarro, Mexico, about halfway between Guadalajara and Manzanillo. In 1955, his family moved to the border town of Tijuana, where he learned about blues guitar. In 1961, he moved to San Francisco, where he became part of the emerging rock scene, forming the Santana Blues Band in 1966. Santana's breakthrough came with his debut album in 1969, which featured hits like the bugaloo-esque *Evil Ways* and the rumba-flavored *Jingo*. After his legendary appearance at the 1969 Woodstock festival, Santana ascended to the heights of guitar heroes Jimi Hendrix, Eric Clapton, and Frank Zappa. Santana's version of the Tito Puente mambo *Oye Como Va*, a Top 20 single in 1969 and one of Santana's most famous songs, brought one of the ruling sounds of the 1950s abruptly into the 1970s. Santana crossed over not only to acid rock and pop audiences, but also to U.S. Latinos caught between the stillborn fate of bugaloo and the onset of the golden age of salsa.

Santana was also at the center of another 1970s musical revolution: jazz-fusion. Like Hendrix, Santana gravitated toward alumni of the classic Miles Davis bands such as guitarist John McLaughlin, keyboardist Herbie Hancock, and saxophonist Wayne Shorter. While Hendrix's rumored sessions with Miles Davis never materialized, Santana's cover of the title track to Davis's *In a Silent Way*, which appears on the 1972 *Fillmore: The Last Days* compilation, is a classic of the era. His 1972 collaboration with Davis's band member John McLaughlin, *Love, Devotion, Surrender*, inspired by their tutelage under Hindu mystic Sri Chinmoy, helped to usher in the new age movement.

A popular topic of discussion in the 1970s was whether Carlos brother Jorge's band Malo—a less acid-tinged, jazzy, purer Latin soul pop machine—was actually better than Santana. Malo's *Suavecito*, from his group's 1972 self-titled debut, was the make-out standard of the day, but the band didn't last, recording its last album in 1974. Carlos's own star began to decline in the '80s and '90s. His strong involvement in Buddhism and the new age movement tended to take him out of the spotlight. But he staged one of the greatest comebacks in pop history in 1999, when his Clive Davis-engineered album *Supernatural* swept the 2000 Grammy awards. Rather than rehashing the undistinguished soul/jazz/rock style he had been doing for several years, Santana patched together several genres popular with college-age listeners (alternative rock, hip-hop) and put out an album whose only organizing thread was his guitar. *Shaman*, released in 2002, is essentially *Supernatural* redux, with even less room for guitar solos. Still, both these albums feature lively performances by emerging stars (Rob Thomas, Michelle Branch) and in many ways expand the mainstream audience's idea of the Latin (or as Santana himself likes to stress, Afro-Cuban) influence on pop music.

Bands like Santana and Malo, as well as ex-Animal frontman Eric Burdon's quirky single *Spill the Wine* helped keep the Latin influence very much alive as the 1960s became the 1970s. The Rolling Stones' *Sympathy for the Devil* was a signature song about the 1960s apocalyptic climax and a harbinger of the group's ill-fated concert at Altamont, California, in which an audience member was stabbed to death by a Hell's Angels motorcycle club member employed as a security guard. *Sympathy for the Devil* might have been an attempt to invoke dread through "jungle" rhythms (note Jagger's ape-like howling that begins the song), but the band actually plays the song in a kind of modified mambo tempo, complete with conga and bongó rhythm section.

In a more amiable vein, early 1970s Stones touring mate, Stevie Wonder, recorded *Don't You Worry 'Bout a Thing* (featured on 1973's *Innervisions*), using an Afro-Cuban piano tumbao often used in cha-cha and bugaloo. He also actually improvised several Spanish slang words, including *chévere*, the Spanglish equivalent of "groovy" at the time. In 1974, when Steely Dan recorded *Rikki Don't Lose That Number*, which begins with an Afro-Latin piano figure written by Cape Verdean-Portuguese jazz pianist Horace Silver, it seemed part and parcel of the mainstream pop vocabulary.

The Latino influence was also present in 1970s pop rock. The early '70s group Redbone, which had a soul-derived hit, *Come and Get Your Love*, often appeared in Native American garb, but the members were really Chicanos. In 1976, Bob Dylan released *Desire* which included *Romance in Durango* and several solos by violinist Scarlet Rivera. Tony Orlando, who is half-Puerto Rican, got his chance by hanging around the Brill Building and gaining an audition with promoter Don Kirshner. Tony Orlando and Dawn's first hit singles, *Candida* and *Knock Three Times*, released in 1970, loped along to a kind of son with Mexican marimba beat.

By the time of the emergence of American and British punk in the late 1970s, the Latin influence began to express itself in the form of rock revivalism, which rescued past Latin-influenced rock hits, and in active participation by Latino members in some of the genre's seminal groups. The New York Dolls's first drummer, Billy Murcia, who died and was replaced by Jerry Nolan for the band's first album in 1973, was an immigrant from Medellín, Colombia. An early lead singer of Black Flag, which became one of Los Angeles's major contributions to hard-core punk, was Ron Reyes (a.k.a. Chavo Pederast), a rare, L.A.-based Puerto Rican, and one of the band's original drummers was Robo (a.k.a. Roberto Valverde), originally from Colombia. (The Black Flag website stated that Ron Reyes quit the group two songs into an early gig and that the band compensated for his absence by playing an instrumental version of *Louie Louie* for an hour and a half.) *Blitzkrieg Bop*, one of the Ramones' signature tunes, is a dead ringer for Ritchie Valens's *Come On Let's Go*. Even the artistic director of the Ramones, the man who designed the famous pseudo-military logo, was Arturo Vega. Los Angeles rock groups the Zeros and Oingo Boingo were led by Mexican-American personnel. The lead guitarist of Roxy Music, one of London's seminal post-glam, modern rock bands, was Phil Manzanera, of Colombian descent, who was raised English.

A Puerto Rican guitarist named Carlos Alomar deserves at least partial credit for helping to resurrect David Bowie's career after the British rock idol dissolved his Spiders of Mars band. Alomar co-wrote the song *Fame* with Bowie in 1975, a song featured on *Young Americans*. Alomar had once played with James Brown, and when he joined Bowie's band on *Young Americans* he helped create a version of rock-disco that predated the Bee Gee's work on *Saturday Night Fever.* Alomar also anchored Bowie's trilogy of *Low,* *Heroes,* and *Scary Monsters,* and worked with Iggy Pop in the late 1970s, playing on songs like *Lust for Life.*

While many Latinos who have been involved in the development of alternative rock and heavy metal may not have added a Latin-music influence to those genres, their presence should be noted. Mia Zapata, lead singer of the Gits, was tragically murdered in 1993 in Seattle. Her associations with local bands (she was good friends with Babes in Toyland, among others), as well as fleeting acquaintances Courtney Love and Kurt Cobain may have been a root of rrriot girl. The album recorded as a tribute to her, *Viva Zapata,* by Seven Year Bitch, was required listening for groups like Bratmobile. Mazzy Star, one of the most influential L.A. post-punk groups, was led by Hope Sandoval, a Chicana from East Los Angeles. Sandoval is a model for many alternative rock singers who succeeded her, even mainstreamers like Gwen Stefani. In the heavy metal world, much of the current thrash scene is made up of bands with sizable Latino representation: Incubus, Suicidal Tendencies, Downset, Fear Factory, and Puya all have Latinos in key roles. Los Angeles Chicano Dave Navarro may have been the strongest hard-rock guitarist of the '90s, with his classic work in both Jane's Addiction and the Red Hot Chili Peppers. And, for what it's worth, Metallica's bass player Robert Trujillo, originally of Suicidal Tendencies, joined the band for 2003's *St. Anger.*

Latin music in almost any form was very unpopular in the mainstream in the early 1980s. Although Rubén Blades's Seis del Solar albums drew a certain amount of interest because of their political content, the watering down of salsa and the disappearance of popular genres like cha-cha, mambo, and bugaloo, as well as

jazz's post-fusion metamorphosis into "historic" music, made
Latin music a purely ethnic phenomenon. The most important
Latin rock band of the '80s and '90s was one formed by a group of
friends from East Los Angeles, Los Lobos. Los Lobos made its
debut with an EP, *And a Time to Dance*, in 1983. While the music is
primarily derived from blues and psychedelic rock, Los Lobos incorporated roots music like Mexican rancheras, conjunto music,
and cumbia; on occasion the band has invited Tex-Mex veterans
like Flaco Jimenez to play with them.

And a Time to Dance and *How Will the Wolf Survive?*, Los Lobos's first LP, released in 1984, both contain typical Lobos tunes,
blues-rockers, as well as roots-rock songs like Ritchie Valens's
C'Mon Let's Go and norteño standards like *Ay te Dejo San Antonio*.
Its version of Ritchie Valens's *La Bamba* for the 1987 soundtrack of
the movie directed by Luis Valdez was inspired, but added little to
the legacy of the song. Standard blues-rock songs predominated
on releases like *By the Light of the Moon* (1987) and *The Neighborhood* (1990), which sandwiched an album of traditional norteño
songs, *La Pistola y el Corazón* (1988). In 1992, Los Lobos released a
daring album, *Kiko*, which came off as avant-garde and psychedelic, evoking disparate sources like Tom Waits and Captain Beef-
heart. The album's use of eccentric accordion soloing and very
funky Delta blues meters was said to be an influence on Tijuana
rocker Julieta Venegas.

Excellent instrumentalists, bandleaders David Hidalgo and Cesar Rojas can write a decent song, and their corridos and ranchera
are serviceable tributes to their inherited tradition. *This Time* was
released to critical acclaim in 1999, and a side project, the Latin
Playboys (which was formed in 1994 to pursue the textured experimentalism hinted at on *Kiko*) followed up with *Dose*, in 1999. In
the early 2000s touring members of Los Lobos were more often
seen with Los Super Seven, a supergroup that included Tex-Mex
veterans Freddy Fender and Flaco Jimenez and concentrated on
covering Latin American and Tex-Mex classics.

Hip-hop a lo Latino

Hip-hop today is known as the creation of African Americans. But Latinos made significant contributions to the origins of hip-hop that are not generally known. By most accounts hip-hop originated in the South Bronx, where dance parties held by DJ Afrika Bambaata acted as an alternative to the street gang warfare going on in New York City at the time. Just as graffiti, used to mark turf of various gangs, became a form of artistic expression for inner city youth, breakdancing became a way for them to act out violent behavior—practitioners still call it "battling"—and rapping a way to make music out of confrontational boasting.

In this atmosphere, the early star of hip-hop was the DJ, or the turntablist, and not the MC, as it is presently. The early turntable whizzes of the era were African-Americans of Caribbean descent, Kool DJ Herc (Jamaica) and Grandmaster Flash (Barbados). These DJs demonstrated their skill by alternating between two copies of the same record to extend instrumental breaks. Those instrumental breaks were often Afro-Caribbean–flavored percussion jams by acts like "It's Just Begun" by the Jimmy Castor Bunch, with timbál breaks often being a favorite. The two-turntable jam, the underpinning of the hip-hop musical aesthetic, thus began with breaks that were analogous to the Afro-Cuban descarga and to salsa's percussive montuno improvisations.

Latin music has been sampled since the early days of hip-hop, from a Tito Puente riff on 1991's *I'm Still Number One* by Boogie Down Productions, back to the early 1980s days of Sugar Hill, where the studio bands would have timbál and conga players. There was a timbál break on Kurtis Blow's *The Breaks*, released in 1980. In filmmaker Charlie Ahearn's 1982 documentary about hip-hop, *Wild Style*, Charlie Chase (a.k.a. Carlos Mandes) of the Cold Crush Brothers manifested a Latino presence. But even though graffiti artist Lee Quiñones and several of the break-dancers featured in the film are also Latino, the twenty-odd year history of hip-hop has yielded few Latino stars. Most Latino rappers have preferred to avoid the language of their ancestors. "I don't make rap in Spanish," said Fat Joe Cartagena on his website. "I'm just a rapper that happens to be Spanish." Although Cartagena has since changed this philosophy, because of peer pressure that equates Latin-ness with being an outsider, many New York Latinos tried not to call attention to their ethnicity. Many, like Queens natives the Beatnuts, have been overlooked.

The Beatnuts, who have been issuing albums since 1993, are a hip-hop underground favorite. While their only overt Spanglish foray is Se Acabó (It's Over), set to the tune of a famous La Lupe torch song, it's the jazzy bass break beat driving *Props Over Here* that nails down the Beatnuts' place in hip-hop lore. Tolerance for thuggish lyrics is necessary to appreciate their early hit *Off the Books*, which features the late Big Pun and Cuban Link, both Latino rappers from a posse called the Terror Squad.

The story of how rap spread to Latin America (see Chapter 10) and takes on a Spanish-language flavor began in California. When L.A.-based Cypress Hill made its debut in 1991, it became the first mainstream hip-hop success to flaunt its Latinness, with songs like *Latin Lingo*. Cypress Hill rapper Sen Dog's brother, who goes by the name of Mellow Man Ace, scored with a single called *Mentirosa* (Liar). Cypress Hill's affinity with Latino listeners spurred the group to eventually release *Los Grandes Éxitos en Español*, an entire album with Spanish-language versions of their songs, in 1999. That album featured a collaboration with rapper Fermin Caballero of Control Machete, based in Monterrey, Mexico, whose story will be examined in the next chapter.

In the late 1990s, because of increasing contact between Latinos and African-Americans in New York and other parts of the country, mainstream hip-hop began incorporating Latin music and Spanglish slang in its hit formulas. In Ruff Ryders' *What Ya Want*, Eve and Nokio rap over a slinky syncopated piano sound, the Afro-Cuban rumba rhythm called guaguancó. Latin flavor started popping up in tunes like East Sidaz' *Got Beef*, Lil' Wayne's *Respect Us*, and Lil' Kim's *No Matter What They Say*, bringing a bellyful of tricky beats and tongue-twisting Spanglish rhymes.

The late 1990s flurry of Latin beats, which could also be attributed to the commercial sales excitement created by the Latin pop explosion, was fueled by Wyclef Jean's collaborations with Celia Cruz and Santana, Puff Daddy's 1998 single *Señorita*, and producer Swiss Beatz. Puff Daddy protégé Black Rob scored with the single *Dame Espacio* (Give Me Space). On *My Story* he described growing up "talking wild shit to Spanish immigrants" and saying "bendición to my mother." Lil' Kim's single *No Matter What They Say* includes a sample from an old tune by salsa vocalist Cheo Feliciano, *Esto Es El Guaguancó*.

In the early 2000s, the inclusion of Spanglish lyrics in hip-hop has abated somewhat, but Latinos have been participating in some of the latest trends in the field. On the West Coast, crews like Dilated Peoples and Jurassic 5, who are at the forefront of the movement to return to older hip-hop values, getting away from the gangsta imperative, feature some Latino members. DJ Rob Swift, at the center of a movement to re-establish the importance of the DJ in hip-hop music, is a Colombian with African roots. And, as will be detailed in the following chapter, "Latin Alternative," hip-hop has taken deep root in countries all over Latin America and Spain.

The Latin influence on rock and hip-hop encompasses direct influences of Latin music on these genres as well as the direct participation of Latinos. The linking of African cultures from Latin America and North America in rock and hip-hop is key to understanding how this happens, and the Latin propensity for mixing musical styles aids in this. But the actual process of Latinos becoming Americans, actively participating in North American culture while adding conscious or unconscious elements from their ethnic origins, is perhaps the most central element here.

10

Latin Alternative

One summer day in 1997, thousands of young Latinos had filled a small amphitheater in New York's Central Park to capacity. From the stage, lead singer Rubén Albarrán of the Mexican alternative pop group, Café Tacuba, addressed a sea of young, hopeful, mostly brown faces. "From the window of my house in Mexico City I could see a volcano, Popocatépetl, erupting right in front of me," shouted Albarrán messianically. "And I wondered . . . If this volcano is waking up, why aren't the Latin American people waking up?" The crowd, which had been wildly cheering throughout, seemed to think about it for a minute, then burst into a sustained roar.

Whether they recently fled hostile governments or disastrous economies, or long fought for a voice as a part of a disdained Immigrant America, a growing number of Latinos are taking part in a rebellious youth culture with its own countercultural music heroes. Bands like Café Tacuba, Jaguares, and Los Fabulosos Cadillacs draw substantial crowds in North America's larger cities, but they're even bigger in Latin America. While rock music has existed in Latin America as far back as the 1950s and '60s, the increasing penetration of North American youth culture south of the border has in the last fifteen years created a new phenomenon.

These days the preferred term in the United States is Latin alternative, to be more inclusive of the hip-hop and rock-salsa fusion bands that have appeared, but in Latin America, the music is still often referred to as simply rock, or roc.

While the development of rock in Latin America was clearly inspired by doings in the United States, the emergence of Latin alternative was foreshadowed in London in the early 1980s. Ska, a music that preceded reggae in '60s Jamaica, was reborn in London as the result of a cross-bred cultural phenomenon between immigrant West Indians and working-class whites at the dawn of Prime Minister Margaret Thatcher's era. Ska, originally the party music of Rude Boys in downtown Kingston, Jamaica, had become a form of political protest against the Tory policies that signaled the end of Britain's welfare state. The adoption of ska by Mexican and Argentine bands was a key development in those countries' rock scenes, which had until then been slavishly imitative of Anglo rock. The political charge that dominated the London ska scene was easily transferable to Mexico and Argentina, where class antagonisms are as pronounced as in Europe. Latin American universities, which feature the same European-style arts education that was the backdrop of English punk music, were also hotbeds of youth activism, factors that helped spur the mid-1980s rock en Español explosion.

Rock music per se, that is the standard format of electric guitar, bass, and drums, reached Latin America as an import in the 1950s and 1960s, and rock's emphasis on the guitar meant it wasn't entirely foreign to a Spanish-based culture, since Spain is key to the development of the guitar. What was new to Latin ears were the blues-based chord progressions, which were grounded in the African-American post-slavery experience. Rock took hold in Mexico because of the guitar-driven cowboy country-western music that developed in the American Southwest partly as a result of contact with Mexican-American culture; in Argentina, which is influenced greatly by European fads, it produced Beatles' imitators. Rock was slower to take hold in Caribbean nations like Cuba, Puerto Rico, and the Dominican Republic because the rhythms of salsa and merengue were so deeply embedded in popular taste. The rock music that was played in those countries was closer to pop-rock and vocalists were more important than instrumental sound.

In Argentina, rock and roll emulators began performing soon after the genre's initial spurts in the mid to late 1950s. Early bands like Los Shakers, Los Gatos Salvajes, and Los Beatniks recorded singles and played in clubs in Buenos Aires. A downtown club called La Cueva sprouted a scene of sorts by the early 1970s, which later expanded into large-scale rock festivals, featuring what Argentine rock historians call the big three: Almendra, Manal, and Los Gatos Salvajes. Many of these groups performed in English, such as Los Mockers (see Chapter 9); some went back and forth. But in the 1980s, everything changed.

While many who lived through the 1980s remember it for its rekindling, and then dissolution of, the Cold War, as well the horrifying carnage in Central America, for Latin alternative, the most consequential event may have been an incident that everyone seems to have forgotten. Because of a breakdown in diplomacy between England and Argentina, two countries with a strong relationship, in 1983, they went to war over an archipelago in the South Atlantic known as the Falkland Islands (Las Malvinas, to the Argentines). One of the silliest wars of the twentieth century, the Falkland conflict had a major effect on music in Argentina—out of a renewed sense of isolationist nationalism, Argentinians tuned out on English and North American rock and started to create their own rock music.

In Buenos Aires, the capital city of Argentina, Los porteños (the term used for Buenos Aires natives) had been absorbing fashion, music, and literature from London, Paris, Madrid, and Rome all along, but now they embarked on creating their own blues, psychedelic, and art rock bands. In the early 1980s, a scraggly haired progressive-blues-rock songwriter named Charly García, co-founder of influential '70s bands Sui Generis and Seru Giran, went solo. He turned Buenos Aires into the backdrop for a Spanish-language Sergeant Pepper with albums like *Clics Modernos*, *Piano Bar*, and *Como Conseguir Chicas*. Luis Alberto Spinetta emerged as his axe-wielding alter ego during stints as a sideman for García and the irrepressible singer-songwriter Fito Paez.

In Spain, the years following Generalissimo Francisco Franco's death were unimaginably wild, indulgent ones, as the Spanish violently threw off forty years of suffocating patriarchal repression. Most of the evidence for Spain's sudden art explosion came through the cinema, which made Pedro Almodóvar and Antonio Banderas national heroes. But on a smaller scale, Spain's rock scene, dotted with progressive rock bands and pseudo-Clash poseurs, as well as the occasional flamenco fusion outfit, produced bands such as Heroes de Silencio, Seguridad Social, Ketama, and La Ultima de la Fila. These bands had styles that ranged from British art rock to punk to reggae and flamenco-rock. Most importantly, they had the effect of galvanizing a public for rock in Spanish in the mid to late 1980s. This explosion of rock from Spain also sold records in Mexico and Argentina, and entrepreneurs and music industry people first began referring to a genre called rock en Español.

Rock en Español is mostly defined by the language of its lyrics, but makes little reference to the traditional rhythms of the band's native countries. Even as rock en Español spread to Mexico, a country where rock had been banned since the early 1970s because of government disapproval, and continued to grow in Argentina, the music didn't diverge much from standard, North American/Euro guitar-oriented rock. In Mexico, groups like Dangerous Rhythms and Three Souls in My Mind, who covered American rock songs in English, were popular, building on the

'50s and '60s audiences that danced to Los Teen Tops, replete with the pompadours and styles of that era.

The New Mexican Rock

The new Mexican rock was born from the ashes of the death of about 200 students protesting governmental repression, mowed down by police bullets in the summer of 1968 in an effort to make the city presentable for that year's Olympic Games, and from the governmental repression that followed a Woodstock-like concert in the suburb of Avándaro in 1971. The Massacre at Tlatleco, as the 1968 incident was called, followed a period when Mexican social conservatives were threatened by the growing jipi (hippie) movement among adolescents. The continuing protests centered in the UNAM (the National Autonomous University of Mexico) also concerned a government that wanted to present a problem-free environment for the Olympic Games during a year when disorder prevailed on the streets of cities around the world.

The Avándaro concert provoked a strong backlash from both social conservatives, who objected to the free-spirited attitudes about sexuality and personal grooming, to leftists, who objected to the Americanization of Mexico through rock and youth culture. Forced underground, over the next decade rock survived in the proletarian periphery of the city with impromptu street concerts and a series of gigs in funky holes-in-the wall that were called *Los Hoyos Fónquis* (Funky Holes-in-the-Wall).

In this mid-'70s era the chavos banda (street kids) aesthetic took hold, through the exhortations of Alex Lora, a burly, bikerish rocker who led Three Souls in My Mind. When Lora greeted a crowd of working-class youth by telling them to go to hell, they felt loved, as British punks did when Johnny Rotten of the Sex Pistols spat at them. Their old English-language records, replete with parodic psychedelic cover artwork, are still big collectors' items at

El Chopo, a huge open-air record market that, despite its illegal status, thrived every Saturday afternoon in the heart of Mexico City. Singing in English was partly a way for Mexicans to emulate North Americans or Europeans, and partly a rebellion against the official national culture of the Mexican Institutional Revolutionary Party. The official culture had a skepticism, if not disdain, for U.S. culture that mirrored the old left's critique of "capitalist decadence." The music of the nueva canción social protest songs was officially promoted by the government, which, despite its social conservatism, supported the Cuban revolution and leftist movements throughout Latin America.

Since rock music was restricted to the hoyos fónquis in the poor communities, it became directly concerned with and more intimate with its lower-class audience. Cover bands singing in English disappeared. Dangerous Rhythms changed its name to Ritmos Peligrosos and Three Souls in My Mind became El Tri, a group now the granddaddy of the movement, invoking a fierce loyalty among working-class, mestizo youth. Though accustomed to not understanding English lyrics (to them, Beebop-alula was just as incomprehensible as *La Bamba* was to Anglo youth), these young people welcomed the development. A compilation put out by Comrock, an independent label, featuring El Tri, Ritmos Peligrosos, and Kenny y los Electricos creeped into the suburbs, becoming a big hit at teenage parties. The music of these bands became fodder for the childhood of groups like Café Tacuba, whose members were beginning to imagine a pop cultural future as hip as the north but tinged with Mexican flavor.

In the mid-'80s a series of developments shocked Mexicans into changing the way they saw themselves. The massive 1985 Mexico City earthquake stirred a new grassroots activism that helped to organize the repair of neighborhoods when the government and other outside forces failed or responded too slowly. One of the heroes of that moment, El Super Barrio, was an iconic figure dressed as a superhero who led activists in drawing attention and help to neighborhoods. After having been relegated to the working and underclass periphery of the hoyos fónquis, rock music was no longer a blatant imitation of imperialist decadence, it was infused with working-class angst, much as it was in England in the mid to late 1970s punk era, and it was no longer sung in English. The oil-driven economy, and the passage of over fifteen years since the repression of youth culture in 1968, contributed to a strong desire to create a new Mexican alternative culture.

But something else was happening with Mexican youth. They had began to watch more and more American television, and as voyeurs of the bloated, self-absorbed TV culture to the North, they developed a healthy sense of irony about stardom. Enter Botellita de Jérez (Little Bottle of Sherry), a Mexico City band that singlehandedly revolutionized Mexican rock, both musically and attitudinally. The activism that grew in the post-earthquake era had become a cause celebre on the campuses and in the union halls of the city, and Botellita became a house band of the scene. A flaky goofball trio consisting of Francisco Barrios, Armando Vega-Gil, and Sergio Arau, Botellita invented guacarock (short for "guacamole-rock") in 1983, which started as a self-effacing joke, but became a prototype of a new kind of Mexican rock that many groups would follow. By reaching out to the petit-bourgeois intellectuals reared on nueva canción and folklorica with absurdist, quirkily intelligent songs, Botellita helped to create a new rock circuit at clubs and coffee houses that surrounded the immense university in the south of the city.

The group's third album, *Naco Es Chido* (roughly, The Masses' Aesthetic Is Cool, Trash Is a Gas, or Brown Is Beautiful), released in 1986, was its peak. The musicians employed the Naco aesthetic as a way of expressing solidarity with the working class. *Naco*, sometimes a crude word that refers to Mexicans with indigenous features and skin color, can refer to a charmingly kitschy taste in furniture and home decorations and clothing. It is basically an unpretentious, working-class attitude or posture in life. To be proud

of the Naco aesthetic, for Mexico City university students, is not
unlike some New York Puerto Ricans' fondness for transparent
plastic slipcovers or Rheingold beer paraphernalia or, for that matter, the taste for used knickknacks that keeps stores like White
Trash in the East Village in business.

But the Naco es Chido era also signaled the beginning of the
end for Botellita. Its tradition of hyperbolic humor and roots in
carpa (folkloric tent theater) humor was difficult to sustain on a
broad popular level. By taking it upon themselves to vindicate
working-class tastes, Botellita at once encouraged a reintegration
of the lower and middle classes in a rock context. But it also opened
up a contradiction that the English punk rockers, the Clash, stum-
bled upon: How much credibility could bourgeois intellectuals
have in championing a class they didn't belong to? While Botellita
infused the middle class with a renewed dose of what the members
called "Mexican kitsch, double entendres, and rudeness," eventually they began to parody themselves. Botellita never achieved the
fame of its immediate successors, Caifanes, Maldita Vecindad, and
Café Tacuba, and broke up in the late 1990s.

The Botellita era coincided with a trickle of rock imports from
Spain and Argentina like Radio Futura, Charly García, and Soda
Stereo. Spanish pop-rockers La Union had recorded a song, *Lobo
Hombre en Paris* (1984), that amounted to a Spanish remake of
Warren Zevon's *Werewolves of London*, and the Spanish-speaking
world began to sing along. In 1987 Heroes de Silencio, a long-
haired quartet that played gothic rock ballads about teen romance,
released its first album, *Heroes de Legenda*, using a kind of English
progressive sound to gain a widespread following.

Back in Mexico, Caifanes, a group that looked and sounded
reminiscent of Heroes but wrote more political songs, was beginning to take off. Caifanes, formed in 1986 by singer/songwriter
Saul Hernández, guitarist Alejandro Marcovich, and drummer Alfonso André, was spawned from an earlier group, Las Insolitas Im-
agenes de Aurora. The first, self-titled album, which appeared in

1988, saw the musicians dressing up in bizarre hairdos, inspired by the hugely popular British group, the Cure. The first single from that album, *Viento* (The Wind), was promoted by an unintentionally funny video, which deployed several wind machines making messes of the band members' mop-tops. But the second single, *La Negra Tomasa* (Black Tomasa) proved to be a huge hit. It was a rock re-take of a traditional cumbia tune and its success was a harbinger of things to come—rock en Español's future would increasingly involve syncopated rhythms.

Caifanes integrated the mystical, magical, and spiritual aspects of Mexican culture (ritual gatherings, worship of demigods and mother earth) into Mexican rock in much the same way that English rockers once incorporated medieval legends in their songs of the late '60s and early '70s. Caifanes is a champion of mythical phenomena such as self-transformation, as in *Metamorféame* (Metamorphosize Me) and *Nos Vamos Juntos* (We Go Together) from their third album, *El Silencio*, released in 1992, the reincarnation of the jaguar and the warrior, and the messages believed to be emanating from volcanoes that loom around the periphery of Mexico City. A Caifanes show is a celebration of occult life in broad daylight, in which pagan themes usually associated with darkly negative metal groups from the United States and Britain become a form of solace and protection from the angst of adolescence—the essence of rock and roll. Caifanes's lead singer and principal songwriter, Saul Hernández, projected himself as a figure of reassurance to Mexican youth, offering his interpretation of indigenous legends as a form of spiritual guidance.

After releasing its most successful record in terms of sales, *El Nervio del Volcán*, in 1994, Caifanes came apart at the seams. With the hit single *Afuera*, inspired by Brit pop, and the folky guitar-driven mid-tempo tune *Detras de los Cielos*, an allusion to the disenfranchised indigenous poor, Caifanes finally broke through to the Mexican music mainstream and garnered considerable U.S. attention. But because of a behind-the-scenes rivalry between guitarist Alejandro Marcovich and Hernández and drummer Alfonso André, Caifanes was dissolved in 1995. In its place, Hernández began Jaguares, which released its first album in 1996, *El Equilibrio*, with guitarist Jorge Manuel Aguilera and André. With Jaguares, Hernández increased his onstage patter and lyrical references to human-animal transformation (most likely alluding to an ancient Mayan cult that used psychedelic roots and herbs to perform rituals in which the shaman would be transformed into a jaguar), astral projection, the use of protective talismans, and a general presumption that the spiritual reigns over the material. In 1999, the double-CD *El Azúl de tu Misterio* scored with poppier hit singles like *Fin* and *Hoy*.

Jaguares's 2001 album, *Cuando la Sangre Galopa*, celebrated some changes in its musical strategy. For about half the album, Hernández, who had always played lead or rhythm guitars, switched to the bass, leaving the lead duties to César "Vampiro" López. The chemistry between the two and drummer André resulted in one of the densest, most imagistic playing of the entire Caifanes/Jaguares oeuvre. Tracks like *El Momento*, *El Secreto*, and *Viaje Astral* capture Hernández's ethereal romanticism. The tropical syncopation of the hit singles *Como Tú* and *La Vida no es Igual* are also innovations, breaking Jaguares out of the prog-rock category. The addition of Chucho Merchán, veteran bassist of Colombian origin who has played with the Eurythmics and lived in London for several years, made Jaguares as formidable as any Latin alternative band.

The band's 2002 album *El Primer Instinto* is a collection of acoustic remakes of classic Hernández tunes. While the album also features two original songs, *Arriésgate*, and *No Importa*, and a cover of Juan Gabriel's *Te lo Pido por Favor*, the primary magic here is in drawing out the essence of Hernández's songs. The stripped-down strategy is equally effective in bringing out the solemnity of *Ante de que nos Olividen*, about the disembodied spirits of young protesters killed by police in 1968, an incident still causing political shockwaves in Mexico. *El Primer Instinto* also fleshes out the traditional Latin underpinnings to *La Célula Que Explota* with mariachi horns and strings, and includes Afro-Cuban conga and piano arrangements for *Como Tú*.

If Caifanes represented the psychedelic, art rock pose of the Mexican scene, Maldita Vecindad was its rhythm-driven underbelly. They are the Rolling Stones, to Caifanes's Beatles, and the argument about who is better is based on almost the same logic that the Beatles versus Stones one is. Formed in 1985, Maldita Vecindad are a ska-punk-funk melange who trade on their homeboy-from-the-hood image. Their obvious constituency was mestizos from the barrio—their full name, Maldita Vecindad y los Hijos del Quinto Patio (Damned Neighborhood and the Sons of the Fifth Patio) makes an explicit reference to class structure within the housing projects of Mexico City. They were from the damned projects, sons of the fifth level of those projects, the level reserved for citizens with the lowest incomes. But instead of the unadulterated rage of gangsta rap, Maldita chose to highlight the underclass culture's difficult economic status, as well as to celebrate the kitschy aesthetic of the working-class households. While the goal mirrors that of Botellita de Jérez, the members of Maldita were more authentically working class, and they used a wide array of Afro-Caribbean rhythms to propel their music.

Maldita's first two albums, the self-titled debut (1988) and 1991's *El Circo*, are classics in Latin ska-rock. The electric presence of lead singer Roco, with his long, straight black hair swinging in a circle, and the dynamism of the rhythmic section made the band an instant underground success. Maldita Vecindad took subversive Mexican comic figures like Tin Tan and Cantinflas, famous for debunking the privileged class, as inspirations and gave Mexican rock a political soul. Because most rock en Español groups from Spain and Argentina were at least on the surface representations of white-skin privilege, Maldita's urban indio reality created a link to the reggae and two-tone subcultures of 1980s London.

The extended rhythm section, which included Latin percussion and horns, gave the group the only pseudo-salsa tinge in the genre, besides Argentina's Fabulosos Cadillacs.

Anchored by drummer Pacho (real name José Luis Paredes), a voracious reader of cultural politics tracts like Marshal Berman's *All That Is Solid Melts Into Air*, Maldita's presentation had an important air of class consciousness. In its classic early hit, *Pachuco*, Maldita stakes rock en Español's claim to a new rebellious subculture that fuses the Mexican-American experience with that of the class-conscious English punk movement, as well as the pent-up rage of the marginalized Mexico City denizen. The song is narrated by the son of a pachuco (Mexican-American street hero) who insists that he must free himself of parental repression to establish his own rebel identity. The title track of *Circo* describes the circus atmosphere of Mexico City's streets, where beggars are dressed in clown costumes and beg for change with organ grinders and monkeys. Because of Mexico's paternalist government, instituted by the PRI party, which until recently enjoyed a seventy-five-year rule and had historically tried to homogenize rock, Maldita's unabashed class antagonism and unbridled punk attitude made the group a phenomenon. But although Maldita released three albums between 1991 and 1998, and continued to tour in a limited capacity, it never captured the excitement of its early run. Record company problems, poor sales and distribution, and the defection of some members left drummer Pacho, a noted activist and journalist in Mexico City, as Maldita's most prominent voice. Vocalist Roco also appeared as a guest vocalist on a song by ska band Inspector, based in Monterrey, Mexico, in 2003.

Rock in Argentina

With a wealth of venues in Buenos Aires for groups to play and extensive media coverage, the Argentine rock scene is as vital as there is in Latin America. While the tango remained at the core of the Argentine music aesthetic, there was also a strong Anglophilia that resulted in a straight-ahead rock aesthetic that worships the blues-based music venerated by the greats of English rock. The end of a seven-year military dictatorship in 1983 also opened up doors to a new rock movement. Groups like the Butthole Surfers-like Sumo, the punk-inspired Los Divididos, and pop rockers Los Twist and Virus gave Buenos Aires a new rock charge.

Bridging the generations that produced stars like Charly García and Luis Alberto Spinetta was the inspirational and idiosyncratic talent of Fito Paez. The piano player/songwriter, born in 1963 in the city of Rosario, Che Guevara's birthplace and decidedly less cosmopolitan than Buenos Aires, was a standout in his hometown. His first solo album, *Del '63*, was released in 1984. His second album, *La La La La*, was a 1986 duet with Spinetta. A dynamic songwriter embittered by the assassination of his aunt and grand-mother by the military dictatorship but somehow resolutely opti-mistic, Paez updated aspects of the nueva canción tradition, top-loading his songwriting with a kind of Prince-ish intensity and dense pop wall of sound. His most impressive album, *El Amor Despues del Amor*, was produced by Phil Manzanera, the London-based former Roxy Music guitarist who has a Colombian lineage and has produced some of Latin Alternative's finest albums. Al-though Paez usually avoided explicit references to politics, he managed to shine a light on the dark past of Argentina's repressive dictatorships of the 1970s and 1980s. His songwriting is highly poetic, with nods to divergent sources, including Latin American giants like Neruda and North American rebels like Bob Dylan.

Paez's shows are intensely professional rock shows, with elabo-rate back-up vocals, horn sections, and performance flourishes. He sees himself as a kind of storyteller, with his perspective formed in his upbringing in Rosario, a major city several hours north of

Buenos Aires, more in touch with the rich indigenous heritage of Argentine folkloric music. But Paez has always projected himself as a rock star—from the moment that he first saw García on a visit to his hometown, he knew what he wanted to do with his life. Paez's songs employ innovative storytelling strategies—a song like *La Verónica*, from 1994's *El Amor Despues del Amor*, is written in the format of a screenplay, and *Carabelas Nada*, from *Tercer Mundo*, invokes Brazilian singer Chico Buarque as one of his heroes, demonstrating the little-known solidarity among Southern cone musicians that transcended the Spanish-Portuguese language barrier. In turn, the avant-garde tropicalista composer, Caetano Veloso, included *El Amor*'s *Un Vestido y un amor*, a love song about Paez's wife, actress Cecilia Roth, on his compilation of Latin American popular music classics, *Fina Estampa*. In the company of such hallowed figures as Mexico's Agustín Lara, Puerto Rico's Rafael Hernández, and Cuba's Ernesto Lecuona, the inclusion of Paez, the only contemporary composer on the album, was an extraordinary compliment.

Beginning with 1995's *Circo Beat*, a paean to the pop-psychedelia of the Beatles's middle period, Paez's albums became less consistent. *Abre*, produced in 2001 by Billy Joel collaborator Phil Ramone, and 2002's *Rey Sol* have their moments, but Paez's lyrics become lengthy and meandering, and his music somewhat predictable, if played in a highly polished fashion.

Two major rock groups, Los Fabulosos Cadillacs and Soda Stereo, gained momentum in Argentina and the Latin rock world in the late 1980s, from completely different directions. The Cadillacs traded on a ska-Afro-Latin mixture similar to that of Maldita Vecindad, and Soda Stereo soared to electro-sonic heights in a way similar to Caifanes/Jaguares.

Soda Stereo, which disbanded in late 1997, went through several styles—at first reggae-ska, then 1980s English rock, mixing in elements of reggae, funk, and indigenous pan flute music from Argentina's Andean interior. But more than just a mere imitation of

Anglo styles, Soda Stereo featured the extraordinary poetry and musical experimentalism of Gustavo Cerati, who seemed to want to express mysticism and dream life through various sequencers and feedback machines, making an utterly contemporary music.

With bassist Zeta Bosio and drummer Charly Alberti, guitarist/songwriter Cerati formed Soda Stereo in 1984 and recorded a self-titled debut. The album, with follow-ups *Nada Personal* and *Signos*, featured short, focused reggae-ska and new-wave-inspired songs. While bandmembers Bosio and Alberti shared songwriting chores, the band came across as Cerati's; it was his persona that was projected by his cryptic lyrics and ambiguous sexuality. 1988's horn-laden *Doble Vida*, produced by David Bowie guitarist/collaborator Carlos Alomar, featured the first of Soda Stereo's peak-period classics, *La Ciudad de la Furia*, a song that used vampirism as a metaphor for Buenos Aires's nightlife. ("With the light of the sun/my wings will melt/I only find in darkness/What unites me with the city of fury," suggests Cerati's narrator to his lover.)

Canción Animal in 1990 marked increased maturity for Soda Stereo; songs became longer, with more room for improvisation, and less pop radio design. Cerati's lyrics began to express a kind of poetic sophistication, suggesting the carnivorous aspect of sexuality (*Entre Canibales* urged his lover to "eat of his body"), as well as the loss of self (*Hombre al Agua* announced that there is a man overboard, helpless in a river's current) or mourning his father's illness (*Te Para Tres* noticed an important absence at afternoon tea).

In Soda Stereo's final albums, Cerati is fascinated with the abandonment of the body and the ephemera of sound as a form of energy, trying to capture that moment when the spirit flies out from the body and soars into an electric, sonic plane. It's as if Cerati were engaged in a permanent fantasy that his records would become the world's first audio Mobius strip, vibrating in its final seconds with a sequenced Roxy Music riff layered over a *My Bloody Valentine* drone. The group's fifth album, *Dynamo* (1993), featured several Cerati solos pulled straight out of U2 guitarist Edge's sonic strategies. Both *Canción Animal* and *Dynamo* featured the collaboration of Daniel Melero, an electronica experimentalist, who added many new sonic layers to the band's style. Cerati and Melero's duet album, *Colores Santos* (1993), reveled in distortion-filled electronica and was almost considered part of Soda's oeuvre.

Soda Stereo's last release before the group broke up in 1997, following a much-celebrated final concert tour, was 1995's *Sueño Stereo*, a sonic extravaganza that featured ear-blasting solos, a Stone Temple Pilots-like hit single (*Ella Uso mi Cabeza Como un Revolver*), and the ethereal triumph of *Angel Electrico*. *Comfort y Música Para Volar* in 1996 was a live recording of an MTV Unplugged appearance, containing startling remakes of older songs, including a now-classic duet with Aterciopelados vocalist Andrea Echeverri on *La Ciudad de la Furia*.

Since the band's breakup, Cerati has continued with a successful solo career highlighted by 1998's *Bocanada*, which fused bolero, rock, and electronica (see below). *Bocanada* was followed by 2002's *11 Episodios Sinfonicos*, in which he reprised many of his greatest hits backed by a forty-piece symphonic orchestra, and 2003's *Siempre Es Hoy*. Although not as compelling as *Bocanada*, the album continued Cerati's flair for experimentalism, electronic ecstasy, and well-crafted pop.

The raucous party band Los Fabulosos Cadillacs began in Buenos Aires in 1985, combining a working-class soccer-crowd aesthetic with a big-band, horn-and-percussion driven format to produce a formidable barrage of semi-ska, pseudo-salsa odes to porteño culture. Gabriel Fernández Capello is the Fab Cads' lead vocalist, possessing a homespun nasal tenor that evokes the origins of the tango in the sailors' seedy barrooms. The band's signature song, one of two new releases on a compilation of previous greatest hits, *Vasos Vacios* (1994), was *Matador*, a pummeling pop powerhouse fueled by Brazilian samba drums and a dub-happy reggae bass line. The title track was a memorable duet with salsa diva

Celia Cruz, the first collaboration between a Latin rock band and a salsera.

By 1995, the Cadillacs, whose early four albums are unavailable in the United States (*El León*, released in 1992, is an early-album exception) were in mid-career. The band ventured into something of a psychedelic route by collaborating with Tina Weymouth and Chris Franz, formerly of the Tom Tom Club and Talking Heads, on *Rey Azúcar*, which featured a vocal cameo by Debbie Harry on a Latin ska remake of *Strawberry Fields Forever*. *Mal Bicho*, a *Matador* clone also from that album, featured a guest appearance by ex-Clash guitarist Mick Jones. The next album, *Fabulosos Calavera* (1997), seemed to be a concession to Café Tacuba's influence, since it featured the kind of wild genre shifts that made the band's 1995 album *Re* memorable. Spinning together a bizarre collection of eerie tales about Argentine political mass murders and dreamlike elegies to dead comrades and lost loves, Fabulosos Calavera's lyrics lurk on the dark side. But its eclectic dynamism overwhelms its esoteric subtext—the sledgehammer of death metal chords that open *El Carnicero de Giles/Sueño* segue suddenly into a cool jazz trio groove; *Abraxas*-era Santana riffs slam up against hardcore thrash and Herb Alpert horn charts in *El Muerto*. The band remains true to its roots in *Hoy Lloré Canción*, a danceable rumba duet with Rubén Blades, who plays a Latin Neil Young to the Cadillacs' Pearl Jam. Constantly shifting identities, the Cadillacs variously pose as cowpokes, surfers, and lounge rats—in the album's dreamiest track, the blatant Dave Brubeck-retake *Niño Diamante*, lead singer Capello's wounded croon floats beatnik-like over Traffic-style jazz-rock.

The Cadillacs' *Matador* was a major hit that was one of the first to make an impact in the United States: Its British-influenced new-wave-ska-meets-salsa rhythms came across like world beat rather than rock en Español. (Latin American rock can sound derivative of Anglo rock to North American ears.) But the Cadillacs' Latin ska presence helped pave the way for the boom of new bands in

Mexico, formed in the wake of Caifanes and Maldita Vecindad. The new generation was led by Café Tacuba, a less-jokey variant of Botellita de Jérez, which picked up on that group's eclectic experimentalism. The scene was bursting with several other contenders. Santa Sabina, a goth, progressive rock quintet named after Maria Sabina, a Oaxacan curandera who celebrated the use of psychedelic mushrooms, made waves with its performance-art-influenced concerts. Fobia, a jangly alternative funk rock group, was one of the first to record in Manhattan. Others suddenly appeared on the scene: La Lupita, which featured the daughter of a Mexican opera singer as a female lead vocalist; La Cuca; La Castañeda; Maná; and Las Víctimas del Dr. Cerebro. El Chopo became more crowded by the weekend—a growing array of pop, thrash-metal, punk, and the still-energetic Rock Urbano (prole rock) turned Mexico City into the Seattle that few outside the Latin world knew.

Café Tacuba is Mexico's first second-generation rock group, having grown up during a time when rock was actually being played and listened to in Mexico City, after it emerged from its thirteen-year hiatus as illegal music. The group's members lived in Satél-ito, a Los Angeles-style suburb north of Mexico City, a place where the middle American dream was supposed to be available for an oil-export-driven upper middle class. In fact, during the 1970s and 1980s, many of these Mexican families did make the journey to Disneyland in Southern California, and the nationalism that included a reverence for indigenous tradition in Mexico began to fade.

Rebellious art students, the members of Café Tacuba (lead singer Rubén Albarrán, guitarist Joselo Rangel, his brother, bassist Enrique "Quique" Rangel, and keyboardist Emanuel del Real) were determined to recover those indigenous roots—starting with their name, appropriated from a traditional Mexican restaurant in the old center city. In their first appearances, Tacuba insisted on wearing traditional indigenous costumes and focused on making the connection between ska, the polka-like ebullience of norteño music, and pogo-punk. Soon they adopted California pseudo-punk dress, while continuing to appeal to their traditional roots by using acoustic instruments (notably Joselo Rangel's bajo sexto, a kind of Mexican baritone guitar) and updating styles like son jarrocho electronically.

But with *Re*, along with subsequent albums *Avalancha de Éxitos* and *Reves*, Café Tacuba pulled Mexican rock fans headlong into a new era. By presenting a wildly eclectic repertoire that ranged from hard core punk to disco and salsa, the group ushered in one of the major developments in the genre that helped change its preferred term from rock en Español to Latin alternative. While there had been some forays into tropical music by the ska-dominated Mexican band Maldita Vecindad and the pseudo-salsa rave-ups of Argentina's Fabulosos Cadillacs, Tacuba's *Re* drew from hard-core, ranchera, Bee Gees disco, 1960s British pop, and Dominican merengue, to produce a hip-hop-style cut-and-paste amalgam of Latin rock that was entirely new.

The songs all seemed to flow naturally from the Café Tacuba compositional instinct: *El Puñál y el Corazón*, perhaps the world's first postmodern charanga; *La Negrita*, an easygoing samba somehow stapled onto traditional Mexican harp samples; *El Baile y el Salón*, a strangely beautiful *Saturday Night Fever*-era disco parody; and *24 Horas*, a kind of answer song to the Beatles' *Eight Days a Week*. Using synthesizers and samplers to substitute for a drum kit, the hybridist tropical rock group always finds its way back to a message of postmodern primitivism. At the indigeno-ska crescendo of *El Fin del Infancia* (The End of Childhood) from *Re*, lead singer Rubén Albrarrán screeches out, "When will I stop doubting that I can be the vanguard/Without having to go to New York to see what's happening?/Will we be capable of dancing for ourselves?"

In the cannibalistic spirit of Brazil's tropicalistas, Tacuba allowed the indigenous and mestizo traditions of Latin America to gobble up European conceptions of art and music. It was as if to say, as some scholars interpret the Aztec codices, that the conquest was all part of the plan, but now the wheel has begun to turn in the other direction and it's time for the conquered to do the conquering. After all, as Tacuba proclaimed in the climactic lyric of *Re's* *Ciclón*, "Life always returns to its circular form."

In 1996, Café Tacuba released *Avalancha de Éxitos*, a risky attempt to revive various obscure pop songs from 1960s through 1980s Latin American singers. The album works best with the edgy rap version of Mexico City bohemian folk singer Jaime Lopez's *Chilanga Banda* and Leo Dan's *Como te Extraño mi Amor*. The band's last two efforts, 1999's *Reves/Yo Soy* and the 2002 EP *Vale Callampa*, were very different in scope. The first was a double album divided into one disc of songs and another that was a series of instrumentals. *El Padre* voices fears about turning into the patriarch you hate most; *Dos Niños* reminisces about childhood; and *Espacio* is a spare ballad about being alone with one's thoughts, seemingly composed in a sensory-deprivation tank. Songs like *El Ave*, *Arboles Frutales*, and *El Hombre Impasible* have a mytho-poetic quality. But in contrast to Reves's adventurous dynamism, *Yo Soy* comes off as a series of incomplete, if somewhat brilliant, sketches. *Vale Callampa* is a less successful revisit to covers, this time focusing on the Chilean band Los Tres, whose work resembles the Talking Heads. The material is sketchy, a prelude to the next Tacuba work, 2003's *Cuatro Caminos*, an ambitious work that actually featured a drummer.

Caribbean Rock

Unlike their Mexican and Argentine counterparts, Caribbean rockers come from countries without highly developed rock scenes. They have more of a tendency to fuse rock with Afro-Caribbean dance rhythms, and don't always shy away from the bolero and Latin pop. There probably isn't a more fascinating character in Latin pop and alternative than Robi "Draco" Rosa. He is the producer behind Ricky Martin's worldwide pop success with *María* (1994), *La Copa de Vida* (1998), and *Livin' La Vida Loca*. But in his enigmatic manner, Rosa has also put out three solo albums that straddle the darker side of rock and roll. *Frío* (1994) had hints of Rosa's visionary approach, and *Vagabundo* (1996), a moody metallic clash of guitars streaked with dark poetry borrowed from Baudelaire and the great Mexican bard Jaime Sabines, is a subterranean journey to the core of a man's soul.

Rosa, whose roots are Puerto Rican, was born in 1973 and grew up in suburban Long Island and was deeply influenced by his parents' musical tastes. His mother loved the Beatles, Led Zeppelin, the Who, and the Doors, and his father was a big fan of aggressive salsa brava. When he was twelve, after his family moved back to Puerto Rico in 1983, Rosa jumped at an opportunity to join Menudo, doing background choruses and arranging.

But when the teen pop group refused to let him write songs, Rosa left Menudo at seventeen to pursue a solo career. In 1993, he signed with Sony Latin and went to Spain to record a solo album, *Frío*. Strongly attracted to Spain's rich flamenco tradition, Rosa dedicated one song to the veteran singer Camarón de la Isla. But *Frío* is also brimming with power pop like *Pasión* and *Cruzando Puertas*. In between solo projects, Rosa worked on Ricky Martin's *A Medio Vivir*, with writer/producer K. C. Porter. He co-wrote and co-produced the majority of the songs on the album, including the hit singles, *María*, *Fuego De Noche Nieve De Día*, *Volveras*, and *Revolución*. In 1996, Rosa released *Vagabundo*, which was recorded in England with Phil Manzanera producing. A tour de force of introspectively haunting tunes like *Llanto Subterraneo* and *Penelope*, *Vagabundo* established Rosa as a unique composing talent.

Rosa tried to sustain the promise of *Vagabundo* on his long-delayed project *Mad Love*, released in 2003. The songs are almost all in English, except for the finale, *Como Me Acuerdo*. With typically screeching guitars and Rosa's moody dynamism, the album has an edgy appeal, but is decidedly neither a pop nor Latin alternative project. Still, the album's broad appeal may make people take him more seriously than Ricky Martin as an English-language artist.

In a sudden reversal of fortune, Puerto Rico, which has long been a salsa-only stronghold, has become one of the major hotbeds of Latin alternative rock. Puerto Rico's Fiel a la Vega is making a traditional Latin/rock fusion music that refers to the island's uncertain relationship to the United States and the rest of Latin America. The strong sense of neo-nationalism in Fiel a la Vega's lyrics plays well to the ultra-lefty university crowd, although its presentation is often derivative of groups like Nirvana and Pearl Jam. *Tres*, released in 1999, is emblematic of their jíbaro pastoralism. Other bands like Manjar de los Dioses, a kind of goth version of Puerto Rican existentialism, and Vivanativa, a funk-pop group that traded on the island's major teen-idol fan base, could easily sell out outdoor concert venues. Vivanativa's *Claro*, released in 2002, is its most sophisticated, well-crafted album. Former Manjar de los Dioses singer José Luis Abreu (a.k.a. Fofe), keyboardist Edgardo Santiago, and drummer David Pérez left to form Circo, which released *No Todo Lo Que es Pop es Bueno* (Not All Pop is Good) in 2002, a neatly produced pastiche of electronica, pop-rock, and neo-bolero (with a cover of *Historia de un Amor*, a song recorded by Lucho Gática and Julio Iglesias).

While it was sometimes frowned upon by the government, rock music has an almost clandestine history in Cuba dating back to the dawn of the revolution. The early 1960s bossa nova/doo-wop group Los Zafiros made a kind of rock, and its lead guitarist Manuel Galbán played in a way that recalled surf music. Juan de Marcos González, the Sierra Maestra and Buena Vista Social Club collaborator, once confessed that he had a band that played *Hotel California*–era Eagles covers. And Carlos Alfonso, the leader of Sintésis, a progressive rock take on Yoruban religious music, helped to commission a statue in honor of John Lennon in downtown Havana in 2000.

Although the Cuban rock scene gained a brief notoriety in the early 1990s in underground clubs, where some teens injected themselves with the H.I.V. virus to rebel, most Cuban rockers go to less drastic extremes. Carlos Varela, the Springsteen of Cuba, has managed to play concerts on his native island, but is sometimes prohibited by the authorities. His song *Robinson* is an allegory that questions the Cuban revolution in the slightly backhanded, slightly loving way of the late filmmaker Tomás Gutiérrez Alea (*Memories of Underdevelopment, Strawberry and Chocolate*). Featured on David Byrne's *Cuba Classics 3* compilation, Zeus is a hardcore/heavy metal band that uses a "death metal" musical sound associated in North America with Satanism to make a commentary on what the Cuban revolution considers the Great Satan, U.S. imperialism. "He's avid and lustful, he hungers for profit/He incites wickedness in all the world/He shuns truth, he loves intrigue/All is vanity when his stomach is full," go the lyrics to *Diablo al Infierno!* But the rock scene in Cuba is usually limited to clubs that play U.S. music, and there is more interest in the early 2000s in the country's burgeoning rap scene. Rock is often used by youth in Cuba, who flash group T-shirts as signs of hipness and status, as a vehicle for their desire for more personal freedom than that afforded them by the strict government.

South American Fusion Rock

In the late 1990s, the primacy of the Argentine and Mexican rock giants was fading, and the nostalgia of Latin youth for their cultural roots, as well as their increasing identification with hip-hop, threw open the music to a vast array of influences. The music itself began to be identified through its wild hybridity, a quality that soon eclipsed all other descriptions, and new groups sprang up to play this new fusion.

In 1997, two groups from the northern coast of South America, Aterciopelados from Colombia and Los Amigos Invisibles from Venezuela, began to experiment with Afro-Caribbean and other folkloric beats, incorporating them into their music. Colombia has unfortunately gained notoriety as one of the most dangerous countries in the hemisphere, statistically leading in kidnappings and murders, with serious guerrilla wars erupting throughout the countryside. It is a place where those who run for elected office are routinely outfitted with bulletproof vests, knowing that may not be enough protection. Despite the hazards of its forty-year-long civil war, Colombia's music scene continues to evolve, and its vibrant youth culture absorbs North American influences while continuing to remain "Colombian."

The frenetic call of "LaMúsicaLaMúsicaLaMúsicaLaMúsica!" from street vendors hawking the latest CDs on Bogotá's Avenida Septima (Seventh Avenue) may have been the inspiration for Aterciopelados' *La Música*, from 1997's *La Pipa de la Paz*, which promised the deliverance of Colombia from its problems through the strength of its musical culture. German Espinosa's 1982 novel *La Tejadora de Coronas* told the story of a woman from Mompós who, through her arts and crafts, attempted to bring modernity to Colombia, only to be tried and executed by the Cartagena Inquisition for being a witch. Far from being executed, Aterciopelados lead singer Andrea Echeverri made herself into one of Colombia's reigning pop queens by helping to bring post-modernity to the country. Pierced and tattooed like the hippest of MTV creatures, Echeverri is a one-woman fashion show of Bogotá flea markets. Everywhere she goes, people stare and smile with the reverence reserved for Madonna.

Aterciopelados' founding members Andrea Echeverri and her one-time boyfriend, Héctor Buitrago, teamed up in Bogotá in 1990 as Delia y los Aminoacidos. Buitrago came from a hardcore rock background, heading up a group called La Pesitilencia. Echeverri had been studying ceramics and lurking at the periphery of Bogotá's punk culture. They once ran one of Bogotá's only rock clubs, and although they were at first romantically involved, their relationship became purely an artistic partnership. Their early work, as typified by their first release, *Con El Corazón en la Mano* (1994), which featured the collaboration of drummer Alejandro Duque and guitarist Alejandro Gomezcáceres, is a noisefest of ringing, distorted guitars and a pummeling punk drumbeat. Beginning with their second album, *El Dorado* (1995), Aterciopelados begins to expand its sound, including traditional rhythms of the Colombian llanos, as well as the nouveau-bolero sound of the group's first big hit, *Bolero Falaz*. With its insistent bolero rhythm and ardent lyrics, *Bolero* broke the band on MTV Latino and made the members stars all over Latin America.

After releasing a third album, *La Pipa de la Paz*, Atercio was able to tour in the United States, recording an MTV Uplugged appearance in Miami in early 1997. *La Pipa*'s songs demonstrated an increasing evolution of the band's sound, and Phil Manzanera's production brought out the songs' crisp intensity. After the departure of drummer Duque, Aterciopelados became less of a rock group than a collaboration between Echeverri, Buitrago, and regular guests like Gomezcáceres. The following year, *Caribe Atómico*, recorded in Manhattan with guest appearances by Downtown guitarists Arto Lindsay and Marc Ribot, further expanded Aterciopelados's sound into the world of drum and bass and jungle. Echeverri and Buitrago became one of the best songwriting teams in Latin alternative, creating a bold voice for Latin American women, as well as speaking out against the violence wracking their home country and the threats to its environment.

Half of the songs on Atercio's most riveting album, *La Pipa de la Paz*, a few cowritten with Buitrago, are coyly insistent demands for feminine autonomy. *Baracunátana* is a cover of a 1960s Colombian pop tune in which Echeverri ironically denounces a loose woman with every Spanish slang word imaginable. In *Chica Difícil* she seems almost open to approach when she sings *Soy una chica difícil/pero yo valgo la pena* (I'm a difficult chick, but I'm worth it), dismissing a cheesy Rico Suave type in a tense spoken-word interlude. Echeverri seems to want to confine herself to *Amor Platónico*,(platonic love), which she sings in gentle lullaby fashion.

Mostly employing a husky soprano and only occasionally show-ing a softer side, Echeverri tells one guy, "I don't need your ap-proval," (*No Necesito*); denounces a man who was castrated by a harassed woman; and begs another lovestruck suitor, "Don't ruin my figure with a baby" (*La Culpable*). Meanwhile, she incorporates Latin musics like Colombian vallenato, Mexican mariachi, and Spanish flamenco. Within *Música*, a bonafide rock en Español an-them, the band shuttles from distorto-riffs to acoustic flower-power interludes, and the ghost of Santana suddenly reappears in *Expreso Amazonia*, a spoofy celebration of new age junkets to the rainforest.

The group's fifth album, 2001's *Gozo Poderoso* (Powerful Plea-sure), delivered an edgy trip-hop salsa, with the songwriting be-coming more layered and revealing of deeper spirituality. On *Gozo's* first single, *El Album*, Echeverri poignantly holds on to mental pictures of a lover left behind. On *Esmeralda*, she is intent on at least temporarily trashing material worlds, insisting that she's "fusing with eternity/elevating" over a subtle soul calypso beat. In *Chamánica*, a song that refers to Hector and Andrea's use of the mind-expanding yagé drug, "the cosmic door" opens her "third eye." Echeverri's remarkably agile, full-throated voice floats languidly over three Velvet Underground-ish guitar chords on *Transparente*, where she dreams of having "crystal-clear skin, so my truth would be seen."

Although still fond of the loops and sequences prevalent on 1998's *Caribe Atomico*, Buitrago meant *Gozo Poderoso* to be a return to the band's folk-rock roots, occasionally enlisting rustic percus-sion and flute session players. He is also a major force as a song-writer, contributing the nuevo-bolero love lament *Rompecabezas* and the lounge-hop strut that catapults the title track. The most confrontational song on *Gozo* is Buitrago's spacy dirge *Fantasía*, in which Echeverri intones that the United States is a fattened, decadent Rome, primed for collapse.

Venezuelan groups like the ska-oriented Desorden Público and the acid-jazz-inspired Los Amigos Invisibles both cite their country's petroleum disaster as major impacts on their youths. The failed dreams of prosperity that dominated the 1970s and 1980s hung over the heads of the country's youth like a waking nightmare. Still, the kids found ways to enjoy themselves. Mobile vans with DJs roamed suburban neighborhoods, which had the effect of creating a knowledgeable, dance-oriented music public. Desorden Público, an excellent ska-reggae group, made explicit use of the national trauma in its lyrics, but Los Amigos preferred to present itself as a party band that engaged in a cartoonish recapitulation of macho adolescent fantasies of the James Bond era. Employing the acid-jazz, keyboard- and percussion-driven groove style popular in the United States and Europe, Los Amigos seems poised for a major crossover.

Los Amigos plays an infectious form of dance rock that is true to the members' rhythmic roots. Guitarist José Luis Pardo's wah-wah playing is innovative post-Funkadelic, and for a dance-hall flavor, percussionist Mauricio engages in frequent toasting duels with lead singer Julio Briceño. The first Latin alternative group to be "discovered" by ex-Talking Head David Byrne, Los Amigos released its first album on a U.S. label, *The New Sound of the Venezuelan Gozadera* (*gozadera* loosely translates as "party") in 1998. The rigorous rumbas, cha-chas, and merengues are merely a palette of backbeats that give way to the acid jazz and house that run through the DJ-driven club-crossover compilation *Nuyorican Soul*, released by Little Louie Vega in 1997. If Los Amigos Invisibles depend on heavy sampling of musical kitsch, it's only in theory—the boys really know how to play their instruments, and the bossa nova harmonies they achieve in *The New Sound*'s *Aldemaro en su Camaro* might send you packing up those Sergio Mendes records for good.

The group's second album, *Arepa 3000* (2000), increased the importance of merengue, Europop, funk, and bugaloo, almost to the point where Los Amigos's identity as a rock band disappears. The cover of *Amor*, a '70s classic Venezuelan pop-shlock tune, is astute, and the Amigos groove continues to intensify on songs like *Mujer Policia*. In 2001, the Amigos moved to New York City, the first Latin alternative band to openly immerse itself in a North American stronghold. The group's fourth album, *The Venezuelan Zinga Sound*, was delayed because of the label's financial difficulties.

At the turn of the millennium, the success of Latin alternative came to depend on its ability to incorporate more Afro-Caribbean rhythms. While Mexican rock soared on the wings of Caifanes's airy guitar-play, Caifanes's first hit song was *La Negra Tomasa*, a Colombian cumbia. Bloque, whose name comes from the search party once organized to bring cocaine kingpin Pablo Escobar to justice, seems to wear its Colombian drama on its sleeve. But despite the bohemian working-man pose presented by lead singer/songwriter Ivan Benavides, Bloque's strength is uniting the richly varied musical traditions of coastal, rural, and urban Colombia into one soul-shattering sound.

While its basis is Colombian rhythms like vallenato, cumbia, porro, and others, Bloque was also inspired by the Afro-pop hybrids pioneered by Salif Keata, Angelique Kidjo, and Fela Kuti, as well as classic rock, progressive jazz, and just plain rumba. Bloque greatly expanded the world music idea, bringing it back full circle to (Latin) America. The genesis of Bloque came in the mid-1990s in Bogotá's club scene, where vallenato people meet cumbia people meet rock people meet jazz people, and drummers of all manner of exotic tambores pitch in a plethora of obscure regional dance beats.

Before securing a recording contract as Bloque, several members of the band—guitarist Teto Ocampo, flutist Mayte Montero, Benavides, and bassist Luis Angel Pastór—were invited by Carlos Vives to bring their expertise to his attempts to make mass-market pop out of the folkloric vallenato style. Benavides wound up co-writing many of the lyrics and guitarist Teto Ocampo was musical director for Vives's 1995 release, *La Tierra del Olvido*, which went platinum in Colombia. But Vives was too constraining on Bloque's ideals, and the four players struck out on their own.

What is perhaps most intriguing about Bloque's project is that the group is a bonafide rock band. The members firmly believe that vallenato's funky ethos closely parallels the North American blues, and the fact that their bassist, Luis Angel Pastór, is a vallenato specialist seems to underscore this. The band's leader, Ivan Benavides, with his shaved head and charming-misfit persona, has a rock attitude and even based a song on the writings of Colombian poet Jaime Jaramillo Escobar, a notorious exponent of the country's beat movement. Bloque's genius is its dichotomy between folk and electric music, and the band derives a significant charge when Cartagena native Mayte Montero, the only woman member, takes center stage with her gaita flute and higher-octave nasal vocals. She sings some songs in an Afro-Colombian dialect, recalling the legacy of palenques, towns in Latin America founded by escaped slaves, linking them again to the African diaspora. Much of Colombian coastal music came from interactions between indigenous people and escaped slaves called cimarones, a term that has the same root as Jamaica's Maroons. When Bloque kicks into this danceable, rhythmic barrage of percussion and folk tradition, it's at its most powerful.

A true experimentalist, Benavides has engaged in session work with Richard Blair, a London club DJ who fell in love with Colombia. In 1999 with Blair's project, called Sidestepper, Benavides recorded a song called *Logozo*, mixing Cuban son with drum and bass. Benavides's work with Blair reinforces the connection between London and Colombia—there is a large group of Colombian expatriates in London.

At the beginning of the twenty-first century, both hip-hop and club musics like rave, drum and bass, and jungle have become a significant part of Latin alternative. While Latinos had always been part of the creation of mainstream hip-hop in the late 1970s, certain U.S. Latino artists like Cypress Hill, the Beatnuts, Kid Frost, and A Lighter Shade of Brown pursued Spanish-language rhyming in the 1990s. Most of the early Spanglish rap groups were based in California, where Mexican-Americans took on a kind of parallel identity with African-Americans, needing urban griots to tell their stories. In New York, most Latino rappers assimilated into the dominant African-American culture and there was little overt reference to Latino culture in hip-hop until the late '90s, through mainstream songs by Puffy Combs and Santana's collaboration with Product G&B.

Meanwhile, inspired by mainstream hip-hop as well as rock-rap hybrids like Rage Against the Machine and Limp Bizkit, a Mexican hip-hop scene began to coalesce in 1996 in the northern city of Monterrey, and eventually the capital city. The rappers Control Machete are a natural response to Monterrey's Nafta-inspired Americanization. Originally a rock band, Control released its first album, *Mucho Barato*, in 1997. The group is at its best mixing metal chords with Esquivel lounge interludes on *Somos Humanos*, snarling "We're humans but they call us Mexicans," in Spanish, like buzz-clip gangsta Zapatistas. The hard-edged vocals of Fermin and Pato give Control a kind of ominous feel, reinforcing the contention that northern Mexico, at least, has become an urbanized site of danger. In 1999, Control Machete released *Artillera Pesada*, which featured a groundbreaking collaboration with members of the Buena Vista Social Club like pianist Rubén González and Orlando "Cachaíto" López. But the band seemed to be on hiatus after Fermín went solo in 2002 with *Boomerang*, an uneven groove-laden fusion rap album with an interesting ambiance and a slew of roaring guitars.

Fellow Monterreyans El Gran Silencio, who play a more rustic reinterpretation of hiphop and ska, are skeptical about Control Machete. The mobster pose in songs like *Andamos Armados* (We Walk Around Armed), according Silencio's Tony Hernández, is a virtual gangsta ploy to appeal to young Mexicans lusting for the California lifestyle. Hernández is a Monterrey original—the first kid in his neighborhood to breakdance back in the '80s, when hip-hop was alien in Mexico, he writes songs that act as soulful critiques of class antagonisms. He is also very willing to enter the discourse about *actitud rock* (rock attitude), which is actually more like a hip-hop code. It's a kind of permanent distrust in authority and an acknowledgment that the only way change is going to happen is through the grassroots efforts. Since the group's first album, *Libres y Locos*, Gran Silencio relied heavily on a roots accordion sound to define its music, but after touring Spain in support of 2001's *Chuntaro Radio Poder*, the members drew more heavily from Colombian cumbia and other world-beat influences they picked up from Spanish groups like Macaco and Dusminguet.

Control Machete and Mexico City-based Molotov, which uses a conventional guitar-rock lineup (albeit with two bass guitars) to back up hip-hop vocals, are at the core of Mexican rap in terms of sales and notoriety. While Control worked closely with Cypress Hill producer Jason Roberts, and featured a turntablist named Toy, Molotov is more of a funk-rock band, engaging in dark grooves that are particularly effective in live performance. Molotov was founded by three native chilangos and the son of U.S. Foreign Service staffer based in the Mexican capital. The presence of drummer Randy "El Gringo Loco" Ebright and the rest of the band's facility with English, hip-hop, and heavy metal give Molotov a broad-based appeal. Played in an unusually slow norteño tempo and featuring accordion parts reminiscent of the traditional corrido, *Frijolero*, from 2003's *Dance and Dance Denso*, is delivered with great irony in a voice that sounds like an English-speaker trying to speak Spanish. Verses and choruses are also translated into English and repeated. The rest of the album, whose title roughly translates into "Dance and Slam Yourself Good," is a densely layered, remarkably versatile collection of headbanging chaos and alternative rap and is considerably more melodic than 1999's effort, *Apocalypshit*. While lacking the strong hit singles of 1997's *Dónde Jugarán Las Niñas?* (a parody of a Maná album title), the album is less sophomoric.

Illya Kuryaki and the Valderramas, who hail from Argentina, surprisingly succeed in finding a hip-hop soul in the Argentine psyche. IKV's name is a study in pop culture: Illya Kuryaki was not only the name of a character on the 1960s TV show *The Man From U.N.C.L.E.*, but also a popular breakdancer from hip-hop's early period. Valderrama is the name of one of the most famous soccer players in Latin America, an Afro-Colombian. Led by Dante Spinetta, the son of rock legend Luís Alberto Spinetta, the Vals practice a Southern cone bilingualism that often sounds like a minstrel show of sacred Chicano ritual. "I believe in sudamérica/soy de la raza brotha/vato estoy loco/be cool, don't be culo," they mutter, juxtaposing sarcasm with sincerity. IKV, consisting of Spinetta and Emmanuel Houvielleur, were prodigies, producing their first album, *Fábrico Cuero*, in 1991 when they were fourteen and sixteen, respectively.

Through albums like *Horno Para Calentar* (1994) and *Chaco* (1996), the group's sound evolved rapidly, from early Chili Peppers-style hardcore/funk to a passionate retake on psychedelic 1970s funk. *Versus*, released in 1998, began a maturing process in which IKV searched for their inner funk souls, so that by the time they got to *Leche*, their fifth album, they come up with something like a Parliament-Funkadelic album that was never made. Featuring Funkadelic bassist Bootsy Collins, who sits in as engineer and plays on a couple of tracks, *Leche* seemed to break IKV in the United States, especially through the strength of the single *Coolo*. Emulating the New York post-disco funk best characterized by groups like the Whispers, tunes like *Coolo*, which featured a salsa piano break, and *Lo Que Nos Mata*, a kind of Hall and Oates/Ohio Players love ballad, executed the concept so successfully that IKV can't be accused of parody. But in 2001, after the death of their longtime manager José Miceli, the two decided to indefinitely take a leave of absence from the group. Dante Spinetta released an invigorating, if somewhat uneven, solo album, *Elevado*, in 2002.

Latin alternative bands began to form in the United States in the mid-1990s as a response to the touring efforts of Mexican rock bands like Caifanes, Maldita Vecindad, and Café Tacuba, as well as some other visits by Argentina's Soda Stereo and Colombia's Aterciopelados. California bands like Ley de Hielo and Maria Fatal made unexceptional records, and a ska fad caught on around bands like Los Skarnales and the Voodoo Glow Skulls. In New York, King Changó drew a lot of attention when signed by David Byrne's Luaka Bop label in 1995. Led by vocalist Andrew Blanco, the only consistent member in the group besides fellow Venezuelan Glenda Lee (of Asian descent) on bass, King Changó focuses on ska, but has experimented with a panoply of tropical beats from the Caribbean like soca, cumbia, and son jarrocho. King Changó's main appeal was the spectacle of its performances—Blanco, a graphic designer who created some memorable professional sports logos, liked to experiment with evoking Mexican wrestlers and the Zapatistas. One of Changó's most memorable tunes is a cover of Lynyrd Skynrd's *Sweet Home Alabama* rewritten to describe the plight of the undocumented immigrant.

Los Angeles-based Pastilla's formula is pretty simple—four-piece power punk with lovelorn lyrics in Spanish. With two albums under its belts, Pastilla was making a new kind of noise. Although most of the members of Pastilla were born in Juárez, Mexico, they grew up in places like Pomona, California, and the band comes on like a revved-up driving machine designed to navigate the alienation of SoCal sprawl. Bassist/vocalist Victor Monroy established Pastilla's androgynous punk pose with *Vuelo* (Flight), an echo-y, distortion-filled assertion that he had not lost his wings. Searing sheets of cacophony gave way to trippy reverb rushes as Monroy's plaintive voice begs for release from boredom. Pastilla's second album, *Voz Electra* (1998), is filled with a lot of reverb, distortion, crazy rhythms, and stories about teenage love and frustration. Victor Monroy's weird groans and brother Adrian's slightly off-key guitar-playing sound like California indie rock groups.

Volumen Cero from Florida and Orixa from San Francisco made an impact using two distinct formulas with varying success. Volumen Cero expertly played a drone-y rock patterned after the British band My Bloody Valentine, scoring on space-rock songs like *Andromeda*. Volumen Cero released *Andromeda* in 1998 to mixed critical reaction, but 2002's *Luces* succeeded as a raucous explosion of searing guitar-pop. Orixa is decidedly more interesting, using a lineup that allows the group to go in both hip-hop and rock directions. The members' rapping is often below par, and the use of a DJ and mixer jumbles the rhythmic energy they create with forays into Latin percussion. Still, songs like *Latino Culturízate* and their cover of Jorge Ben's *Umbaparaumba* act as excellent live anthems and have created an enthusiastic Northern California following. *Culturízate* appeared on the group's self-titled debut, released in 1996, and *Umbaparaumba* was on the second album, *2012 E.D.*, which was more experimental and went more in a funk/hip-hop direction.

As described in the previous chapter, Latinos were intricately involved in the birth of hip-hop through mostly Puerto Rican rappers, DJs, breakdancers and graffiti artists in the late 1970s. By the early 1990s, after a long period of invisibility, Latinos began to make bilingual or Spanish-language rap music. The Latin hip-hop moniker never stuck, because of a desire for these artists to be considered part of the larger movement known as hip-hop, as well as possibly negative connotations of that term, previously used to describe big-haired girl groups of the 1980s like Exposé, Brenda K. Starr, Pebbles, and Lisa Lisa (also known as freestyle). Although New York Puerto Ricans like Curious George and Latin Empire had some impact, the bilingual, Latino-oriented rap phenomenon began in the early '90s with California groups like Latin Alliance, Kid Frost, A Lighter Shade of Brown, Mellow Man Ace, and Cypress Hill.

Uniting rappers from both coasts and backgrounds with as varied a roll call as a Rubén Blades coda, the crew of rappers Latin Alliance provided a defining moment in the creation of a nationwide bilingual hip-hop aesthetic. Although Kid Frost's 1990 debut *Hispanic Causing Panic* was the genre's instant classic, Latin Alliance, which teamed up Frost, Mellow Man Ace, and A. L. T., made a more direct statement. *Runnin'*, which appeared on Latin Alliance's self-titled record in 1991, is a parable about the war-zone aura surrounding illegal border crossings, juiced by its edgy horn-filled backing track, reminiscent of Ice-T's *Lethal Weapon*. Underscored by chilling voiceovers that are recordings of actual Immigration Service radio and telephone messages, and exploiting the pervasive sound of choppers overhead to the same eerie effect as in countless L.A. exploitation movies, *Runnin'* traces the harassment of immigrants and American-born Chicanos. The Latin Alliance collaboration was a one-time thing; Kid Frost made one more record in 1992, and A. L. T. two others in 1992 and 1993.

Mellow Man Ace's 1989 *Straight from Havana* established the West Coast as headquarters for the genre. The album's hit single, *Mentirosa*, adeptly incorporated Santana's *Evil Ways* and was the first Latino hip-hop single to get wide airplay. While his 1992 follow-up, *The Brother With Two Tongues*, failed to generate excitement, Mellow Man is riveting in his ability to get across so many aspects of the Latino experience. *The Brother* featured Mellow braggadocio in several guises: nasally tinged Cypress-like home-boy in *Funky Muñeca, Gettin' Funky in the Joint*, and *Hypest from Cypress*; fake Cubano with a theek aaack-cent on *Ricky Ricardo of Rap*; Spanglish rhymemaster on the title track and *Babulú Bad Boy*; and badass Cuban on *Me La Pelas*, a relatively filthy discourse. The first single, *What's It Take To Pull a Hottie (Like You)?*, is a dance-pop meditation on Mellow's perfect woman. As a black Cuban op-erating in a SoCal landscape dominated by African-Americans and Chicanos, he is a resilient chameleon who managed to hold onto a clear sense of who he is. Mellow Man made a comeback of sorts in 2000 with *From the Darkness Into the Light*, which also focused on the dark side of inner-city life. The affecting *Ten la Fe* was featured on the soundtrack of the teen romantic drama *Crazy/Beautiful*.

The mantle of Latin hip-hop would be picked up by a crew that contained Mellow Man Ace's brother, Sen Dog. While not as bilin-gual as Kid Frost and A. L. T., Cypress Hill crew combined the high-pitched snarl identified with the Beastie Boys with the oldies-style backing tracks preferred by Chicanos. When Cypress Hill ap-peared in 1991, not many observers realized that the group featured two L.A.-reared Cubans, Sen Dog, who rapped in Spang-lish on tracks like *Latin Lingo* and *Tres Equis*, and Bread. The record intrigued largely because of its sampling of late 1950s-early 1960s R&B and doo-wop, music that is a ritual among Chicano lowriders.

Cypress Hill continued to evolve, from rappers to rockers, steadily increasing its Spanglish content while retaining hip-hop credibility. The group split up briefly in the mid-'90s, with B-Real fronting Psycho Realm and Sen Dog producing Delinquent Habits (*The Warriors* and *Here Come the Horns*). The Habits, who are only partially Latin, capitalized on the War-meets-low-rider codes that drive the Chicano subculture on California's "Lower East Side," making use of brass section sampling and syncopated piano rhythms to make a formidable statement against Proposi-tion 187, which many felt was anti-immigrant.

The new Latin hip-hop spurred movements in the Caribbean, mostly Puerto Rico, collected in the *Dancehall ReggaeEspañol* (1991). Featuring the megabeats of Panamanian rappers like El General—a product of the cross-pollination of cultures that occurred in Panama, where so many Jamaicans migrated to help build the canal—served to break down the de facto segregation between reggae, the Jamaican dance-hall style, merengue, and even salsa.

The Spanish-speaking Caribbean—Puerto Rico, the Dominican Republic, Panama, Venezuela, and Colombia—developed an appetite for dance-hall's quick-marching pace (akin to merengue) and its vulgar, pun-laden wordplay. Any salsero could appreciate El General's ragamuffin cadences that pepper the senses in *Pu Tun Tun*. And the slow-dancing romantic Latino aesthetic is served by the Panamanian Arzu's *Amor*, which is crooned over Gregory Isaac's lover's rock classic *Night Nurse*.

Another Puerto Rican rap pioneer is the charismatic Vico C., who likes to perform in a suit, eschewing the classic North American baggy gear. His style, which harkens to La Vieja Guardia (the Old School), either recycles old Sugarhill Gang samples or focuses on the vocal pyrotechnics of Jamaican dance-hall rappers. He makes explicit the "philosopher" mode of the rapper, making constant reference to people of the street on an island whose hard streets are harder to find than rural shacks.

In 2002, Vico C.'s album *Emboscada* railed against government corruption, the struggle for the small comforts the consumer society offers the working man, and a general lack of awareness. With complete control over the music, sampling, and arrangements of the album, Vico C. accomplished the rarest of pop music feats: He put together a polished, commercial album with a grassroots feel. The rapper also used powerful elements of Puerto Rican folkloric music and salsa (in addition to subgenres like reggaetón, a hypnotic, repetitive dance-hall beat over which MCs rap lyrics associated with partying) to create an aura of integrity and command over his ample ramblings. Tunes like *Abusando*, which he introduced as a homage to classic songwriter Rafael Hernández and legendary singer Cheo Feliciano, back up such references with a barrage of style and substance.

The title of hip-hop goddess is bestowed on a blessed few Latinas, like Hurricane G, Lisa M, and Ivy Queen. Ivy Queen's second album, *Original Rude Girl* (1998), is most notable for the guest appearance of the Fugees' Wyclef Jean on a track called *In the Zone*. Ivy is a formidable vocalist who sounds as if she can actually sing, although she prefers to relentlessly proclaim Puerto Rican pride and her own fabulousness, as is expected of a hip-hop performer. Ivy Queen herself is forceful and seductive over the various dancehall, merengue-house and hip-hop funk groove over which she raps in Spanglish. On one track, *La Realidad*, she pays tribute to the Puerto Rican oral tradition when she and guest vocalist Alex D'Castro recite a décima.

Latin hip-hop has spread all over the Spanish-speaking world, and the farther it gets from the border, the more it takes on a character that reflects the local life of its performers. Rap en Español is nurturing a return to the older values of hip-hop, something also chronicled in the 2002 movie about the North American turntablist movement called *Scratch*. A new school of rap began in Spain in 1994 when a new label called Yo Gano released an album by CPV (Violent Poets Club) called *Madrid Zona Bruta*. Groups like VKR (The True Believers of the Hip-hop Religion), Sólo Los Solos, and Geronación followed suit, choosing philosophy and politics over gangsta as their subject matter. Further reaction against commercial hip-hop can be found in Mexico, where Caballeros del Plan G stated that "Chicano gangster rappers don't represent us."

A similar story can be found in Puerto Rico, where a new generation of acts with names like El Sindicato, Enemigo, and Shanghai Assassinz provide an alternative to Vico C. Old school MCs try to survive in a scene where local promoters lean heavily toward mixing hip-hop with merengue and reggae rhythms to form the mindless party genre called reggaetón. In 2003, rapper Tego Calderón made use of the rapidly expanding reggaetón craze to break through with a hit album called *El Abayarde*. However, much of the album sidesteps reggaetón to incorporate Puerto Rican bomba and salsa. The son of independence activists, Calderón made several powerful statements against Puerto Rican racism towards its citizens of African descent and sold enough albums to make him a star for years to come. Latin rap is also spreading from Argentina, where rappers are often engaged in experimental projects with electronica and dance music, to Uruguay, which is just beginning to emerge from a period of chronic Chicano imitations, to Brazil, which has one of the most dynamic and rhythmically spectacular rap scenes on the planet.

Hip-hop and Latin music are increasingly fusing together—in 2001, Fulanito's *Americanizao* and A. B. Quintanilla and the Kumbia Kings's *Shhhhh* mixed up breakbeats with merengue and cumbia. Afrika Bambaataa, a founding father of hip-hop, may not have been able to conceive of the exotic lyrics and Afro-Latin percussion on Sindicato Argentino de Hiphop's *Un Paso a la Eternidad* from Argentina or Obsesión's *Un Montón de Cosas* from Cuba. But, as he hinted in Charlie Ahearn's 1982 film *Wild Style*, when South Bronx rappers dropped rhymes over rhythm tracks provided by Germany's Kraftwerk on *Planet Rock*, something truly universal was destined to happen.

Latin Electronica

In 1999, two years after the breakup of Soda Stereo, the Argentinian Gustavo Cerati launched a solo career that left his rock days behind. Following a path that could be termed nuevo bolero or electro-bolero, Cerati's second solo album *Bocanada* (a word referring to wisps of cigarette smoke) is often better than the work he produced as the leader of his old band. The title song is constructed so that Cerati can blow smoke rings into a sweaty legion of Latin rock romantics, coaxing chaos theory out of a lounge-y 1940s style bolero. "When there's nothing left for us to say/I become one with the smoke/snaking through reason," he croons in enunciated Castillian, eschewing guitar solos for his MPC3000 electric keyboard. Cerati has fully embraced electronica, metamorphosing into a kind of South American ambient drama king.

Tabú is a sci-fi spy movie soundtrack that's like James Bond running through a jungle playing Wes Montgomery riffs, fighting a psychological battle with the "savage alchemy" of desire. The most compelling Latin rock incorporates soulful folkloric and African meters, but Cerati's Southern cone aesthetic employs a medium-cool art-rock palette—Andean flute drones and electrobossa nova beats that fuel *Raíz* (Root) notwithstanding. *Verbo Carne* is an eccentric torch song performed with the London Symphony Orchestra.

Fresh from flirtations with hip-hop, acid jazz, and bugaloo, Latin alternative artists have created a new variation on club music by incorporating samples of the funky tubas, trumpets, and two-step dance hooks of norteño music and the hip-shaking rhythms of salsa and cumbia. One of the centers of this movement is Tijuana, a bustling metropolis where strip clubs and drug running are the backdrop for Mexican youth with a bicultural, Spanglish style. The Nortec Collective is a dynamic, engaging posse of Tijuana-based DJs, designers, and graphic artists. Nortec's compilation, *The Tijuana Sessions, Vol. 1*, is a frenzied stew of fat tropical beats and kicky samples that fuse northern Mexican styles with trippy textures. The new Latin electronica school feeds on young Latinos who want to hear their roots pumped all the way up.

The story of Nortec begins in the mid-1990s, when Tijuana-based chemical engineer and club DJ Pepe Mogt couldn't afford to quit his day job. The industrial, ambient house- and techno-influenced music he was spinning was too strange for Mexican record companies, and he didn't stand out enough from his competition to land a recording contract in the United States or Europe. Then, in 1999, he went back to his roots for source material, and in the process, created a spanking new genre in electronic dance music—Nortec.

Nortec, which expresses the marriage between Mexican norteño music and the endless variations of techno music, was born when Vogt found raw, off-tempo demo tapes from local norteño and banda groups at a downtown Tijuana studio and passed them around to his DJ friends. Ramón Amezcua, a.k.a. Bostitch, came back with a track called *Polaris*, a wildly exuberant pastiche of thundering tubas, syncopated snare drum beats, and ambient electronica. Then the rest of the Nortec Collective—DJ bands Terrestre, Panóptica, Plankton Man, Hiperboreal, and Clorofila—mixed fresh tracks, and they began to play in warehouse and club DJ parties that stood out in Tijuana's already crowded nightlife.

The members of the Nortec Collective, like their Tijuana contemporaries, had grown up listening to European electronica like Kraftwerk, Yello, and Depeche Mode on radio stations from San Diego and Los Angeles—Amezcua took his Bostitch moniker from an old Yello track. And like thousands of northern Mexico residents, they occasionally took jobs in California. Since Tijuana is a major center for the light assembly of electronics, it was easy for Mogt to construct portable mini-studios, and his proximity to San Diego allowed him to scan record-store bins for vinyl sources.

But whether it's the accordion or tuba snippets embedded in their grooves, or the gleeful display of norteño iconography at their shows—images of narcocorrido legend Chalino Sánchez, cactus plants, and the black hats of narcogangsters—Nortec is steeped in the Mexican part of the Tijuana experience. It could be said that the corridos of norteño music are like rap music (see Chapter 8). Like the bomba and plena storytellers of Puerto Rico, they're all part of a tradition of passing legends on to people. Tijuana was the birthplace of Carlos Santana, who made one of the most successful bilingual crossovers in American pop music history. It is also where Ritchie Valens first heard the son jarrocho *La Bamba*, and the rest is history. The Nortec Collective made sure that Tijuana became known as the place that changed the way people experienced dance music, and Latin culture.

Sidestepper's Richard Blair, a London-based British DJ who spends a lot of time in Latin America, is a leading force in Latin electronica and alternative salsa, mixing Afro-Cuban sounds with drum and bass and dub. Blair caught the Latin bug when he visited Colombia in the mid-'90s to engineer a record by folklore diva Totó la Momposina. He stayed on to get his "doctorate in rumba." He realized that the African call and response embedded in Totó's music was similar to the rhythmic base of trance music and decided to exploit that connection in his albums *Logozo* (1998), *More Grip* (2000), and *3 AM* (2003). Sidestepper featured Latin alternative singers Ivan Benavides of Bloque and Andrea Echeverri of Aterciopelados.

DJ (Ramón) Nova, a Dominican beatmaster from the Bronx, was the driving force behind the drum 'n' space of *Tu verás*, a highlight of King Changó's *The Return of El Santo* (2000), and with Lata and Postdata, Ivan Benavides's solo projects, manipulating samples of Colombian chandé and porro rhythms. Si Se, whose eponymous album was released in 2001, qualify as Latin alternative, although they are more grounded in the multicultural New York that produced them. Combining the spacey bilingual lyrics of Carol Cardenas, of Dominican extraction, with both trip-hop and hip-hop influences, plus a mélange of Afro-Caribbean sources, Si Se made a singularly eclectic, urban music.

The concept behind Kinky, a group from Monterrey, Mexico, whose debut album was released in 2002, is relatively simple: Take one drummer into jazz and Latin percussion, a bass player who digs cumbia and norteño, a vocalist and guitarist who are unrepentant punk rockers, and a DJ who eats, drinks, and sleeps Euro-style club music and mix them all together to get a revolutionary brand of smart electro-pop. Kinky made its debut in New York as winners of the Battle of the Bands at the Latin Alternative Music Conference in August 2000, but at that time it was primarily an experimental band.

In 2001, the band hired Chris Allison, an English producer and musical entrepreneur whose Sonic 360 label puts out electronica-oriented CDs. Allison also staged a roving Latin electronica club night called La Leche in London, New York, and Los Angeles. *Kinky*, the band's self-titled album, is a garden of electronic delights, a multilingual, eclectic genre-crunch that gives the listener a glimpse into an international music future. While the group seems like the ultimate studio band, *Kinky* has a visceral, funky feel. The frenetic, oddly paced *Soun Tha Primer Amor* uses a synthetic brass section to flirt with timbales and robotic choruses. Guitarist/turntablist/vocalist Gil Cerezo stays back in the mix, murmuring poetic asides and crooning ecstatic dance commands. On *San Antonio*, he explains how to ask a Mexican saint for help in finding a lover, navigating ethereal keyboard runs and jazzy flute riffs.

Whether the members dabble in deconstructed samba (*Sol [Batucada]*), old school break beats (*Más*), or the funky accordion sound on the norteño-cumbia disco tune *Cornman*, the bottom line for Kinky is booty-shaking. Like Los Amigos Invisibles, Kinky manages to take dance-floor ideals and present them in an ecstatic, live-band fashion.

Latin Alternative's New Blood— the Singer-Songwriter

Much of Latin alternative's energy stemmed from youth rebellion expressed through music and lifestyle. Like North American rock and hip-hop, the attitude is sometimes more important than the music itself. But Latin America's songwriting tradition is so pervasive that many young musicians are determined to create songs with as much formal and thematic integrity as the bolero.

Julieta Venegas, who was first inspired to pick up an accordion by Tom Waits and Los Lobos, and not local norteño artists, is Tijuana's most vital singer/songwriter. Venegas, like the Nortec Collective, is as bilingual as any Nuyorican or Miami Cuban. Although all of Venegas's lyrics are in Spanish, they tell stories familiar on both sides on the border, and although she is also influenced by a very Mexican folk tradition, her raspy voice can cut like P. J. Harvey and haunt like Waits.

A self-described quiet type with a very loud talent, Venegas has released two albums, the second, *Bueninvento* (2000), using some North American musicians and causing a bit of a stir north of the border. Her songs are often penetrating, mournful narratives that represent the ambivalence of the Mexican soul in the post-Nafta age. *Casa Abandonado* features her plaintive accordion playing, embellishing her musings about unanswered phone calls to an abandoned house. Switching to acoustic guitar, she strums archetypal folkie chords on *Hoy No Quiero*, an angry lament that mutates into an edgy modern rock anthem. Venegas's range is so powerful, her singing so finely textured and emotionally generous that she can pull your guts right out of you, as she does on the first album, *Aquí* (1998). Whether surrounded in the studio by sessionists like bassist Fernando Saunders and drummer Joey Waronker or in solo live performance, she generates a huge enthusiasm from her fans. She has the intensity of a ranchera singer or bolerista, but translates that feeling into thoroughly modern rock arrangements.

Manu Chao

Born in 1961 to Spanish parents, Manu Chao is a self-styled anarchist traveling nomad musician, known to set up shop in various towns around Latin America and record local musicians on a four-track, sometimes right in the street, to create his albums. Manu was a one-time leader of the late 1980s Spanish ska-punk group Mano Negra, which had a great influence on the Latin alternative scene in general. His two solo albums, *Clandestino* (1998) and *Proxima Estación: Esperanza* (2001), are big favorites among the Latin alternative crowd, and have more crossover appeal than most Latin alternative because of their basic reggae conventions and happily delivered, easy-to-remember lyrics.

Manu Chao's best songs, like *Hombre Clandestino*, convey his strong identification with the poor of Latin America, who don't have the luxury to travel from country to country, and when they do, it's usually in a desperate attempt to get work that lasts only for a couple of months. These songs lope along at an infectious reggae beat, with Chao's signature sprinklings of found sounds from radio, TV broadcasts, and the street. On *Próxima Estación: Esperanza*, he extended the found-music concept, announcing his band as Radio Bemba, which is Afro-Caribbean slang for "word on the street."

While Manu Chao's songs offer penetrating insights into the Latin American underground most would prefer to overlook, his work can suffer from repetition, so that you swear you've heard the same song in several different versions. When his music revels in the upbeat, there is cause for celebration of some sort of internationalist empowerment à la Bob Marley. But when it is mournful, Manu Chao's voice can drag and seem forced. *Radio Bemba 2002*, released that year, is a free-flowing live album reflecting all the raucous charm of Manu Chao's overflowing concerts.

Juanes

Juanes was the first act to emerge from the Latin alternative scene as a major force on Latin pop. Formerly the lead vocalist of the Colombian rock band Ekhymosis, Juan Esteban Aristizabal sings about the joy and pain of living through a virtual civil war and still finding the time for the angst of post-adolescence. His first album, *Fíjate Bien* (2000), was an invigorating mix of pop-rock, traditional

Colombian rhythms like cumbia and vallenato, and strong song-writing that showed his artistic maturation.

Born in 1972 in Medellín, Colombia, Juanes grew up in the city's surrounding rural area, where he was strongly influenced by the folk music of the Antioquia region. Instead of the typical urban Colombian mix of salsa, cumbia, and rock and pop, as the son of a cattle rancher, Juanes grew up listening to rustic vallenatos, bambucos, and pasillos, as well as the tangos of Carlos Gardel. But like many of his North American contemporaries, Juanes had his head turned around when he heard Metallica for the first time as a teenager in Medellín. In a matter of weeks he formed his first rock group, Ekhymosis, but after twelve years and five albums the band broke up.

In September 1999, Juanes flew to Los Angeles without a record label but with some key contacts and a strong demo tape. He wound up in the La Casa recording studio of Gustavo Santoalalla, one of Latin alternative's most accomplished producers, having worked with Café Tacuba, Caifanes, and many others, and fulfilled his vision. By adding punky, funky edge to rhythms made famous by Carlos Vives, Juanes finally made a record true to who he was.

Although it's cutting edge twenty-first century hybrid-pop, *Fíjate Bien* has more than just a musical message. The title, which means "look closely," or even "pay attention," is about the loss of meaning that Colombian youth experienced in the face of the numbing violence of that country's civil war. It's about not losing the ability to be surprised by everyday life.

When *Fíjate Bien* won the Latin Grammy for best rock solo album in 2001, it gave a clear message to the Latin music industry that for a Latin alternative album to capture widespread support, some form of traditional influence is needed. In 2002, Juanes released *Un Día Normal*, which made him a breakthrough Latin pop star, the first with a background in Latin alternative. There is nothing groundbreaking in Juanes's choice of instrumentation or song structure on the album, but what he started on *Fíjate Bien* is fully realized on *Un Día Normal*.

In search of a "normal day," as the album's title and title track imply, Juanes is at once harkening back to a less complicated time and reveling in the passion of today's dangerous living. Juanes does this by working a classic Latin American theme: Survival in an unstable world requires a deep, unshakeable faith. On the album's first single, the cumbia-rocking *A Dios le Pido*, he asks God for his mother to survive, his girlfriend to stay forever, and for his "people not to shed too much blood and to rise." And when on the title track, a warm-hued rock ballad, Juanes sings, "You never know what you have until you lose it," he acknowledges that our "normal" reality is tinged by the possibility of sudden loss, and you have to have faith to live with that. This sentiment has long been a Latin American reality, and now it's a North American one.

Un Día Normal is filled with free-and-easy choruses and intricately lush guitar work—it's the inspiration for a different kind of summer of love. But as much as Juanes adores his women on string-embellished ballads (*La Única* is dedicated to his mother), he playfully admonishes them on the reggae-tinged *La Paga* and the flamenco blues-rock *Mala Gente*, a subtle echo of Santana's *Evil Ways*.

The formidable production team of Gustavo Santoalalla and Anibal Kerpel do some of their best work here. With a mini-moog or melodica riff here and there, they balance Juanes's English rock dreams with his folkloric memories (see *Luna*, which features Beatles harmonies, some fancy plucking on the tiple, a traditional Colombian four-string guitar, and an infectious reggae beat). And though Juanes does fine on his own, there is a stunning duet with the fabulous Nelly Furtado on *Fotografía* replete with intoxicating choruses evoking the melancholy the Brazilians call saudade. To wrap things up, Juanes toasts Colombian tropical music hero Joe Arroyo with a salsa-rock cover of *La Noche*.

The Future of Latin Music

In its essence, Latin music is a joyful intersection between the worlds that came together in forming what we know as the New World, and this joining is only a precursor to the future intermingling of the world's cultures in the global information age. Whereas previous cultural expressions of modernity involved displacing the past in order to create the new, today Latin music, like Latin culture, seeks to establish the new even as it resuscitates the traditional. For that reason, the contradiction between the increasing modernization of Latin music through mixtures with pop, rock, hip-hop, and electronica and the quest of Latin musicians to unearth forgotten rhythms, harmonies, and melodies rooted in African, indigenous, and even Iberian traditions is not a problematic one.

So the juxtaposition of ninety-ish Buena Vista Social Club pianist Rubén González and the postmodern urban hip-hop of Monterrey's Control Machete makes sense. The appropriation of an Andean dance form by an Afro-Argentine, Spain-based rapper named King Africa to create a wildly popular hit is true to form. The long-overlooked rhythms and dances of Colombia, from the cumbia to the esoteric Pacific Coast chandé, are transformed into the latest influences on Miami-based Latin pop, driven by that area's increasing Colombian population.

In New York, a series of new bands has formed that pay tribute to vintage Afro-Caribbean rhythms, such as Yerba Buena does with bomba and Cumbiamba does with Colombian dances, or place them in a modern conjunto context, like Bryan Vargas's Ya Está. Another band called Yerba Buena, which released *President Alien* in 2003, mixes Afro-Cuban rumba, Afro-beat from Nigeria, and even hip-hop influences in a revolutionary way, showcasing vocalist Xiomara Laugaurt, a queen of filin who left Cuba in the mid-1990s.

The increasing importance of Spain, and to a lesser extent, Portugal, in the current trajectory of Latin music is also notable in the early years of the new century. Alternative groups such as Macaco, Dusminguet, Peret: El Rey de la Rumba, and Ojos de Brujo, the latter a jazz-rock-flamenco band that mixes in hip-hop and electronica, are influencing Latinos from Europe to the Americas. The revival of the Portuguese folk music fado, through groups like Madredeus and singers like Amalia Rodrigues and Mariza, has rejuvenated the genre and made it more relevant to the Latin music-listening public than it ever has been.

Speculating on whether or not Latin music will persist even if the Latin pop explosion of the late 1990s fades is pointless. The unbridled power of its appeal through its driving percussion, seductive melodies, and careful symmetry between verse and song structure is already embedded in North American pop music. The increasing popularity of Afro-Cuban music in Europe, and the fact that there is no sign that the taste for dancing to Latin music is abating in the Americas, are more evidence of the music's entrenched reality. And with Latinos becoming the largest minority in the United States, sheer consumer power will guarantee continued investment by multinational record companies to keep the whole enterprise afloat.

In a hemisphere where the two Americas are most clearly distinguished by material wealth, Latin music will continue to thrive because Latin America's riches are measured in cultural capital. As long as its economies are precariously perched on the edge of upheaval, and its large mass of people remains unprotected by First World safety nets, there will be a need for music to keep spirits happy. The song of Andalucía and West Africa, passing through the darkness of the slave trade into the New World, where it broke bread with a new set of nomadic cultures native to the Americas and replenished by immigrants from Europe and Asia, seems to only gain strength in serving that need.

Bibliography

Austerlitz, Paul. *Merengue: Dominican Music and Dominican Identity*. Temple University Press, 1997.

Boggs, Vernon. *Salsiology: Afro-Cuban Music and the Evolution of Salsa in New York City*. Greenwood, 1992.

Burr, Ramiro. *The Billboard Guide to Tejano and Regional Mexican Music*. Watson-Guptill, 1999.

Carpentier, Alejo. *Music in Cuba*. Translated by Alan West-Durán. University of Minnesota Press, 2001.

Castro, Ruy. *Bossa Nova: The Story of the Brazilian Music That Seduced the World*. Chicago Review Press, 2003.

Chediak, Nat. *Diccionario de Jazz Latino*. Fundación Autor, 1998.

Dunn, Christopher. *Brutality Garden: Tropicália and the Emergence of a Brazilian Counterculture*. University of North Carolina, 2001.

Évora, Tony. *Música cubana: Los últimos 50 años*. Alianza Editorial, 2003.

_____. *Origines de la música cubana*. Alianza Editorial, 1994.

Farr, Jory. *Rites of Rhythm: The Music of Cuba*. Regan Books, 2003.

Fernandez, Raul A. *Latin Jazz: The Perfect Combination/La Combinacion Perfecta*. Chronicle Books, 2002.

Flores, Juan. *From Bomba to Hiphop*. Columbia University Press, 2000.

Giro, Radamés, ed. *Panorama de la Música Popular Cubana*. Editorial Letras Cubanas, 1995.

Glaser, Ruth. *My Music Is My Flag: Puerto Rican Musicians and Their New York Communities 1917–1940*. University of California Press, 1995.

Leymaire, Isabelle. *Cuban Fire: The Story of Salsa and Latin Jazz*. Continuum, 2002.

Loza, Steven. *Tito Puente and the Making of Salsa*. University of Illinois Press, 1999.

Martínez, García, and José María. *La Música Étnica: Un Viaje por las Músicas del Mundo*. Alianza Editorial, 2002.

Orovio, Helio. *Diccionario de la Música Cubana*. Letras Cubanas, 1992.

Ortiz, Fernando. *Etnia y Sociedad*. Editorial de las Sciencias Sociales, 1993.

_____. *La Africaná de la Música Folklorica de Cuba*. Editorial de las Sciencias Sociales, 1992.

Pacini Hernandez, Deborah. *Bachata: A Social History of a Dominican Popular Music*. Temple University Press, 1995.

Peña, Manuel. *The Texas-Mexican Conjunto: History of a Working-Class Music*. University of Texas Press, 1985.

Perrone, Charles A., and Christopher Dunn, eds. *Brazilian Popular Music and Globalization*. Routledge, 2002.

Reyes, David, and Tom Waldman. *Land of a Thousand Dances: Chicano Rock 'n' Roll from Southern California*. University of New Mexico Press, 1998.

Rivera, Raquel Z. *New York Ricans from the Hip Hop Zone*. Palgrave MacMillan, 2003.

Roberts, John Storm. *Black Music of Two Worlds: African, Caribbean, Latin, and African-American Traditions*. Thomson Schirmer, 1998.

_____. *Latin Jazz: The First of the Fusions 1880s to Today*. Thomson Schirmer, 1999.

_____. *The Latin Tinge: The Impact of Latin American Music in the United States*. Oxford University Press, 1999.

Salazar, Max. *Mambo Kingdom: Latin Music in New York*. Thomson Schirmer, 2002.

Steward, Sue. *Música! The Rhythm of Latin America*. Chronicle Books, 1999.

Sweeney, Phillip. *The Rough Guide to Cuban Music*. Penguin, 2001.

Thompson, Robert Farris. *Flash of the Spirit: African & Afro-American Art & Philosophy*. Vintage, 1983.

Veloso, Caetano. *Tropical Truth: A Story of Music and Revolution in Brazil*. Da Capo Press, 2003.

Vianna, Hermano. *The Mystery of the Samba: Popular Music and National Identity in Brazil*. Translated by John Charles Chasteen. Chapel Hill, 1999.

Wade, Peter. *Music, Race, and Nation: Música Tropical in Colombia*. University of Chicago Press, 2000.

Waxer, Lise, ed. *Situating Salsa: Global Markets and Local Meaning in Latin Popular Music*. Routledge, 2002.

Zolov, Eric. *Refried Elvis: The Rise of the Mexican Counterculture*. University of California Press. 1999

Index

368 Index